TRAINING INTERVENTIONS

Margaret Anne Reid, MA, CIPD, spent 15 years as a training officer in both large and small companies in the clothing and engineering industries before moving into higher education. She directed the Postgraduate Diploma in Personnel Management at the former Leeds Polytechnic and was later appointed director of the MBA programme at the University of Leeds, where, having now retired from full-time academic employment, she holds an honorary appointment. She is a past Vice-President – Education of the (former) Institute of Personnel Management. Having contributed to a number of publications, she also has considerable editorial experience of academic journals such as *Personnel Review*, and currently edits *Training and Management Development Methods*. She was a subject assessor for the Higher Education Funding Council.

Harry Barrington, BA, CIPD, formerly Company Training and Management Development Manager with Lever Brothers and Chairman of the UK Soap and Detergent Industry's Training Committee, is also a past Vice-President of the (former) Institute of Personnel Management, and was the Institute's Chief Examiner for Employee Development between 1986 and 1991. He is perhaps best known as the originator of the 'continuous development' movement. An ex-governor of Kingston College, whose governing body he chaired for several years during the 1980s, he is also the treasurer of an associated educational trust and a director of the college's trading company. He has written and lectured extensively on all aspects of employee development.

The authors wish to express their thanks to John Kenney for his contributions to earlier editions of the work

During publication, the UK government instituted a widespread review of all UK post-16 education and training structures, leading to the appearance at end June 1999 of a White Paper entitled *Learning to Succeed*. The impetus for change stems from developments serving lifelong learning which we note towards the end of Chapter 1 (see pages 27–8), together with the emergence of new regional development agencies. Briefly, the White Paper announces the creation of a single new agency (a 'Learning and Skills [L&S] Council') to run education and training for all over-16 outside schools and universities, and a new Youth Service. The former will take over the work of the FEFC, with 40 to 50 subordinate local L&S Councils replacing the present TECs. The latter will 'modernise' the current Careers Service, introducing a new youth support system providing personal advisers for young people. It seems likely that the new system will be introduced from about spring 2001. Our Chapter 2 continues to describe the institutional set-up as it existed at April 1999.

The Institute of Personnel and Development is the leading publisher of books and reports for personnel and training professionals, students, and all those concerned with the effective management and development of people at work. For details of all our titles, please contact the Publishing Department:

tel. 020-8263 3387

fax 020-8263 3850

e-mail publish@ipd.co.uk

The catalogue of all IPD titles can be viewed on the IPD website:

www.ipd.co.uk

TRAINING INTERVENTIONS

PROMOTING LEARNING
OPPORTUNITIES

Margaret Anne Reid
Harry Barrington

Foreword by Sir Geoffrey Holland

Sixth edition

INSTITUTE OF PERSONNEL AND
DEVELOPMENT

For our long-suffering spouses
Laurie Plews and Maureen Barrington

© Margaret Anne Reid and Harry A. Barrington 1999

First published 1986
Second Edition 1988
Third Edition 1992
Fourth Edition 1994
Reprinted 1995, 1996
Fifth Edition 1997
Reprinted 1998
Sixth Edition 1999

Phototypeset by The Comp-Room, Aylesbury
and printed in Great Britain
by The Cromwell Press, Trowbridge, Wiltshire

British Library Cataloguing in Publication Data

A catalogue record for this book is available from the British Library

ISBN 0-85292-804-1

The views expressed in this book are the authors' own, and may not necessarily reflect those of the IPD.

i)

INSTITUTE OF PERSONNEL
AND DEVELOPMENT

IPD House, Camp Road, London SW19 4UX
Tel: 020 8971 9000   Fax: 020 8263 3333
Registered office as above. Registered Charity No. 1038333
A company limited by guarantee. Registered in England No. 2931892

Contents

PROMOTING LEARNING OPPORTUNITIES:
The operational arena

Contents

List of figures

Foreword

by Sir Geoffrey Holland KCB
Vice-Chancellor, University of Exeter
(formerly Permanent Secretary to the Department of Employment
and to the Department of Education)

As I consider all the developments in vocational education and training in recent years, I am impressed by the growing number of people and organisations committed to the creation of a world-class workforce.

The reasons are simple. Technology can be transferred easily and cheaply throughout the world. The development of global businesses or global business partnerships means that decisions on investment, location and sourcing are now quite different from what they were even a short while ago. Throughout the world, demographic trends mean that there is no shortage of hands to do work, no shortage of young people, but critical shortages of more highly educated and more highly qualified people. And finally the rising expectations of customers and individuals mean that unless we match – and if possible exceed – the standards of quality set by the best in the marketplace, we shall simply drop out of contention.

One of the most significant developments recently has been the establishment, for the first time, of national Learning Targets. They are not the CBI's targets. They are not the Government's targets. They are not targets for the education service. They are targets for all of us. And we all have to work together to achieve them.

Of one thing I am clear: the targets are feasible and are capable of delivery. But the targets will only be achieved if all of us work together consistently, purposefully and with commitment and energy to deliver them. And let us remember, as we do this, that the targets are the minimum we need to achieve to be world class. The best in the world are constantly improving. They will not stand still and wait for us to catch up. They will move on and we must be up with them.

There are six key building-blocks if we are to achieve the targets, and each and every one of them is, at least in outline, in place.

First, we have to ensure that all young people are educated and trained long, broad and to high standards. All the developments in the education service point in that direction, as do developments in youth training.

Next, we must have employer commitment at every level: at national level; at sector level (the industry training organisations); at local level (the Training and Enterprise Councils in England and Wales and the Local Enterprise Companies in Scotland); and at the level of the individual organisation (the critically important seal of approval as an Investor in People).

Third, we must have individuals who are motivated to take an interest in and some responsibility for their own personal development. It is encouraging that increasing numbers of employers are now agreeing with employees arrangements, including entitlements to time and money, to enable their workforce to do just this.

Fourth, we must have a modern, relevant, comprehensible qualification system. The Qualifications and Curriculum Authority is well on course to deliver that framework.

Fifth, we must have high-quality information and advice available to all concerned: employers and individuals alike.

And, finally, we must have a research and development programme, at national, sector, local level – all three – which ensures that we continue to improve and which keeps us at the frontier of developments in learning and learning technology.

Training Interventions shows us how much is on the move. We have a foundation and a framework capable of delivering world-class standards. But we now need to secure performance and results from all parts of that framework.

Above all, we need to carry forward a revolution of higher expectations: by employers of what individual employees are capable of achieving and by individuals of where opportunities can lead – and the rewards, both material and otherwise, that they can bring.

The potential rewards are great – for all of us. The alternative is not one we should remotely contemplate.

Preface to the sixth edition

Each time we begin a new edition, we are faced with the problem of how to introduce all the new material relating to such a rapidly developing and expanding area, keep the content comprehensive, and yet avoid making the book too long and cumbersome. This is a difficult task, because the training and development field is still a blend of the old and the new.

Our philosophy of training and the explanation of our new subtitle are given in the Introduction and elsewhere in the book, so we will not elaborate on them here. Suffice it to say that whilst it is important to keep abreast of new developments and techniques and to take advantage of the advances in technology, more traditional methods cannot be completely discarded. Furthermore, training decisions still need to be taken after careful understanding and consideration of relevant contextual matters. Section A of the book therefore deals with different historical, national, organisational and philosophical perspectives, further details of which are given in the Introduction.

Section B is devoted to the operational arena and the practicalities of assessing training needs, planning, implementing and evaluating training interventions, as well as a consideration of current and future trends. In recognition of the increasing need for continuous self-development and the shifting emphasis from 'training' to 'learning', we have increased our material on experiential learning. Mindful also of the high proportion of small businesses which may not have specialist training staff, we have included a section summarising the role that line managers can play in helping their staff to assess and cater for their own training needs, and we give details of how companies, large and small, are encouraged to integrate training and development with business objectives by taking appropriate steps to meet the standards of Investors in People. We have also included further discussion of new technology, particularly the use of intranets. The final chapter looks to the future, with a discussion of knowledge management; learning organisations; new thought processes centring on reflective behaviour; promoting organisational learning in practice; and a scenario where a continuous development management system integrates learning and knowledge management with work.

The Appendices have been updated, and a note on the European scene has been included, as well as an extract from the IPD Code on Professional Conduct and Disciplinary Procedures.

We hope that readers in Scotland and Ireland will bear with us, in that their education systems have certain unique characteristics that it has not been possible adequately to address in this volume.

We are grateful to Sir Geoffrey Holland for writing a Foreword to this book. We acknowledge our thanks to all authors and their publishers in allowing us to quote from their work. In particular, we thank Prentice-Hall for permission to reproduce the Kolb diagram in Chapter 3; Alan Mumford for permission to reproduce the table in Figure 3.3; Peter Honey and Alan Mumford for allowing us to reproduce parts of their work in Chapter 4; Sylvia Downs for permission to reproduce material covering her 'Four Beliefs about Learning' and 'Ten Principles of Learning'; the Bank of Scotland for allowing us to reproduce the extract from their *Human Resources Review 1998*, relating to the competency framework in Chapter 7, and Ann Jakeman for her kind assistance with this; and Michael Pearn and Rajvinder Kandola for permission to reproduce the job learning analysis question cards in Figure 9.3. Thanks are due also to Chris Williams and to Safeway Stores plc for help and for allowing us to reproduce the material in Figures 11.3, 11.4 and 11.5 relating to their store induction; to John Burgoyne for allowing us to reproduce his material in our Figure 12.3, as well as in various chapters throughout the book. We acknowledge with thanks help provided by the Department for Education and Employment in supporting requests to reproduce material in a number of our Figures and in our text (Crown Copyright is reproduced with the permission of the Controller of Her Majesty's Stationery Office), by Investors in People UK Limited in allowing us to reproduce their copyrighted National Standard, by the National Advisory Council for Education and Training Targets in permitting the latest set of National Learning Targets (those for the year 2002) to be copied, by the Further Education Funding Council in agreeing material collated from an FEFC Chief Inspector's annual report, and – finally – by the Qualifications and Curriculum Authority, who have allowed us to reproduce their detailed definitions of the five NVQ qualification levels. Lastly, we thank Anne Cordwent for her ready help, advice and good humour, as well as Chris Jackson and the staff at the IPD publishing department.

Margaret Reid
Harry Barrington
July 1999

Introduction

In this Introduction we briefly explain the philosophy of our title, and our new sub-title 'promoting learning opportunities'. We also clarify our use of terminology in relation to human resource management and personnel management, and human resource development, and training and development. We offer some explanation of standard terms – education, training and learning – and we emphasise the need to manage training and development processes in a situation-specific way. We provide some initial evidence that managing this function is becoming increasingly complex, purposeful and important within the world of work.

'TRAINING INTERVENTIONS: PROMOTING LEARNING OPPORTUNITIES' – AN EXPLANATION OF THE TITLE OF OUR BOOK

Our central theme has stood the test of time and remains, as in previous editions, that an organisation is a learning environment, and membership of an organisation is a continuous learning experience. At the most basic level, people learn from the reactions of others, particularly their superiors, and formulate attitudes towards them – attitudes which begin to influence the way they do their work. Day-by-day experience is so much more powerful that it tends to overshadow what the individual may learn in other settings. Any deliberate training or learning is therefore an intervention into an ongoing process: the task is to promote learning in the most effective and advantageous way – hence our subtitle. We believe that now, more than ever, those who are responsible for training and development need to have regard to contextual factors when determining the way in which they assess training needs and objectives, plan strategies and choose methodologies.

A 'TOP-DOWN' OR 'BOTTOM-UP' APPROACH?

Our title, *Training Interventions*, may seem to imply a mainly 'top-down' approach, where management take entire responsibility for assessing training needs and providing courses and opportunities for learning. However, downsizing and today's leaner organisations and flatter structures, together with rapid change, have created situations where individuals have to be prepared for multi-skilling and/or greater job mobility. This has brought greater emphasis on self-development and self-managed learning, and the acquisition of portable skills, and means that managers have to take more responsibility for their own development, and that of their subordinates.

1

Traditionally, the 'ideal' approach has been that training should start with top management, often on the recommendation of a training and development specialist, and 'filter' down the organisation. This is the case in many organisations, and it is difficult to carry out successful training interventions without some support from top management, but we take a wide view of the type of support required and the role of management. Cultures where people take responsibility for their own learning, and where the workplace itself becomes a vehicle for positive personal growth, do not 'just happen'. They require a supportive and facilitating management style, and the removal of organisational barriers to learning may be regarded as one of the most important 'training interventions'.

More flexible organisation structures and the necessity for rapid changes mean that the impetus for training can come from middle management faced with reorganisation, from innovative project teams, from production workers faced with changes in material or process, or new demands for quality, or from individual workers who see the need to widen or update their range of skills. There is an increasing recognition of the need not only for *training* in the formal sense but also for *learning*. Our title and our book, therefore, embrace learning, whether directly instigated by training specialists or line managers, self-managed, or arising directly from workplace activities. It is still necessary for those responsible for training to be able to analyse training needs and plan and implement training programmes where required, and we provide information on how to do this. We also discuss experiential learning, and suggest ways in which people can assess their own learning, and how their managers can coach them and assist them to do so. We are also aware of the fact that organisation boundaries have become more permeable, with an increase in franchising, contracting and outsourcing, and it may be necessary to be concerned not only with the training and development of direct employees but also of anyone who contributes to organisational success.

TERMINOLOGY – HUMAN RESOURCE MANAGEMENT, PERSONNEL MANAGEMENT, HUMAN RESOURCE DEVELOPMENT, TRAINING AND DEVELOPMENT

In recent years authors, tutors and practitioners have increasingly used the terms 'human resource management' (HRM) and 'human resource development' (HRD) in preference to 'personnel management' (PM) and 'training and development' (T&D). These preferences stem partly from what seems to us the reasonable belief that employees are properly viewed as *assets* and should be regarded as 'resources' rather than mere costs; but they also reflect the conviction that the management of people involves much wider responsibilities than ensuring employee welfare and even workplace efficiency. Armstrong (1990) defines HRM as:

> a strategic approach to acquiring, motivating, developing and managing the organisation's human resources . . . to shaping appropriate corporate cultures, and introducing programmes that reflect and support the core values of the organisation and ensure its success.

The word 'strategic' is often added to the mainstream HRM title, reinforcing the view that this function is an essential element in the process by which an organisation attains its business objectives, a view that the many professionals now in jobs which carry the 'human resource' label will be quick to support and confirm.

We share this view, and might have been expected to move to employ HRM and HRD terms generally throughout this book. But we must still acknowledge that many 'personnel managers' and 'training managers' have been striving towards and serving similar ends for many years, and it takes more than a change of title to ensure that the function takes its proper place as an important means of attaining business objectives. The traditional terms have stood the test of time, and remain in common use. The relevant professional institute, which happens to be our publisher (the IPD), still honours the use of the term 'personnel' while simultaneously defining its members' professional responsibilities and roles in the widest terms.

With regard to our specific subject area, we regard both 'HRD' and 'T&D' as justifying wide terms of reference, embracing anything relating to the development of people, including promotion policies, career development and advice, staff appraisal, skills definition, forward organisation planning, and ethical policies, together with (as we said above) any and all interventions which promote learning – and we see all these things as rightly directed at the efficient functioning of the organisation. Our text will show that we believe all management, and not merely specialists, to have relevant responsibilities. Moreover, it will be apparent that we include important dimensions beyond the 'narrow' business objective, strategic or otherwise: for example, employers have long been expected to contribute appropriately to the national pool of skills, to assist in employing, training and providing work experience for young people, and to help adult staff in lifelong learning.

With all this in mind, we have chosen for the purposes of our book to use HRM and PM terms as interchangeable, and similarly we use HRD and T&D without any intention to imply different meanings or preferences. The important point is that HRM/PM and HRD/T&D policies and procedures must be well integrated and coherent with each other and with other aspects of organisation strategy and objectives. People learn from *all* experience within their organisations, and the promotion of learning opportunities remains an organisation-specific and situation-specific art involving the use of whatever terms are considered realistic at the particular workplace.

WHAT DO WE MEAN BY 'TRAINING', 'LEARNING', 'DEVELOPMENT' AND 'EDUCATION'?

The training field is not characterised by a set of terms with unique meanings, used consistently to explain the same things. In practice, the 'real-life' meaning of terms often depends on the context within which they are used. For example, a group of training and development managers who are discussing 'management training' may be:

- assessing the strengths of a formal programme for others who are formally called 'management trainees'; or
- reviewing their own informal learning experiences among themselves; or
- criticising an external training course one of their number has attended; or even
- exploring what the nation might do to educate the next generation of managers.

The list is far from exhaustive; similar examples could be offered relating to any category of employee, and to most types of learning. We know, for example, of one organisation that uses the term 'training event' for six different types of planned learning activity, and we know of another organisation that uses the term 'development' with different meanings in at least five of its job descriptions.

This immediately leads us into problem areas. Textbooks traditionally suggest standard approaches and norms, implying that the reader might remember or copy them with confidence. But the student of training and development needs to build and respond to a 'moving dictionary'. The need can perhaps be appreciated in practical terms by looking at the following six examples:

1 Imagine you are a so-called training manager, who is *en route* to a local College of Further Education to discuss with a lecturer a course that trainee employees are following and that is said to teach engineering practice (and which incidentally appears in the college prospectus under a heading 'vocational education'). Will it help your discussion if you stick rigidly to definitions of 'vocation' and 'education' that you have acquired in your past experience?

2 Now imagine you are a chairman of a company with a high turnover of management staff. You have a personnel manager reporting to you, but you believe that line management holds the prime responsibility for the performance of the workforce. You have taken to heart government and CBI pronouncements to the effect that 'the nation's human resources are the nation's prime resource', and you want education and training activity to serve better the key aim of economic health in order to provide a new, competitive cutting edge – especially at manager level. You have taken a position on the local Training and Enterprise Council (TEC) and are keen that that body should stimulate the creation of good-quality management in the area, not least because you feel that you might not lose so many managers

from your own company, and you might have replacements more easily available if they do leave. Within your own company you have promoted a form of team development which has involved ongoing discussions, aimed both at welding departmental units together and at finding answers for real problems. Will your contribution in the TEC be about creating specific plans for individuals? Or will it take the group, or the firm, or the local community, or perhaps even the nation, as its unit? Will you call such plans 'training' plans, or 'educational' initiatives, or 'development programmes', or indeed something else?

3 Now imagine you are a Cabinet minister about to engage in discussion with your colleagues on the contents of a forthcoming 'Competitiveness' White Paper. You believe strongly that training activity can contribute significantly to national economic health – that it is a key instrument of competitiveness which all employers should be urged to use and develop. You are, however, aware that the nation's many small employers find training costs hard to absorb (especially the time involved), and that all employers have recently been reducing their intakes of young people. Low-skilled jobs are also disappearing rapidly. You used to see economic growth as the central aim; now you see it as the reduction of unemployment through the development of skills. Most advisers seem to think that the rich/poor gap reflects educational performance, and that employers in the future will tend to ignore unqualified and unskilled workers. You have therefore supported the introduction of the national vocational qualifications system, which you believe can make education more useful for all – the learner, the employer, and the nation. But you would also like to find new ways of prompting organisations to increase their own commitment to workplace training.

4 You are a specialist in the production of 'open learning' or self-study materials, creating TV programmes for the Open University or computer-based learning packages for mail order sale. You are talking to a training manager who plans a course in French for sales representatives. You see both education and training in a new and somewhat different light from that which assumes the existence of teachers and trainers; you challenge whether education and training should be of the 'autocratic' or 'telling people what to do' kind. You are delighted that greater emphasis is now being given to encouraging self-learning, ie individuals are increasingly being asked and expected to identify their own learning needs and are increasingly being given more responsibility for planning and managing their own learning. In this context, how do you define the roles of the teacher and the trainer? Will you perhaps expect the former to balance lecturing with questions, discussion and exercises? Will you want the latter to provide self-study facilities as well as mount courses? And what will you say if the latter says that this will mean much time 'being diverted to removing structural or cultural barriers to learning'?

5 Now spare a thought for the people who may buy self-study material: the sales representative who wants to learn French and is hoping for promotion; the trainee accountant who is starting on the long haul to becoming qualified; the housewife who intends to return to work when her second child reaches school age and who is teaching herself word processing with the aid

of a new word processor and a 'user guide'. Will they expect all their future learning to be self-directed? Do they expect future employees to find ways to dovetail or merge learning and work?

6 Finally, imagine you are a young personnel manager who is beginning to treat change as normal in working life. In the past four years you have experienced a change of ownership for your organisation, which has brought with it a range of new procedures; you have moved your head office; you have assimilated various changes in the law relating to personnel at work; your department has introduced computerised administrative systems; you have devised and introduced a new joint consultation scheme covering all levels of employee; and you have seen four major technical research projects produce four new products for sale. You are aware that each of these changes has demanded new learning on the part of existing staff, and that most of this learning has had to happen 'as part of work'. The rate of change has been such that separating out the training needs and planning formal courses have not been possible. How can you steer this organisation towards a 'continuous employee development' culture, with learning integrated with work?

These examples demonstrate the use of the term 'training interventions' in its widest sense, encompassing ways in which learning might be helped to happen in the service of work goals – including any which aim at group (not just individual) learning, any that aim at developing self-study and self-development, and even any that aim at changing the work or the work environment to stimulate learning.

It is our intention to encourage and help the 'moving dictionary' process: our text aims continuously to expand its subject, and as it progresses the meaning of terms and concepts will become less 'standard' and more context-related. You will increasingly need to form your own conclusions. So, although we start by providing a few simple definitions and conclusions, we hope to stimulate a learning process that will eventually lead you to acquire a unique and personal view of what training and development means and how it might be further developed.

SOME STANDARD DEFINITIONS

The three most important concepts covered by training and development are *education*, *training* and *learning*. The last, learning, is critical and we shall explore its meanings in a separate chapter (see Chapter 3). For the time being it should be noted that there is no universally accepted theory of learning. Until recently most writers on the subject thought in terms of the acquisition (usually by some form of teaching process) of new knowledge, which is certainly one acceptable form of learning. But a learner may acquire new knowledge by memorising words which do not have meaning for that learner; learning may happen without understanding, or without sufficient understanding to allow the learning to be 'applied'. A person may learn to walk, swim, recognise objects, spot defects or develop any of a wide range of skills without consciously retaining the understanding of what is involved in practising it. At this stage, we suggest simply that *learning must yield the ability to do something that was not previously within the learner's capability*. Precisely what the new ability is, and whether it has been acquired via a teaching process, and whether the 'learner' is a person or a team or a nation – these things are subordinate to a simple definition of learning as *the process whereby a new capability is attained*. They may of course become more critical as we move into other, more sophisticated, definitions which relate to specific aims and interventions, but for the present a simple definition will suffice.

Training and development is essentially about 'making learning happen' – any form of learning, although usually in the service of some work goal or goals. Learning can and does occur naturally as a by-product of everyday experience, but random learning is somewhat unpredictable, slow in performance, and may even be counterproductive (eg a random route to learning that an electric drill is a dangerous instrument may involve a nasty injury). Training and development usually involves ways of abandoning random learning routes in favour of more productive, planned routes.

'Education' and 'training' are ways of doing just that – abandoning random learning routes in favour of more productive, planned routes. The (now defunct) Manpower Services Commission's 'Glossary of Training Terms' offered the following definitions in 1981:

> *Education* is defined as 'activities which aim at developing the knowledge, skills, moral values and understanding required in all aspects of life rather than a knowledge and skill relating to only a limited field of activity. The purpose of education is to provide the conditions essential to young people and adults to develop an understanding of the traditions and ideas influencing the society in which they live and to enable them to make a contribution to it. It involves the study of their own cultures and of the laws of nature, as well as the acquisition of linguistic and other skills which are basic to learning, personal development, creativity and communication'.
>
> *Training* is 'a planned process to modify attitude, knowledge or skill behaviour through learning experience to achieve effective performance in an activity or range of activities. Its purpose, in the work situation, is to develop the abilities of the individual and to satisfy the current and future needs of the organisation.'

Both education and training are achieved by creating conditions in which the necessary attitudes, skill and knowledge can be effectively acquired by a learner who, as a result, becomes relatively confident of his or her abilities to apply them. It is important to understand that although confidence is not the only outcome of learning, and not the only generator of the will to develop further, it is central to the learner's ability to transfer what has been learned to novel situations – in a very real sense, it is the learner's confidence that allows the learning to be 'used'.

The underlying philosophy in these definitions is that education gives the general basis for living, and that training modifies and directs one's abilities towards a particular activity or activities. It can be seen that this philosophy assumes that the learner is an individual, and that plans are created by teachers or trainers to help, if not guarantee, learners' learning.

We can now offer a tentative early definition of training and development. It is part of personnel (or human resource) management and involves the planning and management of people's learning – including ways to help them manage their own – with the aim of making the learning process more effective, increasingly efficient, properly directed and therefore useful. People's learning is typically classsified as either education or training; education is 'for life', while training is for work. It all sounds logical and fairly easy to remember.

We are, however, in danger of ignoring our early words of warning. Our definition remains based on generalised concepts. The reality is situation-specific. You might now like to revisit the examples given above, questioning whether our early definitions are 'contextually adequate'. For example, our first training manager visited a College of Further Education to discuss with a lecturer trainees' progress in engineering practice. This does not sound much like separating education and training, the former being 'for life', the latter 'for work'. The essential point is that training and development is a situation-specific art, and must be managed as such; a doctrinaire approach is likely to make communication difficult, and the biggest achievements rest with those who can observe, describe and promote change in ways that others find realistic.

AN INCREASINGLY IMPORTANT AND COMPLEX SUBJECT

Our six examples also illustrate how our subject has grown – in importance, and in complexity and purpose – during the past few decades. They show that education and training are no longer in watertight compartments; that individual training is no longer the only aim; that national economic health is in the frame alongside individual rewards; that teaching is not the only way to ensure that learning happens; that training and development concerns *all* employees, not just managers, and certainly not just personnel or training managers; and that the rate and pace of change have made our subject a fundamental part of work, not just an adjunct to it.

We shall explore these ideas further in Section A, where we shall extend our understanding of:

- how the national and local scenes have developed
- the many institutions that now promote training and development activity
- evolved and evolving attitudes and approaches to learning
- relationships between learners and employing organisations
- organisational learning systems.

Throughout the remainder of this book, each chapter will include a summary of its main contents under the chapter heading and, at the end of each chapter, a number of questions 'for further reflection and discussion', and a suggested 'reading list'. For now, you might like to address this question:

Given the ideas presented in this Introduction, is this book an educational aid or a training aid?

TRAINING
INTERVENTIONS

Perspectives

1 An historical perspective

Introduction – approaches to training interventions – the early decades – the 1940s, 1950s and 1960s – the 1970s and early 1980s – recent developments – extension, variety and diversity

INTRODUCTION

From our point of view, the answer to the question at the end of the Introduction is 'Both'. This book aims both to educate and to train: to offer generalised knowledge; to modify and expand the reader's attitudes and opinions; and also to provide practical guidance. In this chapter, however, the emphasis will be on the former aim through the presentation of an historical account of 'how things came to be the way they are'. We will explore the development of ideas, of training practices, of employer interest, and of national interventions. We will visit bureaucracy and instruction, human relations and formal courses, change management and experiential learning, learning organisations and national vocational qualifications – and the Internet. All these developments have conditioned our present scene, and indeed most of what we describe still exists.

> **Why do you think we have chosen to present an historical account of UK training as the first main chapter in this book?**

APPROACHES TO TRAINING INTERVENTIONS

The twentieth century has seen dramatic changes within the world of work. Organisations have evolved in terms of purpose, size, structure, management philosophy, and relationships with the outside world. Technological advances have revolutionised all work methods, especially those involving planning, communicating and monitoring progress. For many organisations, the operational horizon has moved from a small geographical area to literally the world; for government, 'being competitive' is now a global (as opposed to a selective international) requirement. Everything has speeded up, including the pace of change itself.

In such a dynamic century, it was natural that approaches to training interventions grew in importance, broadened in scope, and became more sophisticated in method. At the start, it was normally assumed that the object of training would be the individual employee, and that the training method would involve teaching. Now, the picture is much more complex:

13

training plans may be aimed at any grouping up to and including the nation itself, and learner-centred activities are developing alongside those that are teacher- or tutor-led. Learning is no longer mainly the province of the psychologist or sociologist: researchers in fields such as systems engineering, artificial intelligence, cybernetics, communications technology, management and even biology have extended relevant theory by drawing on their own specialisms, extending and modifying ideas originally geared only to a human dimension. We now think of organisations as well as individuals as being 'able to learn', and indeed of both as being capable of 'learning to learn' – which means much more than acquiring knowledge of how learning happens.

Three fundamental (and to some extent contrasting) ideas have steadily grown in importance. The first is that the continuously changing environment demands lifelong learning on the part of all. The second is that real-life experience itself offers significant learning opportunities, and can be designed to stimulate learning. The third is that national vocational standards should exist to describe and improve occupational competence, which itself should be recognised by the award of national vocational qualifications.

To understand the reasons for these diverse developments, and how they have gathered pace, it is appropriate to review their evolution in some detail. The following historical account also effectively offers a summary of the main training interventions that have occurred in the UK during the twentieth century.

THE EARLY DECADES: MECHANISTIC STRUCTURES, BUREAUCRACY, INSTRUCTION

Figure 1.1 An historical perspective: the early decades

Background ideas on: organisation/management *people at work/learning*	Employer–led/backed training activity *Training/learning methods*	National training interventions
Scientific management Bureaucracy *Hierarchy*	'Sitting by Nellie' *Unplanned tuition* Craft apprenticeship *Workplace instruction* *+ College-based education*	Vocational education in FE Colleges

During the early decades of this century, psychology, which was still a young academic discipline, yielded new ideas on specific aspects of learning, the primary aim being to support and improve teaching processes, almost exclusively restricted to the world of education. The spotlight was on such matters as perception, memory retention, co-ordination of senses, and behaviour conditioning, the last of these initially involving experiments on animals or birds, who could be brought to adopt regular habits of behaviour by carefully planned stimuli and rewards.

In so far as ideas of behaviour conditioning were related to the world of work, they fitted well with classical management theory, which was itself better established and understood. Classical management theory assumed static, mechanistic organisations, led by managers who taught and disciplined workers to conform to imposed routines which they, the managers, believed to be appropriate and efficient. F W Taylor's principles of 'scientific management' (see Morgan, 1997), which had their origins in the US engineering industry, put all the responsibility for the organisation of work into the management role, including specifying the precise way in which the work should be done, selecting the best persons to do it, and training those people once they were engaged. Taylor's ideas became the cornerstone of work organisation in the UK in the early part of the century, and they remain influential to this day. Management theorists in the UK built on these ideas, creating the hierarchical structures, functional divisions of work, and procedural 'rules' which typified the standard 'bureaucratic' model of organisation. (It is worth noting that the UK has always been quick to absorb ideas from the USA on management and organisation.)

The most prolific of writers on sociology, Max Weber, who made bureaucracy his lifetime specialism, described it in 1947 as the 'ideal' form of organisation – implying not operational success, but rather a standard against which all organisational realities might be compared. Weber also noted that managing in a bureaucracy involved increasing one's professional superiority by keeping knowledge and aims secret: managers were not expected to enlighten outsiders or subordinates on the reasoning behind decisions. Very little attention was given to the human needs of workers: the contract of employment made the individual fit the 'task' requirements of the work unit, and ensured worker commitment through its reward elements. Leadership was primarily a matter of being clear, precise and concise in giving instructions.

It is not surprising that in this environment little planned training took place. Newly engaged employees were either expected to master their work by copying what they saw established workers doing, or, in the case of complex tasks, via instruction. The most visible UK training 'programme' was the indentured craft apprenticeship, which offered young male school leavers a learning route into 'trades' such as engineering or printing, via some five or six years of 'time-serving' under the watchful eyes of tradesmen. Instruction typically involved face-to-face instruction 'on the job' by a card-carrying tradesman to whom the apprentice was attached, plus part-time educational study at a local technical college. A similar approach, without the educational element and invariably implemented with less consistency and commitment, existed in the more labour-intensive manufacturing and packaging fields, where established operatives were assumed to be capable of instructing newcomers for brief periods on repetitive jobs that were considered basically 'unskilled'.

A four-stage approach to instruction was favoured by the few who took enough interest to give advice on the subject. The four stages were:

Tell→Show→Do→Review

The learner was told in detail what must be done and how to do it (great store was set on splitting the material into short stages, each comprising what could be assimilated and retained); then the instructor performed what had just been described; then the learner tried to repeat what had been demonstrated; and, finally, the instructor explained and praised or criticised the learner's performance, leading into a repeat of the cycle or movement to the next stage. Note the assumptions, negative as well as positive: the instructor was always right and fully competent in the worker's roles; all learners were equal; training plans were considered unimportant, and certainly not agreed in advance with learners; the learner should copy and should not be invited to innovate; reasons for any given method were not needed; repetition was the way to handle any who did not learn quickly. A common approach involved building up stages: first stage one, then one plus two, then one plus two plus three, and so on. This ensured repetition, which helped memory and cemented routine. Where information (rather than skill) was the subject of instruction, the norm was simply to teach it – ie to present the information in an ordered way, wherever possible with visual aids, the teacher asking questions to ascertain whether the information had been retained and understood.

THE 1940s, 1950s AND 1960s: HUMAN RELATIONS, A DYNAMIC ENVIRONMENT, TRAINING COURSES, TRAINING SYSTEMS

Figure 1.2 An historical perspective: the 1940s, 1950s and 1960s

Background ideas on: organisation/management people at work/learning	Employer-led/backed training activity Training/learning methods	National training interventions
Human relations	Supervisory/training courses *Lectures*	Training Within Industry (TWI)
Motivation theory	Job enrichment Job rotation Management courses *Lectures + syndicate discussions*	
	Management seminars + conferences *Lectures, visual aids discussions + case studies* Management Traineeships	Business Schools
Management by objectives Organic structures *Theory X/theory Y* Participation/consultation	'Systematic Training' *Policy, needs identification appraisal, records etc.*	Industry Training Boards [to early 1980s]
	Induction programmes Operational courses – [eg Marketing, Safety]	

Note: Entries in Figure 1.1 still apply throughout this period. The precise timing and sequence of new entries should not be assumed from their positions in the chart.

The four-stage instruction process was recommended in a 'Job Instruction' teaching programme drawn up and mounted nationwide by the Ministry of Labour during the Second World War – part of a supervisory training package collectively entitled *Training Within Industry*, or TWI for short. The TWI package was a wholly scripted programme which TWI trainers learned verbatim.

While proving that *some* training was planned nationally during the 1940s, TWI was aimed only at management – in this case, at first-level management. It was nevertheless unusual in addressing people established in their jobs, and contributed towards the establishment of management training centres by several large employers, to be used primarily as venues for training courses for newly promoted managers or supervisors. Here a standard course menu was a battery of lectures – on the nature of (scientific) management, on the formal organisation chart, on creating job descriptions, on company aims and routines, on cost control, and so on. Personnel management *was* usually included: it typically offered course members an opportunity to explore the industrial relations scene, conditions of employment, discipline procedures, and the annual negotiation round. Training was only rarely covered as a specific subject for a lecture.

Prime among the contributions from pre-Second World War sociologists was the work of Elton Mayo, who gave international publicity to research studies carried out in the1920s and early 1930s at the Hawthorne plant of the Western Electric Company in Chicago. Initially, the studies had looked into the relationship between workers' physical working conditions and problems of fatigue, sickness and absenteeism; increasingly the spotlight extended into the wider conditions of employment and the less tangible issues of workers' commitment, boredom, aspirations and preoccupations. The researchers concluded that despite the existence of a clearly defined formal organisation, workers collectively colluded in sustaining many unplanned, unauthorised activities which satisfied their social needs, and that these social needs were at least as important in maintaining morale as anything in their paypackets. Mayo's research suggested that, in most work organisations, the relationships between people and between management and workers were critical to maintaining interest in work which offered no physical or intellectual challenge.

After the war, American psychologists and sociologists continued to research these themes, and developed new theories of motivation. Maslow (1943) defined a 'hierarchy' of needs for the individual in the workplace, at the top of which was an ideal termed 'self-actualisation', which implied both the ability to create and the opportunity to develop. Argyris (1957) explained how workers in authoritarian cultures often worked to the lowest level of their ability, saving their creativity and enthusiasm for periods outside work. McGregor (1960) contrasted management styles based on 'Theory X' (basically Taylor's scientific management approach) and 'Theory Y' (consultation, leading to objectives which served both the organisation's and the worker's needs). Herzberg (1959) preached 'job enrichment', which involved making work tasks challenging and meaningful for the worker. These 'human relations' ideas and medicines came to occupy centre stage in management (and especially personnel management) courses. And training activity was often quoted as evidence of 'human relations in action'.

The world of work was simultaneously becoming more competitive, more complex, more innovative. The large 'front-runner' organisations that made up its most visible elements steadily adopted and built into their structures new operational functions, some of which assumed much less consistent or 'static' procedures. Marketing departments produced plans which followed consumer preferences, not merely manufacturing dictat or sales department demands for volume. Sales departments devised promotions campaigns with short-term variations to standard products, multipurchase deals, and so on. Development departments created new products and adapted technical processes. Cost-accounting rivalled financial accounting in its demands on acountants' time, and new management information systems began to emerge. Specialist departments appeared alongside their traditional functional neighbours. Short-term project teams, often multi-departmental, sometimes part-time, were appointed with special terms of reference. Innovation and change began to be accepted as normal. Matrix organisation charts began to appear alongside hierarchical charts in basic management textbooks. 'Management by Objectives' was preached by management gurus like Drucker (1964) in the USA and Humble (1967) in the UK; organisations formalised forward plans, short-, medium- and long-term. Today's work started to become a function of a planned future, with past norms downvalued, if not openly criticised.

Hard on the heels of the US organisational psychologists came UK sociologists' and management theorists' descriptions of new forms of organisation. Burns and Stalker (1961) looked at a variety of industries and concluded that some organisations could no longer properly be described as 'mechanistic': 'organic' was a more appropriate term, as they managed change by minimising formal rules and allowing authority to rest where problems needed to be solved, or again via a 'meetings' culture which allowed new tasks and processes to be adopted without regard for past norms. Woodward (1965) suggested links between technology and structure, the key lesson being that each organisation must determine the form of organisation most suited to its needs. In the USA, Lawrence and Lorsch (1967) went a stage further, explaining that organisations need to cope internally with varying needs, and justifying a 'contingency theory' approach, with departments managed variably through time, dependent upon their different degrees of stability or complexity. Management course and conference agendas thrived on this type of material, which could be guaranteed to stimulate post-lecture discussion.

In the increasingly dynamic environment, it was perhaps inevitable that training activity should grow and develop within the larger organisations, where employees of most types, and especially those in management grades, attended specially planned courses of many kinds, from marketing appreciation to merchandising techniques, from energy-saving methods to safety legislation. Plumbers were introduced to plastic pipeworking, joiners to machine-woodworking, clerks to calculators. Management traineeships (usually involving specially recruited graduates on 'fast-track' routes to junior, and in some cases higher, management posts) appeared, typically providing planned job experience in several departments before the first management appointment. Newly created business schools offered new business degrees for graduates looking for a fast track into senior management and shorter programmes for young promotable managers. Such programmes usually incorporated lectures on economics, sociology, marketing philosophy, accounting practice, and human relations; and much time was given to discussions, often based on real-life case material. A less sophisticated but equally discursive method, employed also internally by organisations which instituted regular conferences, was to split members into several syndicates, each of which met privately to debate a given topic or problem, and then to mount a plenary session at which each group reported its conclusions. The syndicate/plenary approach generated both new joint experience and reflection on it, with decision making helped by a variety of proposed solutions – all within the 'safe' training conference environment. Believed benefits were found not only in the variety of generated opinions: departmental boundaries became blurred, narrow loyalties broadened, perceived aims changed, and individual confidence grew.

Not all these training interventions involved managers, and not all new methods were collective. Employee handbooks grew in number and complexity; self-study books, and even teaching machines, which led the learner 'frame by frame' through a planned series of questions and (usually) multi-choice answers, appeared in recently created training units within the larger private-sector firms. (Although some organisations persevered with programmed learning and self-study, it rarely became popular: programmes almost always lacked humour, and seemed unable to keep most learners motivated for long.) Most learners, however, seemed conditioned to expect a teacher in front of them: some form of teacher or 'tutor' seemed the only sure way that a learner's questions could be answered properly, and equally the only way a learner's doubts, fears and self-imposed distractions could be resolved or diverted. If lectures were still the mainstay of formal courses, visual aids became a central focus of, or at least a major supporting vehicle within, these courses. A new tool, the overhead projector, allowed the trainer to present prepared *and spontaneously to create* images on a screen while still looking at the course membership – and of course allowed syndicate members to improve presentation skills.

In the larger organisations, therefore, training processes were growing and becoming more sophisticated, and trainers were taking over from management some of the latter's communication roles. This trend was accelerated by Industrial Training Boards (ITBs), created by the Industrial Training Act 1964; the ITBs typically advised in-scope employers to copy a larger competitor in training matters. But their guidance was essentially mechanistic in nature, limited to such things as induction training for new starters and 'systematic' procedures – for example, policy creation, training needs identification, appraisal, records. With all that, the 1960s saw a significant increase within medium-sized organisations (small employers were outside ITB scope) in the number of staff with explicit responsibility for promoting training, and again in the formal identification of training needs, plus their conversion into paper plans. There remained the problem of implementation: plans often remained proposals, with managers uncommitted or just too busy with other priorities to make learning happen.

It is nevertheless wrong to think that bureaucratic ideals disappeared in this changing world of work. Well-defined structures and procedures continued to be prized by top management. 'Closed-system' assumptions, which basically ignored the impact of the outside world on internal management decisions, remained the norm, especially in the small enterprise.

THE 1970s AND EARLY 1980s: TECHNOLOGICAL CHANGE, CHANGE MANAGEMENT, GROUP DYNAMICS, EXPERIENTIAL LEARNING, STRATEGIC MANAGEMENT.

Figure 1.3 An historical perspective: the 1970s and early 1980s

Background ideas on: organisation/management *people at work/learning*	Employer-led/backed training activity *Training/learning methods*	National training interventions
Socio-technical theory		
Contingency theory	Organisation development	
Experiential learning		Manpower Services
Productivity		Commission
Management development	Pre-appointment programmes	Training Services
Organisation development	OD seminars	Agency
	Group problem-solving	Youth Training
	Brainstorming	Schemes
Change management	New management courses	
	Structured exercises	
Barriers to learning	*simulations, discussion*	
Learning styles	Study groups	
	Process review	
Strategic management	Action learning	
	'Sets', projects, tutorials	
Continuous development	Outdoor training	

Note: A 'carry-over' of relevant entries from Figures 1.1 and 1.2 is assumed. As in Figure 1.2, precise timing and sequence of new entries is not implied.

If the scene in the 1960s was one of increasing change, that in the 1970s and 1980s was even more so. New products and processes were introduced with increasing frequency and internal work methods were constantly under review. The larger organisations began to develop strategic ideas and instruments: mission statements, corporate objectives, medium-term plans and budgets started appearing, initial drafts sometimes being prepared by new forward-planning departments. Personnel issues increasingly merited coverage in such documents. This was also a time of high inflation and low profits, fuelled by hikes in the price of oil and upward pressure from workers on wages. The larger employers quickly attacked overmanning situations and restrictive practices, increasingly negotiating 'productivity deals', revising work schedules (notably erasing 'standard' overtime practices), and reducing numbers in return for improved rewards. A decline in the recruitment of young people alarmed government and led to the creation of a nationwide youth training scheme, which quickly gained employer support while costs were borne by the state but later slumped when it became clear that government aimed to shift the costs onto employers.

The wider world was simultaneously intruding in a big way. Competition came from the revitalised continent of Europe, especially Germany, and from the emerging economies of the Far East, where Japan showed near-genius ability in copying Western electronics and automobile technology and then improving creatively on what it copied, and lesser Pacific Rim countries exploited the benefits of cheap labour while developing their own manufacturing operations. Employers were urged – by government, by the CBI, by trade associations, and of course by the ITBs – to train for economic reasons.

The London-based Tavistock Institute of Human Relations, which housed a formidable team of psychologists, psychotherapists and sociologists, developed their own contingency approach (see especially Trist, 1981), pioneering theories of 'open systems' (ie systems open to their environments), and 'socio-technical systems' (ie systems in which the key management task was continuously to balance the relationships between human and technical elements). Socio-technical theory proposed among other things that management must learn how to understand and adjust changing relationships between people, tasks, technology, and structure – indeed, that team management requires that very responsibility above all else. 'Worker participation' became respectable, consultative and representative systems being naturally promoted.

Contingency theory suggested that whereas management might be learnt, it could not be taught as a set of rigid constructs; the approach implied that competence as a manager must naturally be learnt 'by experience'. Kolb's (1974) experiential learning theory rapidly gained ground among academics and personnel management in the USA and Britain: it described a four-stage sequential process for learning at work without a teacher or tutor. (See Chapter 3, page 67.) The newly identified critical element was reflection, which allows the individual to translate real-life experience into abstract concepts and valued 'lessons' which can be stored in the memory for future use. Kolb did not, however, offer answers to the problems of motivating the experiential learner, except to stress the importance to all of 'learning about learning'. In the UK, Honey and Mumford (1986) built on Kolb's theoretical base, defining learning 'styles' and offering ways whereby learners might understand and work on what they themselves perceive as strengths and weaknesses.

In the USA, Argyris and Schon had for years been researching the realities of learning and decision-making. In 1978 they publicised characteristics within landmark organisations that they labelled 'defensive routines' – individuals' ways of protecting themselves, deflecting attention from themselves by obscuring issues and problems that might harm their images – and concluded that such behaviour acted as a brake on learning at the levels of both individual and group, and on creativity at the level of the organisation. They presented their 'theory of action perspective', the centrepiece of which was an explanation of how 'unlearning' and 'creative reflection' should take place via what later came to be termed 'double-loop' learning. (See Chapter 4, page 97 for a more detailed explanation.) The key to the double-loop learning process is the questioning of operating norms at the time information is received (or, more properly, immediately thereafter). Argyris and Schon suggested that top management should consciously devote time to double-loop learning activity and should require their middle management to do the same in cross-functional group discussions mounted for this purpose.

In the UK, management courses, seminars and conferences continued to proliferate, many addressing a new central issue of *strategic* change management, all stressing the critical need to be flexible, and some using new learning methods. 'Organisation development' consultants were in demand, often introduced to lead internal seminars in which managers reviewed their goals, structures, responsibilities, and procedural norms. Enthusiasm for cultural change stimulated interest in brainstorming techniques – typically developed in small, *ad hoc* groups rather than via individual challenges or departmental edicts. Developments in simulation facilitated the creation of business games, offering competitive experience – usually allied to group decision-making. Externally, consultants such as Adair (1978) and Coverdale (see Taylor, 1979) offered short courses involving structured exercises which allowed managers to practise team leadership in a changing environment and with innovative goals. 'Study groups' offered leaderless group experiences in which members, with the aid of a 'facilitator', could review and reassess their behaviour as team members. 'Action learning' (see Revans, 1980, and Chapter 5 page 108) allowed individual managers to work for sustained periods on significant real-life problems in new organisational surroundings, with tutorial assistance. Open-air management courses (known variously by such terms as 'adventure education' and 'outdoor training') also became popular, aiming at improving members' understanding of team-building and team leadership via physically challenging group experiences. In short, management training blossomed, diversifying in many directions and introducing discovery methods alongside the more traditional lecture and syndicate discussion methods.

Trainers who themselves became experienced in these new forms of training were very different from the typical ITB adviser, and indeed the new breed quickly outstripped the latter as advisers on training methods. (The ITBs never extricated themselves from their bureaucratic image, unable to modify their levy-grant or levy-exemption schemes away from formalised training procedures towards more creative learning practices; with one or two exceptions, the ITBs were abolished early in the 1980s.) These new 'professional' trainers, employed mainly within larger organisations, also exerted a wider influence on personnel management through their membership of the relevant professional institute, the then Institute of Personnel Management (IPM), and its innovative national committee for employee development. In the early 1980s, the IPM launched a campaign for 'continuous development' (CD), the main goals of which promoted (a) self-development (meaning learner-centred plans and learner-managed learning) and (b) the integration of learning with work (requiring an ongoing attitude that endless learning opportunities exist at the workplace). CD quickly gained supporters within academic circles and professional bodies, but personnel management in general were slow to sell the campaign to their line-management colleagues. The IPM joined forces with the Institute of Training and Development in the early 1990s to become the Institute of Personnel and Development (IPD); henceforth its largest cohort of members were training professionals, many of whom were developing an interest in new, collective and/or learner-managed forms of learning. Personnel management was now dropping its 'human relations' image, actively preaching a 'human resources' philosophy which put the personnel function into the boardroom and aimed at new strategic rather than traditional negotiation roles.

RECENT DEVELOPMENTS : THE LEARNING ORGANISATION CONCEPT, NATIONAL VOCATIONAL QUALIFICATIONS, THE INTERNET

Figure 1.4 An historical perspective: recent developments

Background ideas on: organisation/management *people at work/learning*	Employer–led/backed training activity *Training/learning methods*	National training interventions
Total Quality Management	Youth Training Programmes *Guided work experience + college-based education*	
Information technology	IT training *Lectures + simulations + hands-on experience*	Training and Enterprise Councils
Competence theory		National Vocational Qualifications (NVQs) Industry Training Organisations National Training Targets
The learning organisation	Teamwork seminars *Dialoguing*	
Multi-skilling	Job enlargement	
Empowerment/re-engineering		Investors in People
Knowledge Management	Continuing Professional	The Internet
Lifelong Learning	Development	
Organisations as brains	*Self-paced, self-planned learning*	University for Industry

Note: A 'carry-over' of relevant entries from earlier Figures is assumed. As previously, precise timing and sequence of new entries is not implied.

In the industrial world of the UK, the 1980s and 1990s have been 'recovery' years: inflation and unemployment have steadily diminished, industry has become more profitable, and although internal change has continued to be the norm for most large organisations, that change has stemmed more from technological advances and 'downsizing' than from cultural aims. Fibre optics have yielded enormous communications improvements. Information-processing has made the desk-top computer the single most indispensable item of inventory equipment. Both have led to redundancies at all levels except the top, with positions amalgamated in reorganisation plans that serve immediate, or at least short-term, financial gains. The employment of young people has also dwindled; in the engineering industry in particular, the number of apprenticeships quickly dropped in the 1980s (the then government relaunched state-funded youth training programmes). The notion of life-time service to an organisation accordingly weakened: it gradually became normal for young, capable, ambitious managers (now of both sexes, thanks to equal opportunities and changing lifestyles) to serve their ambitions by becoming mobile and moving between employers. OD programmes disappeared in favour of more prescriptive restructuring plans; the 'pursuit of excellence' often meant a benchmarking operation in which specialists were detailed to find a superior set of procedures that could be copied and internally imposed. In such a climate it was inevitable that sophisticated management development programmes should tend to be reserved for a select minority, and that the specialist post of management development manager, which had blossomed to some extent during the 1970s, should decline. Computer training, usually teacher- or consultant-led, tended for several years to predominate in internal training activities, despite involving much hands-on practice; it predominated especially (but not exclusively) in firms with personnel and training departments.

Academic interest in links between commercial success and internal learning systems has nevertheless continued to develop, in several notable instances confirming the relationship between strategic management and employee learning. In the UK, Garratt (1994) and Burgoyne (1995) described organisational *patterns* that seemed appropriate to generating change on a continuing basis and stressed the critical importance of teams' self-development activity at the workplace. In the USA, the first director of a Systems Thinking and Organisational Learning programme at Massachusetts Institute of Technology's Sloan School of Management, Peter Senge (1990), drew the 'component technologies' of an ideal 'learning organisation', defining requirements for team learning and newly describing the role of leadership to cover above all the management of a corporate learning process – which he claimed could enable an organisation to manage its external environment in its own interest. Senge showed how traditional, 'top-down' management prevents the all-important double-loop learning that is needed for evolution by its insistence on clearly defined targets which must not be challenged. Nonaka and Takeuchi (1995) later described, using Japanese firms as examples, ways whereby a 'knowledge-creating' culture might similarly allow Western firms to dominate their futures; the essence of the culture is a 'middle-up-down' flow of ideas, authority attaching to the *ideas* rather than any particular position in the organisational hierarchy. The process of exploring and understanding the ideas is seen as the means whereby authority is established. Morgan (1997) has since likened this process to the working of any human brain; he presents a long list of 'critical principles of holographic design' as the basic requirements for organisational learning, among which are the design of networked information systems, the structuring of 'complete process' work teams, and the habit of double-loop learning.

We saw in the last section that UK personnel managers were slow to champion continuous development ideals. With a few exceptions, UK employers have been equally slow to adopt the concept of an ideal learning organisation. Yesterday's passion for cultural change waned with improving short-term economic opportunities, and employers concentrated on reducing payrolls, cutting staff levels, increasing contracted-out work, introducing part-time workers, and adopting more flexible patterns/hours of work, often with less flexible methods of work. In many ways, industry shelved its interest in academic theories and moved back towards more traditional 'man-management' concepts. The 1980s brought interest in 'Total Quality Management' (TQM – see Collard, 1989), a set of disciplines that urged formal definition and redefinition of 'high-quality' procedures and routines. TQM fitted easily into a scene that had largely lost its participative gearing; the approach openly preached a learning culture but generally assumed that managers should simply establish 'best practice' and teach it. A number of new 'service-industry' organisations (eg McDonald's, which Morgan describes as 'perfecting' Taylor's principles) which rapidly grew during this period have made it clear that they view scientific management principles as the only way to organise. The same emphasis on efficiency, quantification, control, predictability, and even de-skilled jobs – sometimes described now as 'McJobs' – can be seen within hospitals, factories, retail outlets, schools, universities and other institutions that have been forced to rationalise their operations and have known no other way to do it. And 'on-the-job' instruction, given to new starters by established workers who make no claim to understanding learning processes, is still the most likely norm in the mass of medium-sized organisations, where training specialists rarely exist and managers usually aim to recruit experienced staff who can quickly commit new routines to memory.

Faced with large employers who seemed to be losing their support for youth training schemes, with small employers who have no training facilities of their own, and with employers of all sizes not recruiting, the UK government has stepped up its own national training interventions. Having abolished virtually all the ITBs, government introduced new national programmes for the young and the unemployed run by the (then) Department of Employment (DE) via a new geographical network of Training and Enterprise Councils (the TECs – known in Scotland as Local Enterprise Companies, or LECs). Once these TECs were in place, the DE assumed the lead position in developing a new national vocational system of *qualifications*

(National Vocational Qualifications, or NVQs, in England, and Scottish Vocational Qualifications, or SVQs, north of the border). (See Appendix 4, page 329, where we explain that throughout this book we use the term NVQ to additionally relate to its Scottish SVQ equivalent.) NVQs are based upon prescribed written standards for specifically named jobs.

NVQs were essentially government's way of updating and upgrading workplace skills via traditional vocational education methods – the classroom and the examination. A sizeable body of literature was produced – by both government departments and by consultants working on government contracts – preaching a new 'competences' approach to skills development. 'Skill' was defined essentially in terms of work outcomes. A body of literature explaining competences theory (see especially Jessup, 1991) maintained that learning methods were not critical: the key to competence was seen as its precise definition.

In the early 1990s, the DE was merged with the Department of Education to form the Department for Education and Employment (DfEE); this new department set up alongside NVQs a new set of 'generalised' National Vocational Qualifications (GNVQs), available to young people in full-time education. New national training targets were henceforth set primarily in terms of achievements against educational targets, and a new national skills task force was established to co-ordinate the work of the standard-setting bodies. The need for employers to plan and implement training internally was not totally forgotten, however: the TECs were given the right/responsibility to dispense an 'Investor in People' (IiP) award to any work establishment which claimed the award and was able to convince an independent examiner on four counts – commitment to, planning of, action on, and evaluation of training. Some TECs have been able to forge alliances with their local Chambers of Commerce and most have pioneered ways of bringing NVQs (and external training resources generally) to the attention of small- and medium-sized employers.

TEC-administered 'Modern Apprenticeships' and 'national traineeships' have also been introduced (with a mandatory NVQ study element) in an attempt to improve the eventual flow of technicians. These state moves have been further developed by the 1997 Labour government, which has introduced a range of 'Welfare to Work' options for the young unemployed.

All these government-led moves have been geared more to improving the nation's economic health by minimising unemployment statistics than by improving profitablility or stimulating growth. Employers have showed some interest but have typically reduced their recruitment of young people further, effectively leaving the education and training of many to the further education sector. Personnel professionals have also in the main accepted NVQs' national standards in place of more specific definitions of workplace needs. In truth, most had little choice but to accept the national standards – and the IPD, which co-ordinated the creation of NVQs in areas relevant to its own work, led the way by adjusting its membership scheme to accept NVQ routes into membership. Its earlier advocacy of continuous development has been transformed into a 'continuing professional development' members' obligation, which requires members to keep an ongoing log of learning achievements but makes no assumptions about either self-development or learning within work.

Those who championed learner-centred learning have been cheered by the rapid international development of the Internet, with its endless reference and forum facilities. Those in full-time education have also shown enthusiasm for surfing the Net, notably when gathering material for projects. This is perhaps a new phenomenon: motivation to learn has until recently not been marked among the mass of young people who do not cope easily with traditional school methods and hence do not aspire to anything beyond secondary education. It is promising to find that young people with a wide range of intellectual abilities can enjoy the process of collecting information on the personal-computer screen, and it is at least possible that this will provide a fillip to self-development in the early years of the next millennium.

Interest in 'lifelong learning' has also blossomed, at least among institutions: the European Commission declared 1996 as their 'Year of Lifelong Learning', spawning a wide variety of initiatives dedicated to stimulating adult learning. Warwick University appointed the first Professor of Lifelong Learning in 1998. But in line with its developing stance on vocational education, the UK government has initially had problems with the concept of *self-directed* lifelong learning. A 1996 report by the Further Education Funding Council (FEFC 1996) on 'inclusive learning' (courses tailored to the individual need rather than the common curriculum) has been largely ignored; another report (FEFC 1997) on 'widening participation', which similarly called for a 'new learning pathway' with imaginative new methods and support for low achievers, was deemed overambitious on cost grounds; and a promised 1998 White Paper on lifelong learning was quickly transformed into a consultative Green Paper (DfEE, 1998) when, at the last minute, Downing Street condemned it as 'lacking rigour', with 'too little commitment to standards and examinations' (TES, 13 February 1998).

The key proposals in the 1998 Green Paper nevertheless remain of great importance, because they report or hint at government-led developments that are already emerging or are likely to emerge in the near future. These developments are:

- a University for Industry (UfI), which uses leading technology to make learning available at work, in learning centres or at home. The development was actually announced 'for real' within days of the Green Paper's appearance; a Pathfinder Prospectus soon followed. The UfI will be launched in 1999 and will provide a networked system of information and advice on learning opportunities, and a 'brokerage' facility that connects individuals and employers with training providers.
- a freephone 'Learning Direct' helpline on qualifications and courses. This service was launched in 1998.
- 'Individual Learning Accounts' – promised for introduction in 2002. Treasury money is to be provided to start these accounts, to which

employers and individuals must also contribute. Course payments can be spread and credit levels secured. These are called in the Green Paper 'the centrepiece of adult learning in the future'.

- more money for higher education (HE) and further education (FE), and again for the Careers Service, including a new learning fund to improve literacy and numeracy among adults.
- a new Institute of Learning and Teaching – to provide courses and qualifications to improve the standard of HE teaching.

EXTENSION, VARIETY AND DIVERSITY

Our subject has 'come of age' during the hundred years covered by this chapter. Its scope has extended from a few to virtually all occupations and to all levels of employee. Its application has broadened from the individual to groups and organisations of all kinds, and even to the nation. Its management has produced a large number of new specialist posts, usually (but not always) located within the personnel management sphere, in turn refining earlier views of line management. New approaches have regularly appeared, usually running alongside – as opposed to replacing – existing approaches. New methods, new resources and new technology have similarly extended the range of training opportunities, notably those allowing learner-centred learning alongside simple instruction and teaching.

The main lesson to be learnt from all this development is that whereas any given training intervention can be reasonably seen as simultaneously contributing towards the improved performance of the individual, the group, the organisation and the nation, there is no single approach or practice that can exist as a standard discipline to serve the all-time needs of all individuals, all organisations, and the nation. Training, like management, is a situation-specific art: as we said in our Introduction, 'those who are responsible for training and development need to have regard to contextual factors when determining the way they assess training needs and objectives, plan strategies and choose methodologies'.

This key lesson is clear from our historical review, and it applies to all types and levels of training activity. The state's own training interventions over the years have varied dramatically in terms of purpose and method. Employers' preferences have varied and diversified, new technology, new structures and new employment levels yielding training plans that have individually pioneered cultural change. The academic world has similarly been reviewing on a continuing basis the nature of management and organisation within new horizons, producing a stream of new conceptual approaches. Individual learners have, especially since the advent of the personal computer, become much less dependent upon teachers, and indeed many are keen to engage in new learning methods.

The implications for the future are clear and strong. We have a century of empirical evidence why training interventions should continue to vary in purpose and design in the future. Although there are many comments to make, many things to criticise, and many suggestions to put forward, there is no ground for advocating a return to scientific management principles or a new 'doctrinaire' discipline to be imposed on all. Each individual training intervention in the future must serve its own up-to-date, realistic appraisal of the twin 'purpose and design' essentials. The best training and development, in short, will continue to be strategic, relevant and unique.

Now we can return to the question we posed at the start of this chapter:

Why do you think we have chosen to present a historical account of UK training as the first main chapter in this book?

Like many propositions in the training and development field, there are several reasons for our strategy – which is aimed at helping the reader to learn, not simply at communicating information.

1 The first reason springs from the point made immediately before we posed our question. History proves this point better than any series of theoretical statements. We suggest that you might like to read again both the last few paragraphs and our Introduction to establish firmly your own stance on the issue, but we hope that at least you will be able to accept that 'any deliberate training or learning is an intervention in an ongoing process'.

2 Our second reason is less philosophical. The mainstream themes of the chapter chart the evolution of what we see as the most important issues in the UK training sphere as we approach the end of the second millennium. The central aim is that of economic progress: training is managed primarily to improve the ecomomic performance of the individual, the employing organisation, and ultimately the nation. Subordinate themes are mirrored in the headings to the Figures: one philosophical, one operational, one political. Summarised as questions, these issues are as follows:

   • What are the main ideas governing UK employers' expectations of how they will manage their organisations in the future, and especially how they will ensure that employees are capable, up-to-date and efficient?
   • What forms can we expect future training or learning activities to take?
   • To what extent will organisations be helped or influenced to adopt a standard 'national' approach to education and training?

Answers to these questions are not easily conjured up in a crystal ball. They can best be determined by reflecting on trends, by remembering past norms that seem too strong to be dropped, and by judging the extent to which *today's* ideas, practices and standards must be modified to meet what the future can realistically be expected to bring.

> A day in the life of Samantha Bloggs, personnel manager for Random Articles Limited, may include any of the following: shopfloor conversations with first-level management, who may have conflicting views on workplace competence as described at industry level, and equally conflicting views on the desirability of workplace assessment; a telephone call from the managing director, who does not understand papers sent to him by the local TEC director; and a trip to the local Further Education College, where information about new courses is shared. It will help Samantha considerably if she has answers, however tenuous, to the three questions above. She will quickly sense whether her contacts are forward-looking or not and, if the former, whether their own views of the future complement her own. It is her job to *feel* and understand employment issues more sharply than her contacts, who – however much they may appear to be trying to convince her otherwise – actually expect her to be able to advise them.

3   The ability to explain 'how things came to be this way' is a major strength for any adviser. Since the world now moves faster and improved communications have made it smaller, management discussions now (ie at the end of the twentieth century) thrive if the dialogue is not confined to communicating information or diagnosing problems but developed in the wider context of 'what the world at large is doing'.

> Sam's job is partly boundary management – defining the boundary in terms of both geography and time. Sam must help her contacts on both sides of Random Articles' geographical boundary to work out what should be done, what might be done, what should not be done, and what cannot be done. Sam will often explain trends as reasons why RA should move to develop a new practice, and will equally cite external experience or movement as the case against something. Gone are the days when RA wanted to be a closed system: RA management generally does now want to be 'open', 'modern', and even 'innovative' – and hence Sam needs continually to help them to judge whether their assumptions are becoming outdated.

4   Observation and understanding of substantial national developments can help managers to understand their own roles.

> Jack James, a production manager in Random Articles, can remember when he first made this connection. The occasion was a branch meeting of his professional institute. The theme of the meeting was the 'Management of Change', and proceedings livened up when members who worked in the public sector challenged others from the private sector, the latter having asserted that 'the only stimulus for change is

competition'. Jack learned several truths: that change happens at national as well as organisational level, that governments and boards of directors try equally to make change work for them; that strategies to make change happen do not always work in the same direction; that political decisions are needed from all managers at all levels; and that the most effective stimulus for change is management itself. Jack has since realised that some training and development decisions taken in Random Articles are similar in content to those taken at national level. How can we get learning to happen: do carrots work better than sticks? Should we build up resources in case they are needed or wait until we are sure, then run crash programmes? Should managers be treated differently from others? Should standards be laid down at the centre, or indeed from the top, or should everyone be urged continuously to develop, setting new standards as soon as old ones are achieved? Should responsibility for training be carried by all or given to one or two special units, or should we have a mixture of the two?

Sam and Jack often share views on training matters, and regularly criticise the way things are moving, but they do not always agree – except, in the final analysis, on the need to manage, and not be managed by, change. Right now they are debating several specific ideas – all put forward by Sam – which have had interesting histories:

- Should we be increasing or decreasing the level of 'employee participation' in decisions on their training?
- Should we make new recruits study to match certain basic requirements in subjects like English and Mathematics?
- Are we spending too much on external course attendances?
- Should we encourage (or make?) established employees study for vocational qualifications – notably for NVQs?
- Should we still arrange separate training events for managers?
- Should we search for ways to allow self-study and distance learning?
- What exactly is this government initiative called the 'University for Industry'?

5 Learning from life is often superior to learning from theory. Indeed, most managers do not learn the art of management by coming to terms with abstract concepts and then finding ways to apply them; they learn by deducing mainstream ideas from what they see happening.

Jack has made a habit of 'learning from practice'. His ideal learning ground is biography. He has read Harvey-Jones, Iaocca and Branson, and would not recognise such names as Argyris, Senge and Morgan. Sam finds she cannot easily discuss her specific RA development ideas with him if she talks theoretically. It is not difficult to see how their current discussions can be more productive if she shows she can discuss RA's history – and can place it in the wider overall national context.

And, perhaps, it is now not difficult for you to see why we chose this as our first main chapter.

FOR FURTHER REFLECTION AND DISCUSSION

1   If you were Sam or Jack, how might your attitudes towards education and training have changed over the last few years?

2   What would you yourself like or expect to see in a statement on national policy in the field of education and training?

3   In an ideal world, what would you expect each of the following to welcome regarding training interventions:
    (a) individual workers   (b) trade unions
    (c) middle managers   (d) senior executives
    (e) employer organisations and trade
        associations
    (f) universities   (g) government

4   Why do you think UK society has tended to expect young people to be 'ready for work' at whatever time they complete their full-time education?

5   To what extent do you see changes in training and education at national level during the past generation demanding changes in the management of training and development at the workplace?

6   How do you think information technology and the Internet will change learning habits into the twenty-first century?

7   Create (a) at least one more 'proposal' to sit alongside those in the 1998 Green Paper (see pages 27–8) and then (b) at least one nation-wide initiative to serve each 'proposal'.

SUGGESTED READING

We do not know of any standard texts which cover the material in this chapter. Most texts on personnel management cover the 'human relations' and 'human resources' approaches to their subject, but without exploring the evolution of training norms as the one moved to the other. Morgan (1997) offers a useful commentary on the development of theories of management and organisation, but covers only the issue of organisational learning as it has emerged from the 1970s onwards. More detailed coverage of many specific training topics in this chapter may however be found in this book by using the index, or elsewhere by following the bibliographical references.

2 An 'institutional' perspective

Introduction – a nationwide institutional network – employees – trade unions – employers – training and education providers – awarding bodies and qualifications – Training and Enterprise Councils – targets – potential employees – central government – Europe – summary

INTRODUCTION

It will have been apparent during the last chapter that much of the commentary was not about training interventions per se *but about what organisations were doing and how they were developing, and about the emergence of new institutions dedicated to vocational education and training – indeed, many twentieth-century training interventions themselves created institutions the essential purpose of which was to make further or future training interventions.*

This chapter aims to describe and explain the main 'institutions' that grace the UK training scene as the twentieth century reaches its close. The word 'institution' is defined loosely, extending beyond organisations per se *to include anything that might reasonably be defined as exerting a significant influence on those who make training interventions – policies, principles, publications, targets, schemes, qualifications, and even people.*

A NATIONWIDE INSTITUTIONAL NETWORK

If our book had been written 50 years ago, there would have been insufficient material to warrant a chapter on this topic; indeed, only a few pages would have been possible. Something would have been written about apprenticeships, which in the engineering and printing industries had long been established as the traditional way of entering craft occupations. We might also have noted the post-Second-World-War establishment by a few large UK employers of management training centres, where short-term internal management and supervision courses and conferences were mounted, mainly for newly promoted or newly recruited management. Technical Colleges and Colleges of Commerce would have merited a mention for their wide range of vocational courses, attended by employees (usually in their own time and at their own expense) who aspired to qualifications that would enhance their job prospects. A very wide range of examining and awarding bodies existed at that time, and colleges often provided their own certificates where national examinations did not exist. It would also have been desirable to explain a part of the Education Act 1944, which placed on employers the obligation to release young people to attend 'further education and liberal studies' classes in 'County Colleges' which were due to be created throughout the land (the legal obligation was never enforced, and only a few of the colleges were established).

But beyond those entries, there would have been little to write: employee development was essentially left as something to be determined or ignored by the employer and/or the adult, without any other 'institutions' established at local or regional or national level to help decision-making or to meet specific needs.

The current picture is very different. Over the past few decades, government-led and other nationwide initiatives have reflected the growing beliefs that employee development can and should make a contribution to solving national economic problems, that lifelong learning is both a natural product and a requirement of continuing change, and that a central stimulus is needed to ensure learning goals of a reasonably high standard. The UK now has a national system of vocational qualifications, a national industry-based network of occupational standard-setting training organisations, a geographical network of Training and Enterprise Councils (TECs), nationally ordered but locally administered 'modern' apprenticeships and youth traineeships, annual national training awards, national training targets, and easy, open telephone or electronic access to information on training providers and resources.

As an aid to understanding the current national scene, Figure 2.1 presents the national training scene in the form of a 'network' chart displaying links between the various institutions that are covered in this chapter. Terms and abbreviations appearing in the chart are explained in Appendices 1 and 2. It is perhaps necessary to stress at the outset several points about its contents:

- Although the central assumption is that the chart names 'institutions' that are responsible for promoting or enhancing employee development in some way, it should not of course be assumed that in every case this is their main function or concern.
- Each box in the chart represents a mainstream category, correlating with our text. 'Institutions' which are not themselves organisations but which are creations of, or systems managed by, specific organisations are italicised within each box.
- Our approach is selective: although the chart includes all 'institutions' that are mentioned in this chapter, it omits many that appear in Appendix 2, which offers a more comprehensive 'quick guide' to training schemes, programmes, initiatives and organisations.
- Dotted lines in the chart do not imply command or subordinate relationships; they do however suggest what might be termed 'operational links', suggesting that regular direct contact and dialogue can be expected.
- Although generally similar, the Scottish and Northern Ireland scenes involve some differently titled institutions.

At the end of each category of 'institution' we offer a few examples of typical training interventions that might be initiated by such 'institutions'. If unfamiliar, terms appearing in these examples are explained in Appendix 2.

Figure 2.1 **The UK's national training network**

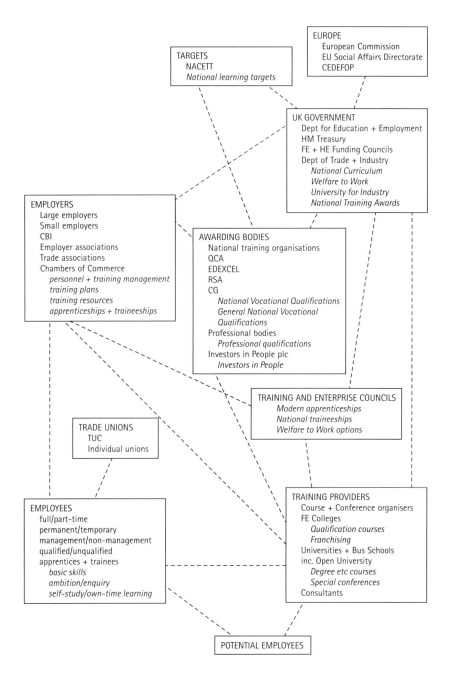

EMPLOYEES

It may seem strange to include employees as 'institutions'. They neverthe-less remain collectively the keystone to which all training institutions relate, and their behaviour or performance is the target of virtually all training interventions. Man-made machines can store data, can 'read' data and adjust routines, can communicate with each other, and can offer alternatives for future decision, but their creative role is limited to their internal man-made programs. If researchers and observers have recently explored new meanings for the term 'learning organisation', they still stress that in the end it is the workforce who must do the learning – using the term 'workforce' to include all who are employed, including (of course) top management.

At the end of 1998, from a total UK population of about 56 million people there were approximately 28 million people in paid employment – somewhat less than half the total. The female share of employment is cur-rently a little below 50 per cent, but is growing steadily (it has increased by 22 per cent since 1990), and is forecast to exceed that of males by the year 2007. Part-time employment, which is mainly undertaken by women, now accounts for about a third of all work, having increased from about a fifth in the last 20 years. (*Source:* DfEE, 1998.)

There is little doubt that only a minority of employees actively seek train-ing opportunities. It seems that, for the most part, UK society still sees training in the mould of formal education – essentially an alternative to work, something to be determined and planned by someone else, something involving dependency, and indeed something difficult and unpleasant. This attitude has been established during full-time education, which of course ends for most at age 16 or shortly thereafter. It is perhaps unsurprising therefore that, if we ignore induction and safety training activities, training is most likely to be aimed at those employees who were the most successful in full-time education – professional staff, technologists, technicians, and management generally, most of whom have successful higher education backgrounds (see Figure 2.2). (Some professions – personnel management and nursing, for example – do now require 'continuing professional devel-opment' (CPD) if their members are to retain their professional qualifica-tions.)

These employees are more likely to press for learning opportunities, espe-cially if they are seen to be linked with professional status and promotional opportunities at work. It is also interesting that such employees are often used in the larger organisations as trainers on internal courses – and that they frequently see their trainer role as that of lecturer.

The relevant percentage statistics have not changed dramatically in the past 40 years, despite boardroom debates on training. In other words, train-ing is disproportionately concentrated on those already in higher-level jobs and on those who are already at least part-qualified. Another report (NIACE, 1998) confirms our original view, speaking of a 'wide gap between the learning-rich and the learning-poor', and stressing the following find-ings:

Figure 2.2 **Employee training by occupation**

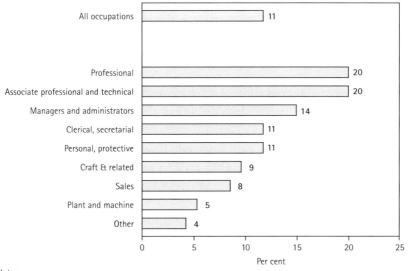

Note:
Men aged 16–64 and women aged 16–59
This figure refers to training provided/funded by employers

Source: DE Labour Force Survey, spring 1996, reported in the DfEE's *Labour Market and Skill Trends 1997/8.*
© Crown copyright.

- Three in five adults have not participated in learning over the last three years.
- More than half those surveyed had no real intention of taking up learning.
- Three key factors affecting people's decisions not to learn, or causing them to give up early, are 'pressures of work', 'finance' and – for women – 'pressure of family commitments'.

One statistic *has* changed during the past 40 years. There is little distinction now to be made between the incidence of planned training for female as against male employees.

Typical training interventions that might be made by employees include:

- seeking new or updated knowledge (eg asking questions)
- self-study (eg reading, personal project activity)
- enrolling as a student on a formal college-based 'own-time' course
- attending branch meetings of a professional body
- joining an Internet-based forum group.

37

TRADE UNIONS

About a third of all UK employees are members of trade unions. Despite the unions' participation as equal partners in the Industrial Training Boards of the 1960s and 1970s, and perhaps because of their members' relative lack of enthusiasm for training, they have not campaigned hard for employee training rights, limiting their strongest challenges to the training aspects of health and safety. Some unions have nevertheless established active training centres, essentially to provide courses for their own shop stewards. And, recently, the Trades Union Council (TUC) has declared strong commitment to the lifelong learning ideal, and specifically to the University for Industry initiative.

A good example of training interventions from the trade-union sector came at the 1998 TUC annual conference, which received and supported a call for union learning representatives at the workplace, plus learning centres in union offices, to bring learning into the bargaining process and promote the UfI development.

EMPLOYERS

The term 'employers' is normally used to mean 'employing organisations', but occasionally it refers to their key decision makers – the chairmen, managing directors, directors and senior executives who are generally thought to lead those employing organisations. Here we use the term in both ways: where we discuss statistics or practices, we are thinking impersonally, but when we refer to policy or aims or attitudes, we are essentially thinking of the people whose thinking governs these matters.

For a country with a mere 28 million workers, it is perhaps surprising that the number of enterprises is as many as 3.7 million – and perhaps even more surprising that over 99 per cent of these employ individually fewer than 50 employees. These 'small' employers account collectively for about half of all employment; in contrast, a mere 6,000 organisations employing over 250 (whom we shall call the 'large' employers) account for 40 per cent of the total. (See Figure 2.3.)

The low incidence of employee training which we outlined earlier is explained partly by the high incidence of small employers, few if any of whom employ specialist personnel or training staff, and – if we ignore family links – few of whom attract young people direct from full-time education with high qualifications. Moreover, a Cambridge research study (DfEE (3), 1998) which analysed data covering the years 1987 to 1995 from some 1,640 small firms who had reported in 1991 that they *did* provide formal training for their staff, could find no consistent links between training and growth or profitability, and could find no evidence that the provision of training improved the prospects for survival. There was however some evidence that *management* training in these firms could contribute to growth.

Figure 2.3 Share of employment by employer size and industry 1996

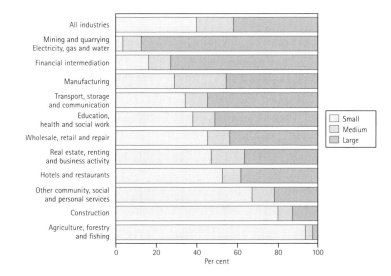

Small employers are often members of their local Chambers of Commerce, who apart from organising regular meetings which offer learning opportunities maintain links with local educational institutions and are in continuing contact with local training providers, schools, careers advisers, and public services generally.

Larger employers tend to look at growth differently: they have established markets, suppliers, brands, distribution systems and so on, and seek growth via innovation and 'the competitive edge', ie improved performance, which means being internally more efficient than one's competitors, and/or finding new ways to do old things. Hence competence may mean something specific to their own unique methods, and tailor-made training may be seen as superior to external courses and even to education aimed at standardised vocational qualifications (a few very large firms now have their own company-based 'masters' degrees and certificates in management, devised and offered in conjunction with academic institutions). Hence also internal training specialists are often employed, training centres are built, training resources are acquired, and detailed training budgets are produced. Where employed, training specialists can be expected to run induction programmes for new staff, to run appraisal systems and collate data on training needs, and even to plan internal courses for established employees, buying in external speakers if necessary but often drawing upon colleagues to provide specialist inputs.

Employers' overall preferences in terms of *types* of training emerged from a 1997 skill needs survey as heavily weighted towards:

Figure 2.4 **Types of training funded or arranged by employers***

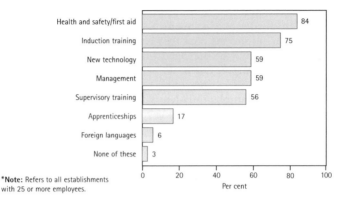

Note: Refers to all establishments
with 25 or more employees.

Source: *Skill Needs in Britain 1998*, reported in the DfEE's *Labour Market and Skill Trends 1998/99*.
© Crown copyright.

- health and safety training
- induction training
- training linked with new technology
- management and supervisory training.

It may be noted that the percentages in Figure 2.4, which summarise employers' own returns and purport to cover only training away from the workplace, challenge those which we reported above from employees. The discrepancy is explained partly by the fact that the employers' survey covered a period of *three* years. Unfortunately, employer involvement in a given type of training does not guarantee its frequency – evidence of a single event is accepted as evidence of employer involvement throughout the period.

We should not forget that some 'household name' employers provide endless evidence of continuing commitment to a wide variety of types of training. The same employers have usually also been ready to offer facilities for work experience for those not yet in employment. Here again, however, the national picture is very patchy: it remains true to say that most employers are for the most part unwilling to fund training for the non-employed, and hence government has had to accept its responsibility to provide funds to stimulate employers' interest. Generally speaking, employers expect the state to equip the unemployed with the basic skills which they look for in a new recruit – primarily numeracy, literacy, communication skills, and a clear commitment to work norms.

Employers of all sizes have however installed computer terminals in their premises, and in recent years the growing use at the workplace of the Internet, and of 'intranets' (groups of networked terminals), has been significant, especially in medium and large organisations. Accessing information via the computer is likely to play a large part in employers' future plans and expectations regarding training.

Later in this book, when we look at the training and development scene from an organisational perspective, we will present a number of learning systems that employers maintain – from an unplanned 'sitting by Nellie' model to firmly designed 'knowledge management' structures. The reality varies considerably between organisations, and we shall see later again that each element in any given model may be managed with widely varying degrees of sophistication. One critical variant lies in the extent to which line management is involved. Where there is no personnel or training management and requirements (such as, for example, the identification of training needs and priorities, or the advance budgeting of training costs) must be met, then 'the line' is expected to find the time to do the work – as indeed it is in many organisations with formal training departments. This in turn means that in such organisations senior management periodically prompts its subordinate management to carry out these responsibilities. And in organisations which see training as a key strategic instrument, senior management itself spends time agonising over the organisation's learning goals, the marriage of training with operational imperatives, the adequacy of training budgets, and so on. It cannot be assumed that the existence of training specialists implies devolution of responsibility for training from line management. Indeed, the most frequently observed principle in organisations of all shapes and sizes is that management is expected to carry the prime responsibility for ensuring the continuing competence of subordinates – a point that we will explain further in Chapters 6 and 9.

One thing that may well be delegated to specialist personnel and training management is ongoing contact with local schools, further education colleges, universities, and a host of potential training providers. In the largest corporations, managers may well be wooed through their superiors by their national trade organisations, who in many cases during the past two decades have created 'lead bodies', or 'industry training organisations' (ITOs), responsible for defining industry-wide standards which are now the basis of approved national vocational qualifications (NVQs). (We will explore later the system surrounding these qualifications, when we will also see that the ITOs have now become 'national training organisations', or NTOs, paid for by government and additionally responsible for overseeing the content of state-sponsored 'modern apprenticeships' and 'national traineeships'.) Large employers also form the majority of organisations in membership of employer organisations (notably the Confederation of British Industry or CBI) and again of trade associations, which exist in virtually all sectors to promote trade in their specific fields. Because it is a prime aim of any such representative body to promote its members' interests at national level, the trade associations and the CBI can be relied upon to maintain ongoing dialogues with government departments of all kinds, with professional bodies, and indeed with any organisation that might present proposals for nation-wide change – and they can be relied upon to present employer views on any and all consultative papers issued. The CBI has perhaps been more proactive than most: it was for example initially responsible for suggesting the idea of 'world-class training targets' (which, as we shall see, government has now

Figure 2.5 Investors in People: the National Standard

INVESTORS IN PEOPLE – NATIONAL STANDARD

PRINCIPLE ONE: An Investor in People makes a commitment from the top to develop all
COMMITMENT employees to achieve its business objectives.

1.1   The commitment from top management to train and develop employees is communicated effectively throughout the organisation.
1.2   Employees at all levels are aware of the broad aims or vision of the organisation.
1.3   The organisation has considered what employees at all levels will contribute to the success of the organisation, and has communicated this effectively to them.
1.4   Where representative structures exist, communication takes place between management and representatives on the vision of where the organisation is going and the contribution employees (and their representatives) will make to its success.

PRINCIPLE TWO: An Investor in People regularly reviews the needs and
PLANNING plans the training and development of all employees.

2.1   A written but flexible plan sets out the organisation's goals and targets.
2.2   A written plan identifies the organisation's training and development needs, and specifies what actions will be taken to meet these needs.
2.3   Training and development needs are regularly reviewed against goals and targets at the organisation, team and individual level.
2.4   A written plan identifies the resources that will be used to meet training and development needs.
2.5   Responsibility for training and developing employees is clearly identified and understood throughout the organisation, starting at the top.
2.6   Objectives are set for training and development actions at organisation, team and individual level.
2.7   Where appropriate, training and development objectives are linked to external standards, such as National Vocational Qualifications (NVQs) or Scottish Vocational Qualifications (SVQs) and units.

PRINCIPLE THREE: An investor in People takes action to train and develop individuals
ACTION recruitment and throughout their employment.

3.1   All new employees are introduced effectively to the organisation and all employees new to a job are given the training and development they need to do that job.
3.2   Managers are effective in carrying out their responsibilities for training and developing employees.
3.3   Managers are actively involved in supporting their employees to meet their training and development needs.
3.4   All employees are made aware of the training and development opportunities open to them.
3.5   All employees are encouraged to help identify and meet their job-related training and development needs.
3.6   Action takes place to meet the training and development needs of individuals, teams and the organisation.

PRINCIPLE FOUR: An Investor in People evaluates the investment in training and
EVALUATION development to assess achievement and improve future effectiveness.

4.1 The organisation evaluates the impact of training and development actions on knowledge, skills and attitude.

4.2 The organisation evaluates the impact of training and development actions on performance.

4.3 The organisation evaluates the contribution of training and development to the achievement of its goals and targets.

4.4 Top management understands the broad cost and benefits of training and developing employees.

4.5 Action takes place to implement improvements to training and development identified as a result of evaluation.

4.6 Top management's continuing commitment to training and developing employees is demonstrated to all employees.

---

adopted as a main plank of its own strategy), and in 1998 it proposed a 'world-class qualifications framework' which would bring together all academic, vocational and competence qualifications.

Nominees from large companies also often sit on their representative bodies' councils and committees; where training committees are concerned, such nominees are, once again, typically personnel or training managers. The same people may also be asked to sit on governmental bodies, on professional body committees, on further education college boards of governors, and so on; if the employer gets a significant track record in the employee development sphere, the nominee may be asked to appear as a speaker at external courses or conferences, or to author articles in the personnel press. In such ways the large employer role expands and extends into the environment.

Since the early 1990s it has been possible for an employer to obtain a training award as a so-called 'Investor in People' (IiP). By July 1998, 10,000 employers were reported as having achieved these awards. We will explain later how they are administered; the process involves satisfying independent assessors that the employer matches a number of nationally prescribed standards. The 'national standard' required of, and demonstrated by, an Investor in People is set out in Figure 2.5. The wording in this national standard is carefully chosen and effectively summarises in its principles and statements everything an employer might be expected to do in relation to employee training and development.

More specifically, typical training interventions by employers include:

- sponsoring attendance at external training courses/conferences
- mounting tailor-made internal training courses
- creating or adjusting the internal training needs identification system
- offering 'Modern Apprenticeships', or 'National Traineeships', or engaging one or more unemployed people under the state-sponsored 'New Deal' welfare-to-work scheme

- creating or developing a training department
- creating a learning resources unit.

TRAINING AND EDUCATION PROVIDERS

Although learning resources units, or indeed specialised training departments, seem likely to make employees more learning-conscious and employers less dependent upon the outside world for training provision, additional
external provision will almost certainly still be sought and used. A glance
at the pages of any personnel management journal or at the list of exhibitors
at any of the UK's periodic national personnel or training conferences will
confirm that the training provision industry is large and buoyant.

Private providers offer everything from consultancy to equipment to film
hire to meeting rooms to programmed texts to ready-made or newly planned
courses – even to services involving expensive technology such as video-con-
ferencing – and a lot more besides. Educational institutions offer even more:
they cater extensively not only for their full-time students but also for part-
time students from the world of work, preparing them for vocational
qualifications. Virtually all universities now have business schools and offer
part-time degrees in business as well as professional studies and short management courses; some ape the Open University in offering distance learning facilities. Further education colleges provide the educational element in
the vast mass of Modern Apprenticeships, National Traineeships, and 'wel-
fare-to work' schemes; they also prepare 'released from work' students for a
wide range of nationally approved examinations, including many set by professional bodies. Some professional bodies have their own student schemes,
these days including distance learning facilities.

Of all these providers, the 400 or more further education colleges are collectively by far the lead provider in post-16 education and training, catering
for four million students (of whom about half a million are in full-time
education), which represents an increase of more than 35 per cent since
1993–4. Since 1994 they have been independent of state and local government, although they still receive the bulk of their income as public funds via
a central Further Education Funding Council (FEFC). Funding for state-
sponsored youth and anti-unemployment schemes is received separately via
local Training and Enterprise Councils, which we will cover in the next section. Employers are charged fees direct for their employees attending
courses. Despite the increase in student numbers, financial pressures on colleges have steadily grown, influencing colleges to negotiate special (sometimes termed 'franchising') arrangements with employers, sometimes in
partnership with private training providers; such arrangements now account
for about a fifth of all colleges' revenue. (In recent years colleges have often
moved into employer premises to take over some of the work-related training alongside the more traditional classroom lectures.)

Figure 2.6 FE programme areas

Programme area	Approximate student numbers
Sciences	500,000
Agriculture	50,000
Construction	125,000
Engineering	300,000
Business studies	700,000
Hotel and catering	225,000
Health and community care	550,000
Art and design	350,000
Humanities	900,000
Basic education	225,000

Data collated from Further Education Funding Council. *Quality and Standards in Further Education in England, 1996–7.*

Each college has its unique internal departmental organisation, each department offering its own range of courses. The main programme areas can be seen in Figure 2.6 (where figures have been 'rounded off'). 'Modern' subjects – such as information technology, motor vehicle maintenance, tourism, design studies, and sports studies – now draw large enrolments. In the current decade there has been an increasing attempt to address employer concerns that 'basic skills', tuition in number and communication skills, and again in information technology, should be offered as part of the curriculum.

Further Education (FE) has been the subject of several major reports in recent years. Two stand out, each identified with the name of the person who chaired the investigating committee, and each gaining widespread support in both political and educational circles. The FEFC's 1996 Tomlinson Report argued forcibly for a new 'inclusive' approach to learning for all FE students, proposing substantial increases in funding to allow students to learn at their own pace and in support of their own objectives – basically suggesting a much more flexible adult learning approach than currently applies. A year later the Kennedy Report (FEFC, 1997) demanded with equal force that much wider participation in FE be available for all ages, and to that end demanded more money, new technology, and new learning 'pathways' – basically a national commitment to promote learning for all with a new system for recognising achievement.

The range of external options for an employee or an employer is enormous. To help navigate the jungle, a free telephone helpline has been opened nationally under the title 'Learning Direct'. Staffed by experienced careers advisors who have immediate on-line access to a national 'learning opportunities' database, it offers information and advice on courses and learning facilities throughout the UK.

Typical training interventions by providers are:

- drafting a new course
- liaising with an employer to supply refresher training for established staff
- devising new projects and exercises within a course schedule
- supplying customised computer-based training programmes.

AWARDING BODIES AND QUALIFICATIONS

Virtually all students attending further education colleges are attempting to obtain a recognised qualification. A large number of organisations, including universities, further education colleges, professional institutes and associations, industry lead bodies, occupational standards councils, training boards and councils, project groups, a variety of examining boards, a national management forum, and even the Ministry of Defence, can and do award qualifications. Three bodies in this varied picture are pre-eminent, being more extensively involved and having the longest experience: the City and Guilds Institute (CG – whose traditional work was mainly in the fields of engineering and science), the Royal Society of Arts (RSA – who similarly pioneered qualifications in clerical, secretarial and office work), and EDEX-CEL (the recently renamed Business and Technology Education Council (BTEC), offering a mix of business and technician awards). These three are represented on the nation's Qualifications and Curriculum Authority (QCA), which oversees all 'officially recognised and approved' academic and vocational programmes and awards.

Employers, employees and even training specialists have always had difficulty in charting the vocational qualifications minefield. Since the mid-1980s, however, several developments have combined to make the overall picture easier to understand and to relate its parts more consistently to each other. Acting in line with a central government strategy, industry lead bodies and occupational standards councils have reviewed and newly defined the necessary content of qualifications within their fields of interest, and awarding bodies have revised their syllabuses to match centrally devised 'national vocational qualification' standards. The NVQ system ensures that all such qualifications – also colloquially now known as 'NVQs' – aim at reflecting actual workplace *competence* and not just relevant knowledge. (Scotland has a similar but technically separate *SVQ* system; we use the term NVQ throughout this book to relate to both.) Appendix 4 outlines the basic conceptual framework for, and the institutional system supporting, these qualifications.

A collective approach to planning future vocational qualifications and a consistent approach to standards-setting were ensured during 1998 by transforming the employer-owned, industry-based ITOs, plus state-owned occupational standards councils, into a new network of state-funded but employer-*driven* 'national training organisations', or NTOs. An NTO National Council exists to maintain a collective two-way dialogue with government and to provide services to the NTOs.

Provided it sticks rigidly to the standards set by the NTO, any awarding body can design an NVQ course or learning programme, and once it has obtained NTO endorsement it can submit its design to the QCA for accreditation. Elements can be imported from established NVQs to cover management and other occupational competences that are considered generic or common to most work sectors. Once accredited, the new qualification will be placed by the QCA in one of five NVQ levels, thus positioning it within the overall national framework (see Appendix 4 for a detailed explanation of the various levels).

The millionth NVQ was awarded in 1995 and the two-millionth in mid-1998, at which time the QCA estimated that some 2.1 million candidates were working towards an NVQ or NVQ units. These qualifications are now the central focus of all government youth training and welfare-to-work schemes; funding arrangements ensure that providers, especially the further education colleges, offer and support NVQs. We will hear later about a sister group named *General* National Vocational Qualifications (GNVQs), related less specifically to the workplace but aiming to prepare those still in full-time education – at school or in further education – for work within a particular industry; although these GNVQs are 'unit-based' (ie a certificate is issued for each unit completed) and based on knowledge rather than workplace competence, they are, like NVQs, approved by the QCA but are exclusively awarded by the 'big three' national awarding bodies – the CG, the RSA and EDEXCEL.

Government funding rules have effectively forced further education institutions to promote NVQs (and GNVQs), and the vast majority of ambitious young employees can now expect an NVQ future. Most young people seem happy with NVQ courses, although some full-time post-16 students who have aimed at both NVQs and A-level examinations seem to have found difficulty in handling simultaneously two different types of study and assessment. College lecturers have also had problems with the need to incorporate workplace realities into their study plans and have complained of the bureaucratic nature of many NVQ standards, but in general they seem to have accepted the competence approach to learning. Small employers – or at least those who patronise further education – seem to be steadily coming to accept the idea of national standards. But some large employers are less sure: their own idea of competence is linked more to their unique needs than to any national denominator, and some have been slow to encourage their established workers to respect the new qualifications. It is probably true that these large employers will come to accept higher-level NVQs for their management as these appear (to date, fewer than 1 per cent of all NVQs are at the highest level), but it is doubtful whether government calls for 'widening participation' or 'lifelong learning' via NVQ enrolments will be supported by large employers unless nationally recognised achievement can somehow be taken to reflect actual workplace performance.

A less permanent but perhaps more immediately visible opportunity for the employer is the annual presentation of 'National Training Awards' (NTAs), determined by a government committee and ensuring wide coverage in the national and personnel press. NTAs are given in each of several categories, one of which recognises innovative training methods.

We have already mentioned the one nationally-recognised *employers'* training qualification – the Investors in People (IiP) award. This is administered by a private limited company (Investors in People UK Ltd), specially set up for the purpose by government. Its positioning in the private sector can be taken to reflect an acceptance by government that employers flinch from the idea of assessment by the public sector. The actual assessment of an employer's application for the IiP award is carried out via arrangements by the local Training and Enterprise Council, at which we will now look in more detail.

Awarding bodies must make training interventions if they are obliged to amend or update their qualifications in any way – for example, changing a syllabus. Every examination that is set is effectively a training intervention of sorts.

TRAINING AND ENTERPRISE COUNCILS

Government has acknowledged the training reputation of some (usually large) firms and has capitalised on their readiness to allow their managements to play a community role by liaising with employer representative bodies and inviting their nominees to sit on the 'TECs' or 'LECs' – Training and Enterprise Councils or (in Scotland) Local Enterprise Companies – which dispense government money in the locality in support of a number of state-led schemes.

The TECs/LECs, of which there are in all about 100, are geographically sited. They are theoretically independent of government, have their own representative national council, and are free to enter into contractual arrangements with third parties (some have joined forces with their local Chambers of Commerce, for example, in an attempt to improve links with small employers). But like many other institutions established by government, they derive their purpose from government initiatives, their full-time staff are civil servants, and their funds come from the Treasury, with strict conditions as to their use. Basically, they are empowered to use these funds in support of government's published aims – in particular, those aimed at reducing unemployment, especially youth unemployment.

Initially the TEC basic role was planned, as the name implies, to combine training and enterprise: new local commercial initiatives were to be supported by local training and related vocational education. Training providers were excluded from TEC boards, but liaison with providers, and especially the further education colleges, was to be creative and critical. But there has been little central money to encourage enterprise (regional councils appeared in 1998 to develop local economies in collaboration with the Department of Trade and Industry), TEC funds becoming almost wholly geared to national youth training and welfare-to-work developments. TECs are now effectively the local custodians of national frameworks developed for Modern Apprenticeships and National Traineeships by the NTOs (frameworks incorporating NVQs now cover over 60 sectors); they are also the on-the-spot co-ordinators of detailed arrangements for these schemes, bringing together (as needed) individual schools, careers advisors, further education colleges, employers and the young people themselves.

The Labour Government's 1998 'New Deal' welfare-to-work programme for the unemployed 18–24 age group, plus similar 'New Start' projects for the 14–17-year-olds, have expanded the TEC role further. We will discuss these developments later in this chapter when we explore the role of the Department for Education and Employment (DfEE) and its Employment Service (ES). These government initiatives, which rely in part on TEC resources, offer the TECs an enhanced influence through their dialogues with the local world of education and training, as well as with employers and employment exchanges. It nevertheless remains to be seen whether the strong image that is so necessary for young peoples' interest and employer co-operation can be sustained.

TECs also provide the administration and assessment requirements in connection with the employers' IiP awards (see Figure 2.5 pp42–3). An employer's application must be accompanied by extensive evidence against a long list of specific criteria; an independent assessor, appointed by the TEC, then visits the employer's premises to gather supplementary evidence, largely via a series of face-to-face interviews, before making a final recommendation to the TEC. When an organisation is awarded its IiP, the presentation is invariably made by a TEC official at a special TEC-arranged event, with the local media invited to be present.

TECs' training interventions are many and varied. They include:

- initiating discussions with one or more employers with a view to adding to their 'Welfare to Work' register
- recommending a local employer for appointment to a further education college governing body
- liaising with the regional enterprise council on the latter's plans, and their effect on the local labour market
- publicising arrangements for modern apprenticeships
- setting up a task force which sets local targets for raising skill levels
- arranging IiP presentations and publicity.

TARGETS

Targets are now a well-established aspect of the UK training scene. National target figures exist for apprenticeships and apprentices, for national traineeships, for 'New Deal employers', for 'employees receiving job-related training', for further education student registrations, and especially for the attainment of vocational qualifications.

A National Advisory Council for Education and Training Targets (NACETT) has been established to review continuously both the main targets and achievement against them. These main targets are now termed 'National Learning Targets' and were revised and expanded in late 1998 to cover – in addition to organisations gaining IiP status – both academic and vocational qualification attainments from age 11 upwards. Figure 2.7 presents the targets geared to the year 2002.

Figure 2.7 **The national learning targets to year 2002**

Target	Autumn 2002
11-year-olds	80 per cent reaching the 'expected standard' for their age in literacy, and 75 per cent in numeracy
16-year-olds	50 per cent achieving 5 higher grade GCSEs 95 per cent achieving at least one GCSE
Young people	85 per cent of 19-year-olds with a Level 2 qualification 60 per cent of 21-year-olds with a Level 3 qualification
Adults	50 per cent with a Level 3 qualification 24 per cent with a Level 4 qualification (a third target – 'Learning Participation' – is promised.)
Organisations	45 per cent of medium-sized or large IiP-recognised 10,000 small IiP-recognised

Notes:
- *11-year-olds* 'expected standard' = level 4 in national tests
- *16+* higher-grade GCSEs = GCSEs at Grades A to C equivalent
- *YP* Level 2 = 5 GCSEs at Grades A–C, an NVQ Level 2, an Intermediate GNVQ or equivalent
  Level 3 = 2 A-levels, an NVQ Level 3, an Advanced Level or equivalent
- *Adults* Level 3 = (same as for 19-year-olds)
  Level 4 = NVQ Level 4, ie degree or higher-level vocational award
- *Organisations* medium-sized = 50+ employees; small = 10 to 49 employees.

It can be seen that the targets are demanding but again that they bring together as 'equals' academic, vocational and competence-based qualifications. Earlier targets addressing 'core skills' at age 19 have been dropped, perhaps because the 11+ and 16+ targets are now expected to satisfy this need. The key point remains that qualifications are seen as the main yardstick against which to judge UK vocational education and training progress – and, more generally, the level of skill attained by the nation's workforce and the level of commitment to training by employers.

NACETT meets regularly to review the national training targets and the progress towards them. If it recommends changes to the former, it makes a training intervention. But it also maintains a set of 'priorities for action' and recommends to a wide variety of bodies ways to improve progress – for example, on national testing, on performance tables, on further education college inspections, on possible actions by NTOs and IiPs, and even on arrangements for funding the TECs.

POTENTIAL EMPLOYEES

It may seem peculiar to include in this chapter a section on people who are not in employment – and to incorporate in the definition of that term those who are in full-time education, including schoolchildren. The rationale for including them lies partly in the 'standard' trainer view that training is usually best completed before it is operationally needed, but also partly because in recent years pre-employment learning has grown in importance, itself due to the already noted belief that many young people emerge from full-time education without the essential employment skills of communication, numeracy and IT, and again without real commitment to work.

Until recently, pre-16 education was essentially academic and each school adopted its own curriculum. The Education Act 1988 changed all that: since then a National Curriculum has been imposed, defining 'core' subjects (science, mathematics and English) and 'foundation' subjects (including information and communication technology) and ensuring that these subjects occupy the majority of the learner's school time. And in the wake of NVQs, as we noted on page 26, in 1992 there appeared a set of 'preparation for employment' qualifications called *General* National Vocational Qualifications, or GNVQs. These new-style qualifications were introduced into schools and further education colleges essentially to cater for full-time pupils who seem unsuited to an academic future. Lead Bodies from 14 selected areas (eg manufacturing, catering, art and design, tourism – overlapping but not identical with the NTOs, which create the national standards for NVQs) have drafted the study content, covering basic skills within their specified vocational areas; the awards are made by the three main national awarding bodies. Assessment is via assessed work rather than traditional examinations, an important distinction aimed at aiding those who are less academically gifted and more in line with workplace realities. GNVQs can now be followed in school from age 14, can be continued or started in post-16 further education colleges, and carry equal value with academic awards for later movement. (See Appendix 4 for more detail.)

The term 'potential employees' must of course include adults who are out of work, people seeking a change of employment, and perhaps even women completing a period of maternity leave. The range of learning options for such people is now large, from Open University courses to adult education programmes to distance learning packages to the Internet. The free telephone helpline 'Learning Direct' is an important resource here (see page 320).

We will cover the topic of potential employees at much greater length under the heading 'Preparing Tomorrow's Workforce' in Chapter 11.

CENTRAL GOVERNMENT

The picture concerning training 'institutions' created, funded and managed by the state itself has in recent decades been a highly volatile one. Over the years, successive administrations have created (and abolished, replaced or adjusted) many and varied training 'institutions'. Interventions have been frequent as policies and priorities have changed, Green and White Papers have been issued, special project reports have been completed, and organisational adjustments have been made.

The merging of two major departments in 1995 to create the current Department for Education and Employment (DfEE) recognised and reflected, as we explained in our first chapter, the political view that government cannot leave employers and employees to provide the skills that the future demands, that problems of unemployment cannot wait for economic growth for their solution, that education must become more vocational to serve the 'small employer' economy, and that a buoyant qualifications system will serve the country better than imposed levy/grant schemes, pump-priming or simple injunctions to learn. Old assumptions about lifetime careers within one organisation, and indeed within one occupation, have increasingly been challenged; it is becoming more important now for the individual to have multiple marketable skills, including the ability to learn in changing conditions, than for the employing organisation to create long-term robots. Within this context it is arguable that the central theme of recent UK training interventions has been the creation of versatile individuals who own personal portfolios of experience and portable qualifications. If we add other influences such as open learning, the personal computer and self-development, it can be seen that whatever the intentions of those who might formally be regarded as the leaders of the evolving system, the UK may be moving towards a culture in which individuals manage their own development rather than simply 'join' organisations and rely upon them to look after their learning needs. At the very least, it must be understood that the overall approach of government is moving away from addressing the employing organisation towards serving and influencing the individual – and that corporate-sector institutions are adjusting to promote that move.

Most corporate-sector institutions are now managed as part of the DfEE operation, although some are quangos – quasi *non*-governmental organisations, technically led by people appointed from outside government. Such bodies remain dependent upon the Treasury for their funds, and their day-to-day adminstrative activities are managed by full-time civil servants in the DfEE; their ongoing roles and powers are to a major extent dependent upon Treasury–DfEE relations.

We have already noted several of these institutions that are 'of' government but not in it. We have seen how NTOs create national training standards and the content of youth training programmes but are financed via the DfEE, which effectively imposes a corporate conceptual approach. Similarly, further education colleges are largely funded from a central funding council, which has to date biased its funding tariff in support of government aims, and which also imposes upon each college a periodic inspection routine and makes the resulting reports available to the public. And although TECs remain legally independent local companies led by local business people, the vast mass of their revenues are tied to government-imposed conditions; as with the further education colleges, private-sector training providers who receive TEC monies are now subject to visits from Training Standards Council inspectors, the resulting reports now being available to all via the Internet.

The DfEE's Employment Service (ES) also affects the national training scene, especially now through the introduction of the 'New Deal' programme and 'New Start' projects in 1998. The former of these is a major initiative aimed at improving the employability of young people aged

Figure 2.8 **The UK government's 'New Deal' options**

The New Deal options for unemployed 18- to 24-year-olds

The employment option – a subsidised full- or part-time job with a private- or public-sector employer, with training for the equivalent of one day a week, leading to a recognised qualification. Full-time jobs must be for an average of 30 hours a week or more; part-time jobs for 24–29 hours a week. The employer is expected to pay the going rate for the job and receives a subsidy of £60 per week (£40 for part-timers) and £750 towards the cost of training. The subsidy lasts for six months, and although there is no obligation to continue employing the young person after this, employers [*are*] encouraged to retain New Dealers as regular employees.

The environment task force option – up to six months' work experience in projects such as recycling schemes or restoring and renovating old buildings for use by local people. It includes one day's training a week (or equivalent) towards a recognised qualification. Participants either receive a wage or their normal benefits, plus up to £400 for the six-month period.

The voluntary sector option – this involves work on a very wide range of projects of value to the community (this is not 'volunteering'). Conditions are the same as for the environment task force.

The full-time education and training option – this option lasts for up to a year. It is intended primarily for young people without NVQ/SVQ Level 2 ro equivalent qualifications, but it can lead to more advanced qualifications if there is a demonstrable link between the course an individual wants to take and their chances of finding a job. The option is delivered by colleges of further education or private training providers and includes study for a recognised qualification or support for pre-vocational or basic skills, training in job-search skills and a period of work experience. Participants receive their normal benefit plus books, equipment and clothing needed for the course.

Source: DfEE *Insight 42*, Summer 1998 © Crown Copyright

between 18 and 24, effectively redirecting national social security funds to serve that purpose. The New Deal welfare-to-work programme takes away the unconditional right of an unemployed person in the age group concerned (government statistics currently record well over 100,000 such young people) to receive unemployment benefit: if six unemployed months are completed, anyone in this group must either enter full-time education or accept one of three other options, which provide six months' part-time work experience and vocational education. (See Figure 2.8.)

The management of the nationwide New Deal programme is complex. The programme provides a number of routes into employment for these young people, who are each offered a personal advisor (usually from the Careers Service) during a 'gateway' counselling period of up to four months, at the end of which – if still unemployed – they move into one of four work and/or education options for a six-month period. A critical innovation is the payment of a weekly wage subsidy to participating employers. Because options are not equal in kind, and movement between options may happen, and expectations generated at counselling interviews need to be understood by programme providers, the need for efficient administration is great, and communication between participating institutions must be consistently accurate. The delivery of particular elements of the programme is not standardised but varies from area to area, depending upon 'local partnership' arrangements agreed between a variety of bodies involved – government's employment offices typically, but not always, co-ordinate the involvement of employers, careers services, training providers, environmental groups, and voluntary organisations, in addition to the TECs.

New Start projects (over 50 of which existed by the end of 1998) similarly depend upon 'local partnerships' and are even less standardised in management terms, in so far as they do not depend upon the ES as the co-ordinating instrument. New Start proposals individually incorporate a 'leading member' of the local partnership, which may be a TEC or a local authority or even a school, and if the proposal is approved, that leading member assumes the key position, notably in connection with the routing of government funds. New Start projects are aimed primarily at young people 'disaffected' with traditional education methods and usually create new-style learning facilities leading towards vocational qualifications. It is possible that these projects will at some future date be consolidated into a national programme on lines similar to those of the older age group's New Deal.

The DfEE has other roles, too. It is of course a body that drafts consultative papers, commissions surveys, maintains statistical records and above all communicates information on what is available nationally. Its quarterly *Labour Market Report* publishes definitive figures on employment, unemployment, training outcomes and official estimates of skills shortages; 'special features' address such issues as progress towards NACETT targets, small-firm training needs, and UK links with the EU Commission and the EU's Social Affairs activities, including the distribution of Social Fund monies.

The DfEE also accepts a central reference role for people who are seeking learning opportunities and for employers wanting to tap into existing resources. Its 'Learning Direct' telephone operation gives free, confidential helpline advice, including information on existing courses and how they can be accessed. The 'University for Industry' moves a technological step further in pioneering a 'national multi-media network' – which aims eventually to offer self-managed, computer-based learning with the aid of the PC, the Internet, and a battery of online tutors and forums. Similarly, the 'National Grid for Learning' aims to offer teachers a 'virtual teacher centre', allowing a forum for the exchange of ideas, a library of documents on learning methods, and resources for teacher/trainer development. If the techniques of delivering online learning are still in their infancy, attempts at dialogue being ponderous and even information-gathering slow, young people in particular do seem attracted by these methods, and committed professionals can be expected to devise new ways for networks to work on data, and indeed for the training world to sharpen its awareness of what can be achieved.

Perhaps the most significant of the DfEE's many training interventions is one that is virtually continuous. Its Skills and Enterprise unit at Sheffield runs a registration scheme that ensures members receive copies of the *Labour Market Quarterly Report*, plus a digest which provides update material on all national training and vocational education matters and abstracts of major reports, plus again a series of pamphlets summarising new research findings. The same unit publishes annually government's *Labour Market and Skill Trends* report, which effectively brings together all aspects of government policy and strategy in this field. Partnership activities involving education, the TECs and employers are also publicised via the DfEE's quarterly *Insight* journal.

EUROPE

Another governmental role involves managing its links with the European Union (EU), and indeed ensuring that the UK observes its responsibilities as a member state. A note on the 'European scene' can be found as Appendix 7, which presents historical data, a comparison of the UK's national training system with those of Germany and France, and a commentary on the EU's aims and actions to date.

Employment and training have always been a key aspect of EU social affairs policy. The original Treaty of Rome (1957) included a 'social chapter' which sets out the EU's social affairs objectives; the EU's Social Affairs Directorate is responsible for drafting 'Directives', which are the EU's way of imposing new law (all Directives must be implemented through national law, which means that an employer who complies with national law is also complying with EU law), and also White Papers, within its areas of interest. There is also a social *charter*, which is a non-binding declaration of community-wide social aims, and which has prompted an action programme driven by the Social Affairs Directorate. And the Commission can itself prompt national action via 'Recommendations', 'Opinions', and 'Communications', all of which member states are obliged to consider.

To date, the only major effect of EU legislation in the training sphere has been related to health and safety. A Movement of Workers Directive does however assume that work will progress on a common comparison of qualifications – this is a major reason for the DfEE's simplification and rationalisation of qualifications. In this development, the DfEE has worked with the European Commission's own training agency (based in Berlin and colloquially known as 'CEDEFOP'), which offers a free information service on all aspects of training throughout the EU, commissions research, publishes monographs, and reports on qualifications systems. The UK contact point for CEDEFOP is the Institute of Personnel and Development.

A number of EU training programmes have been promoted, contributing to mainstream objectives such as language training, co-operation between education and industry, and lifelong learning. (See Appendices 2 and 7 for more detail; the main, multi-stranded programmes have been code-named 'Socrates' and 'Leonardo Da Vinci'.) These programmes have usually involved co-operation across state borders and cross-border exchange of learners; funds and places are (naturally) limited, and the criteria for gaining both are strict. The DfEE must be involved in and must support any UK application, and may also require local support (eg from the local TEC) before deciding whether to process an application.

SUMMARY

If our coverage of the 'institutional' picture is inevitably limited, several key themes can still be seen to run through it. First, the state is assumed to carry responsibility for preparing people for work and for promoting the employability of the unemployed. Second, employers are deemed to be responsible for workplace competence, but only a small percentage of employers (albeit accounting for about half the nation's workforce) are large enough to afford their own professional personnel or training management and to mount their own training activity. Large employers do generally promote training, especially for management, and *all* employers regardless of size look to external training providers (of whom the further education colleges are the most visible) for relevant services, which consist primarily of teacher-led courses. In a concentrated and sustained attempt to promote vocational learning during and after full-time education, and recognising that most employers (and employees) relate competence to qualifications, government has, with the aid of the larger employer and awarding bodies developed a new system of national vocational qualifications to sit alongside and carry equal status with academic awards. Government funds are now used to promote these qualifications, and government schemes automatically incorporate them. Further state incentives exist in the form of national training targets and national training awards. The system anticipates and meets the probable requirements of any forthcoming EU legislation. Government has also stood four-square with the EU in promoting (a) lifelong learning ideals and (b) the development of computer-based learning methods and resources.

Do you remember Sam and Jack of Random Articles? And do you remember the first question we posed at the end of the last chapter, which asked how your own attitudes to education and training might have changed over the last few years if you had been Sam or Jack?

Sam's job demands that she visits the local further education college. The company has recently decided to move towards a claim for IiP status, which will mean for Sam direct contact with the TEC. Sam's discussions with the college have included ideas on how college staff might mount lectures and supervise some coursework on company premises, and how much this might cost. Jack is meanwhile talking with his own production supervisors about the likely appearance of several 'New Deal' participants, who will work only some 24 hours a week, including time at the local college; Jack is wondering whether the government subsidy might justify putting one supervisor in full-time charge of the New Deal programme. Jack and Sam have already been talking about the TUC's stated intention to work towards the appointment of 'learning representatives' at the workplace. Sam is interested in the University for Industry and Learning Direct developments, which she hopes will promote distance learning activity for employees, and also in new TV channels said to be preparing interactive management training programmes. The days are long gone when training interventions at RA were inevitably unique internal creations or bespoke external courses.

FOR FURTHER REFLECTION AND DISCUSSION

1   What do you consider the main reasons UK employees tend to wait for others to decide on their training?

2   Imagine you are in charge of the personnel function in the head office of a multi-national company which has several UK subsidiaries. The subsidiaries are managed independently, subject only to corporate operational targets and advance agreement on major policy changes; they each have their own personnel departments and create and implement their own training plans. What do you think should be your main roles relating to training, and how do they compare with the roles currently accepted by the DfEE in relation to the UK as a whole?

3   How many operational contacts can you list for the full-time Director of a Training and Enterprise Council?

4   What ideas do you expect the EU to promote relating to lifelong learning?

5   Do you think the UK will achieve its Year 2002 National Training Targets? Why/why not?

SUGGESTED READING

There are no standard texts covering the material in this chapter. The DfEE's Skills and Enterprise Unit at Moorfoot, Sheffield S1 4PQ operates a 'Network' membership scheme, which ensures that members regularly receive the DfEE's *Labour Market Quarterly Report*, the annual *Labour Market and Skill Trends*, plus executive briefing papers and updating material. The DfEE's *Insight* journal is available from the DfEE's publications centre at PO Box 5000, Sudbury, Suffolk CO10 6YJ.

3 Learning and training

What do we understand by learning? – reinforcement theories – cybernetic and information theories – cognitive theories and problem-solving – experiential learning theories – learning to learn and self-development – mental processes – other horizons.

INTRODUCTION

Learning theory merits a detailed study in its own right, and a comprehensive overview would be beyond the scope of this book. For this we would refer the reader to a psychology text such as one of those given in the Suggested Reading at the end of this chapter. Our aim is to whet your appetite to pursue more specialised texts by demonstrating some of the ways in which learning theory can be related to training processes and to some of the training methods and techniques that will be found in Appendix 5.

Six main groups or sets of learning theory will be outlined:

- *reinforcement theories*
- *cybernetic and information theories*
- *cognitive theories and problem-solving*
- *experiential learning theories*
- *learning to learn and self-development*
- *mental processes.*

The chapter concludes with two examples of the ways in which trainers are endeavouring to build upon the findings of researchers.

> **Think of three recent occasions when you think you learned something.**
>
> **Does a consideration of what happened help you to define learning?**
>
> **How did your learning take place?**
>
> **Was it the same kind of learning in each case?**

WHAT DO WE UNDERSTAND BY LEARNING?

It might help to consider the following examples:

1 Mary is a trainee in the sales department. Her first boss never seemed to notice when she attracted new business, and so she concentrated on

looking after her 'regulars'. She now has a new boss, who makes a point of congratulating her immediately she gains a new customer, and if a large order ensues she is straightway given a bonus. Mary has now set herself a monthly target of new customers and has brought considerable business to her company.

2   A child picking wild flowers innocently grasps a nettle and stings his fingers and cries. After having made the same mistake two or three times he recognises the nettle and avoids it.

3   The experienced car driver has learned to recognise the condition of the road surface and potential hazards and monitors her speed accordingly.

4   While sitting in his bath, the Greek scientist Archimedes suddenly shouted out 'Eureka!' (I have found it), when he had a flash of inspiration which enabled him to formulate his famous principle concerning the displacement of water.

5   Martin was sitting at a computer logged onto the Internet. He was one of a group of sixth-form pupils trying to find information about the oldest rock formations in the north-west of Scotland as part of an assessed group project. He found hundreds of entries under 'rock' and did not know which to choose, but was fascinated by one relating to a personal contribution from a climber in the Himalayas and started to pursue another relating to rock music and its development. The rest of the group became angry, and one of the others demanded to take over the computer to find something more relevant. The next day, Martin logged onto the Internet by himself and spent an hour following up the entries on the Himalayas and rock music. He subsequently bought a book about the Himalayas, and started a computer dialogue with the author of the personal contribution on the Internet.

These examples have at least one common factor: they all involve a change in behaviour. How did your own examples compare? Did they support the definition given by Bass and Vaughan (1966) that learning is 'a relatively permanent change in behaviour that occurs as a result of practice or experience'? This appears to be a very simple definition, and how one interprets 'behaviour' is an important point, because learning has been said to consist of knowledge, skills and attitudes, and if the learning relates to *attitudes and/or knowledge*, the behaviour may be confined to merely showing interest in a particular topic, such as an open style of management, because the learner may not have the *skills* to change his behaviour appropriately. In addition, there may be a considerable time lag between the learning taking place and the opportunity to display behaviour change. To give a comprehensive definition of learning would be neither short nor simple, and recently in fact a group of well-known 'authorities' on learning met to see 'how far they could agree upon statements about learning that would be of benefit to policy makers and leaders in organisations' and to promote discussion. The result was not a definition but a two-page 'Declaration on Learning', which appeared in *People Management* (Honey *et al* 1998) and caused a vast amount of comment and correspondence. It would be a foolish person indeed who would attempt a short definition of learning but we hope that, by reading this book, the reader will begin to grasp and understand its many facets.

The Bass and Vaughan definition is helpful in distinguishing two different aspects: 'practice', which tends to be related to events that are deliberately planned, and 'experience', which may have been intentionally arranged (such as a short secondment to another organisation/department) or may have occurred spontaneously in the natural course of events. People cannot be brought together in an organisation to achieve any kind of common purpose without this 'spontaneous' learning taking place. As a result they will change their behaviour in various ways. At the simplest level, they learn each others' names, technical terms and the location of equipment; and at a more sophisticated level, they learn about the behaviour of their colleagues, supervisors and management and thus develop attitudes that can have complex effects on their behaviour. This in turn will confirm or alter the manager's attitude towards the subordinate. The process is interactive, both learning about each other and modifying their behaviour accordingly. People learn by imitating others (modelling), by perceiving and interpreting what happens in the organisation and by the cumulative experience of trial and error. In this sense, therefore, learning is an inevitable organisational activity. Later in this chapter we shall show that many of the learning opportunities presented by the organisation pass by untapped because they are unrecognised, and we shall suggest that the ability to identify them is the 'take-off runway' for the process of 'learning to learn'.

This book derives its title from the fact that in managing the training and development function we are continually attempting to decide whether some kind of deliberate training intervention is required into the natural learning process. If we decide that this is the case, the next question is what specific form the intervention might take. Prior to examining the range of possibilities (see Chapters 5, 9 and 10, and Appendix 5) we first consider some of the ways in which the intervention might reflect the assumptions made by the trainer about how people learn. These assumptions may be well informed, on the basis of careful study and deliberation, or they may be implicit, the trainer or learner relying solely on intuition, or purely anecdotal sources. Anyone responsible for training should have a working knowledge of the processes which are involved before committing an organisation to considerable expenditure.

This brings us to the third of our questions above, as to whether the learning was the same in each of the cases. Even the few examples we quoted demonstrate that there is a variety of different kinds of learning. The range of human abilities is extremely wide, from psychomotor skills, such as operating a keyboard or styling a client's hair, to the negotiating skills of an industrial relations expert, the symbolic skills of a computer programmer, or the decision-making skills of a financier. The training specialist searching for one set of simple rules that adequately encompasses such varied activity is going to be disappointed. Researchers have concentrated on different aspects of this complex process and have been able to demonstrate certain principles, but no one theory is in itself complete and none can claim to cover all eventualities. We have selected four main types of theory for discussion.

REINFORCEMENT THEORIES

> On a television programme a volunteer was told to watch the numbers moving round on a counter on the wall. He was promised £20 every time the counter moved to a new number. He was not told what caused the counter to move, but it actually did so every time he blinked his eyes. The camera showed a rapidly increasing rate of blinking as the counter moved around. After a few minutes he was asked if he could state what caused the counter to turn or if he could suggest how his behaviour had changed since the beginning of the programme. He replied that he did not know.

A very basic concept in learning is that of 'conditioning' or 'shaping' behaviour, the main exponent being Skinner (1965), who tested his theory by carrying out numerous experiments, the most famous of which concerned pigeons. By means of rewarding his experimental subjects with corn every time they made an appropriate movement, he was able to teach them many things, even including how to play 'ping pong' with each other. Although behaviour in animal experiments cannot be considered an infallible and accurate reflection of complicated and sophisticated human conduct, it has been claimed that conditioning is an essential ingredient in many types of learning. In fact, the first of our examples (about Mary and her new customers) may be seen to incorporate this type of learning. Praise or reinforcing feedback from her new boss engenders confidence, which acts as a strong motivator for her to continue and extend the desired behaviour.

Another instance is provided by techniques of programmed learning and its current, more sophisticated development into computer-assisted learning. The assumption is that receiving a 'reward' (which for humans is not corn, but might be feedback in the form of being told that they have answered correctly or 'done well') gives positive reinforcement to that response and so motivates them to continue and extend their learning.

Conditioning applied to social systems

Skinner (1976) extended the application of his theory from experimenter and subject (trainer and trainee) to the whole area of the structure of social systems. In his novel, *Walden Two*, he developed the concept of an entire society based on the use of positive reinforcement. He conceived systems that were designed to reward behaviour functional to the society. In other words, the citizens were not controlled by law but by the way in which the environment was designed. Other writers, eg Nord (1969), have attempted to apply Skinner's ideas to management through positive reinforcement, embracing items such as job design, compensation and rewards, organisational design and change. The reinforcement must take place in such a way that the link between the behaviour and the reward is apparent. For instance, Nord suggests that annual merit interviews and salary increments are very inefficient development techniques, because the rewards are so delayed that they have little feedback value.

This brings us back once more to the title of this book. Training is an intervention into an ongoing learning process; the culture, philosophy, policies and procedures of the organisation form a very powerful learning environment, which must be taken into consideration. We shall discuss the influence of organisational culture on approaches to training later in this book (see Chapters 5, 7 and 10). On a note of caution, however, Skinnerian theory goes only a limited way towards assisting understanding of the process by which human beings acquire a whole range of knowledge and skills. His concept of 'social engineering' by the provision of positive reinforcement is now regarded as too simplistic, but it constitutes an important reminder of the need to consider the organisation's culture and to provide feedback or knowledge of results, without which planned learning is unlikely to be effective.

Punishment

Now consider example 2 of the child and the nettle. In this case a particular action was *suppressed*, not promoted. Some researchers, eg Estes (1970), have investigated the effect of punishment in suppressing an inappropriate response. His experiments (which mainly involved giving mild electric shocks to rats) demonstrated the principle that punishment may temporarily suppress a response but will not *extinguish* it. After having been 'punished' for pressing a bar, the rats made fewer trials, but later, after the punishment was withdrawn, they resumed their original behaviour patterns.

Although positive feedback can bring about a relatively permanent learning outcome, negative feedback or harsh criticism may be effective only as long as some threat appears imminent. What then are the implications for safety training, where it might be said that the trainee is being taught to avoid possible punishment (in the form of accident or injury)? The nettle stung the child every time it was touched and would always do so even if further trial attempts were made. Accidents, however, have a different characteristic. They have been described as chains of events when a number of different conditions all coincide at one fatal moment. Because these events do not normally all happen together, the threat does not continuously appear imminent; it may be possible to ignore certain safety features for a considerable time without necessarily meeting with an accident, and therefore on occasions malpractices go 'unpunished'. If safety equipment is irksome to wear, and a worker has managed to do without it and no accident has occurred, the habit of neglect will be reinforced as thoughts of danger recede. An illustration is provided by car seat belts which, until legislation was introduced, large sections of the population refused to wear for the sake of their own safety (largely because the habit of ignoring them had been reinforced – it was easier and no accident had 'happened to them'). It was not until the threat of prosecution became constantly imminent that the correct usage began to approach 100 per cent!

This is one of the major reasons why safety training is often ineffective, and you might like to think of ways in which the imminence or possibility of danger can be *constantly* emphasised. For instance, in some countries there is a practice of leaving a wrecked car at the side of a road that features particularly dangerous hairpin bends. We shall return to the question of making safety training more efficient later in the chapter.

CYBERNETIC AND INFORMATION THEORIES

A trainee sewing machinist finds that he is unable to concentrate on controlling the foot treadle and at the same time guide the material correctly through the machine. After special exercises in machine control and demonstrations and supervised practice in handling the material, he gradually becomes proficient and is able to increase the speed and quality of his performance.

These theories concentrate on how information is received and monitored. Stammers and Patrick (1975) and Duncan and Kelly (1983) liken the way in which feedback can control human performance to the manner in which a thermostat controls a heating system. The temperature is monitored and regulated because information fed back from the thermostat determines the level of power input to the system. See Figure 3.1, which is based on Stammers and Patrick's model.

Figure 3.1 **The monitoring and regulating process**

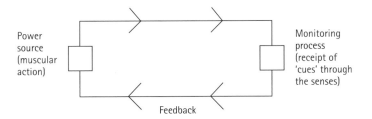

This monitoring is a constant process in all activities. For example, someone who is profoundly deaf may develop an unusual speaking voice because he cannot hear it and must monitor it in some other way, possibly by the feel of muscles in the mouth and throat. The motorist in our example 3 was receiving 'stimuli' from the environment, by which she monitored and regulated her performance or, in other words, her input to the system. She received these stimuli through the senses – touch, sight, hearing, kinaesthesis (the sense of muscular effort or the 'feel' that one's limbs are in the correct position) and balance. For instance, the machinist above might interpret the sound of the machine, the pressure required by his foot to operate at the correct speed and the appearance of the work in the machine. Similarly, a cook or a wine taster might be relying on his or her sense of smell and taste to monitor performance.

In a training situation the most usual form of feedback is provided by comments from an instructor, but sometimes it can be given by simulators which act as artificial 'thermostats' and help the trainee monitor his or her performance.

An important part of skills analysis (see Chapter 9) is to determine by which 'cues' or 'stimuli' an experienced worker is being guided and by which of the senses they are being received. Probably the best-known example is to be found in the job of a typist. Observation of a skilled performer reveals heavy reliance on kinaesthesis, or the 'feel' and positioning of the fingers on the keyboard. Left to his own devices, it is likely that a beginner would rely upon sight, looking intensely at the keyboard and using what has been described as the 'hunt and peck' method. Anyone who has taught himself to type in this way finds it difficult to learn to touch type because he has to unlearn all his bad habits. A skills analysis, which includes not only a record of exactly what is done but also the details of exactly what 'cues' or stimuli are being used to monitor performance and trigger action, can provide the basis for an efficient training programme for many psychomotor jobs. The training time can be shortened by providing practice in recognising and reacting to the stimuli used by those with experience, rather than allowing the learner to work unsupervised and thereby reinforcing less efficient habits, such as the 'hunt and peck' method.

Since recognising stimuli is central to learning, a trainer should understand the process of perception. For instance, training for inspection tasks is largely a matter of organising the perception to highlight certain stimuli or details and ignore others. During the learning process the 'selectivity' of stimuli becomes increasingly automatic, and the experienced worker ceases to think consciously about it (in other words 'sheds the perceptual load'). Think of a learner car driver, who initially has to concentrate hard on braking, accelerating and changing gear; after sufficient practice these operations become second nature and are carried out almost without thought. Similarly, when learning to ski, the beginner has to concentrate hard on cues which assist his or her balance, the correct position of the body in relation to the skis, how to traverse, how to turn or stop. After a number of painful experiences, he or she may look wistfully at the experienced performer, who seems to carry out all these operations naturally and apparently without thought, although possibly observing other matters such as the texture of the snow or the position of other skiers on the piste. In other words, certain of the experienced skier's actions have been 'pre-programmed'.

You should now be in a better position to answer the question posed earlier in this chapter:

How can safety training be made more efficient?

Far more effective than the threat of punishment to persuade people to avoid accidents is the positive aspect of ensuring that from the beginning the trainee will always perform in a safe manner (compare the example above of the use of car seat belts). Cultivation of safe working methods and habits must therefore be the prime concern and will help to ensure that, even when the perceptual load is 'shed', the *safe* way has become automatic.

Kay (1983) gives a useful explanation of accidents as enforced changes from programmed to unprogrammed activity. For example, someone walking along a pavement is carrying out an activity that has been programmed since childhood; she therefore does not need to think consciously about it. If, however, her foot slips on a banana skin, the programmed activity will not suffice and she has to concentrate rapidly on new-style evasive action. Injury may result if she cannot think out and effect this action in time. Someone trained in the art of falling could probably manage this because her mind is pre-programmed to do so, but the rest of us would most likely fail!

An important part of safety training, therefore, is to pre-programme trainees for possible hazardous situations (eg training vehicle drivers on a skid pan) so that they can more rapidly recognise and interpret the stimuli they receive in the monitoring process (eg the first feel of the vehicle's wheels sliding); because an appropriate response pattern has been pre-programmed, the trainees have a much improved chance of avoiding an accident. This theory has a further implication for safety: because learners have to concentrate on many items at once and cannot shed the perceptual load, they have less ability to anticipate potential hazards and are thus more prone to accidents. Trainers need to pay special attention to this fact, particularly when dealing with young employees and students and schoolchildren on work experience, where the trainee is not only attempting to cope with cues and signals from the job itself but also has to become acclimatised to a whole new work environment, as opposed to the familiar background of school or college.

COGNITIVE THEORIES AND PROBLEM-SOLVING

Craft trainees are confronted with a model of a live electrical wiring system. By operating levers and watching the results, they can work out the principles of electricity for themselves and apply them to their work.

In direct contrast to reinforcement theories, which are concerned with the establishment of particular behaviour patterns, cognitive theories draw attention to behaviour that we might ordinarily describe as 'insight'. They reflect the way in which we learn to recognise and define problems or experiment to find solutions, whether by trial and error, by deductive reasoning, by seeking information and help or by a combination of all three. We see the situation as a whole and begin to organise it. Eventually we conceptualise or 'internalise' the solution and methodology, so that we are able to extend their use and adapt them to future situations. Sometimes the solution comes by sudden insight, as in the case of Archimedes in example 4 above.

These theories are not new. In 1925, Kohler was experimenting with an ape which was required to solve the problem of retrieving a banana placed beyond its reach outside the cage. It first tried to grasp it by frantically stretching its arms through the bars but gave up after several unsuccessful attempts. After retreating to the back of the cage for some time, the ape returned to the bars, reached for a stick which was lying outside, and managed to poke the banana and pull it nearer the cage. The experiment was then repeated but this time the banana was further away and the ape had to use a short stick to pull in a longer stick before being able to reach the desired food (see Kohler 1973). This experiment demonstrates the close relationship between cognitive theories and the training technique called discovery learning. In this technique the trainee is given tasks that require him to search for and select stimuli or 'clues' on how to proceed. The aim is to provide a means of unassisted learning and appropriate experience to develop insights into key relationships. The success of this method obviously depends upon the effectiveness of the task design.

The craft trainees in our example learn with the aid of a practical working model, but the technique is very versatile. For instance, depending upon the method of presentation, a case-study, a project or assigned task can provide discovery learning. This training technique has the advantage of assisting transfer of learning to the job because, as the learner has found an answer for himself, it becomes internalised. However, this method requires careful structuring of the situation to the learner's needs, because long periods spent in vain pursuit of a solution that is well beyond his current capability can prove an extremely frustrating and demotivating experience. In these circumstances, anger and irritation are likely to be turned upon the trainer. As we have seen from reinforcement theory, however, finding the solution acts as a well-earned reward to reinforce the learning. Obviously it is usually quicker to tell the learner than to let him find out for himself, and therefore discovery learning sessions tend to be time-consuming, although by providing better learning transfer they are likely to be more effective in the long term.

EXPERIENTIAL LEARNING

A personnel manager conducts a disciplinary interview, and when writing up the results for her records discovers that she does not really know enough about the offender's side of the story. Upon reflection, she realises that she did not give him the opportunity to explain, most of her questions having required a yes or no answer. She then decides that in principle when she needs to obtain information in an interview, she will ask at least some questions that are open-ended to encourage the interviewee to talk. She tries out this idea at the next interview and discovers that it works; she therefore resolves to do this on all future occasions.

We can see that there are really four stages here: the experience; observation

66

and reflection; theorising and conceptualisation; and testing and experimentation. To be effective, the learner correspondingly needs four different but complementary kinds of abilities. This is how Kolb (1974) conceived the learning process, which he illustrated in the model in Figure 3.2 below.

Figure 3.2 **The Kolb learning cycle**

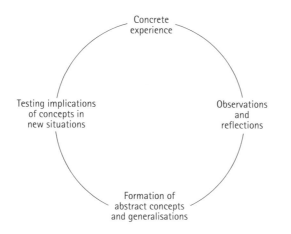

Source: David A. Kolb, 'On Management and the Learning Process', in *Organizational Psychology: A book of readings*, ed. Kolb, Rubin and McIntyre, 2nd edition, 1974, page 28. Reprinted by permission of Prentice Hall, Englewood Cliffs, New Jersey.

Kolb suggests that this ideal is difficult to achieve and argues that in fact the required abilities might even be in conflict. He claims that:

> as a result of our hereditary equipment, our particular life experience, and the demands of our present environment, most people develop learning styles that emphasise some learning abilities over others.

In other words, most people are better at, and prefer, some of the four stages rather than others. For instance, a mathematician might give preference to abstract conceptualisation and active experimentation, whereas a manager may have greater concern for concrete experience and the active application of ideas.

Building on Kolb's theoretical base, Honey and Mumford (1992 and 1986) defined four major categories of learning styles: activist; reflector; theorist; and pragmatist. These correspond with the four stages in the Kolb Cycle, viz. concrete experience; observations and reflections; formation of abstract concepts and generalisations; and testing implications of concepts in new situations. Honey and Mumford have kindly given us permission to reproduce in full their descriptions of people strong in each of their four styles:

Activists
Involve themselves fully and without bias in new experiences. They enjoy the here and now and are happy to be dominated by immediate experiences. They are open-minded, not sceptical, and this tends to make them enthusiastic about anything new. Their philosophy is 'I'll try anything once.' They tend to act first and consider the consequences afterwards. Their days are filled with activity. They tackle problems by brainstorming. As soon as the excitement from one activity has died down they are busy looking for the next. They tend to thrive on the challenge of new experiences but are bored with implementation and longer-term consolidation. They are gregarious people constantly involving themselves with others but, in doing so, they seek to centre all activities around themselves.

Reflectors
Like to stand back to ponder experiences and observe them from many different perspectives. They collect data, both first hand and from others, and prefer to think about it thoroughly before coming to any conclusion. The thorough collection and analysis of data about experiences and events is what counts, so they tend to postpone reaching definitive conclusions for as long as possible. Their philosophy is to be cautious. They are thoughtful people who like to consider all possible angles and implications before making a move. They prefer to take a back seat in meetings and discussions. They enjoy observing other people in action. They listen to others and get the drift of the discussion before making their own points. They tend to adopt a low profile and have a slightly distant, tolerant, unruffled air about them. When they act it is part of a wider picture which includes the past as well as the present and others' observations as well as their own.

Theorists
Adapt and integrate observations into complex but logically sound theories. They think problems through in a vertical, step-by-step, logical way. They assimilate disparate facts into coherent theories. They tend to be perfectionists who will not rest easy until things are tidy and fit into a rational scheme. They like to analyse and synthesise. They are keen on basic assumptions, principles, theories, models and systems thinking. Their philosophy prizes rationality and logic. 'If it's logical it's good.' Questions they frequently ask are: 'Does it make sense?' 'How does this fit in with that?' 'What are the basic assumptions?' They tend to be detached, analytical and dedicated to rational objectivity rather than anything subjective or ambiguous. Their approach to problems is consistently logical. This is their 'mental set' and they rigidly reject anything that does not fit with it. They prefer to maximise certainty and feel uncomfortable with subjective judgements, lateral thinking and anything flippant.

Pragmatists
Are keen on trying out ideas, theories and techniques to see if they work in practice. They positively search out new ideas and take the first opportunity

to experiment with applications. They are the sort of people who return from management courses brimming with new ideas that they want to try out in practice. They like to get on with things and act quickly and confidently on ideas that attract them. They tend to be impatient with ruminating and open-ended discussions. They are essentially practical, down-to-earth people who like making practical decisions and solving problems. They respond to problems and opportunities 'as a challenge'. Their philosophy is: 'There is always a better way' and 'If it *works* it's good.'

The concept of learning styles is an important development because it helps to throw light on how people learn from experience. It indicates firstly that a variety of training methods might be planned in sequence. In the example of the interview situation above, immediate experience requires a practical interview session (either 'for real' as part of the learner's daily work, or as a simulated exercise in a classroom situation), whereas observing and reflecting might take place by individual thought or by discussion with a coach or mentor, or observer and tutor in the case of the classroom exercise. Generalising and theorising might involve the learner in comparing her findings with relevant literature and formulating and re-examining her own principles and guidelines on, for example, the use of specific techniques and strategies. The next stage would be testing out these perceptions in a new situation and so back to experience. This example demonstrates the need for all four stages. However, when planning specific learning programmes or selecting participants for external courses, it is wise to allow for the fact that some people learn better by one style than another and some may reject certain styles altogether; hence programmes will ideally be planned with a knowledge of learners' own preferences, and diagnostic activity will be built into the early stages of (flexible) plans.

It is also important for the trainer to realise that she has a natural learning/teaching style and that in choosing appropriate techniques she should consider the trainees' preferred or desired learning style as well as her own, insofar as it is practical to do so.

A rich menu is on offer to those who can take advantage of all four learning styles. For instance, consider in how many ways we can learn a sport such as tennis or golf. Your list is likely to include methods such as practising, experimenting, coaching, reading, watching others, watching oneself on video cassette, talking to other people, thinking about one's game and, of course, playing. Each of these methods involves one or more of the four learning styles and, taken collectively, they encompass the whole of the experiential learning cycle. The successful professional will ideally take advantage of them all.

Similarly, many learning opportunities are available to managers. Mumford (1989) points out that learning opportunities do not have to be manufactured: they already exist in the real environment. Many of them pass unnoticed and unused, and managers need help in learning to recognise and take advantage of them. Figure 3.3 lists examples of situations that may provide these opportunities within organisations and in private life. The right-hand column lists the *processes* by which managers can learn, and again it will be seen that taken together they embrace all four learning styles. Managers who rely on only one learning style are restricting themselves unnecessarily to just one course on the menu.

Figure 3.3 Learning opportunities

Situations within the organisation	
Meetings	Modelling
Task – familiar	Problem-solving
– unfamiliar	Observing
Task force	Questioning
Customer visit	Reading
Visit to plant/office	Negotiating
Managing a change	Mentoring
Social occasions	Public speaking
Foreign travel	Reviewing/auditing
Acquisitions/mergers	Clarifying responsibilities
Closing something down	Walking the floor
	Visioning
	Strategic planning
Situations outside your organisation	Problem diagnosis
	Decision-making
Charity	Selling
Domestic life	
Industry committee	
Professional meetings	**People**
Sports club	
	Boss
	Mentor
Processes	Network contacts
	Peers
Coaching	Consultants
Counselling	Subordinates
Listening	

The opportunities identified here are not necessarily separate. You may, for example, think of something first in terms of something happening at a meeting – or you may think of the way in which one of your colleagues achieved success at a meeting.

Source: *Management Development: Strategies for action* (IPM, 1989). Reproduced by kind permission of Alan Mumford.

Considerable developmental work on learning styles has already taken place and there is now a wide range of literature. For example, Richardson and Bennett (1984) have examined the structural and cultural barriers to behaviour at each of the stages in the experiential learning cycle. They suggest that one can think of the organisation itself as having a preferred learning style, which influences those within it. You might compare this concept with the discussion of the different approaches to training in Chapter 5. Although further research and validation of this work is still necessary, it is important for the trainer to realise that her own natural training style may be at variance with the culture of her organisation and with that of the learners.

Furthermore, a traditional difficulty of group training activities is the effect of the composition or 'chemistry' of the group and the influence it can have upon individual learning. Although the concept of learning styles does not produce instant answers to this problem, it nevertheless contributes an explanation, and may help to promote useful discussion and understanding within the group. During the course of their research, Honey and Mumford (1986 and 1992) developed a Learning Styles Questionnaire based on self-description and established norms for different types of manager, such as those engaged in research and development, production or finance. Such a questionnaire is a useful measuring instrument for the trainer and could ultimately yield data relating to the influence of different learning styles on group activity, thereby constituting a valuable guide in, for instance, determining an optimum composition of learning groups. For the individual it provides a tool for self-diagnosis as a guide to building on strengths (best learning styles) and overcoming weaknesses (least favoured learning styles), leading to the use of a richer variety of methods. Honey and Mumford (1986) give advice on making the best use of your learning strengths and how to improve and practise each of the four styles.

LEARNING TO LEARN AND SELF-DEVELOPMENT

In 1979, we wrote: 'Our cyclical economy and the speed of technical change suggest that "learning to learn" is the central training problem of our time' (Kenney, Donnelly and Reid 1979), and we suggested the need for further research in this area. Attention has been gradually focused on the activities of the learner and the means of equipping him with strategies and a range of styles that are not only appropriate for present learning but will transfer to future situations and enable learning from experience to take place. The emphasis has moved from activities largely controlled by the trainer to the learning process and, where possible, to self-directed and self-managed learning using opportunities provided by new technology such as computer-assisted programmes.

In 1981 a report 'How do I Learn?' was produced for the Further Education Unit (FEU) by a team from the then Industrial Training Research Unit (ITRU); the team had been asked to look into what the FEU called 'doing' learning (as opposed to 'memory' and 'understanding' learning). The team made two important points:

- learning is something one does for oneself
- the most effective ways of learning involve conscious mental activities such as checking, self-testing and questioning.

These points emphasise the fact that whatever the activities of a trainer, it is the learner who is really in the driving seat.

Much training theory assumes that learning objectives represent a static work state, in which case competence depends largely upon memory and the acquisition of basic skills which will last a lifetime. Knowing 'what' and 'how' and 'when' is a matter of remembering what the manual (or text book) says; and/or what worked last time. However, memory proves unrewarding if the content, or indeed the context, of work is constantly changing. For example, if manual bookkeeping changes to computerised book-keeping, the individual's memory of mental arithmetic will not suffice: the computer now performs this task. Confidence in the relevance of one's knowledge base diminishes and must be replaced by some new knowledge (eg how to make the computer perform calculations), plus keyboard skills. The whole process is illustrated in Figure 3.4.

It will be seen that there are both positive and negative factors affecting attitudes: initial confidence and sense of achievement in attaining competence, which in terms of reinforcement theory act as a motivator to further learning, followed by apprehension and fear of change which would demotivate. In ideal circumstances, the desire to learn might be regarded as self-generating, the sense of achievement from successful learning giving rise to confidence in one's ability *as a learner* and reinforcing the desire for further learning. The learner remains competent and 'learns to learn', eventually creating new 'improved performance' objectives and managing the learning process required to realise those objectives. This is the essence of self-development.

Curiosity is a strong motivator (see page 84), and learning is like opening a door in a corridor that gives a view into a room beyond; the room has other doors that had not previously been in view; on opening these doors further doors appear. This phenomenon becomes very apparent to users of the Internet international computer link, where the skill often lies not in finding a door, but in choosing which one to open and which corridor to enter, as Martin's experience in our fifth example at the beginning of this chapter shows. As the Internet becomes more readily available it will be an increasingly important tool for self-development. The conflict between a highly structured learning style of formulating and pursuing precise objectives, and one which is more open, creative and exploratory is made apparent when the user is confronted with the dilemma of adhering strictly to what appears to be totally relevant material at the expense of missing something that could lead to exciting and unpredictable learning outcomes. Depending upon circumstance the latter might well be the more rewarding in the long term by opening up new perspectives that might otherwise never have been contemplated.

Although an important means of self-development, the Internet offers a great deal more than the opportunity for the individual user to obtain almost unlimited information by means of a computer. It can provide continuous learning in the form of contact and exchange of views and information with people with similar interests and problems throughout the world. However, to access and use the information they have gained, users need to develop specific and sophisticated skills such as reading, editing and drafting, those of research (eg posing the right questions, evaluating the data, evaluating the search, selecting, storing and saving information) as well as co-operation and collaboration with other users internationally.

The Internet should not be regarded merely as a medium for the lone user, because it can be an invaluable vehicle for a collaborative and co-operation learning environment, such as that described in example 5. This is particularly likely to happen in schools, where it is increasingly being used to enable small groups of pupils to take part in investigations for themselves and negotiate how to proceed. Discussion is in progress in many parts of the world to identify the issues that arise from use of the Internet, and to

Figure 3.4 **The continuous development spiral**

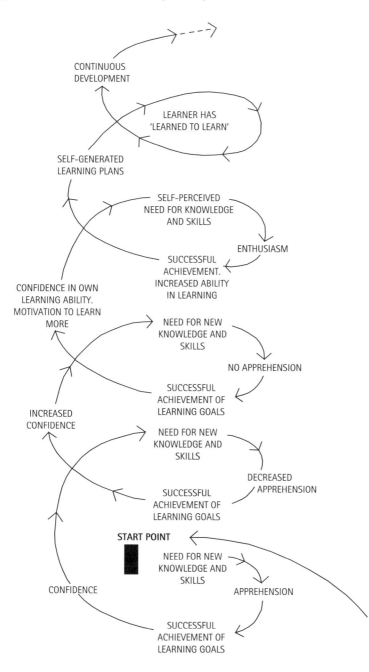

explore the implications for those involved in teaching and learning. There are a number of barriers to learning, for example fear of failure, inability or unwillingness to expend the time and effort. In a rapidly changing environment it is not sufficient to acquire the standard knowledge and skills. The process has to be constant; the successful organisation will be one where attention is paid to minimising the demotivating factors by creating a supportive climate and by developing employees' confidence in their ability to tackle and overcome barriers to learning – in other words a 'learning organisation' which fosters and encourages the natural self-generating learning process. This is a critical aim. Learners who have grown to believe that they are competent as learners take the lead in managing change and develop themselves in the process. Writers such as Hayes, Anderson and Fonda (1984) have stressed that interest in continuous development is one of the main features that distinguishes workforces in countries such as Japan and the USA from those in the UK, where the training emphasis tends to be placed more upon short-term considerations. The concept of continuous development is discussed more fully in Chapter 12. There is a need not only for 'learning organisations' but also for individuals who can readily move from organisation to organisation, or even take part in several 'virtual organisations' at once. Awareness is growing of the economic necessity for continuous self-development, as security lies increasingly in marketable skills rather than in a 'safe' job, and training is seen as an important part of the total employment contract.

MENTAL PROCESSES

We start with a consideration of memory, and the dual memory theory which has important implications for trainers. It is possible, however, that exciting discoveries about learning may lie in extending our knowledge of cerebral processes, and a fruitful avenue of exploration has been the study of the effect of brain damage on cerebral functions. In more recent times new technology, particularly the use of sophisticated scanners, has facilitated more comprehensive investigations into the functioning of various areas of the brain. We give an outline of the activities of the right and left hemispheres of the brain, followed by examples of the ways in which educationalists and trainers claim to have built upon research findings.

Memory

Think of the last time you looked up a telephone number in the directory. Unless you wrote it down you may well have forgotten the number while you looked up the code. If the number was engaged and your telephone did not have a memory facility, you would probably have had to look it up again to redial. If you want to remember a friend's number, you have to keep repeating it. This is explained by the *dual memory theory* which distinguishes between short-term and long-term memory and postulates that rehearsal is necessary if we wish to transfer material from short-term to long-term memory. The average number of discrete items that the human mind can comfortably take in at one time is seven. We can remember much more if we combine small items into larger 'bits'. For instance, it is only possible to remember about seven random letters of the alphabet, but if we combine them into meaningful words or sentences we can remember many more. The implication for the trainer is that meaning assists memory. It is very difficult and time-consuming to remember something we do not understand.

Retention

The two factors of long-term and short-term memory have serious implications for trainers. Any matters that learners cannot recall shortly after a training session are unlikely to have entered into long-term memory: such matters will therefore 'decay' and not be retained. Four phenomena are worthy of note:

- *memory decay* – the rate of decay slows down with time, and prompt reinforcement of what has been learned is therefore an advantage
- *interference* – learning one piece of material or skill can hinder learning another
- *levelling* – after a time-lapse, the material is remembered in very general terms, and much of the detail is glossed over
- *sharpening* – certain items and details are remembered for their peculiarity or particular interest (although they may not necessarily be the most important items of content). Jokes or amusing stories may be remembered long after the serious content of a presentation has been forgotten and care should be taken to ensure that it is the important items that are 'sharpened' in the learners' minds.

The implications are that a trainer should present material logically, ensure that every point is clear and easily understood, and summarise the main points succinctly at the end. Other ways of assisting retention are mental imagery (see the example of electrical coding in Chapter 10), appealing to more than one sense (for example, the use of slides in a presentation involves sight as well as hearing and helps to 'sharpen' the main points), and finally, overlearning (see page 92). A good account of the process of memory can be found in Atkinson and Atkinson (1996).

The right and left hemispheres of the brain

Researchers have found that the two hemispheres of the brain have very different ways of processing information. The connecting network that sends messages from one side of the brain to the other is called the 'corpus collosum'. When this is unimpaired the two hemispheres are effectively integrated, but studies of patients in whom the 'corpus collosum' has been severed have indicated separate awareness in right and left halves of the visual field and for objects in the right and left hands. For instance, it has been found that such patients cannot match an object felt in the left hand out of sight with the same kind of object felt separately and unseen in the right hand. By studying these patients, researchers have been able to demonstrate that each side of the brain appears to have its own specialisations. Experimental work indicates that the left hemisphere is analytical; logical; associated with spoken language skills; number and scientific skills; and reasoning. The right hemisphere is related to art; three-dimensional forms; music awareness; imagination; creativity; insight; and holistic perception. The right side also has a visual learning capability. There are still many questions to be answered concerning these complementary abilities and the way in which the two hemispheres are co-ordinated. It must be emphasised that neither has a complete monopoly of its particular cognitive style, the specialisms of the two hemispheres now being regarded as a matter of degree rather than as an absolute. Studies have shown that individuals vary greatly in the ways in which the hemispheres are habitually activated, and such factors as sex, age, handedness, education and special training appear to have an effect.

New technology has enabled more extensive and accurate research in scanning the brain and measuring its electrical activity while the subject is exposed to different kinds of stimuli such as a conversation, a piece of music or synchronised words and music. Researchers claim that by this means they have obtained scans that show the particular areas of the brain which are activated by these different stimuli (see Rose, 1991).

Johnson and Indvik (1991) consider the implications of these findings in relation to the job of a manager, and suggest that the integration and synthesis of both the analytical left- *and* the intuitive right-brain activity are critical. For instance, too heavy reliance on the analytical left can result in loss of intuitive powers on the right side of the brain. They indicate that left-brain-oriented managers pursue rational and logical reasoning and work in a highly structured way, but may quosh imaginative ideas generated by more intuitive right-brain-oriented colleagues. It is suggested that where policy issues are complex, right-hemisphere and integrative skills are needed more than purely left-hemisphere skills, because the complete data on which to base a totally calculated and logical decision is not always available. In addition, advances in computer technology will diminish the need for managers possessing left-hemisphere analytical skills, while the demand for those with creativity, imagination and the ability to take a holistic perspective will increase.

What, then, are the implications for employee development? First, it would seem important that employees are aware of the functioning of the two hemispheres and of their own particular dominant skills, as well as of the effect they might have on colleagues and subordinates. Johnson and Indvik suggest that this knowledge might be used in career management, to ensure that people are placed in jobs appropriate to their particular mental strengths. Secondly, they indicate that the advantage possessed by 'great minds' lies in the inclination to use both hemispheres effectively and they suggest exercises to enhance brain interaction.

Thirdly, from a training perspective, it would seem sensible to attempt to involve both hemispheres in any structured learning activities. For instance, learning that relies upon logical interpretation appeals to the left hemisphere and can be effectively reinforced by the use of visual aids, imagery, or sensory stimuli which relate to the right side of the brain.

From work with patients who have suffered brain damage researchers have discovered that certain mental functions appear to be associated with particular areas of the brain. These discoveries have led to theories that types of mental processes may be discrete activities, and to the hypothesis that ability (whether learned or innate) in one activity does not necessarily transfer to another activity. These theories obviously have important implications for learning transfer.

However, despite this functional characteristic, researchers (eg Jensen, 1995) have pointed out that the brain works holistically and by parallel processing. It does not function in a discrete manner, concentrating on one thing at a time, but has the capacity simultaneously to take in and interpret many things whilst also controlling subconscious activities such as breathing, digesting etc. It is multi-functional, operating on many levels of consciousness at once, observing the world around, selecting what appears to be important and matching and comparing it with past experience. And, as Jensen points out, 'In addition, the brain is attaching emotions to each event and thought, forming patterns of meaning to construct the larger picture and inferring conclusions about the information acquired.' The exponents of 'Accelerated Learning' (see below) postulate that the ability and capacity of the brain is massive but greatly underutilised, and that by exploiting the phenomenon of parallel processing and emotional aspects, learning can be greatly enhanced.

OTHER HORIZONS

Trainers and educationalists have endeavoured to devise techniques based on the interpretation and application of research findings such as those described above. Within the context of this book it is not possible to describe any of these in detail, but we conclude the chapter with a brief outline of two examples.

Accelerated Learning

The exponents of Accelerated Learning have devised methods for which they claim spectacular results. These are described in detail by Rose (1991), who suggests that the average human uses only 4 per cent of his or her potential brain power, maintaining that we have a cultural legacy of self-imposed limitation, produced in part by the way in which we are taught to learn at school. Rose claims that most schools relegate right-brain activities to two or three hours a week, the main emphasis being on the left-brain functions required by verbal and deductive subject matter. Furthermore, as a society we tend to value logical and analytical thinking more highly than artistic or intuitive ability, and in the main we do not reward independence of thought or creativity. Thus we starve the right hemisphere of development and *systematically damage* the brain. Accelerated Learning methods stimulate the whole brain, not just one hemisphere, and emphasise the role played by emotional content in learning because it effects a higher state of arousal, thereby making the learning more likely to be retained. If the whole brain is to be used there is a need for imagery as well as logical thought, and (as we exemplify in Chapter 10) visual association assists memory.

A novel feature of Accelerated Learning is the use of music as part of the learning event because it is claimed to stimulate right-brain functioning. In particular, it is suggested that the Baroque composers produced exactly the right frequency and sound to harmonise with the rhythm of the brain, thereby inducing a state of relaxed alertness and calm conducive to learning.

It is also maintained that in every learning activity there is a focused and central component, but also an area of peripheral activity, in which the brain subconsciously processes more than the learner realises (peripheral, subconscious and paraconscious often being used interchangeably). Peripheral learning contributes strongly to what is retained, and therefore Accelerated Learning builds in techniques that appeal to the subconscious. These include visual presentations which take into account peripheral vision; the use of posters and cards arranged around the room; materials directed to visual, auditory and, where possible, kinaesthetic channels; games and role-playing which distract the attention and allow information to be subconsciously assimilated.

It is not possible here to give more than this brief summary of the underlying concept of Accelerated Learning, but a much fuller account will be found in Rose (1991).

Neuro Linguistic Programming (NLP)

NLP was developed from research in the USA in the early 1970s by John Grinder, a professor of linguistics, and Richard Bandler, a mathematician. They selected three communicators (all of whom were therapists renowned for their excellence) and studied them at work with their clients. The purpose of the research was to identify the precise behaviours that contributed to this excellence, and to produce a framework or model of excellence in one-to-one communication which could be used by others. By combining the skills of linguistic analysis and mathematical notation, they were able to organise their data into a set of hypothetical 'rules' which could be used by other therapists, who thereby improved their performance (see Bandler and Grinder 1976).

Since this original work, practitioners have applied the use of NLP to education, training and development. Although the original work related to self-management and one-to-one communication, later work by Dilts and Grinder extended the scope to leadership and management of groups and organisations. The exponents of NLP draw attention to the fact that each person's concept of reality is actually his or her subjective interpretation, because the mind is a filtering mechanism. The interpretations made by each individual are influenced by their experiences and attitudes relating to other people and the world around. From birth onwards, individuals learn to programme their reactions and develop strategies, which are then likely to become automatic or unconscious. These strategies are of two kinds: those involving language, and those relating to body movements and physical reactions. From their studies of the strategies used by 'excellent performers', the researchers developed a framework that can be used to help an individual identify his or her own strategies and those of others. Having been made consciously aware of his or her own strategies, the individual can begin to have choice and control by adjusting what would previously have been 'automatic' responses and behaviour.

A recent study (Routledge, 1995) used NLP methodology to investigate the critical behaviours and strategies used by effective learners on an interpersonal skills programme. The model was based on the assumption that, consciously or unconsciously, we set goals and develop a test to indicate to ourselves whether the goal has been achieved. If it has not been reached we change and do something to get closer to it. This process was the basis of the data collection, and it was found that effective learners had the following characteristics.

- realisation that interpersonal skills are useful not only at work but also in a number of aspects of their lives
- validation of the learning process took place outside the formal class – effective learners felt that the true test of the course was whether the skills could be used successfully in the work/social environment
- use of visual and kinaesthetic senses – effective learners could 'go inside themselves' and visualise occasions when they would be able to use the skill
- judgement of success was not a matter of pass/fail, but of moving towards ideal performance, or an opportunity for feedback on how to improve
- natural inclination to plan – effective learners were outcome-oriented (set themselves targets) conscious of what they were trying to achieve and of the level of skill required
- motivation to develop themselves personally.

NLP embraces many different techniques and approaches, which cannot all be described here. Some of them relate to self-management, an example being 'outcome thinking' – thinking of the positive outcome required in a particular situation, and rehearsing it by imagining it through as many senses (sight, sound, feeling etc) as possible. The next stage is to identify the personal resources (eg confidence) needed to bring about that outcome, and to summon those resources using stimulus/response techniques which require the individual to think of a time when he possessed the particular resource, to relive how it felt and to recall how he reached that state, in order to help himself recreate it. The final stage is to rehearse the use of that resource in the new situation in order to bring about a positive outcome. Other skills are concerned with the micro-skills of communication, to enable the individual to become aware of how he or she is progressing towards the desired outcome, and to help him acquire the flexibility to adapt as necessary. For fuller accounts see Johnson (1991) and Kamp (1991).

It must be obvious that no one theory explains the complex processes of learning in all situations. This chapter was intended to provide a background to help you to choose and devise training strategies which will be discussed in more detail in Chapter 10. In the meantime, the discussion of the value of curiosity and the barriers to learning leads to a consideration of contextual factors, which are the subject of Chapter 4.

By now you should have realised the importance of feedback (or knowledge of results) in the learning process. Its role in guiding the learner towards certain behaviours and in gradually enabling self-monitoring to take place will also be discussed further in the next chapter. In preparation for this, you might like to think of as many ways as you can in which feedback, both positive and negative, occurs in your organisation.

FOR FURTHER REFLECTION AND DISCUSSION

1   **'Health and safety training never ends.' Why should this be so? What arrangements would you recommend to ensure that on a regular basis workplace behaviour does not contribute to sickness and/or lost-time accidents?**

2   **Study the 'Quick guide to training methods and techniques' to be found in Appendix 5 of this book, and see if you can identify the different learning styles to which they might appeal. Select any subject matter (or skill), with which you are familiar, and identify training methods which could be used:**

   (a) appealing to only one learning style
   (b) involving all four learning styles.

   Compare method (a) with method (b) in terms of potential interest/ enjoyment and effectiveness, when related to different groups of learners.

3   **A child is backward at reading. Is the suspicion that he cannot learn likely to be extended to learning and training in general? What can be done to help him?**

4   **To what extent do you think it is desirable for learners to know about theories of learning? What would you recommend to enable adult learners in your organisation to develop their own learning plans?**

5   **How would you reflect what you know about learning styles in the
    design of:**

    (a)   **a *seminar* for mid-career managers who need a new job after
          redundancy**
    (b)   **a *policy* for open learning in your organisation?**

(Adapted from IPD Examination Stage 2, Employee Development.)

SUGGESTED READING

ATKINSON R. L., ATKINSON R. C. *et al. Introduction to Psychology.* 12th edn.
Harcourt & Co., Brace, Florida, 1996. A good general introduction.

BANDLER R., GRINDER J., DILTS R. *and* DELOZIER J. *Neuro-linguistic programming.* Volume I: *The Study of the Structure of Subject Experience.* Meta
Publications, California, 1980.

DOBSON C. B. *and* HARDY M. *et al. Understanding Psychology.* Weidenfeld
and Nicolson, London, 1990. Chapter 3, 'Learning and conditioning',
Chapter 4 'Remembering and forgetting'.

HONEY P. *and* MUMFORD A. *Manual of Learning Styles.* 3rd edn, Honey,
Maidenhead, 1992.

PATRICK J. *Training: Research and practice.* Academic Press, London, 1992.
Covers many aspects and relates them in a practical way.

ROUTLEDGE C. 'Brains, learners and trainers – a three-part series'. *Training
and Management Development Methods.* Vol. 13, section 7, 1999. Examines
the structure and processes of the brain, and the strategies and methods that
trainers can use to facilitate learning.

4 The learner and the organisation

The learner – the organisation as a learning environment – the organisation can learn and learn to learn.

INTRODUCTION

As we have explained in the preface, and indeed stress throughout this book, the learner does not exist in a vacuum but in an environment that influences the behaviour and learning of its inhabitants, and which is in turn influenced and shaped by them. This interaction is reflected in the first two sections of this chapter: the first section deals with contextual factors with an emphasis on how they affect the individual: in the second section we recognise the organisation as a learning environment, which both influences, and can be influenced by, learning/training events; in the third section we discuss the concept of double-loop learning and the way in which the organisation can learn to learn.

THE LEARNER

The aspects we have chosen to highlight are as follows:

- motivation
- knowledge of results (or feedback)
- attitude formation and change
- the age factor
- learning transfer.

Motivation

A large manufacturing company wished to provide the best possible training for school-leavers enrolled as trainee machinists. Accordingly, an off-the-job induction programme was provided for them during the first week of their employment. It was held in a classroom away from the noise of production and consisted of films, discussion and talks by various managers in the company. The trainees appeared to have little interest in the programme and from the difficulties they experienced later it was obvious that they had not absorbed the information that was given to them, and the results of a 'quiz' to test their knowledge of the company left much to be desired. Occasionally trainees handed in their notice at the end of the first week, saying that they were bored.

As part of the programme evaluation, they were asked to write a short description of their feelings the night before they started work. They produced comments such as:

'I was frightened; I wondered whether I would be able to do what they asked me.'
'I wanted to get to a machine and have a go.'
'I wondered what my supervisor would be like.'

Because of these comments, the programme was reorganised and trainees were taken straight to the training department workshop and introduced to their supervisors, who showed them their machines (already labelled with their names). They then learned how to operate them in a completely safe manner, and were allowed to try them out on a specially designed exercise. At a later stage, the films, discussions and talks provided a welcome break at appropriate times from skills training sessions; for instance a session explaining a pay slip was given in the afternoon before the first pay day. Trainees were also given a checklist of items to find out for themselves.

Under the new scheme trainees reached target performance much quicker and the results of the knowledge 'quiz' were greatly improved.

Motivation is a complex concept and it is most important to recognise that, as this example shows, people are multi-motivated and that they can be motivated towards or against specific behaviours.

Otto and Glaser (1970) suggest a useful classification of motivational factors based on the kind of rewards that are involved in learning:

- achievement motivation, for which the reward is success
- anxiety, for which the reward is the avoidance of failure
- approval motivation, for which the reward is approval in its many forms
- curiosity, for which the reward is to explore the environment and be exposed to novel stimuli
- acquisitiveness, for which the reward is something tangible, such as money or material benefits.

None of these classification groups should be regarded as excluding the other: for instance, both achievement and anxiety motivation are possible in the same person at the same time. The trainees in our case-study were motivated by both curiosity and anxiety. All the factors are influenced by the immediate experience of the learner, and as motivation is a personal matter, the case for careful discussion of individual programmes is obvious. Frequently, however, a variety of people are undertaking the same programme and it is necessary to bear all the general motivational factors in mind. For instance, achievement motivation requires that learning should be a successful experience. This has implications for the size of the learning 'steps' in relation to the target population; for timing; for the provision of ample knowledge of results or feedback to learner and trainer, and assistance in case of difficulty. If the training is lengthy, and possibly daunting, the setting of intermediate targets can be a useful means of effecting a sense of achievement, as can the introduction of a competitive element for younger trainees, although older learners tend to react unfavourably to that type of atmosphere. Approval is also concerned with knowledge of results, and psychological theory suggests that it is more effective to approve, and so reinforce, correct actions, than to punish and ridicule incorrect ones (see page 62).

It is likely, however, that there is an optimum level of motivation. Learners who are too eager can suffer from excessive anxiety, which may inhibit learning. This can apply particularly to older workers, who may be anxious for financial reasons, for prestige, or because of domestic problems; a good trainer should be prepared for this and allay any fears. As in the case above, it is useful to help the trainee to face the cause of the anxiety and thus overcome it. If this does not happen, the learner either wastes time worrying about failure or practises very hard. This is beneficial if he is practising an effective method but, if not, he may be reinforcing errors that may be difficult to eradicate. It is not always true that 'practice makes perfect'.

> An office supervisor took delivery of a new piece of technical equipment which he wanted all staff to learn to use. He left it covered up in the office and claimed that within two weeks every member of staff had found out what it was and how to use it!

Curiosity can be a very powerful motivator, as experience with small children will show; for this reason, discovery methods (see pages 65ff) are often very effective. They have been applied in machine-handling, with colouring and numerical cues being used to minimise the safety risk. Curiosity is one of the trainer's most powerful allies and should be nurtured by building on the learners' interests whenever practicable rather than destroying them by a rigorous insistence on logicality. Our induction course case-study illustrates the importance of considering motivational factors such as curiosity and anxiety when timing learning events so that as far as possible they occur at the most appropriate point for the learner.

There can be difficulties in establishing a direct link between the acquisitive instinct and successful completion of training. The relationship is probably at its most obvious in the field of operator-training for pieceworkers, where a resultant increase in output will be reflected in a higher overall wage. In management development, however, the outcome is likely to be less clear; the relationship is more likely to be indirect, in that if the training leads to better performance, an increase of salary or promotion may result, but as many factors contribute to improved managerial achievement, it can be extremely difficult to attribute cause and effect.

Knowledge of results

Knowledge of results

This is a form of reinforcement, without which it is difficult for learning to be retained and applied. It has important implications for the way learning situations are structured. The more prompt and specific the reinforcement, the more effective it is likely to be. For instance, in the case of learning the piano it is more effective to hear a wrong note at the time of hitting the key than for someone to tell you of your error three weeks later. In the case of development where results are longer term (such as certain managerial skills) it is useful to set criteria for adequate performance to act as subgoals to final achievement. There are also obvious relationships with continuous assessment of progress, behavioural objectives, target-setting or goals in managerial jobs.

Extrinsic knowledge of results

Is provided artificially, for example, by comment from the manager, trainer or fellow trainees, or by information derived from a simulator such as a monitoring screen in simulated pilot-training.

Intrinsic knowledge of results

Relates to the monitoring and guidance the learner is able to gain from cues within the job itself. Unless the learner can internalise knowledge of results, ie convert it from extrinsic to intrinsic, and know himself whether he is performing well or badly, the effects may not last after removal of the extrinsic provision and may not transfer to the working situation. Success depends upon drawing attention to the intrinsic cues so that the trainee recognises them. For example, a learner driver may initially look at the speedometer to decide when to change gear but, with trainer help and experience, will learn to know instantly from the feel and sound of the engine.

A good tutor or a manager well trained in coaching skills will help to convert extrinsic knowledge of results to intrinsic by the manner in which feedback is given to his subordinate.

> Frank sent for his subordinate, Jim, and told him that the job he had completed was unsatisfactory and that he must do better with the current one or he would have to go. John, however, opened a discussion with Peter, his assistant, by asking him how he thought his latest job had turned out. Together they identified and agreed the *criteria* for success, how far they had been met, and what Peter should have been watching and monitoring during the course of the job. This enabled Peter to estimate the quality of his work *through John's eyes*, and when doing a similar job on future occasions he could monitor for himself how well it was going and decide what corrective action he should be taking.

In this case the criteria could be related to predetermined goals, and obviously the more explicit the objectives and related feedback, the better the subordinate can learn to monitor his own performance.

Learning curves

These depict the rate at which learning takes place, thus providing knowledge of results to trainer and trainee. Progress is plotted on a graph, with the vertical axis representing a measure of achievement, such as output per hour, and the horizontal axis denoting the time period or number of attempts made (see Figure 4.1).

The curvature can be described by the way the gains vary from trial to trial – in the case of sensorimotor skill the curves are most often of decreasing gains (the change in performance from the current trial to the next is frequently less than the change that took place on the previous trial): this is one reason why the learning of a skill is often discouraging. Sometimes it is practicable for trainees to plot their own learning curves, and seeing their own progress can act as a motivator.

Fleishman and Hempel (1955) have suggested that as the attainment of skill level in a task increases, the importance of certain ability dimensions can vary. For instance, having gained more competence in the task, the learner's further progress may be affected by his reaction time and rate of movement, while other abilities, such as spatial relations, may have a decreasing influence on performance improvement. The learning curve may therefore not be measuring the acquisition of one skill but of different skills which are called in to use as the learning progresses. This may be one cause of a plateau of learning.

Plateaux of learning

These are periods of no improvement. They can sometimes be explained by a shift from a lower order of learning to a higher order (eg from letter habit in typing to word habit, ie learning to type familiar words as a single unit rather than concentrating on one letter at a time). A plateau is often followed by a rapid burst of progress. The trainer should attempt to discover the causes of plateaux, particularly those which occur regularly, in order to assist the trainees to overcome them. For instance, there may be certain stages when trainees become demotivated, indicating an alteration should be made to the training programme. They may need to concentrate more on one aspect – perhaps, in the example above, in learning to type particular combinations of letters where errors are most frequently made or, as Fleishman and Hempel maintain, they may have reached a stage when they are dependent on a different type of ability that has not yet been adequately developed.

Attitude formation and change

Attitudinal aspects of training are extremely important because they predispose learners to action. The relationship between attitudes and action is, however, by no means a simple one: in outline, we would state that attitudes are formed through our relationships with other people and are notoriously difficult to change. The concept of cognitive dissonance (Festinger, 1957) provides an explanation based on the premise that we normally like our attitudes to be in harmony with each other. Admiring a superior who actively supports an organisational practice of which I strongly disapprove, I am left

Figure 4.1 **A learning curve**

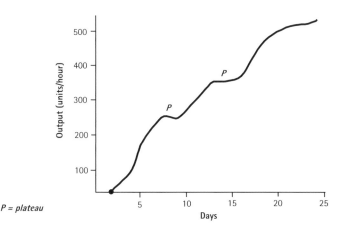

P = plateau

in an uncomfortable and dissonant state of internal inconsistency, in that someone whom I admire is supporting something I dislike. The problem can be resolved by modifying my attitude about my superior, or about the organisational practice, or by a decision that the practice is not very important anyway. Whatever the outcome, I shall have altered my attitude in some way. In a training situation, cognitive dissonance can occur in role-playing where, while acting to a brief, I may be required to give a convincing argument from a standpoint other than my own (such as that of a subordinate). If this is done in public, I am left with an uncomfortable state of dissonance and may begin to move slightly nearer my subordinate's viewpoint. In other circumstances, however, it may cause me to reject new learning as unimportant, possibly even subconsciously, because it is inconsistent with my other firmly held attitudes. A useful discussion of this phenomenon in relation to management development is given by Mumford (1980).

Group discussion has been found to be one of the effective ways of attempting to modify attitudes. Examples may be found in Study Groups, and other forms of social skills and leadership training.

Another method of attitude change is by providing new information. For instance, people's attitudes towards certain medicinal drugs can change radically when they learn of research that indicates harmful consequences. This fact is particularly important in training as preparation for organisational change. If little or no information is given on important issues, people may develop attitudes to the change that may harden and be difficult to alter. When a particular attitude has been adopted, the natural tendency is to seek confirmation that reinforces it, unless there is extremely strong evidence to the contrary. For a fuller discussion of attitudes see Hewstone (1990).

The Age Factor

The climate and the approach to teaching in schools is usually different from that in industry, and school-leavers can experience considerable difficulty in adjusting to a different kind of learning situation. Trainers must take this into account when designing programmes if young people's natural enthusiasm is to be channelled in the right direction. Young trainees usually react favourably to intergroup competition and appreciate variety in their programmes. They prefer to keep within their original training groups, membership of which gives them confidence. Leaving school and looking for work is a big and worrying step for many young people and self-destructive behaviour, such as overconfidence or shyness, often results from a feeling of insecurity. A patient and supportive trainer can do a great deal to help; this is particularly true with those taking part in temporary work experience, who may be discouraged if they see little hope of obtaining a permanent job. A perceived and desired outcome is an essential motivator, and it is important that learners are consulted about their programmes and are thus participating in training that is seen by them as interesting and relevant.

Research on the effect of ageing on learning shows the interplay of a number of factors, and that the effect is by no means totally adverse. Gradually, as we become older, the reproduction of new cells to replace those which die slows down and those which continue to reproduce start yielding a higher proportion of unhealthy offspring. The result is that speed of performance can decline. For example, as they grow older the majority of people will perform less well on a timed test. Welford (1962) found that the process of ageing impairs the central decision processes. This affects the time taken to reorganise information, monitor movements and deal with a number of matters at one time. Short-term memory deteriorates, resulting in time increase and errors in complex cognitive tasks. On tasks involving number matrices, Welford's older subjects were unable to cope with a large amount of information arranged according to different criteria. This involved not only short-term memory but the reorganisation of behaviour to shift from one aspect of the task to another. This appears to emphasise the potential value to the older worker of certain types of modern computer software such as spreadsheets. Certain tests, such as those of vocabulary and comprehension, demonstrated an improvement with age, but reasoning and numerical sections of intelligence tests showed a decline for older people and therefore, although they were able to score as well as (or possibly even better than) in their youth, the marks were obtained in different ways.

It is generally agreed that a number of factors are likely to affect achievement in later years and that age is by no means the sole determinant. The first of these is the original level of intelligence. Vernon (1960) gives evidence that the rate of decline is slowest among those whose original score was high. There is therefore an accentuation of individual differences.

The second factor is stimulation. A number of studies suggest a slow decline among those who make the greatest use of their intellectual ability and a more rapid decline in intelligence among those who do not. There is also evidence that stimulation can increase mental ability and may have physical consequences for the brain. Evidence from animal studies shows that the weight of cerebral cortex is affected by stimulation from the environment (Bromley, 1990). Evidence was found by Vogt (1951) of slower deterioration in brain cells of those whose level of intellectual activity had been high. A third factor is education and training. Welford (1962) suggests that the manipulative, occupational, mental and social skills acquired through experience help to offset a decline in abilities as a result of the ageing process. Other important factors are state of health and motivation.

For information on designing training programmes for older people, see page 254 and Plett and Lester (1991).

Our knowledge of the ageing process is imperfect, but there are a number of important implications for the trainer. Demographic trends indicate the availability of fewer young people in the workforce and an increasing dependence upon the services of older people. There may have been a time when people of 50 and over were deemed to be unsuitable for job change and retraining but organisations of the future are unlikely to be able to take this view. In fact one supermarket has opened a store staffed entirely by people over 50 (see page 267 ff); there is evidence that employees in their late 40s and early 50s tend to stay with the organisation much longer than those in their early 20s, that they have lower absenteeism and accident rates, often have greater spirit and reliability, and may already possess useful skills (Worsley 1996). Fear of difficulties in training should not therefore be used as a barrier or discriminatory factor in recruiting more mature workers.

If people are at their most receptive to learning in youth, and in later years draw upon their attainments, it is essential that the young are given every opportunity to learn. If those with lower cognitive ability are likely to show greater deterioration than those with above-average potential, it is extremely important that a broadly based training is given to young people so that through vertical transfer (see below) they may find it easier to learn a variety of skills when they are older. These arguments also provide a strong case for national traineeships and supply a justification for the prevention, although at a high cost in financial terms, of a young unemployed workforce.

Learning transfer

Having learned to drive a particular model of car, we expect to be able to drive different models; although some of the controls may be alien to us, we can adjust ourselves to them without having to repeat the entire learning process. This is because of *positive learning transfer*, which is said to occur when learning that has already taken place on one task assists later learning on another. Positive transfer can be either vertical or lateral. We shall discuss each type in turn.

Vertical transfer

Occurs when one subject area acts as a basis for another. For example, a basic knowledge of mathematics can transfer vertically to make it easier to learn statistics. The justification for starting many training schemes with a basic foundation course before allowing the learner to accept specific modules is that, as well as providing an overview, the content will transfer vertically in a number of different ways. This is also the rationale of providing a broader general education in schools. In a rapidly changing environment, pupils can make better use of vertical transfer to assist in the acquisition of a wider range of knowledge and skills later in life.

Lateral transfer

Occurs when the same type of stimulus requires the same response. Training simulators are devices for teaching a skill that will transfer, usually laterally, to the real task. For example, a trainee pilot can practise in a 'safe' situation provided by a computer-controlled flight simulator which imitates the effect of using different controls. Care is required, however, in the provision of simulators, because the extent of transfer obtained by their use is complex (see Annett 1974).

On- and off-the-job training

At one time there was a tendency to regard training off-the-job more highly than that which took place on-the-job, or 'sitting with Nellie' as it was sometimes called. (See page 105.) This was because 'Nellie' was often paid mainly for doing her own job, not for training others, and the trainee was left to watch and pick up the skills as best he or she could. In addition, Nellie might have had little or no training in the skills of tuition. Gradually, however, attention has been paid to the training of trainers and instructors and to the coaching skills of managers. On-the-job training has the advantage that the question of learning transfer to the actual job and the working environment does not arise, and, if properly planned and carried out by well-trained people in a safe environment, it can be very effective for some jobs. The emphasis on experiential learning, based on the work of Kolb and Honey and Mumford (see pages 67 ff, 226, and Fig. 12.5) is enabling managers to 'learn how to learn' from their experience at work, and it is also seen that there can be much advantage in arranging special assignments at work as an integral part of individual management development. The concept of 'cascading' (pages 151 ff) has devolved more responsibility to managers for training their subordinates and given some impetus to coaching on-the-job. 'Learning organisations' and continuous development necessitate the integration of learning with work and, although not precluding opportunities for learning off-the-job, place a high premium on self-development by learning from working experience. This capability is increasingly important as the pace of change accelerates. The organisation itself is a powerful learning environment (see pages 92 ff), and although there are many extremely valuable forms of off-the-job training, the advantage of the learning opportunities on the job cannot be underestimated. Very often the ideal is a combination of both. (See also page 239 for a discussion of on-the-job training.)

Off-the-job training relies upon lateral transfer to the working situation. It can have many obvious advantages, including the provision of conditions conducive to learning away from the noisy rush of the workplace; properly trained instructors; planned training methods; a carefully prepared programme at a pace governed by the trainees' needs; the creation of safe and inexpensive situations in which to try out and practise newly acquired skills and techniques; use of a greater variety of training techniques (eg discovery learning, case-studies, films, closed circuit television, simulators and interactive computer programs) and the opportunity to emphasise all four stages of the Kolb learning cycle, particularly observation and conceptualisation.

On the negative side, learning undertaken in a specialised environment may hinder the learner's ability to cope with the actual situation. For example, case-studies are useful in the consideration of a variety of possible courses of action, and of principles and concepts, but they can be criticised on the grounds that in the 'real' world we frequently have to decide on one best course of action and undertake personal responsibility for the results. What is learned during a leisurely contemplation of alternatives may not transfer to a stress situation. Furthermore, if the on-the-job climate is not supportive of what has been learned in the training situation, it is unlikely to be transferred.

Although it is generally agreed that off-the-job training can often be beneficial, it is necessary to introduce factors from the 'real' world (e.g. workplace jargon) and on-the-job experience when it becomes appropriate. There has, for instance, been a progressive increase in the number of 'organisational placement periods' as an essential part of educational courses, and a significant increase in the on-the-job element of teacher training. The NVQ requirement that training shall be carried out and tested to workplace standards emphasises the importance of obtaining learning transfer.

Negative transfer

Sometimes, however, old learning or past experience can hinder performance on a new task, that is when the same stimulus requires a different response. For instance, having learned to drive on one side of the road can make it difficult to drive on the other side when touring abroad. Literature suggests that although negative transfer can interfere, it quickly gives way to positive transfer and may actually result in more flexible performance in the long term (see Duncan and Kelly, 1983).

In matters relating to safety, as in our driving example above, or where dangerous or expensive material may be involved, it is necessary to overcome negative effects immediately. Duncan and Kelly (1983) indicate that the more similar the responses required in the two tasks, the greater is the likelihood of negative transfer: it increases with response similarity until the point is reached where the required responses are identical and transfer becomes positive. There is no guaranteed method of overcoming the problem; one precaution is to check the learner's previous experience of similar tasks and carefully point out the differences and possible consequences of

ve transfer. It is worth noting that it is most likely to occur when the
's attention is distracted by, for example, situational factors or new
its of the task, such as approaching a roundabout when driving
, as in the example above.

Factors that assist transfer

Transfer of knowledge and skills to new situations is essential for continuing development and the attainment of flexibility. It is a complex area and
there is no one set of infallible rules but the following points may be helpful:

Understanding of general principles: transfer occurs through the understanding of general principles and concepts rather than by concentration on
one narrow application. It can be facilitated by discovery learning. It is necessary both to understand the general principle and to be able to apply it
under different conditions. For example, a knowledge of employment law is
less likely to transfer to the working situation if the learner has had no practice in applying it to the actual procedures in an organisation. Examples of
training methods that might assist this process are discovery learning, case-
studies and histories, structured exercises, assignments and projects. Group
discussions and any means of associating and integrating new learning with
existing knowledge help too. You might also like to consider the relationship
of learning transfer with the reflection and conceptualisation stages of the
Kolb learning cycle described above.

Overlearning (ie practising beyond the level of minimum competence): in
situations where confusion could be caused by the acquisition of several
similar skills, minimum negative transfer will occur if the learner obtains a
really good grasp of the first step before proceeding to the others. Systematic
rehearsal and mental practice assist in the maintenance of skills already
acquired.

Association factors: the transfer of learning will be assisted if the trainee can
associate and integrate new learning with other learning that has already
taken place. Any structured exercises that help to achieve this aim are therefore useful.

THE ORGANISATION AS A LEARNING ENVIRONMENT

If we accept the link between experience and learning in Bass and Vaughan's
(1966) definition of learning (quoted at the beginning of the last chapter)
and consider Nord's (1969) application of Skinnerian theory of reinforcement
to organisations, we find a number of important implications for the training and development manager.

A continuous learning process

The first implication is that the training and development manager is really
intervening in a continuous learning process, and therefore requires diagnostic and analytical skills of a far higher order than is commonly realised.

People learn by example and reinforcement, and the influence of a superior upon his subordinate is very powerful. It is particularly strong when the superior holds the key to what may be termed the rewards and punishments of the organisation. Successful training requires active management support – ideally it should start at the top and filter down through the organisation, each superior being involved in the training of his subordinate. McGregor (1960) maintains that:

> every encounter between a superior and subordinate involves learning of some kind for the subordinate (and should for the superior too). The attitudes, habits and expectations of the subordinate will be reinforced or modified to some degree as a result of every encounter with the boss . . . Day by day experience is so much more powerful that it tends to overshadow what the individual may learn in other settings.

Range of training interventions

Secondly, the term 'training intervention' embraces much more than the provision of courses and off-the-job training: it includes any activity initiated by a training specialist, owner/line manager, or the learner himself. Such activities range widely and include: short periods of work in different organisations, jobs or roles; problem-solving discussion groups; projects; action learning sets; giving advice; feedback on performance; coaching; and mentoring. Measures to remove barriers to learning constitute important interventions and can include attempts to overcome attitudinal and cultural constraints, as well as practical assistance such as the granting of day release to attend classes or the provision of open learning facilities. A highly skilled training and development manager can act as facilitator and consultant, helping the whole organisation to learn more effectively.

Influence of organisational culture

Thirdly, off-the-job training requires reinforcement at the workplace: the attitude of the superior and the culture of the organisation are both powerful influences in determining whether training is likely to be transferred to the working situation. For instance, it is difficult for a manager to put into practice what he has just learned about the adoption of a participative and democratic style if the organisational structure and atmosphere is autocratic.

Everyone in the organisation, not least management, already has, and is constantly formulating, attitudes towards training. Views do not have to be expressed, and often remain hidden within assumptions that are themselves accepted uncritically by those whose own views are unclear or equivocal. These attitudes and assumptions are perhaps the most important factor within the working environment. Many observers have suggested that cultural variations explain the differences in organisations' ability to innovate; others have criticised the existence in UK organisations of 'anti-development' assumptions, which threaten developmental forms of organisation through discrediting new ideas before they have a chance to take hold. Dore and Sako (1989) wrote:

> If we were to single out just one salient point . . . the one for a British audience would probably be this: by such criteria as training expenditure and man-hours in off-the-job training, Japanese firms would come rather badly out of any international comparison. Where they do seem to be distinctive is in the way they motivate . . . to learn in order to gain in competence.

In other words, Japanese attitudes naturally promote workplace learning whereas British attitudes often block it. Similarly we have seen that all the political parties and social partners involved with the German economy give frequent vocal support to Germany's 'dual' training system, and that French society appears strongly committed to its educational framework. By contrast, UK attitudes seem much less certain about the value of spending time and money on planned training once full-time education has ended.

One person who spent a considerable portion of her working life in the now-defunct Industrial Training Research Unit (ITRU) at Cambridge has presented her 'collective' views on how to remove or diminish the blockages and stimulate learning activity *at work*. Downs (1995) sets out four basic 'beliefs about learning' and follows them up with 10 'principles of learning'; her interest throughout is cultural – that is, she is more interested in what the workplace might offer to help learning than in how an individual learner should set about the learning process. However, her conclusions are essentially related to the way people think and are not geared to specific procedures.

Downs' four 'beliefs about learning' maintain that:

- *Learning at work is largely a social activity.* In other words, the competitive bases of full-time education (eg tests, grades, pressures to succeed) should give way to *collaborative* learning activity. Comparisons between adults' achievements tend to prevent development.
- *Everyone has a role to play in helping people to learn.* Checking people have understood is as important as instructing; giving feedback and encouragement are as important as answering questions. Keeping knowledge to oneself is at best unproductive, at worst, sabotage.
- *Everyone has something to contribute and something to gain when learning.* It is an error to assume that others have no previous experience or relevant knowledge. Interactive learning processes are more effective than passive ones.
- *Colleagues, trainers, parents and teachers sometimes unwittingly prevent people from learning.* Making instructions or lectures difficult, laughing at others' mistakes, viewing questions as disruptions – these and many other responses kill learner motivation.

(Downs' 10 principles of learning (see page 99) are each linked to long lists of 'pitfalls' and 'remedies').

If we accept that these beliefs are not unconsciously promoted by the majority of employees, and are not likely to be presented strongly by an organisation's top management, it follows that one of the training and development manager's key operational aims should be to find ways of developing and maintaining them.

Unexpected repercussions

The fourth implication is that training may be likened to a game of skittles where aiming at one target may have repercussions in a variety of other areas. The 'skittle effect' suggests that it may be impossible to train one group of people effectively without changing the behaviour of another group. Apparent inefficiencies on the part of one section of employees may in reality be caused by poorly maintained equipment or defective materials, indicating training needs for a totally different section of the workforce. (See Chapter 5, page 108, and Chapter 7, page 159.) Training of one group of people can sometimes act as a catalyst in triggering change in other parts of the organisation, and may have unexpected consequences: in one instance, a complete redefinition and reappraisal of the organisational structure resulted from an in-house training course for managers.

Attitudes influence political decisions

Favourable management attitudes are particularly important in influencing political decisions about training. The advantages of planned training have to be 'sold' and clearly demonstrated. The ability to do this is the first requirement of a training and development manager; it may be no easy task, and there is no one recipe for success. Deciding where in the organisation to start can be a critical decision, and although straightforward discussion and debate might be the obvious first route, and a convincing and detailed demonstration of the cost benefits be all-important, ultimately minds are likely to be swayed by *successful training results*; this in turn means that decisions on where and how to train must at least be influenced by estimates of likely success and of attitudinal outcomes. The logical starting-place is at the top, so that training can 'cascade' down the organisation; during courses for supervisors a common cry is, 'It's our managers you ought to have here.' Notwithstanding its obvious advantages, depending upon the attitude of management, such a simple recommendation might not always be practicable or culturally profitable. In such a case, it might be more expedient to start where success in demonstrating financial return appears the most likely, or where an acute organisational problem might be solved, with the aim of creating a more favourable climate.

Necessity for commitment

The sixth implication is expressed by McGregor (1960), who suggests that:

> knowledge cannot be pumped into human beings the way grease is forced into a machine. The individual may learn; he is not taught. Programmes do not produce managers; we cannot produce managers as we do products – we can only grow them.

Skill and knowledge are required in the design of training programmes to meet specific needs, but the most difficult task is often that of gaining enthusiasm and whole-hearted co-operation, because people will normally learn only if they want to do so. It is all too easy to pay lip service to training. We could extend McGregor's horticultural analogy a little further and suggest that a gardener will succeed in cultivating a delicate plant if he starts by allowing it to grow in appropriate conditions and encourages and feeds it to help it bloom. We must never lose sight of the fact that commitment comes from involvement, and if we involve people we must attempt to use their suggestions, even if they do not necessarily accord with neat and tidy models of systematic training. It is necessary for a training and development manager to be fully conversant with planned methods but the skill of adapting them to specific situations is paramount.

THE ORGANISATION CAN LEARN AND LEARN TO LEARN

The final implication is that whilst the organisation is a learning environment for the people within it, they, collectively, constitute an entity which itself can learn, and learn to learn, the collective experience of the whole being greater than that of any of its members. To consider one of the ways in which this learning takes place we turn back to cybernetic and information theories in Chapter 3 and the example of the thermostat. If this model were applied to an organisation and its controls, such as performance indicators and budgets, it would ensure that any deviation from operating norms was discovered and adjusted. Many organisations have become good at devising and monitoring controls which do this effectively. However, this is a description of a system which maintains the status quo, and is described by Argyris (1977) as single-loop learning. Figure 4.2 illustrates this three stage process.

Figure 4.2 Single-loop learning

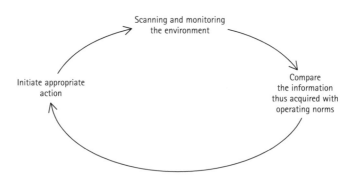

Figure 4.3 Double-loop learning

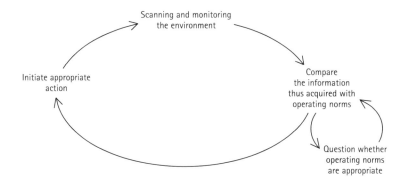

Double-loop learning involves questioning the relevance of the specified operating norms. In the case of the thermostat, these questions might refer to whether the temperature at which it was set was the most efficient and economical for the purpose, or even whether the thermostat was placed in the right location to be typical of the environment. See Figure 4.3.

In other words, single-loop learning occurs when addressing the surface symptoms of a problem and double-loop learning occurs when we ask why the problem arose. It is much more difficult to introduce double-loop learning into organisations and only a very small proportion of them have managed to achieve it. People's behaviour tends to be determined primarily by previous events and experience, and there are many barriers such as inertia, bureaucracy, defensive routines (some of which are described by Argyris as 'the organisational games that inhibit learning'), the inability to see beyond the status quo and/or vested interest in maintaining it. Argyris later cites the US Space shuttle disaster of January 1986 as an example where serious problems with the O-ring seals were buried by the desire to conform with plans and launch on time. In some types of organisation, controls and procedures can be sources of managerial power and there may be strong resistance to anyone who questions them or suggests changes; it may take a serious disaster such as the one above, a 'revolution' from within (new management) or without (political interference or takeover) to trigger an effective 'rethink'.

We have, however, seen double-loop learning come about in a small owner-managed company which had been run the same way for years. The staff all knew their jobs and there did not appear to be any learning needs. The owner-manager attended an external training programme and, beginning to see the potential of his company in a different light, he started to question the operating norms. The staff had to acquire new skills, began to query their own procedures, and a new organisation structure emerged. Learning needs thus became apparent at the second level and the whole operation changed from a relatively static to a dynamic process. It was the beginning of a learning culture, and the company started to learn to learn.

We will be returning to the concept of double-loop learning and developing it further in Chapter 12.

Some of the ideas in this chapter may seem very conceptual, and it may need considerable thought to turn them into practicalities. You should be able to draw upon the concepts and ideas and examples and apply them to the design of situation-specific training/learning programmes and opportunities and to be able to relate them to the concept of the 'learning organisation'. Considering the questions below should help you to put into practice what you have learned.

FOR FURTHER REFLECTION AND DISCUSSION

1   What do you consider to be the main reasons why a person is, or is not, motivated to learn? What action would you recommend within your own organisation to ensure a higher commitment to learning? This question can be considered in general terms or in relation to a specific example.

2   What arrangements can you suggest to assist the transfer of learning from a formal off-the-job course into a work situation? What do you recommend to make this transfer process more effective?

3   Suggest ways in which line managers can give positive feedback to assist the learning of their subordinates.

4   What do you understand by 'barriers to learning'? Using the headings 'Personal' and 'Organisational' list any barriers you encounter in your own learning. Is there anything you can do about them? Do you need to add any further headings? What 'barriers to learning' do you think might apply to a new entrant to your organisation? Could anything be done about them?

5   At the end of Chapter 3 you were asked to think of as many ways as possible in which feedback, positive or negative, occurs in your organisation. Try now to use this information to answer the following questions:

   What feedback do *you* receive?
   How does it affect you?
   How could it be improved?
   What additional feedback would be helpful?

6   Now consider these questions in relation to your subordinate, then ask your subordinate the questions, and compare his answers with yours.

(Adapted from IPD examination stage 2 Employee Development Nov. 1994.)
Can you relate any of your findings to theories of learning and reinforcement?

7   Describe the purpose(s) for which feedback can be used and *how* it could be used in two of the following situations:

    (a)   an appraisal interview
    (b)   a seminar on oral behaviour
    (c)   a weekend programme to develop interactive skills
    (d)   coaching to improve performance in a sport of your choice.

8   Below we give Downs (1995) '10 Principles of Learning'. Consider them carefully and, for each one, list any organisational or training features which might constitute *barriers to learning* and any features which would be *helpful and promote learning*. You may use your own organisation as a reference point if you wish. Save your list until you have read Chapter 10.

1   Learners need to know where they are going and have a sense of progress towards their objectives.
2   The learning environment has to be one of trust, respect, openness and acceptance of differences.
3   Being aware of and owning the responsibility for learning lies with the learner. Others can only give information and support, and provide feedback.
4   Learners need to participate actively in the learning process.
5   Learning should be related to and use the learner's experience and knowledge.
6   Learning is not only a basic capability but also a group of skills that can be developed/learned.
7   Facts, concepts and skills are learned in different ways.
8   Getting ideas wrong can be a valuable aid to developing understanding.
9   For learning to be processed and assimilated, time must be allowed for reflection.
10 Effective learning depends on realistic, objective and constructive feedback.

(Reproduced with kind permission from Sylvia Downs, *Learning at Work*, Kogan Page, London, 1995.)

SUGGESTED READING

ATKINSON R. L. *and* ATKINSON R. C. *Introduction to Psychology.* 12th edn. Harcourt Brace & Co, Florida, 1996.

BROMLEY D. B. *Behavioural Gerontology: Central issues in the psychology of ageing.* Wiley, Chichester, 1990.

DOBSON C. B. *and* HARDY M. *Understanding Psychology.* Weidenfeld and Nicolson, London, 1990. Chapter 13, 'Attitude Change'.

Downs S. *Learning at Work*. Kogan Page, London, 1995.

Patrick J. *Training: Research and practice*. Academic Press, London, 1992. Useful all-round text. With reference to the content of this chapter, see learning transfer, retention of skill and knowledge of results.

Pedler M. *and* Aspinwall K. *Learning in Company*. McGraw-Hill, UK, 1995.

5 An organisational perspective

Introduction – the dimensions of organisational learning systems – specific learning systems – other organisational variables.

INTRODUCTION

Chapters 3 and 4 reviewed what we know about individuals' learning behaviour. In the last analysis all learning is performed by individuals: a machine may be programmed to collect and store data, and to adjust its future responses to newly received messages, but its programme will still be based upon assumptions and decisions made by its human programmer. But individual learning is itself to some extent influenced, conditioned and moulded by the environment in which the individual moves.

We must here repeat once again our mainstream propositions: that each organisation is a learning environment, and that training interventions are made within that environment to promote learning, or to direct learning to specific purposes, or to make learning processes more efficient. In much the same way that a machine's behaviour reflects programming assumptions made by humans, so training interventions often reflect human assumptions built into the organisations in which people work.

This chapter will first outline conceptual models which researchers have drawn to describe key cultural differences between organisations, and key differences between organisational learning systems; it will then explore a variety of specific learning systems – such as 'sitting by Nellie', 'competence-based' and 'problem-centred' systems, the 'training process' and 'knowledge management' – which reflect these differences.

Throughout the chapter, the word 'system' is used somewhat flexibly to cover a wide variety of formal and informal groups of activity norms, with widely differing degrees of explicitness and sophistication. It should not be assumed that we are at any time equating the concept of a learning system with that of a formal and systematic management control system that has clear-cut inputs and outputs; in many ways, our notion is that of an ongoing process with characteristics that are observable on a regular basis.

> **Think (again) about your own environments – your family, their workplaces, your old school, the local supermarket, the local football club, and so on. These are all organisations in which people live and work. Are they 'organised' to promote learning – or does it just 'happen'?**

THE DIMENSIONS OF ORGANISATIONAL LEARNING SYSTEMS

Unlike research into the psychology of individual learning, and despite sociologists' interest in organisational models, research into organisations' learning systems *per se* has not been widespread. The norm has been for sociologists to address problems in the structuring of work tasks or procedures, or to explore relationships between people and their work, or to analyse political systems. Perhaps because of the wide differences between organisations, alternative 'theories' of organisational learning have not appeared; instead, a variety of complementary ideas or perspectives, albeit widely differing in their basic assumptions, have emerged in the process of describing specific organisational models.

In a lengthy typology of organisations (which extends even to considering organisations as 'psychic prisons' and 'instruments of domination'), Morgan (1997) includes chapters on organisations as 'machines', as 'organisms', and as 'brains'.

'Machine' organisations are of course mechanistic in nature, and operate as bureaucracies, tending to 'scientifically' manage via prescribed rules and procedures. Even if there were no overt rules or procedures relating to learning in this type of organisation, one would expect individuals to conform to a relatively standard approach to learning, which would be that adopted by the key decision makers; their decisions would naturally include decisions on whether formal training arrangements should exist or not. We shall see later that in 'machine' organisations of any size, decisions in favour of such arrangements usually include well defined training routines and who carries responsibility for them, and teaching processes predominate.

'Organisms' are much more open to their environments, and accept that there is no one best way of managing, encouraging a flexible and even enquiring outlook on the part of all. Contingency theory ideas ensure that authority is likely to be informal and to change through time. In such organisations, training activities and methods are also likely to vary through time, with new techniques being encouraged, especially during periods when substantial operational problems are experienced.

'Brains' take flexibility to a higher level, prompting innovation on the back of superior information processing. In such an organisation, individuals endlessly question and challenge their operating norms, and aim to create a trouble-free future by anticipating problems and creating solutions. Learning is not geared to any specific type of training approach, but 'learning to learn' is an endless aim, and indeed the organisation is reasonably described as a 'learning organisation'. Formal training activity tends to give way to creative dialogue between open minds, development being continuously integrated with work itself.

Morgan also describes organisations as 'cultures' and 'political systems' – generalised terms which overlap the three organisation types we have just noted, and which encapsulate first the ethical and social philosophies, and second the distribution of power, within organisations. (For further material on organisations as cultures or political systems, see Morgan's extensive bibliographical commentary). Within each of these new types, variations abound, determining for example whether individual or group learning predominates, and again the extent to which learning is short term or strategic. Cultural and political factors can in fact dominate learning systems, and may indeed be the determinants of how strong any given learning system itself may be.

Shrivastava (1983) studied organisations' learning systems before the brain metaphor had emerged. He first conducted a literature search, and concluded that research in this area had followed four distinct and contrasting perspectives.

- First, organisational learning was viewed as the *gathering of experience*, repetition ensuring improved future performance.
- Second, it was viewed as the *development of a knowledge base*, more and more sophisticated knowledge allowing superior decision making.
- Next, it was viewed as the *sharing and meshing of assumptions* via 'cognitive maps', allowing the correction of naive thinking and concerted action.
- And finally, it was viewed as *adaptation*, allowing resources to be directed to new aims or new problems as they arise.

Shrivastava's synthesis of these perspectives brought him to conclude that although contrasting, they are not mutually exclusive. (We might ourselves now add that the first two seem naturally to serve 'machine' organisations, and the last two naturally to serve 'organisms'; while all four might be employed within 'brains'). All involve individual learning, contributing to the organisation's collective knowledge, skills and attitudes base. This in turn serves wider decision making, thus becoming a part of an *organisational* learning process rather than merely an individual one. This organisational learning process is itself influenced by a broader set of physical, social and political variables, but in a given decision area the developing knowledge, skills and attitudes base allows the organisation to adopt new aims, to pose new solutions for problems, and even to innovate operationally.

Shrivastava identified two 'critical dimensions' that allowed him to generate a typology of organisational learning systems (see Figure 5.1 overleaf). The first critical dimension is the 'Individual–Organisation' dimension. At the one extreme, learning is 'single person dependent': the individual learns in isolation, serving his or her own needs, without any clear shared use in prospect. Bearing in mind our loose definition of the word 'system', and despite the fact that most large organisations have in recent times sought to use training interventions to improve operational performance, a bias towards this extreme remains the norm. 'Learning by exposure' is the prevailing system in most organisations, even where training interventions are frequent and sophisticated. Most learning happens randomly, and is self-centred, self-determined, self-controlled. Attendance at external courses is usually arranged individually, without pre-course briefing to establish how the eventual learning might be used at work, or shared with colleagues.

Figure 5.1 Shrivastava's 'key dimensions'

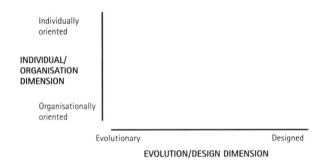

Manuals and textbooks (like this one) are usually compiled with the individual learner in mind, not any particular organisation. This is not to deny that some organisational benefit accrues. It simply means that the link between what is learned and operational performance is assumed as an act of faith, the learner being trusted to implement the learning at the workplace and indeed to 'spread the gospel' through normal, unplanned social contact. A common practice among small organisations is for the chief executive regularly to arrange attendance at external management conferences or trade association meetings, essentially to keep contact with equals; many such people, enjoying substantial decision-making power in their home organisations, can then impose their personal learning output on their return as 'organisationally worthwhile' – or they can simply reject its operational value.

At the other extreme, the system overtly and directly serves the organisation independently of any one person's input. The expressed aims are here described not in terms of what the individual learns, but in product attributes, or operating procedures, or statistics – overall results concerning safety, perhaps, or productivity, or even worker loyalty. Such a system may still involve individual learning, but the content or area of study is prescribed – as for example in a research laboratory engaged on a defined programme of product development. Another example might be integrated with the organisation's safety procedures: after fire drills, safety stewards might be required to meet *en masse* to review their responsibilities collectively and agree amendments. We shall see later how most bureaucratic training activity is aimed in this direction, requiring employees to experience standard learning processes or routines, usually in the cause of explicit work goals.

The second of Shrivastava's critical dimensions describes the degree to which learning is designed or not. At the latter extreme, with literally no planning whatsoever, the learning processes simply evolve as accepted traditions, valued not as the result of any formalised review of results but because they have stood the test of time, appear to be generally respected, and are easily recognised. Many old-style 'time serving' engineering apprenticeships were for long in this mould in so far as workplace learning was concerned (although the mandatory educational element – for many the key training element – was of course planned). Some large private sector companies mount annual top management strategic 'away-days', which are planned in terms of a time programme but not as learning experiences, and hence might be said to fall into the evolutionary category.

The opposite is the scientifically designed planning and information system, dedicated to serving specific information and learning needs identified in equally consistent ways. Perhaps less sophisticated, but still similar in type, is any standardised skills development system which takes newcomers through a series of prepared, supervised exercises with tests establishing the extent to which the skills have been mastered.

It seems reasonable to suggest that in recent years those UK organisations with substantial training activities have tried to develop organisational learning systems as a way of improving upon individual learning systems, simultaneously increasing the planning, and decreasing the evolutionary, elements. Smaller organisations, without the resources to mount substantial training activities of their own, have either left management to determine what to communicate and how, or have relied on using external facilities – which effectively means the perpetuation of an individual and evolutionary approach, albeit one that is now affected by published national standards.

SPECIFIC LEARNING SYSTEMS

We have already hinted that Shrivastava's typology needs to be updated. We offer here our own set of contrasting systems, using Shrivastava's key dimensions to distinguish differences between them. It is perhaps necessary to repeat that (a) our use of the term 'system' can be taken only to imply regular, consistent use, (b) an organisation can exhibit more than one system at any one time, and (c) our list of systems is not exhaustive.

The 'sitting by Nellie' system

XYZ Limited is a manufacturing organisation, the managing director of which believes 'we cannot afford to train'. The firm recruits 'ready made' workers, paying them higher wages than local competitors. Learning happens solely 'on the job', supervisors and and established workers giving new recruits whatever information they (the 'trainers') think is needed, the recruits picking up routines and standards as they go along.

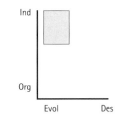

Strictly speaking, this is not a learning system; it is an 'anti-system', since it relies on chance. But, because learning still happens, it can be considered a management option, and it is of course widely preferred, if perhaps by default. In so far as it can be said to reflect any of the values that we have set out above, it assumes an individual and essentially *un*designed, ie evolutionary, set of norms.

In this particular example, the learner is assumed to be able to gather knowledge and to use it without any real help other than that randomly offered by colleagues, who may set other tasks as priorities as they think fit. There are no obvious incentives to train, or disincentives not to do so – indeed, the managing director might be expected to criticise anyone who made training itself a priority. The 'trainers' are not themselves trained, nor are they prepared in any way for their training roles.

The last two sentences suggest ways whereby this approach might be made less haphazard and operationally more useful. First, as we saw in the preceding chapter, experiential learning can be improved *if learner motivation is increased*. This may involve little more than offering to remove probationary status once competence is demonstrated. Another incentive might involve the creation of explicit learning objectives against which the learner can measure progress. Second, *Nellie can be trained to train*. This is likely to change the way Nellie talks, and to introduce learning plans, making it easier to appreciate and copy what Nellie does. It will also identify an 'authority' to whom the learner can direct questions without feeling embarrassed. Such moves would have the effect of developing a more definable (and properly termed) system.

'Competences' and other 'analytical' systems

A small bus company has paid a fee to engage in the Vehicle Engineering Competence Assessment scheme developed by its national training organisation. The fee entitles the company to receive literature explaining the scheme, the forms on which its administration is based, plus the training of its own staff as trainers and assessors. The central aid is a manual which sets out in detail 'standard' elements of vehicle fitter jobs in the industry, including performance criteria. The elements are collected under a number of generic headings; a requirement of the scheme is that each fitter (the scheme applies to all ages) must be trained to master all the essentials of an actual site job, which *must* include some elements from each generic heading. When the learner thinks he or she is 'competent', a claim form must be completed, an assessor then visits the workplace and tests the learner, using real-life materials and processes. Satisfactory results allow the award of national qualifications.

Our example, which represents one of the many in-company systems based on the existing national vocational qualifications system, aims essentially at developing the individual to prescribed and carefully designed competence standards which are set outside the organisation. These standards are described in terms of:

- *elements of competence*, which are evidence of 'what the competent performer can do' – that is, 'an action, behaviour or outcome which a person should be able to demonstrate' (the approach to learning has been labelled by some the 'outcomes' approach)

- *performance criteria*, which are 'statements which describe the quality of outcomes of successful performance', and 'the basis against which an assessor can judge whether an individual can achieve the outcome specified in the element'
- *range statements*, which define the 'breadth of competence required for the individual to be considered occupationally competent'.

(All quotations from the NCVQ's *NVQ Criteria and Guidance*, January 1995)

These three components collectively form the 'standard'. They must however be backed by *evidence requirements*, which detail both performance and knowledge essentials that the assessor must check.

This is a heavily prescriptive system, but has considerable appeal to employers who simply do not have the resources to complete time-consuming analytical work. Similar systems which are geared more specifically to individual organisations can be seen where an employer has produced a unique, organisation-specific manual which is used as the basis for a standardised recruit training programme, and for regular refresher course activities (eg sales training systems); but even here, unless there is provision for regular review and updating of the manual, the learning system still cannot be said to be developing the organisation itself.

Critics have challenged the emphasis on 'outcomes' to the exclusion of learning processes – that is, the lack of interest in learning processes. These critics stress that an outcome can be affected by the learning route (for example, a fitter who has memorised a sequential procedure will operate differently from one who has acquired diagnostic skills). This suggests that the 'competences' system might be most appropriate where the actual job need, the prescribed standards and the training methods can be consciously matched – as indeed might be the case in our example, where the trainers and the assessors are employed by the same employer.

'Problem-centred' systems

An advertising agency includes in its organisation a part-time 'trouble-shooting' team comprising five senior managers, who attend the monthly board meetings as observers and meet immediately thereafter to draft corporate plans stemming from problems identified by the board. Because agency performance levels are often criticised, it is usual for plans to include training interventions. The company does not employ its own training unit, nor has it a dedicated training budget; hence training has usually taken the form of formal in-house departmental 'teach-ins' conducted by external consultants.

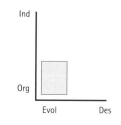

Predominently short-term, pragmatic and *ad hoc* in nature, this system is dominated by operational problems, senior management deciding on change and what this means in learning terms – and dredging their own operational budgets for whatever has to happen. Systems of this kind are often highly acceptable to subordinates: they attack real work problems, produce quick, visible action, and are usually believed to produce cost-effective results. However, their success depends on diagnostic skills rather than the instant panacea of expert knowledge in named spheres. As the example implies, they can tend to adopt 'quick fix' teaching solutions which do not serve real organisational learning needs. A useful example comes from a City office where the output from the audio-typing pool was criticised, the diagnosed need being little more than 'put those typists straight'. In the hastily-mounted ensuing course, the external trainers quickly became convinced of operational faults, line managers lacking the skills to use the pool effectively. These managers never became the subject of a training plan, and a number of typists went to work elsewhere. The main point is that the gearing of training to operational problems often requires careful diagnostic activity.

The 'action learning' (AL) system

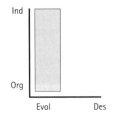

John Smith is currently halfway through a six-month attachment to a large computer software establishment; under normal circumstances he is a shift manager at a power station. Together with three other secondees, he has been asked to look into the methods of distribution of software packages to a variety of types of outlet; the company is concerned at delays in delivery which have been reported by too many clients. John's team has gathered data from several sources, and has set up several more 'action sets', incorporating selected line managers from the host firm and a transport manager from a mail-order house. They are being tutored in their search for solutions by staff from a local business school.

'Action learning' (AL) is basically the study of real-life problems and their resolution within the real-life environment. Its justification as a training system which simultaneously develops individuals (usually managers) and organisations rests on the mix of a motivating challenge for fresh, sharp minds and the transformation of problems into opportunities for flexible organisations. The combination of motivated self-study and high quality tutorial resources is a strong developing force. 'Action learning' has been used in a variety of forms; the approach was pioneered by Revans (see Revans 1980 and 1983), and involved setting up and maintaining 'task cultures'. The experiences involved in achieving this are claimed to develop superior understanding of organisation, leadership and team skills, which advocates of the system see as the prime managerial competences. AL is discussed in more detail in the second section of this book.

The 'training process' system

A local authority has recently appointed a training manager to work within its personnel department. The training manager's job is first and foremost the establishment of annual training plans for all departments; the new manager has already set about the task of systematising the identification of needs, and has linked up with department heads to allow draft plans to be discussed and, it is hoped, agreed. A central training budget has been allocated; all major training expenses except salaries will be charged to it. Once agreed, the training manager is empowered to make implementation arrangements direct with learners and their superiors, both concerning individuals and groups. The training manager is also committed to producing in the future an annual training review document, which will summarise training achievements during the past year and suggest improvements to the training system in the future.

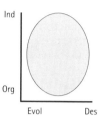

This system owes its origins to Fayol's ('plan-organise-do-review') process theory of management. It was strongly advocated by most industrial training boards during the 1960s and 1970s, and became synonymous with the 'systematic training' ideal widely preached by them. We shall see later that a simple version of the model has been accepted by the lead body for training and development as the basic model used for its definition of competences. A more complex version is offered here as Figure 5.2, from which the four-stage process of (a) identifying training needs (b) designing training plans (c) implementing the plans, and (d) evaluating the results can easily be deduced. Support for this type of system has grown over the years, and the model has steadily become more sophisticated, organisations increasing their adherence to what have come to be known as 'basic system requirements' – accepting that training interventions will be a regular phenomenon throughout an organisation's life, with posts explicitly named as carrying responsibility for seeing that appropriate processes exist and are followed. Typically, those processes are seen as including:

- the promulgation of training and development policy
- the inclusion of training responsibilities in job descriptions
- the regular, periodic definition of training needs
- the creation of training plans
- the provision of training resources
- the training of trainers
- implementation of training plans
- the assessment of results.

Much of Section B of this book explores these processes in more detail.

We have shown this system as oval-shaped in our mini-illustration. This is simply to suggest a fundamental difference between it and the next system we are about to describe. In this, the extent to which training serves the organisation and its employees, and the extent to which development

Figure 5.2 **The 'training process' system**

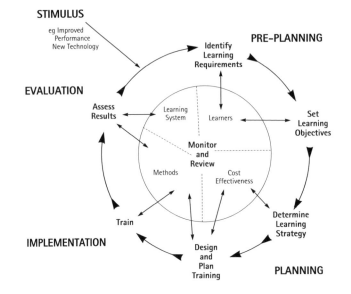

evolves or is designed, are determined essentially by a few key people, notably professional trainers and their leading line contacts, who naturally manage the system in what they consider to be its preferred direction. In our next system, a strong central design has its own evolutionary characteristics, and seeks to maximise both individual and organisational learning.

The 'knowledge management' system

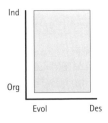

ICL's 'Project Vik' developed an Intranet (an internal computerised network) covering many countries. An initial series of forums was run in which key employees were asked about information needed to do their jobs more effectively. They said they needed information about the company, its customers, its services and products, and most importantly about internal ICL services. They also asked for improved communication aids, even down to copies of site directories. 'Café Vik', a unit with six PCs, plus discussion and meeting facilities, opened 11 weeks later with company-wide management briefings; a mobile roadshow took the message all over Europe, and established 'Café Viks' in most major outlets. A year later, the rapidly developing system was said to be used by about 10,000 of 19,000 employees. A central focussing and development department includes positions with titles such as 'knowledge officer', 'information service provider', and 'web master', while selected operating managers are designated part-time 'knowledge sponsors'.

The concept of knowledge management is a recent innovation, but interest in it has grown rapidly with the development of information technology. In its simplest organisational form, a knowledge management system requires carefully prepared, structured management information systems in which information is recorded, stored and made available to those who are encouraged to retrieve it – 'systems for capturing knowledge and moving it to where it is wanted' (Garratt, 1994). Designated 'knowledge developers' design the computer programs that control the database, and 'Learning Options' guides help employees to find, at any given time, information that serves their personal development and/or work needs. Access to 'classified' information is automatically confined to those whose responsibilities allow it, but the system allows all levels to share unclassified knowledge without the problems that geography or hierarchy normally produce. And there is a much more sophisticated, ambitious version of knowledge management, aimed at not just the sharing of formal data but extending to the sharing and meshing of assumptions and beliefs. We noted this earlier as one of Shrivastava's researched ways in which the organisation learns; proponents of knowledge management now suggest ways in which what is called 'tacit' knowledge (meaning expertise that is stored not in formal management databases but in peoples' heads) can be clarified and shared with others, eventually combining to become 'newly-created knowledge', understood and accepted throughout an organisation. We shall be discussing these ideas in greater detail in the last chapter of this book, which we entitle 'An Agenda for the Future'.

Other systems

We have chosen systems that are visible in present-day UK organisations, omitting several that you yourself may believe are more usual, important, or interesting – for example, the 'political system' (in which learning activity follows the political aims of the key opinion moulders), the 'organisation development' system (in which behavioural science techniques are applied to organisational change), and the 'self-development' system (in which employees with a strong commitment to learning regularly allocate time to exploring things of their own choosing, using their own preferred methods). We have also left the important concepts of 'continuous development' and 'the learning organisation' to be covered along with knowledge management in full in our final chapter; they move beyond the idea of a learning system contained within an organisation to one in which the two become one.

OTHER ORGANISATIONAL VARIABLES

Personnel and training professionals sometimes complain that defining and categorising learning systems is unrealistic and of little value. They argue (and our case examples perhaps confirm) that each organisation develops its own unique system without a particular model in view, that a variety of learning systems coexist side by side at any one time, and indeed that training decisions are always influenced by matters which are operationally, rather than organisationally, important. They suggest a large number of important variables, including

1 *The learners themselves*
Some training systems are specifically geared (in terms of both resources and methods) to employee types – eg graduate management trainees, or technical specialists, or people with disabilities (eg the Royal National Institute for the Blind's centres).

2 *Training methods*
During the 1960s, many large companies bought or built residential training centres, which became the focal centre of their (formal) learning activities. More recently, self-study has become a new focus for some.

3 *The size of the learning unit*
Some organisations define needs in terms of individuals; others group people in departmental units or occupational groupings (eg managers, drivers). The larger the organisation, the more likely it is that group activities will at least have a place in the system.

4 *Training resources*
Many organisations feel they cannot afford their own training resources, preferring to use local providers (eg Further Education Colleges).

5 *Lead times*
Plans can be 'long-term general' or 'short-term specific'. The former are most usually seen in organisations that are internally stable; but even such organisations may abandon long lead times, in periods of recession.

6 *Status and power*
The status and power of those pressing for the learning to take place.

7 *Operational purposes*
Whether mainstream operational priorities are served or not.

8 *Management commitment*
Whether or not the prime responsibility for ensuring that training interventions are made is seen throughout the organisation as resting with line management, and whether or not line management actively support any such intervention.

9 *The training function*
Whether or not training roles are defined and built into the organisation as specialised responsibilities.

A long-established medium-sized food manufacturing company maintained for many years a strategy of recruiting school leavers and graduates, 'growing its future management', and promoting from within to fill all management vacancies. Personnel department handled recruitment, but no formalised induction training was given; line management were responsible for any work-place training. No specialised training unit or management was employed. When local competition for labour increased with the arrival in the area of three major new employers, all of whom had more formal training pro-grammes and a training department, traditional recruitment sources tended to dry up, and top management were forced to review their strategy. Top management concluded that they wished generally to continue with the estab-lished management approach, believing it still had significant operational strengths, but that some improvements should be introduced. Recruitment staff were asked to improve their links with local schools, colleges and uni-versities; a recently recruited graduate was given the task of planning a two-hour induction course, and a team of five supervisors were later briefed on how to present the course. Attendance at the induction course was given priority over workplace needs. First, line management were asked to give priority to initial job training, and to incorporate new training estimates into their budgets.

In this example, top management may not have consciously reviewed their organisational learning system, but they have shown their trust in it. Moreover, they have judged that as potential recruits value training facilities, and competitors are offering it, management must commit themselves more strongly to training, and – most important – new entrants must be able to *see* the commitment. This is important: it is not enough to have a good system if it is not appreciated by those for whom it is intended.

A fast-growing commercial photography business was originally formed by the current director with the aid of two enthusiastic assistants. The firm now employs 35 in premises created from three side-by-side shops. The Director recently introduced new equipment, including high quality colour repro-graphic machines; he talked the suppliers into providing training in the use of these last machines on his premises without charge. A further commercial suc-cess is a contract with the Defence Ministry for a new type of aerial map which combines real-life photographs with three-dimensional map layouts. This has been enabled by part-time secondment arrangements for one of the assistants to the cartography department of a local college, and similar arrangements for the other assistant to a printing college. Both assistants help their respective colleges by handling practical sessions with students, and providing advice on photography for the staff. Neither arrangement has to be paid for. The direc-tor knows that he cannot yet justify internal trainers, nor can he employ tech-nical experts in these new fields. He has therefore searched for them elsewhere, and found them in local FE colleges. The 'cost' to the business is negligible (ignoring the non-availability of the assistant while away from the business), because the secondment arrangement has allowed him to barter some of the firm's own expertise for new technological knowledge – and the assistants have had some useful personal development in the process.

In this example, a small organisation uses its own established strengths to buy in technological and training expertise that it does not possess. They do not already have an organisational learning system – but their commercial growth, which is based in technology, is beginning to make one commercially desirable. The decision maker may not understand this clearly: he thinks operationally, and 'finds' externally the learning the organisation needs, then works out how to import it. In the process, the organisation grows further – technologically, commercially, and in human terms.

> In a London office much discontent was fostered by a sequence of what were seen by clerical and administrative staff as 'unfair' decisions on further education facilities. Some workers were given paid release to attend classes that they, the workers, had chosen; others were refused similar requests. Some refunds of travelling expenses and book expenses were authorised; other, similar, requests were turned down. Most employees' complaints implied that they wanted equal treatment. The training manager believed in equality, but any idea of establishing rights on a collective basis had always been strongly challenged by top management as 'uncommercial', and the training manager had himself insisted in the past that he must be consulted before release was granted to any employee. He talked with various line managers and with several day-release students; virtually all wanted a tighter set of rules. The training manager drafted new 'rules' governing release decisions; these rules were quickly approved by the board. In future, support would be given only for classes that were appropriate to the work that staff were undertaking or expected to undertake in the near future; approval required both the line manager's and the training manager's signatures on a newly designed form. Support would follow prescribed rules concerning paid time away from work, payment of fees, refund of travel and book expenses, payment coming out of the training manager's budget.

In this example the training manager reviewed and re-established his norms as follows: first, learning must be in both the company's *and* the employee's interests as expressed in work arrangements; second, decisions on facilities would be individual, not group; third, the power to decide would rest jointly with the line superior and the training manager; and fourth, resources would be provided from a central budget which the training manager would control. Other variables (eg the nature of the learners, lead times) were not considered important enough to influence the new system which, once agreed, was imposed on and quickly accepted by all. Discontent disappeared overnight. The 'singles versus groups' issue was treated as an important one and resolved in favour of an individualised system; but it was subordinated to the issue of company need and again made subject to the twin issues of management control and available resources.

More fundamentally, the 'educational system' has here been the cause of workplace problems, primarily because different line managements have been interpreting and developing the system in varying ways. Luckily the organisation has a specialist who is well placed to re-establish a common approach: he knows the detail of the learning arrangements, has access to the various parties, and can draft a solution to the problem without damaging the system. It is noteworthy that the solution is a bureaucratic one, involving new rules which must be observed by all, and that it puts him in a critical position to ensure that future arrangements honour those new rules.

The essential points to remember from these three case examples are that:

1   each specific training intervention is an 'operational' one, not to be dominated by philosophy or theory, although both may influence it (it is also a 'political' one, in the sense that it affects the balance of power and authorities in the organisation)

2   unless a major new strategic plan is involved, training interventions will usually be taken within the framework of the (usually undefined) learning system that exists; and – perhaps the key point in this chapter –

3   just as management is a situation-specific art, so the structure and identity of the training and development function is invariably determined in an organisation-specific way.

You will have noticed that we are slipping away from theory and moving into practical language. We are now thinking about real-life operational management, not 'deduced' organisational systems. We are also beginning to explore the training and development function within organisations – which brings us to the end of the background material that forms our first section of the book, and prepares the way for the second section, which is all about promoting learning opportunities in the real life, and requires us first to look at the training and development function more closely.

FOR FURTHER REFLECTION AND DISCUSSION

1   **Can you think of any other 'organisational variables' that might dominate a given organisation's approach to learning? If so, how might they affect each of the specific learning systems that we have outlined?**

2   **What do you think will be the long-term effect of the UK government's strong advocacy of the 'competences' approach to vocational education?**

3   **Study Figure 5.2. Imagine or recall a real-life organisation, and assume that it is introducing a new computerised Intranet facility that will form the basis of a future internal learning system. Work your way round the depicted wheel, transforming each item from a concept into an activity, using words you think can reasonably describe the training process in operational terms.**

SUGGESTED READING

MORGAN, G. *Images of Organisation.* Thousand Oaks, California, London and Delhi; Sage Publications, 1997.

SHRIVASTAVA, P. 'A typology of organisational learning systems', *Journal of Management Studies – Special Issue: Organisational learning*, Vol. 20 No. 1, Basil Blackwell, Oxford, Jan 1983.

JESSUP, G. *Outcomes: NVQs and the emerging model of education and training.* The Farmer Press, London, 1991. Although outdated by more recent developments, this gives the basic philosophy underlying 'competences' systems.

Section B

PROMOTING
LEARNING
OPPORTUNITIES

The operational arena

6 The training and development function

Introduction – the training and development function – line management's responsibility for training and development – specialist training and development resources – positioning and defining dedicated units – political and ethical roles – the national standards' limitations.

INTRODUCTION

The first section of this book presented the background (historical, institutional, theoretical and organisational) to training interventions. We must now turn to our first mainstream theme: the organisation and management of the training and development function.

Most of what follows in Section B will concern the level of the operating organisation. We may at times imply that we assume a standard form of operating organisation, and a logically consistent approach to learning. We should perhaps remind you that management remains a situation-specific art, serving and at the same time being constrained by the environment in which it is carried out, and hence it is more important that the approach to learning should blend with existing operational norms than slavishly copy alien standards.

This chapter aims to outline what the function comprises, the responsibilities of line management, and the justification for, and establishment of, dedicated training and development units – including their structure, positioning, role definitions, and organisation.

> Read the last paragraph again. Now, think of any organisation with which you are in regular contact – for example, your local bank, health centre, supermarket, cinema or leisure centre. Do you know if training activities occur in that organisation? If so, who makes (or should make) them happen? Perhaps you don't know; perhaps they are not managed *formally* at all; perhaps you *assume* they happen, but you are never able to watch them happening. Now assume that *you* are somehow put in charge of the whole operation. Do you want any training activities to happen? Do you want these activities formally defined? Do you want anyone to be formally identified as responsible for making them happen? If the answer to any of these questions is 'Yes', try adding the detail to each – and then think about how these things might fit into a chart or map or picture which describes the organisation as a whole.

THE TRAINING AND DEVELOPMENT FUNCTION

The word 'function' comes from a Latin verb meaning 'to perform or to act', and a useful definition of the training function (based on that contained in the former Manpower Services Commission's *Glossary of Training Terms*, 1981) is:

> the purposes, structure and specialised activity of training and its relationships with other activities within a working organisation.

You should appreciate that this particular function is a relatively recent addition to UK organisational structures compared, for example, with production, accounting or sales. Donnelly (1984), in his review of the evolution of training as a specialist function, drew attention to the fact that, prior to the 1960s, training activities were very restricted and diffused within organisations. Not surprisingly, therefore, there was an almost complete absence of any objective analysis of dedicated training and development jobs and (in the minds of top management) the nature of company training activities rarely justified the status of a 'business function'.

We are then dealing with what is a relatively recent feature of organisational life and, moreover, one which, often from a zero base, enjoyed a spectacular but ephemeral growth.

Although a number of large companies (eg Ford, Lever, Cadbury, Pilkington) had training units in operation before the Second World War, training departments first appeared in quantity during the late 1960s – in the form of off-site course centres or wings of existing personnel departments, and occasionally as mere one-person administrative units. There was no general pattern of organisation, nor was a standard pattern preached by the 1964 Act or the industrial training boards, which were the main stimulus for the development. In later years, when the legislative support was withdrawn, many of these training departments failed to consolidate their position. As might be expected, there were great variations in the ways in which training units evolved, in their perceived purposes and achievements, and in the extent to which they were accepted and valued within their organisations. At one end of the spectrum, they existed simply as a token presence to satisfy minimal internal needs, and perhaps also to justify an ITB grant. At the other extreme, training units were developed that enjoyed a high status and influence, and came to be embedded in the mainstream activities of the organisation.

Bearing in mind the very limited stock of training expertise that was available, the low-calibre staff frequently appointed to the training positions and the limited training they were given, the expectations that organisations had of their training departments at that time were often unrealistically high. A warning note about the range of activities of training officers was sounded by Rodger, Morgan and Guest (1971). In their study, carried out in the mid-1960s, they sought to clarify the function of the training officer and the limits of the function, and they commented that:

> Training is a means of making better use of human resources in the organisation by developing people to meet the requirements of the job to be done . . . Any attempts to extend the expertise of training officers into broader human resource specialist roles is to change the trainer into . . . a more exotic role that would be beyond the aspiration of all but a minority of training officers.
>
> *A Study of the Work of Industrial Training Officers*, 1971

This quotation should not be taken to mean that training *per se* has no part in organisational change and the creation of a flexible workforce. On the contrary, it is a primary vehicle for these developments. But their achievement demands the exercise of a high order of training expertise, and this was in short supply at that time.

The economic recessions of the 1970s and 1980s provided the *coup de grâce* for many weak training departments, especially those in small organisations, typically resulting in the cessation of planned training activities in the host organisation. In more robust organisations, some training departments lost their independent functional status, and the responsibility for the activities that survived cost-cutting was dispersed to other functions. Thus in many small and medium-sized organisations the training function that had enjoyed a departmental state in its own right regressed to its pre-1964 state.

But the seed had germinated: some organisations, particularly those with buoyant personnel departments, had increasingly appointed good-quality human resources to their employee development positions. They found during the 1980s that employee relations problems were less in evidence: hence employee development could wrest more resource time from the personnel professional. The economic recovery of the 1980s, coupled with the success of government's Youth Training programmes, further renewed many organisations' involvement with employee development, and although the recession of the late 1980s and early 1990s hit companies hard, the tendency to ignore the training function has not been so evident; indeed, by 1990 some commentators were coming to describe the function as critical for forward growth.

Rodger, Morgan and Guest (*op. cit.*) noted a wide variety of activities in response to variables such as:

- the status and importance of the function as expressed by top management's interest and support
- the extent to which there is a need and demand for training within the organisation
- the natural development of training in the firm
- the managerial calibre of those in specialist training and development posts.

Similar data emerges from studies 20 years later. We shall see later how strategic, political and organisational constraints influence, if not mould, the function, and how the emergence of 'knowledge management' systems is simultaneously sophisticating the concept of a learning function and making it more generalised in its application; but it is still possible to suggest three main conditions that must be satisfied if the function is to achieve a secure status in the organisation. These three conditions are as follows:

1 Line management should accept responsibility for training.
2 The function should be appropriately structured within the organisation – with roles that are perceived as relevant to such aspects as boundary management, organisational culture, operational strategy, management style and the organisation's geography.
3 Specialist training staff should be seen as professionals – trained, with clearly defined roles.

These prerequisites for success are discussed in the remainder of this chapter.

LINE MANAGEMENT'S RESPONSIBILITY FOR TRAINING AND DEVELOPMENT

Although, as we shall see, there are different types of managerial responsibility for training, all managers, without exception, ought to accept personal responsibility for the training and development of their own staff. This involves taking an active interest in their careers, providing opportunities to improve and extend their abilities, especially by using day-to-day work tasks, and, above all, by encouraging them to continue learning (Singer, 1979). An organisation should ensure that each of its managers accepts the importance of this particular role when contributing to the corporate training effort and that their success in exercising this responsibility will have a bearing on their own career prospects. Unlike other training responsibilities, this cannot be delegated.

These assertions of good practice, however, are not universally accepted by managers. 'More urgent tasks have to be given priority' and 'general pressure of work' are the usual reasons given by managers for not being involved in training and development. Although not discounting these reasons, it is true to say that a critical aspect of the management process is concerned with identifying and dealing with priority tasks, and for many managers training is simply not perceived to be a priority. We have drawn four conclusions from numerous discussions we have had with senior, middle and junior managers attending management development programmes:

- A significant obstacle to progress in exercising this responsibility is that, for many, the task is perceived as being difficult – and is hence avoided.
- It is unusual (perhaps for the same reason) for managers to be assessed rigorously on this aspect of their work (in appraising managers and determining their own training needs, much more emphasis should be placed on expertise – or the lack of it – in this sphere).
- Many training activities (especially those linked with determining training needs – which we shall explore more fully in Chapter 9) demand a heavy and sustained allocation of a manager's time.

- It seems that many managers have adverse feelings about learning which stem from their early experience of formal education – feelings that are both uncomfortable and unpleasant, and that they hoped to leave behind when they entered adulthood. Such feelings act as powerful anti-development influences, and ensure that trainer-training for managers is itself a complex and lengthy process.

The nature of the responsibility for training, and how it is exercised, varies with the level of management. Top management have four main responsibilities as follows:

- They bear the main responsibility for creating and sustaining a positive attitude to human resource development in all its forms.
- They determine the organisation's human resource development policies, and the level of resources to be allocated in support of them.
- Their personal involvement in training decisions, and in formal training events, and their own self-development practices, offer an example to ambitious subordinates.
- Their training interventions (not least via critical comments on what they observe) provide a quality control service for the training function.

Middle and junior managers are responsible for implementing the organisation's training policy within their own spheres of influence. They must themselves communicate information linked with work plans, for example, new work schedules or new output targets. They must ensure workplace competence despite such hazards as raw material variances, machine breakdowns, variable hours of work, sudden workforce sickness and frequently changing specifications – all of which require a flexible workforce with trained deputies available at short notice. They must honour conditions of employment – for example, those allowing leave of absence to attend external courses. But above all, they must encourage subordinates' learning on a continuous basis, to ensure that all these other operational learning processes can flow smoothly. As with their own top management superiors, their own training decisions, their involvement in discussions, their self-development and their training interventions give to their subordinates an ongoing justification for learning.

SPECIALIST TRAINING AND DEVELOPMENT RESOURCES

Paradoxically, an increasing commitment by line management is often the strongest influence leading to the use of specialist, 'dedicated' training and development people and units. We saw in the case studies in the last chapter how an expanding photographic firm bartered for external know-how, how a food manufacturing company selected and briefed supervisors to run formalised induction training courses, and how a London office's need to standardise employee study facilities justified the drafting of 'rules' by an already-appointed 'training officer'.

This last example also showed how important it is for employees in different departments to be treated equally and consistently. The potential problem grows if employees actually move across organisational boundaries to learn. Imagine your own reactions if, as a management trainee on a roving familiarisation programme, you are welcomed in one unit by senior management, given access to strategic material, and regularly allowed to attend management meetings, while in the next unit these opportunities are missing. Imagine the effect of the sales department allowing you to draw sales expenses on sales attachments, while a distant research laboratory provides none. The aftermath of your critical questions at head office is likely to be a standard ruling – which in turn may involve a central budget of some kind, clearly defined within a named manager's span of control.

Results of this kind are not confined to management traineeships, nor to large organisations: any activity that serves, or is commissioned by, a department or departments other than that in which the activity happens, demands a focal point to which problems can be referred for decisions. In a small or medium-sized organisation, this may well be the senior executive him- or herself, or at least a senior manager, who of course has only limited time and specialised knowledge, and is likely to delegate the task if the need recurs regularly. And the need may be for regular action, not just *ad hoc* decisions. This is not to say that wherever training activity grows, full-time training officers and training departments must inevitably appear. Those taking on the new responsibilities may well combine them with more visible existing responsibilities: a safety officer may be asked to handle the ongoing training of safety stewards, an accountant may be asked to coach newly appointed supervisors on cost-effectiveness, and so on. The 'training' tag may not appear in their job titles, and the time to be spent on this aspect of their jobs may remain unspecified.

Nevertheless, many training roles, and especially those which serve more than a single purpose, are often delegated to a 'dedicated' unit or person. We have seen how a 'dedicated' induction unit might be created to ensure recruits are consistently and properly introduced to a company. Again, if 'diagnostic instruction' is needed on several jobs prior to a decision on initial placement, a 'dedicated' technical training unit might handle this. And so on. These units usually do have 'training' in their title, as it is their main task. And if their work spans departments, we may find them placed in a central personnel department, since training and development roles often link with, and in some cases overlap, personnel management roles.

The picture in large, multi-departmental and multi-site organisations is more complex, but the organisational issues are basically the same, especially if organisational change happens frequently. Even if specialist training and development roles already exist, decisions on whether line management roles should be changed (and specialist roles decentralised or redrawn or abandoned) are periodically needed. The need can be crucial, as is clear in the following extensive example:

A well-known multi-national corporation originally organised its operations in one product sphere in separate manufacturing and selling operations. Six manufacturing companies (each comprising one site) existed, each with its own head office. Each of three sales companies had its own regional office and nationwide sales force. All nine companies had central training units, working from and within their central personnel departments. Competition forced a series of major reorganisations: a new marketing-oriented company took over the entire operation, manufacturing being concentrated over several years on two sites, and a new head office, with a newly created marketing department, focussing a single, combined sales force. There were of course many redundancies, but none among training staff, whose workload grew enormously. Extensive training was envisaged over a number of years to train the remaining factory employees to handle newly moved equipment and processes, to retrain sales reps used to 'old' routines, to brief newly recruited marketing staff, and to generate a single corporate identity.

To serve these ends, (a) the three factory sites were each given an enlarged training unit, housed within the site personnel department, which itself reported to the site general manager; (b) the sales department was given both a central training unit (reporting to a sales controller in head office) and a 'regional personnel and training manager' in each regional office (reporting to the regional manager, and independent of the central sales training unit); and (c) a 'company training manager', working from head office and responsible to the new company's newly appointed personnel director, took over management and management trainee training. The key point here is that operational decisions forced existing specialists to relocate at new bases – manufacturing organised geographically, sales geographically and functionally, and head office on the basis of management grade. But some key line management responsibilities also changed in the process.

Further changes evolved during the next few years. In one of the factories, a technical training unit was established within the main production unit, managed by a full-time technical manager who reported to the production manager. A 'head office training manager' post was newly established, responsible for 'determining and where appropriate implementing training plans' for the marketing, commercial and personnel departments in head office; for convenience this new post reported to the company training manager, but most of the person's time was spent in discussions with line management in the three mainstream departments. The sales force introduced 'cycle days' at the end of each four-weekly sales cycle, when reps came together with their area managers; half of each cycle day was given over to training led by the area manager, but uniquely scripted by the regional personnel and training manager in discussion with the regional and area managers concerned. To ensure some overall co-ordination of expense, the company training manager was given the added responsibility of advising annually on all training budgets, of creating a corporate 'annual training review' document, and again of commenting quarterly on actual company-wide training expenditures. The company training manager chaired and controlled the agenda for a new 'standing training committee', which met quarterly and immediately thereafter reported to the board of directors via a written document and a board meeting agenda discussion. Attendance at this board meeting varied, dependent upon the chairman's view of what should be discussed, but the company training manager was always present.

Later again, the title of the company training manager was extended to become 'company training and management development manager', and he was given responsibility for liaising with directors in maintaining ongoing development programmes for specifically listed promotable managers. His first act was to carry through amendments to the formal appraisal processes to ensure that promotability ratings were determined and agreed annually with the directors concerned. A small technical instruction unit was established in the head office to train audio typist and administrative assistant recruits who, when trained, worked in central pools; this unit was led by an instructor reporting to the office manager, but it was also required to handle all administration relating to external training arranged within head office.

This case example shows how complex organisational decisions regarding training and development, taken to complement operational change, can be – roles and reporting responsibilities sometimes must be newly clarified, new base points determined, and even new co-ordination methods arranged. There is no single model to be followed: a new, unique model must be created, and operational and political influences are usually the strongest determinants of specific decisions. Nevertheless, the example does suggest a number of critical lessons:

- Where widespread change is extensive, and the organisation is large, dedicated training responsibilities are usually justified. A worthwhile 'rule' might be that 'in turbulent operating conditions, the responsibility (or reponsibilities) for training must be formally and clearly outlined, and must be both understood and acknowledged by all levels of management'.
- In a large organisation, spread over geographical and functional boundaries, it is unlikely that a single training unit or department can adequately handle the wide variety of training responsibilities that top management will want or need to see managed, and managed professionally, and hence need to delegate.
- It should not be assumed that the creation of one or more 'dedicated' training units or departments involves the total delegation of the training function.
- While the training function might appear to fit naturally within the personnel function, there are often major reasons why formal training units are better placed close to the line management who still carry the prime responsibility for operational results and attempts to improve them.
- *Technical instruction* (including in this instance training in such skills as typing and administration) demands technical know-how, and can reasonably be considered part of technical operations, and hence run by technical staff.
- *Sales training* can involve special geographical problems, and hence often justifies unique arrangements.
- *Management development* (by which we here mean preparation for future promotional moves, and the forward organisational planning that may be dovetailed with them) requires support and commitment from the very top, and a degree of confidentiality that justifies direct links between the

specialist and top management, often bypassing middle management in the process.

- Training *administration* can be handled anywhere, and will ideally be managed by people who are used to managing logistics.

Perhaps the main lesson in the last case example relates to the endless ongoing need for liaison between training and development professionals and line management. A technical training unit may be given sole and complete responsibility for instruction activities, especially where new recruits are concerned; a central induction programme may be installed without reference to future bosses; a management development manager may work directly with top management. But normally, a training and development department established with no more than a generalised responsibility to determine the ongoing learning needs in a geographical or functional area of the business, and to see they are met as well as possible, does not take over sole and unique responsibility for the function. In these circumstances, which are the norm in most medium-sized and large organisations with dedicated and formalised training units, the overall responsibility remains shared with line management. It is simply not possible for job descriptions to divide and prescribe detailed task responsibilities on a permanent basis. What is needed instead is a mutual appreciation of *roles*, or more precisely, *role expectations* – that is, who is expected to carry the *prime* responsibility, and indeed to make the first moves, for and in specific areas of the function. (We shall look much more closely at the definition of roles later in this chapter). What this means is that through time, following some initial structuring of roles, and as a result of an ongoing interplay between the line and the 'professionals', a working relationship between the two evolves. The positioning within the organisation chart of the dedicated unit or units, person or persons, team or teams, is important, but it must also be reviewed regularly: this positioning can promote or hinder the evolutionary process that is so important for operational results.

POSITIONING AND DEFINING DEDICATED UNITS

Arranging the structure

As we have already noted, the need to structure the training function 'appropriately' within the organisation is easy to prescribe and difficult to describe. There is no one correct way of 'positioning' the training and development department within organisations that vary in such respects as employee numbers, employee types, geographical sites, organisation charts, historical tradition and management style.

In a very large number of small organisations, and a minute proportion of large ones, the function is not itself detailed at all. Responsibility is held to rest with line supervision and management, and corporate decisions are taken by the owner, managing director or whoever else is the senior executive. In organisations that number more than 100 but fewer than 250 employees, it is often the case that a personnel function (or department or unit) exists, and the personnel function is taken to subsume that of training and development; in many such organisations, the personnel manager is unlikely to be served by substantial resources, and he or she will not be able to spend a large proportion of working hours on these matters; typically, the department will arrange for external training activity (eg vocational courses at local colleges) to be patronised. Some small companies meet their needs and obtain much valued resources by joining group training schemes or consortia, which plan and manage training for specific categories of staff, or use an external training consultant/adviser on a permanent contract.

But the vast majority of middle- to large-sized organisations, both public and private, do now formally describe and place the function in their charts. Role designations vary considerably, as can be seen from the following list of existing titles (which is by no means exhaustive):

- Personnel director
- Personnel controller
- Human resources director
- Human resources controller
- Human resource development manager
- Personnel development manager
- Personnel operations manager
- Group training director
- Group training manager
- Group training officer
- Group employee development manager
- Company training manager
- Company training and development manager
- Training manager

- General training manager
- Chief knowledge officer
- General training officer
- Training officer
- Training adviser
- Employee development manager
- Management development manager
- Managment development officer
- Sales training manager
- Sales training officer
- Technical training manager
- Apprentice training officer
- Instructor
- Web master.

Figure 6.1 **Organisation chart – example A**

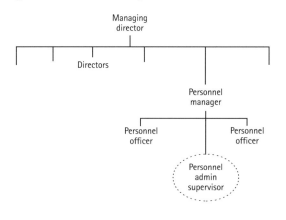

Some of these positions are sometimes observable as 'part-time' posts in specific organisations, or perhaps held in conjunction with other positions (eg the company secretary may also handle the management development role; a regional sales manager may also be the sales training manager).

The essential need for an 'appropriate structure' is not met simply by choosing titles for those carrying responsibilities. The function must attempt to 'fit' all those strategic, political and cultural items already discussed; above all, it must be integrated with the overall personnel management function and, equally importantly, with other operating functions. Here are a few examples of this sort of integration:

> Example A is a smallish company that operates on only one site, apart from a small field salesforce, and it does not itself run training events of any kind. Its basic approach to learning is a mixture of 'sitting by Nellie' and 'competences' systems. Training needs have always been satisfied by sending young entrants on part-time courses at the local College of Further Education or (in the case of supervisors and managers) to selected short external courses run by various providers. The function is not itself to be seen in the formal organisation chart: it is in fact carried by the personnel department.
>
> Induction courses are run about once every two months by either of the two personnel officers, who draw on others (eg the safety officer) to handle individual sessions. The admin supervisor keeps information on external courses, makes all bookings and arranges for the fees to be paid. She also records course attendances on personal files. The admin supervisor also issues blank appraisal report forms (covering only management grades) and reports incorporate salary recommendations, but not training needs. Line management and supervision determine who attends what courses and when.
>
> This is an authoritarian, tight-knit organisation run by management who believe in helping young people to acquire formal qualifications but who have no current belief in the need to plan learning on a continuing basis and do not aspire to any sophisticated employee development plans.

Figure 6.2 **Organisation chart – example B**

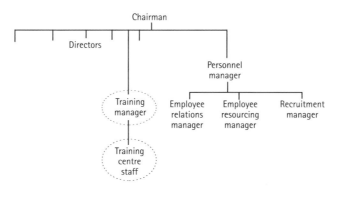

Example B is somewhat larger than A in numbers of employees, although it also operates from a single site; and it does have a specialist training centre. That unit is responsible directly to the chairman, who is an enthusiastic supporter of youth and management training but believes the company should manage these matters internally, to ensure learning is geared to the actual workplace. The training centre comprises a youth training workshop (covering engineering and secretarial skills) and a residential building in which management courses are run. Induction courses are also held in the training centre.

This example does not easily equate with any of the specific systems in Chapter 5. Training serves the organisation and has been 'designed' but it is becoming more evolutionary and less prescriptive. In recent years the chairman has insisted that his training manager develops (mainly by purchasing appropriate hardware and software) a range of self-study facilities, with the result that the training centre is now called a 'learning resources centre': employees can apply to attend and have access to audio-visual and computer-based programmes. Access is guaranteed outside normal working hours; during working hours, the decision to allow the use of these facilities is shared between the training manager and the line manager.

Example C is a small provincial building society, which has 35 branch offices all within about 40 miles of the company's head office. The company is diversifying into a wide range of new customer services; these developments are led by a marketing department, staffed by so-called marketing development managers. Branch offices are closed to the public until 11 am each Tuesday: this time is 'operational training time', and is used both to train people in new procedures and to discuss problems with office staff. Branch office managers lead the Tuesday morning training sessions, but their formal content is agreed in advance with the relevant development manager, who often attends and indeed sometimes operates as an instructor.

This is clearly a 'problem-centred' system. The personnel director, the company personnel manager and a management development officer all operate from head office; they handle all other employee development activities, including central induction, further education regulations, liaison with outside training providers, attendance at management courses and conferences,

Figure 6.3 **Organisation chart – example C**

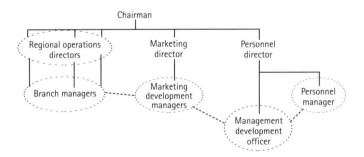

Figure 6.4 **Organisation chart – example D**

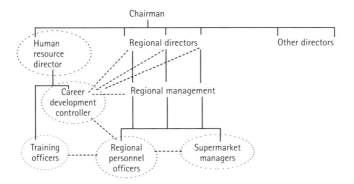

management trainee programmes and 'one-off' programmes created for managers before or on promotion. Line directors have a major role to play in the management development system, maintaining succession plans and mounting periodic interviews with all who are on promotion lists.

Example D is a supermarket chain, with many branches and an annual intake of around 350 retail management trainees, whose recruitment is a major annual operation and whose later development has justified the emergence of a large central training unit. This unit reports to a member of the board known as the human resource director; to him a number of managers are responsible, including a career development controller and several training officers.

Apart from engaging in the annual recruitment 'milkround' and running specific management courses and conferences, the main role of the central training department has been to manage the management training system and its outputs. This involves endless discussions – with trainees and with regional and district personnel office staff – about the objectives and methods in individual programmes. The system is moving towards becoming a 'competences' system. The department has detailed some 40 'areas of competence' (eg stock control, running wines and spirits, opening new stores) that must be mastered by a trainee before an initial management appointment; specific plans are worked out for each individual, the vast mass of actual learning being completed in real-life shop circumstances. The final say on what is included in a personal plan rests with the central career development controller; but in practice, decisions are invariably jointly taken, regional personnel officers handling the liaison with supermarket management (who themselves take on the day-to-day training and instructor roles).

Example E is a large company with several thousand employees (including several hundred managers) and operations involving a head office, two manufacturing sites and a regionally organised national salesforce. The company has a long history of training – applied to all departments and all levels of employee. Full-time training managers exist in each functional department (technical department has one in each factory). Company and departmental training plans are created every six months.

Figure 6.5 **Organisation chart – example E**

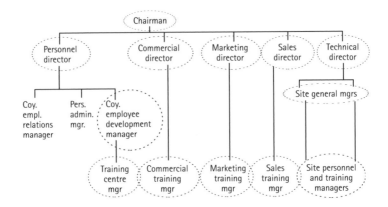

Figure 6.6 **Matrix organisation – example E**

Responsibility	Chairman	Pers'l Director	Other Dir's	Site Gen. Mgr.	Coy. Empl. Dev. Mgr.	Training Centre Mgr.	Functional Training Mgrs.	Site P&T Mgrs.
HR Policy	*	●	*					
Corporate Trg. Needs/Priorities	*	*	●	*	†			
HR Systems		*	*	*	●		†	
HR Budgets		*			†	*	*	*
Mgt Development	†	●	*	*	*			
Mgt Trainee Programmes		*	*		●		†	*
Departmental Training Needs + Plans			●	†	*		†	*
Individual Training Needs + Plans							†	●
Formal Course Management					*	●	*	
Liaison with Outside Training Providers						†	†	†
etc.								
etc.								

Key: * = Some responsibility   † = Major responsibility   ● = Prime responsibility

In this company, a matrix arrangement ensures that responsibilities are often shared, but one person will always carry *prime* responsibility for training within

Figure 6.7 'Outsourcing organisation' – example F

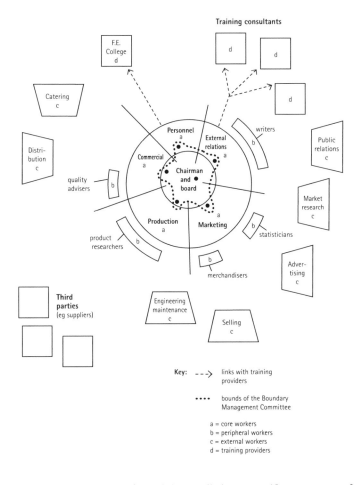

each site or department, or for training applied to a specific category, or for a given training task. The nature of the matrix can be appreciated from the second chart.

Example F is a medium-sized company that during the past five years has doubled its turnover, trebled its profit and reduced by 40 per cent the number of employees on its payroll. The reduction in employees is perhaps more apparent than real: an 'outsourcing' policy has led it to negotiate the transfer of some of its staff to outside companies who have been given rolling three-year contracts to supply services, and again to establish others as self-employed specialists whose fee earnings are underwritten provided they spend a third of their time working for their former employer. In this way, market research, product research, advertising, selling, distribution, engineering maintenance, catering, public relations, advice on quality and even the implementation of training have been 'outsourced'. The policy owes its origin to the 'flexible firm' model put forward during the 1980s by Atkinson (1984) following research by the Institute of Manpower Studies: workers are organised as 'core' (full-time employees), 'peripheral' (part-time, self-employed individuals) and 'external' (employed by contractors and agencies, but working full- or part-time within the company). Forward strategy gives a high value to maintaining control over peripheral and external workers via ongoing training: as part of their agreements, outside companies and specialists are committed to spending the equivalent of at least two days per month in training activity prescribed by the main company. The traditional hierarchical organisation chart is inappropriate, being replaced by a 'doughnut' (see Figure 6.7).

External training facilities are used: three firms of outside consultants are retained and the local FE College provides formal courses. There are no formally designated training staff: training of core staff is the responsibility of line management, whose departmental budgets include training budgets. The training of peripheral and external staff is concerned mainly with (a) identifying needs, (b) deciding priorities and (c) briefing/negotiating methods with the training providers. Training costs in these areas are centrally paid for from the personnel budget.

The chairman chairs a 'boundary management' committee which meets every two months to review non-core operational (which in practice means mainly briefing or training) needs. The committee comprises a senior manager from each main department, including those responsible for managing links with peripheral and external groups, plus the personnel manager; the secretary of this committee is the external relations manager. Once needs and priorities are determined and budgeted funds are confirmed, the external relations manager and the personnel manager jointly establish the detail of what is required, together with how/by whom it should be carried out, plus any funding limits. The dialogue with outside training providers is usually conducted by the external relations manager, although the personnel department handles college

Figure 6.8 **Virtual organisation – example G**

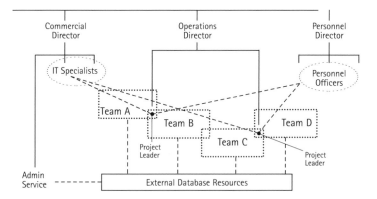

course administration requirements. Over the past three years the practice has grown of monthly 'briefing meetings' for non-core staff held on company premises and organised and run by the training consultants, with inputs from line management. A consequence has been the growth of similar internal meetings mounted and run by line managers themselves.

It can be seen that 'outsourcing', although removing names from the payroll, does not necessarily reduce training activity; indeed, it arguably increases the need for regular, period learning to be managed. In this example, the importance attached to managing outsourcing, plus the decision not to delegate training roles to full-time trainers employed as core staff, has led to increased attention to training by line management, even if the word 'training' is not used.

Example G is perhaps more than a little futuristic in character. It reflects the currently developing concept of the 'virtual organisation' – a term borrowed from computer terminology, where it is defined as 'not physically existing as such, but made by software to appear to do so'. This is not easy to translate into an organisational model, but might typically describe an operational set-up that is project-based, new projects appearing frequently and project teams endlessly re-forming to tackle them. Each change brings with it new roles, new relationships and (most importantly) new and unique information needs. These information needs are satisfied by access to networked intranet databases – which, married to simulation methods, provide new knowledge *and* suggest how it might be used, *and even* offer a forward view of what the results of adopting the information will be (hence 'not existing, but made by software to appear to do so'). In our example, project teams are formed and re-formed by the project leaders, who also operate as team members but carry the prime responsibility for resolving detailed day-to-day problems in the ongoing management of each project; team members access the databases using their own computers and telephones. Project work moves forward as members, operating in 'chains' or networks, feed their personal findings to colleagues via unique processes which are regularly reviewed at team meetings. Training interventions are frequent and commonplace but the word 'training' is rarely used, as the learning system is effectively integrated with the project work. Everyone nevertheless has a 'training function' and a contribution to make to the corporate learning system, even if in most cases they are serving temporary ends. Two key roles exist, however – that of the IT specialists who maintain and develop the information system, and that of the process consultant/s whose job is to understand *and help project leaders and team members to understand* their own process reality. There is no 'training officer' *per se*; personnel officers handle induction training as part of the induction process, and provide the process review expertise.

It can be seen that advanced information technology is a major influence promoting new 'knowledge management' systems; it is also likely to promote flatter and more flexible organisations. It also tends to merge learning with work and to make the individual the master of his or her unique learning process. An article in the *Independent on Sunday* (6 March 1994), discussing recent work by the well-known commentator Tom Peters, drew a picture of an environment in which 'independent contractors such as freelance journalists, software programmers and gardeners wake up knowing that before sunset they must (i) prove themselves again with their clients and (ii) learn a new wrinkle to improve their odds of survival'. The article then went on to suggest that everyone in salaried employment might need to achieve this same attitude. The key point is that the training function effectively becomes a learning function and it is organised as part of work processes, not as an extra.

These seven examples underline the wide variety of possible ways of organising employee development activity in organisations. There is no one model that can be suggested as appropriate for any given size of unit, category of work or type of worker: each organisation must develop its own, aiming to 'fit' dedicated training and development units into its operational activities in line with its policy, its purpose, its environmental constraints and opportunities and the imagination of its personnel and training staff. As we shall see in future chapters, the nature of this 'fit' is an important determinant in the selection of the most appropriate training approach and methodology.

Defining dedicated training and development roles

Far and away the most comprehensive definition of tasks and roles is to be found in the national Training and Development standards published by the Employment National Training Organisation (see EOSC 1995), which are now the established basis for NVQs in this field.

A single statement of purpose was first set down as

> To develop human potential to assist organisations and individuals to achieve their objectives

As with all standards aimed at approval for NVQ use, a functional analysis process (a process that we shall explain later, in Chapter 9) was used to break this statement into functional areas and sub-areas, then into units and elements of competence – the latter being described in terms of what people in relevant positions are expected to be able to do at the workplace. The eventual result was a detailed 'mountain' of statements comprising:

- 1 statement of purpose
- 5 areas of competence
- 14 sub-areas of competence
- 56 units of competence, including 11 'management' and 6 'personnel management' units, and
- over 100 elements of competence, each carrying up to 8 performance criteria, plus range statements and 'evidence required' lists.

The essential framework describing the function is contained in the areas/sub-areas of competence; we reproduce these here as Figure 6.9.

To understand the precise meaning of terms used in the NVQ system, see pages 330–35 in Appendix 4. The important points to note here are simply that the 'unit' briefly defines a specific competence, and each unit is divided

Figure 6.9 **Training and Development National Standards:
The main functional areas and sub–areas**

into a number of 'elements' (which explain in great detail what the person in the role must be able to do). Taken either individually or in groups relating to units of competence, elements of competence are effectively formal statements of role expectations.

But this was not the end of the project, which had to do more than simply describe roles. To convert these roles into a hierarchical set of NVQ qualifications, each unit had also to be aligned with one or more of the three NVQ levels 3, 4 and 5 – which are defined generally as 'supervisory or technician level', 'mainstream managerial level', and 'high managerial level'. The units of competence could then be classified as 'core' or 'optional' against each of these levels. We have extracted here the *core* units of competence (see Figure 6.10), yielding lists which effectively present all the *essential* roles, as viewed by the lead body, that dedicated training and development professionals must perform.

Appendix 3 presents this material in even greater detail. It can be seen that at the mainstream managerial (NVQ 4) level it proved necessary to create *two* groups of units with different headings – one concentrating on the training of individual learners – entitled 'Training and Development

Figure 6.10 **Training and Development National Standards:**
'core' units of competence

NVQs in Training and Development – 'Core Units'

NVQ Level 3 – Training and Development

- Identify individual learning needs
- Design training and development sessions
- Prepare and develop resources to support learning
- Create a climate conducive to learning
- Facilitate learning in groups through presentations and activities
- Evaluate and develop sessions
- Evaluate and develop own practice

NVQ Level 4 – Training and Development (Human Resource Development)

- Identify organisational training and development needs
- Devise a plan for implementing an organisation's training and development needs
- Co-ordinate the provision of learning opportunities with other contributors to the learning programme
- Evaluate training and development programmes
- Improve training and development programmes
- Evaluate and develop own practice
- Manage relationships with colleagues and customers

NVQ Level 4 – Training and Development (Learning Development)

- Identify Individuals' learning aims, needs and styles
- Design learning programmes to meet learners' requirements
- Create a climate conducive to learning
- Agree learning programmes with learners
- Monitor and review progress with learners
- Evaluate training and development programmes
- Evaluate and develop own practice

NVQ Level 5 – Training and Development (Strategy)

- Identify organisational human resource requirements
- Ensure the strategic position of human resource development within an organisation
- Devise human resource development policies
- Implement human resource development plans
- Evaluate the contribution and role of human resource development in an organisation
- Introduce improvements to human resource development in an organisation
- Evaluate and develop own practice
- Monitor and control the use of resources
- Establish and improve organisational culture and values
- Comply with professional and ethical requirements

(Learning Development)', and one related to programmes and systems – entitled 'Training and Development (Human Resource Development).

To allow you to appreciate the extent of the detail mapped out in the functional analysis operation, a sample of a single element of competence is reproduced here as Figure 6.11.

Figure 6.11 Training and Development National Standards: an example of an 'element of competence' or 'standard'

Unit A22　　Identify individual learning needs	**Element A222**
Element A222　　Identify learning needs with individuals	**Evidence requirements**
Performance criteria	**The *performance evidence* required:**
a) Individuals' views about their needs and suitable training and development opportunities are obtained.	Identifying, prioritising and agreeing learning needs with individuals.
b) Identification of needs is based on valid and reliable assessments of all relevant information.	Information obtained. Recommendations on ways of meeting identified needs.
c) The use of the information obtained is clearly explained to individuals.	**The *knowledge evidence* required:**
d) Individuals are encouraged to feel comfortable to ask questions and express their views.	Methods of identifying learning needs. Training and development opportunities available.
e) Identified learning needs and any initial recommendations on ways of meeting them are discussed and agreed with individuals.	How to match learning needs with training and development opportunities.
f) Identified learning needs are prioritised and agreed with individuals.	How to put learners at ease. Interviewing and questioning techniques with individuals and groups.
g) Initial recommendations on ways of meeting the identified learning needs are passed on to the appropriate people.	Resources available.
h) Records are correctly completed and stored in a suitable manner.	Organisational requirements How to sequence and pace information, and gauge appropriateness of language for individual learners.
Range statements	Issues of, and organisational policy on, confidentiality.
1) Relevant information: results of assessments, qualifications, reports, discussions.	Equal opportunities and non-discriminatory practice.
2) Learning needs based on: priorities, current and anticipated demands relating to learner's role.	***Guidance to assessors of this element***
	1　Performance evidence requirements relating to 'identifying and agreeing training needs': the candidate should provide evidence of identifying learning needs in at least two different settings, covering range statement 1.

We are here essentially interested in the potential use of these standards as aids to structuring dedicated training units. It must be said at once that despite the rationalisation of the first T&D competence 'tree', the standards still suffer from their very size and complexity. Although now purporting to cover all aspects of the training and development function, including assessor roles, they still cannot offer an off-the-shelf blueprint for an individual training job or department, and the process of adapting their detail to any given job description – or indeed to 'modern' jobs with flexibility built into these job descriptions (assuming they exist) – demands sustained hard work. It can be seen in Figure 6.11 that performance criteria employ such terms as 'suitable', 'appropriate', and 'correctly completed' without offering precise clues as to their meaning: such criteria must be further defined within the context of a specific work operation if they are to be used to represent workplace, as opposed to general occupational responsibilities. Perhaps more importantly, the bureaucratic assumptions underlying any static or 'perfect' model certainly seem out of touch with some modern organisational norms, as witnessed by the very standards themselves having to be reworked within twelve months of their launch. And an even more fundamental challenge comes from those who argue that management roles must remain flexibly described, because the fundamental management responsibility is that of setting one's own standards on an ever more demanding, endless basis.

But despite such criticisms, the national standards still offer an invaluable aid to anyone who wants a detailed description of what training interventions and their management are all about, or 'what the training and development function comprises'. For anyone or any organisation about to create a dedicated training unit, or needing to review and reorganise what already exists, we recommend obtaining a complete set of the standards documents and working systematically through each individual element, rewriting entries in terms of one's own workplace. This would be a mammoth task, but it would prompt great understanding of the training and development function as it exists in the organisation at the current time, and it can confidently be relied upon to yield many ideas on how to develop what is in place – or missing.

Organising dedicated training and development units

The standards were created with an educational purpose. But they also yield valuable ideas on the organisation of the function. They reflect the most detailed analysis of training and development work ever undertaken, and can be of significant help to anyone wanting to understand, create or amend dedicated training and development units.

The four lists in Figure 6.10 effectively offer the bases for standardised job descriptions at supervisory, management and senior management levels. Moreover, the individual competence units incorporate extensive performance criteria, the range statements expand these criteria to explain such things as resources and contacts needed for competent performance, and the lists of 'evidence required' point directly to training needs. A number of significant organisational conclusions emerge from our own appreciation of these documents:

1 *The function is complex, and covers all management (including supervisory management) levels.* Any attempt to formalise roles within a given organisation should therefore cover all these levels explicitly, regardless of the limits of responsibility allocated to any dedicated unit/s.

2 *Strategic roles include positioning the function, devising policies, establishing values, and determining the organisation's overall personnel needs.* Assuming strategy is not itself imposed by a parent organisation, or in some way delegated, top management responsibilities should incorporate these roles explicitly; if no expertise exists in this field, top management should either create or develop it, or should ensure they have access to it from external sources.

3 *Base-level responsibilities are primarily concerned with identifying individual learning needs, designing or arranging learning activities, and 'running courses'.* If relevant roles are delegated to specialists, eg instructors or training officers, they should be established as junior management rather than technician positions.

4 *Mainstream management roles are many, but divide naturally into those which implement 'top-down' policies and design broad plans to serve 'top-down' strategies (the so-called 'HRD' roles), and those which design programmes to meet individuals' (in the plural) needs and develop learning methods (the so-called 'Learning Development' roles).* The NTO's decision to split the vast number of roles at this mainstream management level may be no more than a compromise device to cope with a numbers problem, but it also acknowledges that in many medium-sized organisations these responsibilities are carried by a personnel department and a training unit (the latter usually established within the former). It seems the lead body favoured this model against an alternative which would make a dedicated training unit responsible for all these management roles, with internal management resources adequate to the need. Another approach consistent with the NTO standards would give the 'HRD' roles to a training manager, within or outside the personnel department, and place the 'Learning Development' roles inside operating departments, either as specialist roles or covered explicitly on a part-time basis by line management.

5 *The only unit of competence which appears in all four NVQ lists is 'Evaluate and develop own practice'.* This suggests that self-development must be a norm throughout the function; if so, it should appear in relevant job descriptions, including those at senior levels.

6   *Units often need amplifying before use.* This is perhaps the most important conclusion to be drawn from the standards: many performance criteria lack operational meaning until words like 'appropriate', 'relevant', and 'correct' are given workplace meaning. In other words, the sophisticated but essentially theoretical ideal must be adjusted to fit in with its own organisational environment.

POLITICAL AND ETHICAL ROLES

The national standards yield another conclusion that seems surprising, to say the least. 'Comply with professional and ethical requirements' is mentioned as a 'core' unit only at the top level, and it is not even given optional status elsewhere. The issue here is an important one, especially in view of the IPD's stress on ethical requirements for members at all levels (see Appendix 6).

If we temporarily translate the term 'professional' into 'political', we can reasonably argue that *all* training and development management roles must be exercised with both political and ethical judgement, and that a person who has neither is unlikely to be viewed as competent by superiors or colleagues. Our multi-national organisation case study showed how important the links are between line management and any specialist training function; put simply, the 'health' of those links goes a long way to determining the strength of the function, conditioning in turn its structure and position. Two important criteria in establishing the priorities of training interventions are (a) whether they appear likely to be successful, and (b) whether they will actually yield their 'promised' returns – which, because interventions always involve discussions on plans, effectively means whether line management, and especially the key decision makers, trust and *know they can trust* what the specialist trainer suggests. One way towards this is to know about and be able to discuss the cost/benefits of 'unplanned learning' against those of planned learning, not least with accountants and senior management. It is also critical to 'market' training and development, which of course means that specialists must have a clear understanding of business as a whole, and take an interest in general organisation matters. Most important of all, they must become '*involved*' in all mainstream activities: those who confine themselves to their own units are unlikely to exert the necessary degree of influence, however good the interventions they might plan.

Ethics are similarly important adjuncts to technical competence, and in real life cannot properly be omitted from role definition. Personal standards and behaviour can greatly affect credibility both among top management and the shop floor. Learners are unlikely to seek advice or guidance from an unsympathetic trainer, or explore blockages with a trainer who seems self-satisfied, biased or critical of others' failings. What this all means is that training is about relationships as well as decisions, about example as well as comparison. Moral dilemmas can and do arise, of course, in the application of any management role (see Marchington and Wilkinson 1996). While there is no suggestion that specialist trainers should ever break the law, or condone any practice which does so, loyalty to the organisation and its objectives is a prime reason for the payment of salary and must take precedence over attempts to 'reform' the organisation by campaigning for specifically personally held beliefs or favoured causes. 'Promoting the function' should not extend to pushing professional standards for their own sake. In the words of the IPD's Code of Professional Conduct and Disciplinary Procedures, professionals

> must within their own or any client organisation and in whatever capacity they are working, seek to adopt in the most appropriate way, the most appropriate people management processes and structures to enable the organisation to best achieve its present and future objectives.

The main contents of this IPD Code relating to professional conduct are reproduced as Appendix 6.

THE NATIONAL STANDARDS' LIMITATIONS

It remains desirable to remember that these standards are essentially based upon the particular approach to the function which we called the 'training process' system approach when introducing it in Chapter 5 (see pages 109–11), albeit overlapping the 'Competences' and 'Analytical' systems which we also described. Thus they omit some roles that might be present in an 'open system' organisation where the dedicated training and development unit is expected to represent the organisation on outside bodies, or to negotiate across boundaries. Thus also they ignore moves towards 'knowledge management' systems, with their emphasis on computerised information flow and the delegating of tasks to IT specialists – such roles as the maintenance of information systems and the cultivation of effective relationships with colleagues, which are included here as optional units, might well need to be rewritten and revalued within a different organisational environment. And, as we have just seen, they inevitably ignore any specific definition of political and ethical conduct.

One final point. The national standards naturally assume a coherent, autonomous, 'watertight' function. Earlier versions of this book have made the same assumption, essentially to assist in describing it. And in certain circumstances, the assumption is a reasonable one: for example, a relatively autonomous apprentice training workshop, or a learning resources centre, or an induction training unit, may be established with an operational role that to all intents and purposes encompasses all the roles in the standards. But we have said enough above to show that these examples are exceptions: where the dedicated training and development unit serves a wider operational purpose, the function will always be bigger than the unit, and it is desirable that the overall organisational design provides for this. Especially important is to ensure that all line management who head major mainstream departments appreciate and accept their own training and development roles, and indeed see them as a branch of their ongoing responsibility for improving performance; one way of achieving this is the establishment of standing training committees, which typically are chaired and attended by non-specialists while being serviced by professionals. The quality of the interplay between the dedicated training and development staff and their line colleagues is the central influence in determining whether the overall function is managed competently or not, a result that no formal definition of specialist roles can independently guarantee.

Nevertheless, the NTO document remains the only comprehensive and sophisticated analysis of what the training and development function involves, and it offers much more detailed material than any organisation can be expected to draw up for itself. Provided the commitment exists to adapt this material for clear-cut operational use, the task of defining the function within specific organisations (not least those smaller ones that cannot justify dedicated units, but who need to define the 'core' responsibilities within line management roles), and that of positioning one or more dedicated training and development units, become much easier to complete.

You might now review your own learning from this chapter by working on the following short tasks:

1 Imagine you are the first training manager appointed by a newly formed company which operates from a single site and includes a small manufacturing unit and an adjoining suite of offices. You work in the personnel department, reporting to the personnel manager. Fill in for yourself the details concerning numbers of staff, type of operation, top management, etc.

(a) List the main work areas for which you expect to be responsible.

(b) List the people with whom you expect to be regularly in contact.

(c) Draw a chart/map describing your place in the organisation.

2 Now imagine you are in the same job five years later – by which time the company has expanded to control two sites plus a small salesforce. People are being recruited regularly and formal courses are being run on site (again, fill in any further details for yourself). You now have three subordinates working for you in what is called the 'training department'.

(a) List your main responsibilities.

(b) List the main work areas for which each of your subordinates is responsible.

(c) Draw a chart/map describing the position of the training department within the company and its internal organisation.

FOR FURTHER REFLECTION AND DISCUSSION

1 You are a personnel manager in an organisation that has just appointed a new training officer who will report to you. You have not previously worked with the newcomer. You feel strongly – on

both 'cost' and 'results' grounds – that training is first and foremost a line management responsibility and that training should be primarily aimed at improving workplace performance. What would you include in your brief to your new subordinate and why?

2 Do you agree that if personnel or training managers publicly criticise line management for their lack of interest in training it damages the image of the personnel and training functions?

3 (a) Look again at Figure 6.1. Imagine that this 'Example A' organisation is expanding, and is about to create a small training unit – to look after induction training and external course administration, *and* to develop departmental on-the-job training. How would you organise for this, and how would you redraw the chart?
   (b) Now choose any one other Example from Figures 6.2 to 6.8, and imagine you are a person shown on the chart with a 'dedicated' training and development role. Try to construct a map which will show and describe your operating links with colleagues.

4 What are the advantages and disadvantages of an organisational arrangement that places the employee development function outside the personnel department?

5 How should small businesses whose top management believe they cannot afford full-time or part-time trainers organise to ensure that training happens?

6 Take any organisation with which you are familiar. How would you expect the training function in this organisation to be influenced by the upgrading of communication and information systems to the point where it operates as a 'virtual organisation'?

SUGGESTED READING

Texts that specialise in the organisation of the training and development function are rare, but here are some you may find useful.

CHILD, J. *Organisation: A guide to problems and practice*. Harper and Row, London, 1982. This is a comprehensive outline of the many choices that must be made when attempting to organise *any* function.

HANDY, C. B. *Understanding Organisations*. Penguin, London, 1985. Another comprehensive general text on organisation, including cultural characteristics and their implications for organisational design.

As our text explains, the Employment National Training Organisation's *National Standards for Training and Development* offers the most detailed descriptions of training roles yet produced.

WALKIN, L. *Training and Development NVQs*. Stanley Thornes, Cheltenham, 1996. This text explores in great detail the content of the Training and Development NVQ Level 3 Further and Adult Education Teachers' Certificate; it offers lengthy descriptions of each unit of competence (and even each activity within each unit) and incorporates many self-assessment questions.

7 Identifying organisational training needs

The levels of training needs – types of organisational reviews – before starting the review – reasons for an organisational review – carrying out an organisation-wide review

INTRODUCTION

'More than £100 million of public money is being wasted on irrelevant police training, according to the Association of Chief Police Officers (Acpo). We spend many hundreds of millions on training. I would say twenty percent of it never needed to have been provided in the first place, or is given too late' said a spokesman for Acpo, who also admitted the 'failure' of the system to identify and meet training needs. He added 'It could be argued that we over-supply training, but often it is not relevant to the role that officers are performing. **We have trained as an end in itself and not as a means to an end***'. A second spokesman states 'Officers are being offered the wrong training in the wrong places, which could be dangerous for them and others.' He fears that they will not be able to cope with the new sensitive roles that will be demanded of them by the Crime and Disorder Bill, which focuses on young offenders, sex offenders and curfews. A separate, independent report commissioned by the Police Federation (University of West of England 1997) claims that the skills gaps of thousands of officers are not being remedied, and little thought is given to necessary skills when promotion or transfers take place. The officers surveyed for this report expressed a widespread lack of confidence in their training and appraisal systems. More than half of them had not been provided with appropriate training through the appraisal system, and two-thirds of senior officers said they had no training in appraisal procedures. Furthermore, the Police Complaints Authority cites lack of training as a key factor in the high level of deaths in custody. Some forces, free to adopt their own standards, decided not to provide control-and-restraint training.*

(Summary of feature article by Welch, 1998)

This case is concerned with spending public money and providing a public service, and is therefore of national interest. A similar situation in private organisations might not be of such general concern, but the case illustrates a number of points which are of equal importance to any organisation, public or private, wishing to maintain a competitive edge in today's climate:

- Human resource development (HRD) is not an end in itself. It should be an essential element of the strategic process by which an organisation achieves its objectives.

- In order to fulfil its strategic role, training and development should be based on a careful analysis of the organisation's present and future needs. (See Figure 5.2 on page 110.)
- Providing training and development which is not directed at the most important needs can be counterproductive and can tarnish its own image. It is demoralising for employees to be sent on unnecessary training courses while being unable to obtain help in acquiring the skills they need for the job, particularly when lack of these skills could lead to being at the centre of an official complaint. Providing inappropriate training costs money and takes up time which could more profitably be channelled elsewhere.
- Identifying these needs and illustrating the possible consequences of failing to meet them, as in the case above, is a persuasive way of gaining support and resources from top management.
- Failure to develop an appropriately trained workforce is likely to have deleterious consequences such as lack of efficiency, costly complaints and poor image, which can affect the whole organisation.
- Training and development is an important facilitator in organisation change. For example, it is implied in the case that the development of new skills and an appropriate culture may be required to carry out the more sensitive roles necessitated by recent legislation.

THE LEVELS OF TRAINING NEEDS

The case also illustrates that training needs occur at a number of levels:

- *at the organisational level* – for example, to ensure a supply of individuals with the skills necessary for promotion and transfer, and a culture which would enable officers to see the bigger picture
- *at the occupational level* – for example, the provision of control-and-restraint training
- *at the individual level* – for example, remedying skill gaps identified during individual appraisal sessions and recognising skills already possessed.

There is a further example of these levels in the case on pages 152–3 and we shall refer to them again when considering evaluation on pages 257 ff. It is important to realise from the outset that the needs at the different levels can sometimes conflict; for instance, school leavers require training to stand them in good stead for future promotion or job-seeking elsewhere, but the short-term organisational need may be very narrow and specific. If there are insufficient promotion prospects or opportunities for wider experience, the long-term development of the employee may be sacrificed to the specific requirements of business objectives. Although management may be aware of the need for new experience and fresh challenges, it is not always possible to provide them at the right moment, particularly in times of recession or fierce competition when budgets are reduced: the enthusiastic may thus become frustrated. However, the current trend towards flatter organisational structures (where the tiers of the hierarchy are reduced and more staff require a broader base of skills, reward often being based on output and value-added contribution rather than rank) should encourage learning contracts and help towards providing wider experience, as may the use of project teams. NVQ programmes, both external and in-company, offer a framework for career progression, providing recognised and 'portable' qualifications for the individual and, possibly, at the same time meeting organisational needs.

In this chapter we are concerned with reviewing the organisation's needs within the training and development sphere. These requirements may be expressed in terms of systems, procedures, priorities and the like, as well as explicit statements of 'training need' which may themselves be linked with specific sites or departments or operations, but not with individual employees. (We shall deal with the individual level in Chapter 9). Before attempting such a review of needs, it would obviously be necessary to be familiar with the overall objectives and goals of the organisation, as this would influence the depth of enquiry in specific areas, and highlight 'priority problems' (see page 153 below). However, because it seems logical to group together such matters as visions, aims, policies , resources and plans, we have deferred discussion of these items until Chapter 8. We referred in Chapters 1 and 2 to a national 'Investors in People' award, which is based on a defined set of national standards governing what might be termed an organisation's internal training and development systems (See Figure 2.5, and its accompanying text). The standards are set in terms of outcomes, not processes: they do not, for example, assume that dedicated training staff must exist, nor that specific documents should be created. They do, however, demand:

- a *written but flexible plan* of business goals and targets
- *recorded* training and development needs
- *clear training plans* to meet those needs
- ongoing *evaluation* of training and development activity.

An organisation really needs to meet these basic standards before it can monitor the extent to which its current training and development activity is adequate to operational health. Different organisations have carried out the task of claiming (or more accurately ensuring they can justify claiming) the IiP award in different ways. For example, Kingston College set up a small working party comprising the principal, the quality assurance manager, the head of personnel, the head of adult education and the head of staff development; this group reviewed what they already had, and proposed developments which were carried into effect before the claim was made (Elms 1998). At Sinai Warren Holiday Village, where the training and development system was less firmly established, a consultant was appointed to oversee the early stages of the project, and to identify key innovative developments. Ten members of staff, including chefs, housekeepers and entertainers, then volunteered to form a working group to keep records of each department's progress towards the establishment of these developments (Merrick 1998).

While these cases demonstrate that any decision to claim, or move towards claiming, the IiP award will itself necessitate an organisation-wide review of the existing training and development system, they also provide the opportunity to develop it further as a worthwhile exercise in its own right. The IiP exercise nevertheless remains a one-off project; regular, periodic, *operational* reviews are additionally needed (and ideally will be demonstrated as 'standard' activities within the IiP claim) to ensure that the system itself continues to develop, and – most importantly - that the prime link between training and development activities and organisation results is being maintained.

TYPES OF ORGANISATIONAL REVIEWS

It will have been seen from Chapters 5 and 6 that there are many different 'organisational learning systems' and a variety of approaches towards training interventions. This diversity presents us with some difficulty in dealing with the operational practicalities. We do not intend to be prescriptive or uncritical: our stance is that each of the methodologies we describe is valuable in appropriate circumstances. We do not suggest that any one of them is intrinsically 'better' than any other; on the contrary, a combination of several methods is often advantageous. We recommend that you bear in mind the content of Chapter 5 and the different organisational forms and structures illustrated in Chapter 6, while reading this chapter.

The next four chapters appear to relate mainly to the 'Training Process System' (see page 109) and we are conscious of the fact that there are other approaches which do not conform to this paradigm. We address the practicalities of some of these at the end of Chapter 9 and in Chapter 12. We suggest, however, that in any case it is still beneficial to consider the four stages of the TPS system, because even in other learning systems these have to be addressed in some way, albeit differently and possibly not in logical discrete steps.

We outline below four different (although not necessarily mutually exclusive) types of organisation review activity. First, however, it is essential to point out that any review of organisational training needs is likely to highlight problems which do not have a training solution: in a production process the cause may be faulty material or inadequate or outdated machinery; in managerial spheres problems may be caused by a wide range of factors such as fluctuations in rates of exchange or government policy. The purpose of the review is to identify the situations where *training*, as opposed to other types of management intervention, could make an important contribution

Global review

This starts with an examination of the organisation's short-term and long-term objectives. Each job category is then analysed (See Chapter 9 for details of this process), its overall purpose is aligned with organisation objectives, and the necessary knowledge and skills are identified. Each employee is then assessed against the appropriate specification, and training provided where a shortfall is identified. In its extreme form this is a very time-consuming exercise, and assumes a certain degree of stability. Many companies exist in rapidly changing markets where speedy adjustment is required and they may require other techniques. This approach can, however, be used differentially, that is, applied in a very detailed way in some departments where there may be specific justification, but not in others.

An approach like this, based on the accumulated analyses of jobs within the organisation may seem deceptively straightforward, but in some of the more recently developed types of organisational structure, such as the 'virtual organisation', or 'outsourcing organisation' illustrated in Chapter 6, the first stage would be to answer such questions as 'who is an employee?' 'where does the boundary of the organisation begin and end?'. In a fiercely competitive environment, it may be necessary for an organisation (which may be only one link in a chain) to provide some types of training for its clients or customers, or even its suppliers. In a 'Matrix Organisation' how do individual needs apply to the teamwork required? Furthermore, an analytical global approach assumes that assessing the skills of individuals and adding them up tells us how good an organisation will be at achieving its goals. For a deeper discussion of this see Hirsh and Reilly (1998), who question this assumption and suggest that organisations are more than the sum of their individuals and ask how, 'even if you measure skills and add them up, you know whether the "quantity" of skill is enough for your future needs?'. We suggest that although a mechanistic analytical approach can be extremely useful in some types of organisation, it possibly needs to be supplemented and supported by other methods and that individual performance must be continually assessed in the ways described at the end of Chapter 9 (pages 221 ff).

Competence and performance management approaches (see also page 106)

A well-known contract catering group announced recently that they have taken a major step from old-style 'systematic' training to a 'performance management' approach. They 'cascaded' the whole philosophy of training throughout the organisation, bringing the improvement of standards down to 'unit level'. Managers were required to draw up job descriptions for every member of staff, specifying competences against which performance was to be reviewed. Line managers accepted that training was an integral part of their management role, and they were expected to possess or acquire the necessary skills. They then had to put together a systematic training programme for new staff, which provided a framework that could be related to NVQs.

This is really a form of global review using competence assessment and key areas as a means of aligning training and development to the achievement of organisation objectives. The current QCA approach (see Appendix 4) requires a specification of competences and standards that could provide a ready-made basis for a review of this type provided that it is borne in mind that the analyses made by the NTOs require adaptation and further detail to be useful for individual organisations. If responsibility for preparing the competency standards is 'cascaded' down the hierarchy in this way, training and development becomes an integral part of the managerial responsibility. It also becomes compatible with the concept of Total Quality Management, and linked with continuous development of staff. The role of the HRD specialist then becomes one of process consultant providing expert skills and advice.

Although it is still subject to the limitations of the global review, this type of approach appears attractive in that it is firmly related to outcomes and provides a potential basis for performance-related pay. There is evidence from the CBI (quoted in *People Management* 13 August 1998, page 15) that around two-thirds of companies are using competences as a way of determining pay levels. This provides a good example of coherent and integrated HRM procedures, the need for which we stressed in our Introduction on page 3. It can easily be imagined that such schemes may involve much detail, and computerised systems can be a great advantage. Several specialist consultant organisations have prepared computer software which includes templates providing a structure and headings for NVQ-type analyses and assessments, to assist large or global organisations to standardise their procedures. As the incidence of organisation-based NVQ programmes, with their emphasis on workplace assessment, increases, this may become a common approach, The IiP standard stipulates that targets and standards should be linked, where appropriate, to the achievement of NVQs, although for a variety of good reasons (not least of which is cost), not all organisations which use this method of analysis have embarked on NVQ programmes.

A further example of the competency approach is provided by the Bank of Scotland. Here, the framework, which was introduced in 1966, is not directly linked to a vocational qualification. It is seen as ' a major opportunity to recognise the value to the Bank of the knowledge and skills of our staff and to provide for them clear guidelines and encouragement to help them develop the skills that will be needed in the future. Competences are now an established and recognised feature of the Bank's make-up. They are used to assess the personal and technical skills of every individual at Customer Service Officer level and how these relate to the job they are in'. The system has recently been extended further up the management hierarchy. To assist with this, role profiling has been carried out. This involved drawing together a profile for every role and linking what competences are required with the role's key result areas. Individuals are then assessed against those competences listed in their role profile:

- At a *bank level* this approach provides a method of comparing the skills currently available with those that will be required in the future. It helps in the identification of training needs and supports the principle of self-development.
- At a *departmental or divisional level*, it provides a way of assessing the skills needed to create an effective team. It also contributes to the design of training programmes.
- On a *personal level*, the competency framework sets out what the Bank requires of individual members of staff now and in the future. It uses a 'common language' of skill definition across the Bank.

'The competency framework is set to become the hub of the bank's people management process as it moves into the next century' (Bank of Scotland Human Resources Review, 1998)

Critical incident or 'priority problem' analysis

A retailing company suffered bad publicity due to press and TV coverage of unfortunate incidents in some of its branches. In a number of cases the company's employees were alleged to have had a very poor attitude towards customers' requests for after-sales service. The chairman called for an urgent investigation. The subsequent report accepted the criticism but showed that in almost every case the employees were competent in selling: however, because of work pressure in the branches and management emphasis on high sales targets, insufficient attention had been paid to the importance of after-sales service. The report stipulated that this weakness must, as a matter of priority, be addressed both by management directives and training, and the HRD manager was instructed to take immediate action. She worked with line management in reviewing and amending, as necessary, the job specifications of both managers and staff, and then provided training for those employees whose assessment showed they required it.

In this model the objective is not to produce a comprehensive list of every possible training need but to identify and prioritise the main problems of the organisation that appear to have a training solution. (See the 'Problem-Centred System' in Chapter 5) An important point to note about the case above is that it was not just the sales staff who required training to higher quality standards but managers also, in that they needed an awareness of the concept of total quality management and the ability to design appropriate procedures. This is an example of the 'skittle' effect described on page 95 where, in order to achieve the desired result , it may be necessary to include other targets before tackling the one that appears to be the most obvious. (See also Chapter 5 page 108) Priority or problem areas therefore require careful examination to determine the *real* source of the difficulty, and whether the solution also necessitates training for levels of staff who did not at first appear to be involved. This approach is extremely important, as the main message must be *to determine which areas are vital to the strategic objectives, or possibly even the survival, of the organisation, and to concentrate the main effort upon them.*

Critical incident analysis is a strategy that is likely to be suitable for small-to medium-sized enterprises (SMEs), particularly at an early stage in their development. A study by Warwick University's Centre for Corporate Strategy and Change (1991) suggested that in an SME, particularly in its early stages, when markets are evolving, goods or services are being refined and the customer base broadened, training needs unfold rapidly and an *ad hoc* approach is required in order to maintain current viability. Flexibility and adaptability are more important than systematic across-the-board analyses of training needs based on job descriptions and specifications. After five to seven years, however, when the organisation has become more complex, and the numbers of staff have increased, new problems can arise, indicating the need for a different approach. For instance, people have not had time to develop their skills and keep up to date, or they have continued to learn on-the-job as the complexity has increased and there are difficulties in training new inexperienced staff to replace them. The findings suggest that 'there may be a natural life cycle of training, which matches the intake and progression of employees', the precise nature of the cycle differing from firm to firm.

Learner-centred analysis

We have implied that these types of analysis require the intervention of an HRD specialist or consultant. Now imagine that you are a member of an organisation-based action learning set with important company goals to achieve (see Chapter 5) where, although (if circumstances demand it) your 'set adviser' might, if reluctantly, act at an appropriate time as a catalyst, an important part of your 'set's' functioning is to work out for yourselves how to determine what training and development you need in order to achieve your objectives, and to take steps (possibly assisted by the 'set adviser') to acquire it. Your learning in the 'set' is essentially targeted directly at organisational needs, because it is encapsulated in the action itself. At the same time it is highly developmental and an embodiment of 'learning to learn', thus bringing together the needs of the organisation and those of the individual. The whole process is an important part of your learning experience, and unless an intervening HRD specialist approached his or her task in a highly participative and democratic manner, the culture and norms gradually developed by your 'set' might cause you to resent the 'external' person probing into your training needs.

Similarly, in a 'task' culture (see Handy, 1985), where knowledge and skill requirements might vary from one project group to another, the first, most important *group task* might be to determine its own learning needs in order to complete the project. Quality Circles are likely to display the same characteristic. Although he or she might be called upon for assistance, the uninvited intervention of an HRD manager might well be regarded as an interference. The approach to identifying training needs and the manner in which the task is carried out will therefore be influenced by the organisational culture. A mechanistic form of global analysis is likely to be most suitable for a 'role culture' or 'training process system' (see Chapter 5), where the content of jobs can be specified in detail, and is likely to remain constant for long enough to make all the necessary analytical work worthwhile. Current trends, particularly those relating to NVQs, are analytical; but is there a contradiction here? The pace of change is accelerating and, in such a climate, will top managers not tend to assign the key problems of the company to project teams, whose responsibility it will be to determine their own needs and possibly those of others whose jobs impinge upon the task in hand? Perhaps the question we should be asking is, 'How can we develop people to develop themselves?' Training needs are never static: they *unfold* as situations develop, even more so in a changing environment. Although it is logical and necessary to produce an overall assessment as a basis for a company training plan targeted at organisational objectives and for boardroom justification of the budget, such a document rarely offers more than a snapshot in time.

BEFORE STARTING THE REVIEW

Now imagine you are the senior training officer of a large national building society which has decided to instigate a formal training review to be carried out every three years; you have been asked to draft proposals for its content and process and to create an appropriate statement for discussion at a future top management meeting. What would your first considerations be? How would you set about your task? Would it be different from that of Joe Brown, who was at the same time undertaking a training review in the small sweet factory in which he was employed?

Congratulations if your first query concerned the purpose of the review! This would determine whether it would require an audit of current skills, and possibly an evaluation, of existing training, or an investigation into current and/or future training needs. It would also help to establish whether the review should be total or partial, as well as who might attend the top management meeting and the items on the agenda on which decisions need to be taken. Every review should relate to the strategic objectives of the organisation, but these are likely to be much wider than the all-important one of achieving profit targets. Most organisations have objectives relating to public image (the public are usually customers!) and to compliance with the law (on matters such as health and safety and equal opportunities). Adapting to national and international developments, such as EU regulations, or coping with government economic policy may well be reasons for companies to consider their training needs. A partial review may relate to one of these or a variety of other objectives. In an industrial relations audit the questions that would arise and the composition of the meeting would probably be different from that convened to discuss a training needs review for Total Quality Management. This very obvious example emphasises the fact that the first step must be to make sure of your objectives, because it is all too easy to waste time in irrelevant discussion and information-gathering.

REASONS FOR AN ORGANISATIONAL REVIEW

Despite the apparent contradictions between analytical, problem-centred and learner-centred approaches, there are circumstances, such as those outlined below, when a review might be necessary in *any* organisation, regardless of its culture.

Corporate planning and longer-term training needs

Organisations monitor trends in the demand for their goods or services and attempt to forecast possible threats and opportunities which would affect their survival or growth. These forecasts should take account of critical factors such as economic conditions, government policies (including possible legislation or entry into the European Monetary Union (see Welch 1998)), financial constraints, expected market changes, competitors' activities, technological developments, investment programmes, new products or services planned and personnel issues. A useful technique is that of SWOT analysis, which involves identifying organisational *s*trengths and *w*eaknesses (internal factors), and *o*pportunities and *t*hreats (external factors).

Data from these sources is used to construct possible future operating scenarios which top management evaluate in deciding the organisation's future policies and strategies. Human resource planning should play an important part in these processes.

Human resource specialists should help to develop the scenarios and offer advice to top management when the strategies are being formulated, and later translate the staffing implications of the agreed strategies into operational plans. The organisation's expected manpower profile, expressed in numbers by occupational category and competences required, is then compared with the existing workforce and, after making adjustments for retirement and other expected staff losses, surpluses and shortages of staff are identified and succession plans are drawn up. This is the first step in developing a comprehensive human resource plan for the organisation which, by co-ordinating recruitment and training, retraining, career development and other personnel responsibilities, will help to ensure that appropriately trained and experienced staff are available when required. For a detailed discussion of human resource planning see Bramham (1988) and also Bennison and Carson (1984).

The preparation of a training budget and plan

The organisation's training requirements may be reviewed annually in order to prepare budget and training plans for the following year. These result in a statement of intent which shows how the specific training objectives required by the company's manpower plan will be met. The draft will specify what has to be achieved, how it will be done, whom it will affect, what benefits will accrue to whom, and what financial expenditure will be required. (It will be remembered that the criteria for the Investors in People standards include a written but flexible business plan in which the resources for training and development should be clearly indicated.)

A major change in an organisation's activities

Training and development play a major organisational role in preparing people to be readier to accept change and, when necessary, in equipping the staff concerned with the expertise they need to do the new work expected of them.

> Imagine you are employed by an airline which has just decided to buy a new type of aircraft, and consider the range of training that will be required. New skills and knowledge will be needed by some of the pilots, navigators, maintenance engineers, marketing and sales staff and, in varying degrees, by other employees. The successful introduction of the new aircraft will depend in part upon all the staff concerned being trained to undertake the new tasks required of them. The training implications must be identified if the changeover problems are to be minimised and the benefits gained at the earliest possible stage and you would want to be involved right from the beginning. Policies, priorities, costs and schedules of training must be determined and co-ordinated at an organisational level and, eventually, detailed training programmes prepared. Working with and using data obtained from planning and senior line management, the HRD specialist examines in turn the list of activities to be undertaken by each function, how each function will interact with other parts of the airline (the boundaries of the subsystems) and with the external environment. It is then possible to clarify the specific and general training that will be needed and prepare a schedule of priorities, sequences of training programmes, costings, etc.

Profound changes or discontinuities that affect the whole of an organisation present formidable challenges to the training and development function, as in the case of the privatisation of a nationalised industry. For instance, one of the new water boards carried out a major review of operations following privatisation. This resulted in an extensive 'upskilling' programme involving the BTEC national certificate in water and water-waste operations for the incumbents of about 700 new operations controller posts. A lower-order but still powerful challenge is presented by a major change in the way part of an organisation operates, for example when a decentralised computer-based management information system is introduced. This type of change can be deceptive in that it may ultimately result in a new style of management, requiring totally different abilities. Many companies are turning to the 'flat organisation', which needs staff with a broader base of skills, thus eliminating the need for many specialisms; traditional boundaries and practices change. A survey by Coulson-Thomas and Coe (1991) for the BIM indicated a wide recognition of training and deveopment needs in this type of organisation, 95 per cent of respondents indicating that 'managers need to be equipped with new skills'. Many of Coulson-Thomas and Coe's recommendations focus on developing these skills. They suggest that the restructuring should begin with a skills audit and that financial resources should be allocated to pay for its recommendations. They contend that in this type of organisation particular attention should be paid to team-building skills; development activity should be linked to the achievement of change; people should be encouraged to identify their own qualities and strengths and relate them to the organisation's objectives; employees should take responsibility for their own learning; the focus should be on learning rather than teaching; flexibility is required to cater for the needs of individuals. It may be noted that these are all characteristics of learning organisations. In some circumstances it may be necessary to consider outsourcing the formal training and development function.

Mergers and takeovers

Usually these require considerable culture and organisation change, and training and development programmes may be crucial in achieving a smooth transition. Where mergers and takeovers are on an international basis, the problems can be writ large, and each national unit may have objectives of its own. An example is provided by a statement from the Rover Group chairman and chief executive, who was shocked to find that when BMW was assessing promotion candidates, none of the five British nationals under consideration could speak another language, whereas all their European candidates could speak at least one other. It is easier for German trainees to come to the UK and gain the benefit of European experience than for British trainees to work in Germany, and if BMW is unable to send British trainees to its units in other countries they are likely to become inward thinking and the credibility and efficiency of the British operation is likely to suffer (Walsh, 1998).

Requests from management

These might indicate the lack of a more systematic approach, but on the other hand training needs can arise suddenly, particularly in small organisations, and may not occur at the time of regular audits. Such requests may have political significance in encouraging line managers to accept responsibility for defining training needs, and in demonstrating that the training department can play a useful role in helping to achieve organisational objectives.

Incorrectly identified training needs

It is necessary to approach an assessment objectively and with an open mind, without being unduly influenced by the assumptions that management and others may make about the cause of a problem and how it should be solved. On occasions it will be found that a difficulty is in fact not a training problem, although it has been presented as such. For example the training officer in a civil engineering company was asked to prepare a training programme for supervisors in the subcontracting department. On investigation he found that the supervisors' apparently inadequate performance was caused by the irregular flow of work into the company and therefore into the department. The problem was an organisational one and could not be solved by supervisory training.

Partial training needs

Help may be sought in tackling such problems as removing bottlenecks in a production department, the assumption being that the shopfloor workers concerned have not been trained to do their jobs correctly. Although this could be the case, an investigation might show that inadequate operator-training is only partly responsible for the poor quality of the work or slow working: the major causes may be poor supervision or machine maintenance, discontent over pay or recruitment of unsuitable employees. It is necessary to distinguish between those problems that are wholly or partly due to ineffective training, and are therefore likely to have training solutions, and those that result from non-training factors, for which other answers must be found.

'Displaced' training needs

Problems are sometimes not initially referred to the training department because they are attributed to other causes and are not recognised by management as training needs. Consider the following example:

> An investigation into the backlog of work in the accounts department of a rapidly expanding company showed that the root of the trouble was not, as the chief accountant had claimed, a shortage of staff but a deterioration in the calibre of accounts clerks which the company had employed. Previously the recruitment position in the area had been favourable and new employees had not needed formal training. When the labour market was tighter, less able staff were recruited and still no attempt was made to train them. The newcomers were eventually able to learn how to do the work (without training) but this took time and in the process they made many more mistakes than their predecessors.

It is necessary to be well in touch with the mainstream of activity, to be aware of such problems and be prepared to offer assistance when the time seems appropriate.

Skills audits for specific purposes

An audit of existing staff's competence in a particular facet of their work is another example of an organisation-wide training-needs analysis. Such an analysis may be undertaken for a variety of reasons, such as an industrial relations audit (Jennings and Undy, 1984) or a discrimination audit or an audit of needs relating to membership of the EU. For a substantial treatment of the 'triggers' of training audits, including case examples, see Pepper (1984).

Benchmarking

This can be defined as the search for the best practices that lead to superior performance, and has been used with such aims as enhancing total quality, product reliability and customer satisfaction. Increasingly it is being applied to the training function. It is a conscious and systematic attempt to compare one's own current reality with what is believed to be 'best practice' somewhere else – leading to judgements on whether to bridge the gap and, if so, how. The two main types of comparison are:

- external – against other organisations, where the choice is legion but is usually confined to those considered similar in some way (by type of work, size etc)
- internal – against other parts of one's own organisation.

Comparisons may be made in terms of what is done or (more usually), where the home organisation already has some expertise and commitment) of how it is done. Both can yield decisions on whether and how to bridge a gap, which by definition will involve some new learning on the part of the home organisation. The main stages of a disciplined benchmarking process are likely to be:

1 initial decisions on the process – who to conduct, what aspects of performance are to be studied and how to define them, where 'best practice' is to be found, how data will be collected and reported, etc
2 production of performance indicators, preferably relating to 'output' rather than 'input'
3 data collection – by reading, arranged visits, attendance at conferences, correspondence, arranged discussions etc.
4 analysis – in which initial comparisons with the home reality are made, and possible new practices, activities or behaviours emerge, to be rejected, modified or confirmed
5 planning (perhaps including a brainstorming element) the route towards what are now confirmed as 'priority needs'
6 implementing any desired new processes.

In a 'continuous development culture', 'review and replan' stages might be added.

Benchmarking has been widely promoted during the early 1990s – to the point where some enthusiasts argue for *joint*-benchmarking practice, in which two or more organisations share information and influence each other towards improvements, the underlying philosophy being that no organisation has a monopoly of best practice and hence a joint review is likely to benefit all who participate. In a competitive environment some organisations fear openness, but others argue that rivals benchmarking 'against' them actually bring in new insight into their own strengths, allowing them to advance further before the rivals have caught up. There is a hint of 'action learning' philosophy (see page 108) here; the benchmarking activity is itself seen as more than the identification of needs, offering a natural, if undefined, learning opportunity in its own right.

It should, however, be viewed more as an operational 'trigger' than a straight training needs assessment tool. An important limitation of benchmarking is that there is no guarantee that by emulating the best training practices in other successful companies, organisational effectiveness or benefits to the bottom line will necessarily accrue. Training effectiveness is situational and one may not be comparing like with like in all respects. Benchmarking will provide *indications* and *ideas for improvement* which must be well thought out and tested before implementation. The correct reason for introducing a training procedure or technique is that the organisation needs it and will benefit from it, not purely because it is fashionable or that other companies do it. Joint benchmarking practice involving discussion and sharing of information is more likely to overcome this difficulty.

Total quality management

The decision to attain Total Quality Management and/or the attempt to reach British Standard 5750 require a careful audit of training needs throughout the organisation. Every facet of work must be performed to the highest standard, and quality targets must be defined and met. This requires not only initial training to make staff aware of the targets and to assist them to attain the necessary competence, but also continuous monitoring to ensure that standards are not allowed to slip and are kept up to date, taking into account the implications of any organisational changes. Procedures for continuing professional updating and 'upskilling' are also required.

Ensuring that statutory requirements are met

Organisations, their executives and employees are variously affected by both new and long-standing statutory obligations. Ignorance of the law is no defence for failure to comply with it. Nor are an organisation's legal obligations necessarily met by a once and for all training intervention. Laws can be changed or amended and, in addition, it is necessary to consider the outcomes and implications for the organisation of current cases and High Court rulings, as the example given below illustrates. The training function has a continuing role to play in helping to ensure improved compliance with legislation, and this can be achieved by the maintenance of a checklist of statutory responsibilities to use in reviewing training needs for a department or for the organisation as a whole. Such a list would include the following areas: health and safety; industrial relations; race relations; sex discrimination; disability discrimination; and working time regulations.

Health and safety

The Health and Safety at Work Act 1974 specifies that it is the duty of every employer to provide:

such information, instruction, training and supervision as necessary to ensure, as far as reasonably practicable, the health and safety at work of his employees.

Part 1 Section 2

Subsequent sections of the Act are concerned with a written statement of policy on health and safety and the 'arrangements' (which presumably include training) for its implementation, together with the appointment in 'prescribed cases' of safety representatives and safety committees. The philosophy of the Act is clearly supportive of employee participation and consultation, and this has training implications. It will also be necessary for employers to be aware of any complementary legislation adopted by the UK in connection with membership of the EU.

It must be emphasised that Part 1 Section 2 of this Act (quoted above) mentions the provision of supervision. It is generally recognised that safety training must be an integral part of a company's training schemes and must be included in programmes for supervisors and managers as well as in induction courses and in operator training. School-leavers and 'work experience' assignees are particularly at risk and require special attention.

A recent High Court ruling (*Walker* v *Northumberland County Council*) illustrates the need for all managers and supervisors to realise the implications not just of bare legal requirements but also of relevant court cases and judgments. Under the above ruling, a social worker received £175,000 in damages after successfully proving that two nervous breakdowns had been caused by the stress of his impossible workload. (See Welch, 1996.) Unless regular training programmes are provided so that supervisory staffs realise their responsibilities to their subordinates, an organisation could find itself required to pay out large sums of money for matters of which top management were previously totally unaware.

Industrial relations

The inept handling of what appear to be relatively minor problems by supervisors and managers unaware of the law can lead to major industrial relations issues. Furthermore, if a case is brought against an organisation at an industrial tribunal, it is extremely damaging if senior managers cannot support the actions of their subordinates. In cases of unfair dismissal because of incompetence, one of the first questions that arises at a tribunal concerns the amount and quality of the training and counselling provided and whether sufficient warnings were given. In addition to a knowledge of the relevant law, skill in devising the procedures necessary to comply with it, and training in company policies and practices, as well as in union agreements, are necessities.

The Employment Protection (Consolidation) Act 1978 places the employer under a legal responsibility to allow trade union officers time off with pay during working hours to take part in industrial relations training relevant to their duties.

Race relations

Training will not solve problems of race relations or equal opportunities, but it has a contribution to make. Awareness of the special needs of particular groups of workers is likely to be achieved most effectively when included as an integral part of the organisation's training plans for managers, supervisors and other employees. There are obvious needs relating to job-centred training. The Race Relations Act 1976 encourages positive action (it is not a legal requirement) to promote entry of racial groups into new areas of work by stipulating that the employer or trade union can provide training facilities exclusively for members of a particular racial group to fit them for work in which they are under-represented. For examples of positive action in this field see Prashar (1983). Another important aspect is induction to the organisation and to the trade union, including knowledge of all relevant procedures. This training can help to prevent the painful consequences that may otherwise arise from later misunderstandings. Language teaching may be necessary and there is evidence that such programmes must be supported by the indigenous English-speaking population and related to shopfloor practices. Race relations audits have shown that ethnic minorities tend to be under-represented in more senior posts and point to the necessity for improved opportunities and training for career development.

Advice on problems, ranging from provision of language training to courses for managers and shop stewards can be obtained from the Commission for Racial Equality.

Working Time Regulations 1998

Traditionally there has been very little statutory control of working time in the UK and employers, managers and supervisors will not be accustomed to taking this into account when planning their work schedules. While large companies may have a central department which can make company regulations to ensure compliance, any member of staff who authorises working hours will need to be made aware of the statutory regulations, and of the consequences of non-adherence. In smaller organisations, it will be particularly important for managers to know the different types of agreement that may be used to supplement or modify the regulations, as well as exactly what constitutes 'working time' and the definition of 'worker'. Such knowledge may be particularly important to those drawing up schedules in certain industries, for instance where unexpected delays could cause expensive disruption to schedules, or where workers may be 'on call'. It may also be particularly necessary for shift supervisors to be knowledgeable about the statutory regulations, if there is any possibility that they might have to make 'on the spot' decisions about individual workers without the advantage of any advice.

Sex discrimination

Organisations have a legal responsibility to comply with the requirements of the Sex Discrimination Act 1975. As in the case of the race relations legislation, an organisation should ensure that its managers and supervisors understand their obligations in this field and, where necessary, they should ensure that appropriate training is provided for their subordinates. Appropriate management development including advice and, where appropriate, mentoring should be available to assist women to progress up the career ladder. As the number of school-leavers declines, women employees are going to constitute an increasing proportion of the workforce, and special measures may be required to ensure that they are adequately represented in the upper levels of management. Special training arrangements during career breaks, as well as for those returning to work after a number of years' absence, are likely to become more commonplace (see Chapter 11).

Disability discrimination

The Disability Discrimination Act 1995 relates to many aspects of employment, including recruitment and selection, terms and conditions, opportunities and benefits, dismissal and any other detriment. It imposes a legal responsibility upon an employer not to treat a disabled person, for a reason relating to his disability, any less favourably than he treats, or would treat, others to whom that reason does not apply. It is the employer's duty to take *reasonable* steps to modify or alter any arrangements or physical features of the premises which place a disabled person at a substantial disadvantage. It is important that all employees, but particularly supervisors and managers, have a good knowledge of the provisions of the Act and their implication for the organisation. Some examples are provided of the steps an employer may have to take in relation to a disabled person. These include such matters as making adjustments to the premises, allocating some duties to another person, allowing time off during working hours for rehabilitation or treatment, or providing a reader or interpreter. Of particular interest to trainers is the inclusion of the following:

- giving him, or arranging for him to be given, training
- acquiring or modifying equipment
- modifying instructions or reference manuals
- modifying procedures for testing or assessment.

To help to ensure that disabled pupils receive the best possible education prior to seeking work, the Act amends the Education Act 1993 to the effect that the annual reports of all county, voluntary or grant-aided schools must contain information pertaining to the arrangements for the admission of disabled pupils, facilities to assist their access, and the steps taken to ensure that they do not receive less favourable treatment than other pupils.

CARRYING OUT AN ORGANISATION-WIDE REVIEW

Although an organisation-wide review can be time-consuming and expensive, it is nevertheless worth considering in closer detail how it might be carried out, as a model or 'standard guide' which can be adapted for many purposes and used differentially. Although sections of the review may be delegated and responsibility for identifying training 'cascaded' throughout the organisation, and collective discussion will often take place, one person normally takes overall responsibility for the review and, for the purposes of this example, we are assuming that the 'reviewer' is the HRD manager.

The usual reason for an organisation-wide review is to provide objective data about the training investments required, in the short- and longer-term, to meet corporate goals. It provides top management with professional advice on human resource development and enables them to decide the nature and extent of the role of training in the achievement of corporate objectives. Top management's decisions determine the operational training policies and plans for the organisation.

The organisation's corporate policies and plans set the context within which the review takes place. It comprises:

- the identification, at all levels in the organisation, of the certain and probable needs for training
- a critical review of this data
- the submission of a report that sets out the priority training and development issues and recommends action plans, supported by cost estimates.

Figure 7.1 shows the sequence of steps that might be followed in reviewing training needs at the level of the organisation.

Figure 7.1 Steps in identifying organisational training needs

---

Step 1
Preparation for the review

Step 2
Collection of data and initial interpretation
Identification of problems with 'non-training' solutions

Step 3
Detailed interpretation of data
Identification of 'key areas'
Development of recommendations

Step 4
Preparation for implementing the recommendations

Step 1: Preparation for the review

The importance of preparation as a key to the success of a training-needs investigation cannot be overstressed. This involves obtaining a clear brief specifying the precise objectives of the exercise. The brief should cover the scope, objectives and the time horizon of the review, the degree to which it is confidential, the authority that the reviewer is given for access to relevant information, when the results are required and the person to whom the final report is to be sent.

When the objectives of the review have been clarified, the next step is to ensure that all employees who are likely to contribute to it are informed. This is necessary for three reasons. First, the reviewer relies on the co-operation of senior managers and others. It is, therefore, important that the purpose of the investigation, and how and when he or she proposes to carry it out, are fully discussed in advance with the appropriate staff. For example, it should be made clear that the review is *not* part of an organisation and methods or work-study exercise. This initial activity has an important part to play in the formation of attitudes and will help determine the acceptability of any resultant training activities.

Second, the investigations may involve asking searching questions, which may cause adverse reactions from some employees who might adopt a less than co-operative attitude if, as can easily happen, they misconstrue the intention. This is particularly likely if the organisation climate is unsettled. A review taking place soon after a company has been taken over, or when a number of people have been made redundant, or during an industrial dispute may well run into difficulties. Even if the organisational climate is favourable, he or she should nonetheless explain the purpose of the review to the staff concerned and their co-operation obtained. The review should be regarded as an opportunity to nurture positive attitudes to training, but training needs are often weak spots in an organisation and those concerned tend to be sensitive when questioned about them, especially if they regard the investigation as an implied criticism.

A third reason for advising those involved of the impending review is that, given advance notice, they can collect the information that will be required, for example, by updating organisation charts or job specifications, where available, and by preparing labour turnover statistics. This can save everyone a great deal of time and is particularly important where line managers are taking responsibility for drawing up job descriptions and standard specifications for their subordinates.

Finally, the most appropriate starting-point must be determined. This will depend upon many variables, such as urgency of action in particular areas, staff availability, the purpose of the investigation, the personal choice of the assessor and the degree to which line management is prepared to co-operate.

An organisation chart showing the relationships of different departments and the formal lines of responsibility is a useful document, but it is important to remember that these charts often show much less information than may be needed. To be of value, they must be up-to-date and indicate the real areas of responsibility and lines of communication, not just those of the formal organisation. If, as is often the case, no chart exists, it may be necessary to draw up new-style 'maps' as the review progresses. The data shown on such 'maps' must be continually cross-checked against the perceptions of other managers. Organisational mapping is an important skill within this context and must be practised as a standard technique; the nature of a given map must reflect management's view on future operational priorities.

Step 2: Collection of data and its initial interpretation

Although, in theory, information has first to be collected before it is interpreted, in practice it is artificial to separate these two processes, as they tend to take place simultaneously. The reviewer interprets and records facts and opinions, at times seeking more detail and at other times deciding that more information is not required. During this process, comments on current and former training policies and interventions will be received. This feedback must be taken into consideration when helping to formulate the organisation's training plan. The amount of support that employees and line managers are prepared to give will certainly influence top management's decision as to the resources that will be made available. Organisations are always faced with the problem of competing claims for limited resources and it is helpful to be able to argue a case which has organisation-wide approval. The case must be based on acknowledged training priorities, the rationale for these priorities must be explicitly expressed, and alternative strategies (for example, job redesign or the recruitment of ready-trained employees) shown to be less cost effective than training interventions.

Methods of collecting information

Depending on the focus of the investigation, information might be obtained by:

- reference to strategic planning documents relating to marketing, production, staffing, etc
- analysing minutes of management meetings
- selecting data from operational records such as personnel statistics, job descriptions, accident records, training reports and staff appraisal forms. Accounting records can often also be very revealing. For example, costs/returns of waste board or metal can yield dramatic evidence on precision in manufacturing, which in turn may reflect on operator competence
- formal and informal interviewing, especially with people in charge of key departments. Senior managers often have major operational aims that are not to be found in the published forward plans
- questionnaire surveys
- discussions with the training and development committee, which can provide information on training requirements and the priority areas. (Do you

recollect that in Chapter 2 Jack and Sam were pondering whether they should be creating internal TECs of their own? These would indeed be invaluable in the situation we are discussing and, as they would be of very senior level, might in fact steer the whole process of the review)

- direct observation of work.

The reviewer often has to ferret out information, because it is not necessarily available in the form in which she needs it. For example, job specifications prepared for recruitment purposes are useful but at best only a starting-point for any training analysis (see Chapter 9).

Sources of information

There is no one correct sequence to follow in collecting relevant data: a potentially successful plan will reflect top management's current views on operational priorities. The following are likely to be the main information sources: external influences, top management, human resources department, other service departments, departmental managers, and their staff and trade unions. But each organisation has its own key sources and idiosyncrasies: for example, XYZ Ltd may have recently developed its Joint Consultative Company Council as a major forum for discussion on efficiency, in which case Company Council minutes and an interview with alternating chairmen might be frontrunners.

External influences

No review should be undertaken without reference to the context in which the organisation operates, as its training needs are directly influenced by the external environment. Economic factors such as interest rates, stock exchange movements or general recession all have an impact on organisational activity, as well as international events, politics, markets, raw material prices and exchange rates. Competitive activity may suggest, and even force, new or more technical development activity, changes in product presentation, etc. The demand for its goods or services provides the *raison d'être* for the organisation's existence, and any changes in demand can have a considerable impact on the training function. The reduction or discontinuation of apprentice recruitment in a recession can have a major effect on a training department, whereas a policy of non-replacement when staff leave eliminates the need for induction and initial job training. Conversely, an increase in demand for the organisation's goods or services can lead to an expansion of training activities, particularly if the organisation has a policy of retraining its staff when jobs become redundant.

Top management

The reviewer should begin the investigation by discussing with each of the directors or senior executives their objectives and the human resource problems likely to emerge in meeting them. However, an organisation's objectives are not always clearly defined; nor will they necessarily be fully disclosed. If senior management do not supply strategic information about the company's present and future operations, ideally making available strategic forward plans, the validity of the review will be in doubt. If the reviewer is not considered a suitable custodian of this type of classified information, the review should be carried out by someone else. Without this information, there is no objective means of assessing the significance of the data collected, no certain basis for determining priorities and other training recommendations, and therefore no satisfactory ways of measuring the standards and effectiveness of existing and future training.

Furthermore, if the organisation's goals have not been clarified it is possible that the company's structure is inappropriate and that operating problems may occur because managers are unknowingly working to different ends. This can give rise to situations where training is apparently being applied successfully to remedy a problem: in reality it is only a palliative which treats the symptoms of a problem while its cause, for example an outdated policy, remains unaltered.

The reviewer must therefore obtain from top management indications of any expected variations in the business, such as technical, product or market changes, future capital expenditure, and any predicted adjustments in the labour force. These variations have training implications if they result in a demand for new expertise or an increased requirement from existing staff categories (eg multi-skilling). The reviewer records these changes in detail and notes when they will be implemented, their scope and estimated effect. At this stage he or she will also be able to list a wide variety of *questions*, answers to which will be sought in the later stages of the review. Armed with this information, he or she will be able to assess the relevant factors when discussing training needs with managers of departments affected by these changes.

Organisation systems

If we recall the case of the police, we can see that one of the reasons for ineffective spending on training and development was the fact that the 'organisation systems', such as staff appraisal and career planning were not working properly. The final document at the end of a training review might well include a report on what systems exist and whether they are adequate and working well. These might include matters such as staff appraisal, assessment centres, personal development files, as well as systems of mentoring and coaching. All of these are discussed in Chapter 9 and 10.

Personnel department

A personnel department can supply valuable information, including job descriptions, job specifications, job evaluation documents, recruitment plans, the industrial relations climate, bonus payment and assessment systems and promotion policy. In addition, it can provide employee statistics of three main kinds: labour turnover, length of service of leavers and age distribution, all by department and section. These statistics are of great importance in an organisation-wide review and are illustrated in Figures 7.2 and 7.3. Obviously a good computerised record system is invaluable in its capacity to provide analyses in many forms.

Local availability of skilled labour is also essential information. The personnel department may have its own list of 'improved performance' priorities (eg timekeeping, lost time, accidents) or procedural changes (eg new appraisal systems, new flexi-time arrangements) or external threats (eg competition for labour in the locality). Industrial relations officers can usually be relied upon to communicate shopfloor attitudes regarding any known innovations or problems.

Labour turnover

Labour turnover statistics are of significance to the investigation because where there is a high turnover of new staff there is also likely to be a substantial need for induction and job training for recruits. An investigation of the reasons for high turnover of labour may reveal that it is caused by inadequate training or by non-training problems. The organisation may need to solve some of the latter, such as low wages or inadequate supervision. If it fails to do so, a disproportionately heavy expenditure on training is the penalty. Organisations sometimes find that the cause of a high labour turnover lies outside their control. For instance, the demand for technicians skilled in a rapidly developing technology is likely to exceed the supply and, in spite of attractive salaries and work conditions, these staff may leave within a year.

It should be noted that staff turnover as an index of labour instability is only valid if related to small, homogenous groups of employees. When dealing with large numbers of staff, marked variations in labour turnover tend to be 'evened out' and their significance lost. Analyses by job category or department category can often be illuminating. Caution is necessary in deciding what constitutes a 'high' or 'low' figure. Comparisons should be made only with the same type of industry and areas that have similar recruitment problems.

Length of service of leavers

An unstable workforce can be expected if staff are not trained correctly and find the work too difficult to learn unaided. The 'length of service of leavers' should be checked to determine whether, as in Figure 7.2, many staff have left within a short period of joining. Even if this pattern emerges from the figures, it cannot be assumed that inadequate training is necessarily to blame, because non-training reasons, such as poor selection or tight bonus, may be the cause.

As with labour turnover figures, the reviewer should initially regard leavers' length of service data as general indicators for further investigation. Finding out why employees leave is not easy; sometimes the departure is multi-causal, or they are often reluctant to give the real reason, and this kind of data can be misleading unless interpreted by experienced staff.

Figure 7.2 'Length of service of leavers' data (taken over a one-year period)

	Length of service					
Job	Up to 3 months	4 to 8 months	9 to 23 months	2 to 5 years	Over 5 years	Total
Sales assistants	48	25	9	6	4	92
Section supervisors	–	3	2	2	1	8
Departmental heads	–	–	–	1	1	2
Buyers	–	1	–	2	4	7

Figure 7.3 Data showing 'age distribution' by job category

	Age range						
Job	Under 25	26–30	31–40	41–50	51–60	61–65	Total
Office supervisors	1	2	2	5	7	8	25
Senior clerks	–	3	3	2	1	–	9
Word processor operators	6	6	3	–	–	–	15
Typists	15	7	4	7	8	6	47
Clerks	32	26	20	17	18	15	128

Age distribution

The purpose of an age distribution analysis, in this context, is twofold: to discover how many employees in a department or staff category fall within certain age groupings, and to interpret the training implications of any imbalances in the age structure.

A department may have a very young labour force, in which case both inexperience and staff mobility are likely to create considerable demands on training resources. Conversely, a department may be staffed largely by older employees, perhaps with a number of its key personnel approaching retirement. For instance, in Figure 7.3, eight out of 25 office supervisors are over

60, and a total of 15 are over 50, a situation that could give rise to problems in the not too distant future unless succession plans are being prepared. An ageing workforce is not revealed by labour turnover statistics; on the contrary, a low staff turnover might appear to suggest that little training is required. Both turnover and age distribution statistics should be considered.

Ideally, the labour force will match the local labour market profile in terms of age, sex and type (eg ethnic minorities); few do so. The extent to which an organisation is 'top heavy' (ie biased towards older workers), or young male dominated, or 'at a management standstill' (ie managed by unpromotable middle-aged people) can strongly influence the later stages of the review.

Other service departments

In medium and large companies there are usually other specialists from whom information can be obtained. For example, planning, maintenance, accounts, management services, quality control, and research and development departments all have data about the company's activities which can be of direct value to the review.

Planning departments accumulate much data on problems – especially regarding manufacturing and distribution, but also in the area of 'lead times', which are often a direct reflection of decision-making abilities and speed of transforming decisions into action.

Maintenance departments have information about machine utilisation and efficiency.

The accounts department may be able to provide such details as: training expenditure in the company, with a breakdown by department, and the system of recording training costs (see Chapter 8). A review of company training, expressed in financial terms, provides a valuable measure of the scale on which training is taking place. However, the level of expenditure must be carefully interpreted. For example, a department's high training costs may be due to inefficient training or fully justified by high demand, whereas low expenditure might indicate inadequate training or little requirement for it; or it might reflect an economical training methodology, such as the use of self-learning packs.

Records in the 'Management Services' department can be an important source of information for certain types of job. Work procedures, job specifications and grades, training times, work standards, all provide a clear picture of the structure and work of a department. Moreover, because these specialists are concerned with analysing existing work as well as implementing new systems, they can often suggest where training requirements already exist in the organisation and where, in the future, training is likely to be needed.

Similar help can be given by the quality control and research and development departments. The former can provide quality standards for particular work and indicate where employees have difficulty in achieving these standards. Research and development staff will know of expected technological changes and when they are likely to be introduced in the company. They may also be able to predict some of the human resource implications of the proposed changes, such as the grades of employee that will be required in the future and the feasibility of retraining existing staff for new jobs, eg operators to undertake more highly skilled work associated with the introduction of higher technology.

The costs of unplanned training are often hidden but are usually well worth investigating, both to help 'sell' an improved scheme and to use as a yardstick in later evaluation. These costs can be expressed in inadequate equipment utilisation, damage to equipment, high scrap levels, time taken by supervisors or others in instruction, lack of recruits and, as already mentioned, in staff turnover and length of training time.

Department managers and their staff

The reviewer is by this stage well prepared to start the major part of the investigation: discussions with line management. Using the information already collected about the organisation's current operations and its objectives, he or she discusses the following questions with each departmental manager:

1 Problems of the department

Many of these may be later ruled out as not having a training solution, but the knowledge gained from discussion can be very helpful in determining training priorities.

2 Present training arrangements in the department

- Who is responsible for training?
- What training has the nominee had to do this job?
- How much is training costing the department?
- What is the scope of the present training?
- What plans are there for training new and existing staff?
- Do these cover job and career training?
- Are these arrangements regarded as satisfactory?

3 Quality of present training

- Have training programmes been based on identified needs?
- Have training standards been established and, if so, on what basis?
- How are trainees assessed?
- What records of training are kept, and why?
- Are training resources adequate, and what is the basis for their allocation?

4 Departmental management's attitude to training

- Is the manager well informed about the training in his department?
- Is he aware of the organisation's training policies?

- Does he regard the policies as satisfactory?
- Has he developed his own departmental policy? For example, is it his practice to train staff to be able to do more than one job?
- Can senior management or the training department give him any further assistance?
- Are there any training problems that are particular to the department?

5 Future training requirements

- What are the likely future developments affecting the department?
- What future training needs have been recognised in the department?
- What plans have been evolved to meet them?
- Which requirements should have priority?
- What departmental and other resources will be required to meet these needs?

The reviewer then interviews the junior managers and supervisors concerned with day-to-day training, who are therefore well qualified to discuss the quality of existing arrangements and recommend improvements. The close involvement of junior managers and supervisors is vital. Their perception of training needs is often insightful, and they are one of the organisation's most important training resources. These discussions also provide an opportunity to assess the managers' actual and potential performance as trainers.

Other employees who can help are staff currently under training or who have recently completed their training. The consumer's point of view is often very illuminating.

Finally the trade union's attitude to, and policies on, training matters are important factors which must be considered both during and after the review process.

Having collected data under these headings, the reviewer should have a comprehensive record for each department's present arrangements, its expected training needs and priorities, and the resources required to meet them. At this stage it is often possible to identify those problem areas which are unlikely to have a training solution, and such information can be discarded.

Step 3: Detailed interpretation of data: determination of 'key' areas and development of recommendations

At this stage the information that has been collected is reviewed and the results analysed. At times, there will be gaps and discrepancies in the data, necessitating a return to particular information sources. Some of the problems that have emerged will be identified as requiring solutions other than training, and can be discarded from the review. An attempt is then made to weigh the relative importance of the identified training needs, initially on a departmental basis and subsequently for the organisation as a whole, bearing long- and short-term objectives constantly in mind.

Ranking training priorities is difficult and requires careful judgement of the organisation's key priorities, and it is helpful to refer to criteria such as the terms of the original brief, existing training policies and strategies, the availability of resources that particular training programmes will require and the benefits that they are expected to yield. Prioritising is important because training budgets are seldom large enough to meet every need. The findings must therefore be synthesised and expressed as recommendations for action. The recommendations should satisfy the following criteria. They should be:

- clearly in support of the organisation's operational plans and objectives
- consistent with the organisation's training and development policies or, where policy changes are needed, reasons should be given
- acceptable to senior management
- justified, with supporting evidence of actual training needs listed in priority terms
- feasible, in that the necessary resources are likely to be made available
- costed and, if appropriate, marked to indicate whether or not the proposed training is eligible for any funding from the local TEC or other grant
- practical and acceptable to those implementing and receiving the training
- specific, in naming who would be responsible for implementing the training and when it is required.

The recommendations and the evidence on which they are based are normally contained in a report for top management. In writing the report, important points to consider include: the initial and likely subsequent readers; the use of confidential information collected during the review; and how to express criticisms of managers who have apparently failed to train their staff, or perhaps of past training plans and/or methods, or even of learners who are resisting change.

Step 4: Preparation for implementing the recommendations

When the review report is completed, there are still two key tasks to perform. First, to follow up recommendations and help to get them accepted within the company and, secondly, to see that they are implemented.

It is unlikely that all the recommendations will be adopted. Some managers will accept the reviewer's specialist advice enthusiastically and use the training department's services fully. Others will disagree with particular findings or recommendations, but will be open to persuasion if the points can be substantiated with facts and figures. The apathetic manager, who superficially accepts the results of the assessment but takes no positive steps to implement them, is more difficult to win over.

The HRD manager should be prepared to spend a great deal of time discussing, persuading and marketing his or her services using the support of senior management, keen departmental managers and the training committee.

If he or she does not carry colleagues with him or her, much of the value of a review will be lost.

After reading this chapter, you should by now be fully aware that:

1 *The training effort must be directed to the most important organisational objectives. A survey of organisational needs or key areas is a logical step to ensure this. How it is carried out, and to what extent, will depend upon a number of factors, such as the culture or the stage of development of the organisation. It is also the basis for the training plan and budget. Without any investigation into real needs, large sums of money might be invested with little positive result. If large capital sums were to be spent on the purchase of a machine, a detailed investigation into the need for it and its use and advantage to the company would be undertaken. The same discipline should be exercised in expenditure on training.*

2 *There are a number of approaches to identifying organisational needs, none of which is inherently 'good' for all situations; there is seldom likely to be one 'right' answer. Identifying 'own training needs' is an important part of some types of organisational activity, such as project groups. In these organisations the design and conduct of any review must take this into consideration.*

3 *The 'best' answer is likely to be that which appears to offer the 'best fit' in all the circumstances. To determine this may well involve the consideration of a number of different variables.*

4 *As well as being skilled in a range of techniques, an HRD manager needs diagnostic abilities of a very high order.*

Do you know of any organisation that completes a systematic analysis of training needs? Can you contrast it with one you know that does not? Why do you think this difference exists? And can you identify any effects of the two approaches?

FOR FURTHER REFLECTION AND DISCUSSION

1 **Acting as a potential provider of training facilities, a local FE College has asked how your organisation's training needs are expected to change and/or develop over the next five years. The request was sent to a senior executive, who is a member of the college governing body, and has been passed to the personnel department to construct an appropriate answer. How should the department set about establishing the facts and drafting the reply to be given to the college?**

2 **What are the essentials to a succession planning system? Who are the key contributors to the system, and how should their work be linked?**

3 In a recent report on management training in the UK researchers concluded that there was no link between organisations' investment in management training activities and their commercial results. You have agreed to introduce a discussion on this topic at an IPD branch meeting, which you know will be attended by practising managers and students. Summarise your planned contribution to the meeting.

4 Who should be the various contributors to a periodic 'Training Audit' in an organisation employing over 1,000 people, and how might their work be integrated? What would you expect/require to be the types of output of such an audit?

5 Identify the main strategic training and development issues facing modern, leaner, flatter and more competitive organisations. Assess the appropriateness of your organisation's approach to the issues identified. (IPD Examination Stage 2, Employee Development, May 1995)

6 Change has become a permanent condition for many organisations. Identify the four or five major changes that you expect will affect your organisation over the next two years. Outline the probable training and development requirements, with a clear indication of programme content for two or three of the changes. (IPM Examination Stage 2, Employee Development, May 1992.)

SUGGESTED READING

BOYDELL T. H. *and* LEARY M. *Identifying Training Needs.* Institute of Personnel and Development, London, 1996.

BRAMHAM J. *Practical Manpower Planning.* Fourth edition. Institute of Personnel Management, London, 1988.

FOWLER A. 'Benchmarking'. *People Management.* 12 June 1997.

HIRSH W. *and* REILLY P. 'Cycling Proficiency'. *People Management.* 9 July 1998, pp36–41.

8 Policy, plans and resources

Organisation vision, aims, strategy and plans – training and development policy – policy development – corporate training plan – training resources – identifying costs and benefits

INTRODUCTION

In Chapter 7 we suggested ways in which the organisation's training needs might be determined in relation to its objectives. We now consider the relationship between these requirements and the underlying policy. We shall then examine how these two factors determine the content of a training plan and some of the typical resources that can be used to implement it. We shall then consider costs and some of the issues that can arise and the kinds of decisions that may have to be made in allocating the budget. This will be followed by an introduction to cost/benefit analysis. As we discuss policy development and its uses, you might like to think of organisations you know, and try to gauge what their approach might be. Do they have a vision statement or a policy? and how formal is it? Not all organisations have written statements; the examples we give below are from large organisations or those that have achieved IiP standard. Should all organisations have formal statements? If they have not, should the training and development specialist formulate them for his or her own unit?

ORGANISATION VISION, AIMS, STRATEGY AND PLANS

If you want to achieve anything you must have a vision of where you are going. It is easy to think of sportsmen and sportswomen who have trained with the utmost dedication because they have had their eyes firmly fixed on 'going for gold'. Exactly the same principle applies to organisations, and the standard set by IiP is a very wise one, namely that organisations should:

> develop and communicate to all employees a vision of where the organisation is going and the contribution employees will make to its success, involving employee representatives as appropriate.

The *Vision Statement* describes what the top executives think the organisation can achieve and how they would like to see it. It is a step in ensuring that everyone is striving for the same ends, and top management's decisions are likely to be more effective if those concerned can understand how they fit into the total picture To be effective the statement is usually ambitious, providing a stimulus to innovation and entrepreneurship, and may be encapsulated in a short challenging sentence, for instance:

To lead the world in integrated communications – Cable and Wireless (1998)

To become the world's leading music company – EMI (1998)

Such a statement is really an expressed wish and is insufficient to be used on its own for planning, and many organisations produce a *Mission Statement* elaborating what this means in more detail. An example of a mission statement will be found in the extract from the Institute of Personnel and Development Code of Professional Conduct & Disciplinary Procedures in Appendix 6. Some organisations produce a statement of their overall *Aim*. For example:

To contribute to high levels of employment and growth, and to individuals leading rewarding working lives, by helping people without a job to find work and employers to fill their vacancies.

Employment Service (1997–1998)

Not all organisations use these terms in precisely the same way. For instance, some do not produce a mission statement, and some combine it with their vision statement, or a statement of *values*. The important thing is that they define the way ahead in a form that employees and all stakeholders, such as shareholders, customers and suppliers, can understand. It is important to remember that organisation visions and values may extend much wider than the 'bottom line'.

The next step is to determine the appropriate *strategies* to bring about the desired results. For instance, one of the strategies to achieve the Cable and Wireless vision is to 'integrate a broad spectrum of services and package them under a single brand, with a single bill, using one network, a common back office and integrated management'. A second strategy is to 'make sure we control, or significantly influence, the business we're in'. Having defined the strategy it is now possible to formulate *policies*. In a work context a policy can be thought of as 'an expression of intention' which gives general guidance for the conduct of affairs and establishes a broad framework for its *plans*. For instance, the last quotation from Cable and Wireless concludes with what might be described as a policy – 'where this isn't the case, we'll exit'. Accordingly the company has disposed of its enterprises in Germany, Sweden and Columbia, (Cable and Wireless 1998) and to do this it would have to draw up detailed plans.

We cannot stress sufficiently the need for an integrated personnel strategy which in turn is aligned with organisation vision and objectives. Imagine an organisation with a vision of leading the world in innovative design, whose product depends essentially upon teamwork. The long-established remuneration system allows for large bonuses awarded in a highly individualistic way, which puts employees in competition with one another. The recruitment policy is to engage personnel at low levels and promote from within. There is, however, no complementary training and development policy to prepare employees to climb the career ladder. When stated in simple terms this case sounds ridiculous, yet in how many organisations do supervisors find themselves promoted to manager overnight without any attention being paid to the competences they require? As a further example, coaching from a superior is one of the most valuable methods of management development, yet managers are seldom awarded any recognition, let alone tangible reward, for excelling in this. On the contrary, they can actually suffer in consequence either by frequently losing highly promotable subordinates, or in some instances, being replaced by the younger protégé they have coached so well! Our philosophy is that the organisation is a learning environment, and ideally the messages that come across from all aspects of that environment should be consistent and in harmony. Although a careful examination of training needs is an important step in the right direction, complete integration of policies cannot be brought about by training and development specialists alone. Directors and senior executives need to take the lead, and unfortunately this does not always happen.

TRAINING AND DEVELOPMENT POLICY

An organisation's philosophy towards the training and development of employees is reflected in its policy: this governs the priorities, standards and scope of its training activities. All organisations have a training and development policy; it may be explicit or implicit. Some policies are the outcome of a planned human resource management approach, others are reactive responses to requests and problems. Some are written, others are not: some are regarded as being semi-confidential, others are promulgated to all staff. Some, where there is no organisational support for training, are negative; some apply only to certain job categories, others concern all employees; some are enforced, others are honoured more in the breach than in the observance.

In addition to the statutory requirement for health and safety training (see pages 161–2 below), organisations develop training and development policies for four main reasons:

- to define the relationship between the organisation's objectives and its commitment to the training and development function
- to provide operational guidelines for management – for example, to state management's responsibilities for planning and implementing training and development, and in particular, to ensure that training and development resources are allocated to priority and statutory requirements (see Chapter 7)
- to provide information for employees. For example, to stress the performance standards expected; to indicate the organisation's commitment to training and development; and to inform employees of opportunities for

training and development (including willingness to grant time off, and/or payment of fees for external courses).

- to enhance public relations – for example, to help attract high-calibre recruits; to reassure clients and the public at large about the quality of the products (eg in pharmaceutical and food companies) or services (an air-line's safety standards); or to protect an image as a caring and progressive employer by taking part in government sponsored 'social' training pro-grammes.

These four purposes overlap and are expressed in policy statements, in the organisation's plans for training and development and in the rules and pro-cedures that govern training access and implementation.

A corporate policy statement that aims to influence the outside world tends to be couched in such broad terms as 'We offer training and develop-ment as part of our equal opportunities programme.' Corporate policy that regulates internal action may be published as a 'free-standing' policy docu-ment or included in the organisation's training and development plan. Both typically include general statements of intent which set the corporate frame of reference for training activities, eg 'The Council will provide appropriate development opportunities for all its employees'; and specific statements which define the organisation's current priorities for training, for example, 'All managers and supervisors will attend a seminar on the company's indus-trial relations procedures'. The policy should also clarify who is responsible, or who shares responsibility for different aspects of the training and devel-opment function and decision-making activities, eg assessing needs, allocat-ing resources, determining strategies, providing training, etc.

> Now put yourself in the shoes of the training director of an electricity board. During the reorganisation that followed privatisation, the training and devel-opment department was designated a profit centre, selling its services and advice to management on request, in competition with external providers. When this change first took place, your staff were extremely concerned because they felt that the new system might not allow them to discharge their responsibilities of adequately meeting all training needs. A policy statement was issued which included a classification that, in general, the onus for ensur-ing that employees were given access to sufficient training was upon line man-agement, *not* the training department, but that to ensure uniformity, some areas, such as certain aspects of health and safety and induction, would remain the responsibility of the training department.

Without this statement much confusion would have arisen, and the training staff would have been in a very difficult position, not knowing where their responsibilities lay.

Corporate policy at departmental level shapes the line manager's action plan by specifying what training and development will be provided for which staff, when it will take place and who will be responsible for ensuring its implementation. It is at this level that policy can play the important role of helping to ensure equality of opportunity between employees working in different parts of the organisation. For example, published policy such as 'Junior office staff should be encouraged to attend day-release further education courses', or 'All employees within two years of retirement are entitled to attend pre-retirement courses', will limit the discretion that a manager might otherwise apply unfairly.

POLICY DEVELOPMENT

An organisation's policy for training and development is influenced by a number of variables, such as:

- aims and strategic objectives of the organisation
- size, traditions and prevailing culture
- products and services
- economic and social objectives
- recruitment policy
- the labour market and the alternative means of acquiring skilled and qualified staff
- obligations to provide professional updating (continuing) training, eg for nurses
- top management's views on the value of training
- availability of information about the organisation's training needs
- past and current training and development policies and practices
- training and experience of its managers
- calibre of its specialist training staff
- resources that can be allocated to the function
- expectations of employees and their representatives
- legislation, eg health and safety, and government-funded schemes.

Training and development policies are therefore unique, varying with the approach and requirement of different organisations. They are more often determined by the prevailing interest than principle, and tend to be impermanent and susceptible to change. This applies whether or not an organisation has adopted a planned approach. If this is the case, top management decide what contribution they want the training and development function to make in the achievement of the organisation's objectives. Their decision provides the framework within which the policy and plans are determined, but effectiveness is likely to be increased if that decision has been reached after consultation at all levels.

In organisations without a planned approach, policy for training and development results from the unsystematic growth of decisions, rules and procedures introduced to deal with particular problems. These decisions are typically made on a piecemeal basis and, with the passage of time, may be accepted as precedents and become 'policy'. *Ad hoc* policy development of this kind can give rise to inappropriate emphases and inconsistencies in application in different parts of the same organisation, particularly if changes in demand for skill and professional competences occur over short periods of time. A regular review of an organisation's training and development policy is essential to assess the relevance of existing priorities, rules and procedures in relation to current objectives. In the Introduction to this edition, we stress the need for these policies to be well integrated with all other organisation policies, and the regular review should take this into account. Other reasons can prompt an organisation to review its policy regularly, including: national developments, eg NVQs; the availability of new methods of delivering training; unexpected demand for training caused, for example, by mergers or restructuring to a flatter organisation (see Chapter 7, pages 157–8); the need for retraining or retrenchment stemming from fluctuations in trading, eg through recession or international developments. The following is an extract from a company's policy statement:

> The directors recognise the important contribution which training makes to the company's continuing efficiency and profitability. They further recognise that the prime responsibility for training rests with management. The Company and Development Manager is accountable to the Managing Director and is responsible for submitting an annual assessment of organisational training needs, as well as advising and assisting all managers on training matters and providing the necessary training services. The annual training budget is approved by the Board and managed by the Company Training and Development Manager.

This company's training and development policy refers to all employees and aims to:

- provide induction training for all new staff and for those transferred to new departments
- provide day-release facilities at the discretion of the appropriate departmental manager in consultation with the company training and development manager
- ensure that appropriate training and development is available to enable individuals to reach and, through updating training, maintain satisfactory performance in their jobs
- provide the training and development required by those selected for promotion so that they are appropriately prepared for their new responsibilities
- provide information, instruction and training to ensure the health and safety of all employees.

There are a number of advantages to be gained from making the training policy widely known in the organisation. This approach clarifies the purpose of training and communicates top management's intentions; defines the organisation's responsibility for the development of the individual employee; helps those responsible for implementing training; clarifies the role and function of the training specialist; states in general terms the training opportunities available to employees; and may indicate priorities. If the contents are progressive, publication enhances employer–employee relationships, but the success of a training policy is likely to be diminished if the 'public rela-tions' element is overplayed or if the employees' expectations are not met. Employee resentment and, as a consequence, the possibility of more difficult problems can result if an organisation fails to honour the develop-ment opportunities promised in published policy statements.

Writing a training policy is a task that requires considerable skill and attention to detail. The starting-point is to clarify the reasons for introduc-ing the policy and the objectives that it is designed to achieve. It is impor-tant that the staff categories to which the policy will apply are clearly stated. Account should be taken of any contingent precedents that may have been established, either in a formal way or by custom and practice. Discussion with representatives of those who will be affected is an essential part of the process of drafting a policy statement. It is important that the policy is writ-ten in an acceptable style, that the statement is positive (avoid using nega-tives) and that it contains no ambiguities.

CORPORATE TRAINING PLAN

An organisation's training plan should be a detailed and authoritative state-ment of the training that will be implemented over a given period. The plan results from a reconciliation of priority training needs, policy for training and development, and available resources, particularly budgets.

A range of requirements for training is identified prior to the preparation of the annual training budget and/or from a detailed investigation of the kind described in Chapter 7. These training needs should then be appraised against the criteria contained in the existing training policy statements: a process that may eliminate some requirements from the proposed plans. For example, a proposal from one department head for certain managers to attend a day-release MBA course would not be included in the plan if there are to be no exemptions from a company's policy that staff over the age of 21 are not granted day release. In other cases, as we saw on page 181, it is the policy that has to be changed to meet new conditions. Finally, training pri-orities have to be established by ranking, in order of importance, all the training requests received. As an organisation never has enough funds to meet all requests in full, it is important to remember that resources for train-ing are likely to be in competition with provision for other purposes and that decisions about respective allocations may well be highly political. Obviously, those requests that appear most closely related to the organisa-tion's strategic objectives are the most likely to be successful. For instance, the board of a company that has limited resources and is introducing an important new range of products in the coming year is more likely to allo-cate money to provide product training for its salesforce than to what appears to be less urgent training in other fields, particularly if such train-ing can be postponed without serious repercussions.

The training plan should be drawn up with extreme care and political acumen. A typical plan would contain the following elements:

- details on a calendar basis (monthly, quarterly, half-yearly) of each department's training requirements by job classification and by number of employees involved, eg accounts department, four clerical staff and two supervisory staff (NVQ junior management course); laboratory, one technician (attachment to raw material supplier); production department, an estimated 25 operatives (induction and initial training) and four managers (computer applications course)
- details on a monthly, quarterly, half-yearly, etc. basis of the projected training for categories of staff not permanently allocated to a department (eg three graduate trainee managers)
- specification, against each item of training, of the standard to be achieved, the person responsible for seeing that it is implemented, the training strategy to be used (eg self-development, on-the-job coaching, internal or external course), how much the training will cost, its duration, when it will take place and its target completion date
- a summary of the organisation's and each department's budget allocation for training: this may be divided into training that is continuing and to which the organisation is already committed, for example, craft trainees who are partway through their apprenticeships, and other training
- possibly a sum set aside for additions to the company learning resource centre, or for the development of material to be used over the organisation intranet.

It should be noted that similar data can be collected and used to develop training plans of longer duration, eg two- or three-year rolling plans.

We know of one large organisation with branches throughout the country that produces such an annual document with 14 sections, starting with a business review and followed by a section dealing with a projection of costs and of activities in each important aspect of the company's operation in the forthcoming year, thus linking all functions closely with corporate objectives. The following extract is the section that deals with training and development. It is a real case, altered only to conceal the identity of the company, and is, of course, backed up by a more detailed plan (too long to reproduce here), which provides a blueprint for the work of the training department.

The main thrust of our efforts during this year and next will be to achieve cost-effective and more sharply focused training covering a wider group of people. Examples of current initiatives, actions and plans include:

1 Development of the Senior Management Team
A series of short lunchtime workshops has been arranged for all Directors and Department Heads. The programme of monthly sessions extending to the end of the year covers all aspects of the organisation under the headings Managing the Business, Managing Others and Managing Ourselves. Material from the Group Learning Resource Centre will be used as a basis for the sessions.

2 Development of Supervisors
A series of training courses for first line supervisors has been launched. Subject areas include: an examination of their role; personal organisation and time

management; effective delegation; use of branch diary; safety, etc. Use of existing materials, including company guidebooks and the Learning Resource Centre will be encouraged.

3 Development of Trainers
Greater emphasis is to be given to the use of senior/more experienced staff to provide guidance and training both on the job and during more formal courses.

4 Performance Review
Training sessions will be held to emphasise the importance of the review in the overall management and improvement of the business. The review is to be extended to include hourly paid supervision.

5 Trainees Under Agreement
Improved monitoring of training will be achieved next year and more of these trainees will be involved in the business review groups set up under the Total Quality Initiative.

6 External Training Professional Bodies
We continue to be involved in a wide variety of external committees and advisory groups covering professional bodies, local institutions of Further and Higher Education, Training and Enterprise Councils and Lead Bodies. The involvement allows us to influence the shape of future training within the industry and to draw on best practice from other industries/companies.

7 Personal Efficiency Programmes
Selected senior management (including Directors) are undergoing individual programmes of guidance on personal efficiency. This is leading to improvements in effectiveness.

At the beginning of this chapter, we pointed out that not all organisations have written training plans, but that some have plans on a less formal basis. This may be because of the factors illustrated by the Warwick University research described on page 154, which make it impossible for some small to medium enterprises to make forward plans with any degree of certainty; could it also be that in times of rapidly developing technology and economic change, or recession, larger organisations no longer experience their former stability, and that their managements, too, are constrained from committing themselves to longer-term planning and adopt an *ad hoc* approach? In this case, plans may well be discussed with managers and constantly reviewed to ensure that most urgent problems are addressed. Alternatively, the training may be phased – the precise pattern and content of each phase depending upon the outcome of those which preceded it. In certain types of organisation, action learning groups or project teams may draw up their own learning plans. The optimum approach to planning may therefore have to be decided according to the context in which the organisation is operating. Whatever approach is used however, even short-term decisions should be recorded in writing with a proposed date for revision, and circulated to all concerned. Such documents can then act as a blueprint against which to monitor progress and evaluate what has been achieved.

TRAINING RESOURCES

We explain in Chapter 10 that when a training and development specialist recommends or chooses a training strategy to meet an identified need he or she strives to achieve the 'best fit' consistent with the learning objectives, the organisation's policy, the learner's preferences and the resources available. Training resources can be thought of as the input required to enable a training plan to be implemented. The range of resources that can be drawn upon are considered later in this chapter and include people (eg the trainer herself), and facilities (eg the self-learning packages, a 'walk-in' open access resource centre, a training room) and money, eg the training budget. However, it is often not so much the resources themselves that achieve results but the skill with which they are managed.

Central to the success of a training and development manager is the function as a manager of learning resources. Credibility and influence are enhanced when she is accepted as the focal point in the organisation for advice and information about training activities (both internal and external); as the source of specialist knowledge and experience about learning in a work context; as the co-ordinator and monitor of the organisation's training policy, plans and budgets; as a competent trainer; and as a successful (line) manager of the training department, its staff, the training centre and learning aids. It is through contacts with top managers that she benefits from the key resource of 'political' support for her activities.

During the last two decades the work of many training and development managers has been dominated by organising and contributing to in-house courses and arranging attendance at external courses. The resources at their command are those required to carry out this restricted function, ie a limited training budget and a training room or area. In recent years, however, the benefits of structured on-the-job learning have gradually become more recognised. This recognition has extended both to the techniques and, through the greater involvement of line managers, the range of resources that an organisation can apply to planned training. Work-based projects, job rotation, and coaching (see pages 85 and 227–8) are examples of activities that can result in effective learning of a kind that, by itself, classroom-based training cannot achieve.

The recognition that successful training does not have to take place in a training centre has been powerfully reinforced by the application to training and development of the new technologies. These technologies are having three main effects.

First, computers, videotape-recorders, compact disc, interactive video systems, access to computerised data bases, intranets and the Internet have greatly increased the choice and flexibility of learning systems available. Wherever there is a computer terminal there is a potential training resource.

Secondly, these applications of the new technologies are changing the perceptions of training. As a result, effective training is no longer so widely perceived to be primarily a classroom-based activity and few would now hold the simplistic view that, to be trained, employees had to attend an in-house course. However, in the right circumstances, the 'course strategy' (see Chapter 10) remains a very important method of achieving training objectives.

Thirdly, new opportunities are being opened up for employees who have in the past been 'disenfranchised' from training and educational programmes because they worked shifts (ie could not attend 'normal' courses on a regular basis), or worked in dispersed units or in small organisations, or could not be released for training, or lived in an area without a local college. The new technologies have enabled the creation of sophisticated 'open learning' systems which make it possible for employees (and employers) to study at home, at work (even in the car on their way to and from work!) or wherever they wish; to embark on their studies when it is suitable for them (as opposed to the fixed enrolment date of an educational institution); to have access to a very wide range of courses, irrespective of where the learner happens to live, and to construct their own learning environment without having to cope with the 'going back to school' anxiety.

The trend to reduce what have come to be accepted as 'artificial' admission barriers to vocational educational courses (for example, traditional and notional minimum or maximum age regulations), and the parallel trend to recognise that in some circumstances adults' 'life experience' and high motivation to learn can more than offset their not having 'A' levels or other paper qualifications, have also opened up training and development opportunities for the 'unqualified' person. This characteristic of open learning is of particular importance in helping less well-qualified technical personnel to acquire improved qualifications in the context of serious shortages of skills in the new technology industries, and in allowing employees in all industries to update their skills and receive certification for units of NVQs. A number of large organisations now have their own open access training centres, where employees can use technology-assisted instruction at times to suit themselves, and many organisations have designed their own learning packages, which can be used by employees across a wide geographical area either as distance learning or as open access material supported by tutoring from local managers.

Clearly, the role and expertise of the training and development manager in influencing and evaluating these approaches to planned training are very different from those required for traditional in-house training activities. For example, the explosive increase in the number and variety of open learning programmes becoming available presents a major challenge for the training officer to give advice on which is the most appropriate programme for a particular employee.

All training resources ultimately cost money, and the training and development manager is responsible for advising on the best use of the available resources to facilitate learning. To do this he or she requires an up-to-date knowledge of the resources on which to draw and how they can best be employed. We now describe the three major categories of training resources: people, internal and external facilities and money.

People as a training resource

Line managers

Many organisation training policies clarify that the training of their staff is ultimately a line management responsibility, and indeed most learning takes place in the day-to-day work situation. Managers can act as coaches, mentors, appraisers and role models for their subordinates, as well as helping them to identify and use the many learning opportunities that occur in the course of normal work, and in the 'learning organisation' (see Chapters 9 and 12) increasing emphasis is being placed upon these aspects. In addition, successful off-the-job training relies heavily upon the trainees' receiving suitable briefing by their managers prior to the training and being given support to transfer their learning to their work. Line managers' commitment to training is crucial not only to maximising the benefits of formal course training, but also a powerful factor in creating and developing a climate that expects and supports training interventions as a normal part of organisational life. At an operational level, line managers, especially if they are good trainers, are an important source of lecturers for induction and other in-house programmes.

Training specialists

An experienced training and development specialist is potentially one of the major contributors to an organisation's training operation. The extent to which her knowledge and skills are put to profitable use depends in practice upon many variables, in particular upon her credibility, technical competence and the degree of co-operation received from fellow managers.

Trainers

Trainers act as the essential link between the learner and the training plan and include managers (when coaching their own staff), company tutors overseeing trainee technologists, craft trainee supervisors and operator instructors.

Former trainees

Satisfied 'customers' are the best ambassadors in helping to create informed opinion about the training and development function. They can also be of great assistance in getting a new form of training accepted, such as outdoor training sponsored by an organisation (see Appendix 5). Again, because of their experience of a former programme and, in particular, its subsequent value to them in their work, past trainees can often make helpful contributions as speakers or syndicate leaders.

Internal training facilities

These can range from residential management centres, off-the-job training rooms (some equipped with simulators), to learning resource centres containing hardware and software of many kinds. Some organisations derive an income from hiring out such facilities to other less-well-equipped organisations, thus providing a welcome addition to the training budget. The availability of general organisation resources such as desk-top PCs, videoconferencing systems, a corporate intranet and/or access to the Internet facilitate a wide choice of methodology and delivery (see Chapter 10). Consultants and external training providers have not been slow to anticipate a considerable potential market, and it appears to be becoming more frequent for organisations to commission templates they can adapt for themselves, or custom-made software for use with the latest technology. Records, such as job descriptions, training undertaken, competences achieved, can also be a useful internal resource, as they can save much time searching through information. Some of the software mentioned above is designed to record automatically for each employee such information as programmes undertaken and standards and competences attained.

External training facilities

Further details of external facilities will be found in Chapter 2. For the purpose of this chapter they can be grouped under six headings:

1 private-sector courses and consultants
2 group training schemes
3 professional associations
4 public-sector education and training services
5 programmes under the auspices of the TECs and the Employment Service
6 courses run by trade unions.

Private-sector courses and consultants

Numerous organisations offer a wide and, at times, bewildering variety of courses on almost every aspect of training. Reduction in the number and size of training and development departments and the sophistication of new methods of delivery have resulted in an increased demand for outsourcing and for external courses. Selecting the right course is a difficult but important task if the company is to benefit from what can be a very considerable financial outlay. (See Chapter 10 page 245 for criteria to use in selecting external courses).

Consultants are a valuable source of expertise and organisations considering employing them should apply similar criteria to those used in selecting courses. An external consultant can often achieve results that would not be possible by using internal staff. It is not only the wider expertise that a consultant is likely to bring, but also the advantage of being unaffected by internal politics and value systems. Techniques such as video conferencing, and multi-media-based on-line training can require expensive equipment, and specialist skills which may not be available in-house.

Group training schemes

These are formed by a group of employers, often in a similar industry, who establish joint training facilities which, individually, they would be unable to afford. These schemes normally offer employers, particularly small employers, the facilities of a training and development specialist, instructors and an off-the-job training centre. Traditionally, group schemes were concentrated in the craft training area, particularly in the first year off-the-job training, and the decline in numbers of craft trainees has affected group training schemes, although some now cover the whole spectrum of training and may also include assistance with employee selection.

Professional associations

The growth in professionalism in many fields of employment in recent years has led to new professional bodies being formed. The training and development specialist needs to be familiar with those professional associations relevant to his or her organisation. They can supply detailed information on training courses and programmes that lead to membership qualifications, and of post-qualification short courses to assist their members to keep up to date in specialist fields – courses an organisation could not normally afford to run internally.

Public-sector education and training services

Universities and Institutions of Further and Higher Education offer vocational courses in a wide variety of subjects and skills. Many of these courses are geared to national examination syllabuses, but there is a trend for colleges to provide courses to meet specialised regional demands and the specific requirements of individual organisations. Some of these courses can, if required, lead to certificates which can be accumulated for NVQs. The availability of courses 'tailor made' to meet an organisation's specific requirements is a well-established feature in management development, where it is closely associated with consultancy. Thus, in addition to their more traditional role as providers of standard courses, colleges and universities are increasingly regarded by industry and the public sector employees as 'resource centres' from which they can commission research and consultancy and obtain guest lecturers. The Open University and The University for Industry (see Chapter 1) should also be considered.

Programmes under the auspices of the TECs and Employment Service (ES)

As well as controlling the local funding for a number of national schemes, TECs offer a variety of different services to assist organisations to develop a training strategy linked to their needs and objectives, as well as measures designed to help overcome perceived local needs. Such provisions will obviously vary from time to time and from locality to locality, and training and development managers should, therefore, be thoroughly aware of the activities of their local TEC and ensure that they are kept completely up to date with funding available. They should also be aware of local link arrangements and consortia involved with initiatives such as those under the New Deal.

Trade unions

Employers should be aware that trade unions run a wide diversity of training course for shop stewards and union officials. Some of these courses are sponsored jointly by employers' associations and trade unions, and are usually oriented towards a particular industry: most, however, are arranged by the TUC or by a trade union, sometimes in conjunction with colleges.

IDENTIFYING COSTS AND BENEFITS

The idea that learning from haphazard or unplanned experience 'on the job' does not incur costs is in nearly all cases a complete misapprehension. The costs that are incurred in this way are normally termed *learning costs* and the usual approach to costing planned training is to consider the various *learning costs* and then to determine how these can be minimised or even replaced by new earnings through expenditure on training. A list of examples of learning costs is given below:

- payments to employees when learning on the job
- the costs of materials wasted, sales lost or incorrect decisions made by employees who are less than competent
- supervision/management cost in dealing with 'incompetence' problems
- costs of reduced output/sales caused by the deleterious effect on an established team of having members who are less than competent
- cost attributable to accidents caused by lack of 'know-how'
- cost resulting from employees leaving – either because they find the work too difficult, or resent the lack of planned learning, or feel they have no prospects.

'Training costs' are defined as those deliberately incurred to facilitate learning and with the intention of reducing learning costs. Some such costs might be aimed not at planned training *per se* but at the learning *system*: for example, a training intervention might involve investing in appraisal procedures in order to get better data on learning needs, and the act of clarifying learning objectives might in itself generate some learning. But most training costs are more directly related to planned training itself. They may be conveniently described as being of two kinds: *fixed costs*, which are not expected to change with the amount of training that takes place (eg salaries of permanent staff): and *variable costs*, which must vary directly with the training (eg materials used or college fees paid).

The following are examples of training costs:

'People' costs:
- wages, salaries of trainers and instructors
- managers'/supervisors' salaries while training/coaching
- fees to external training providers
- fees to external assessors
- fees to assessing bodies for in-house courses
- travel and subsistence of trainees and trainers.

'Equipment' costs:
- training equipment and aids
- depreciation of training, buildings and equipment.

'Admin' costs:
- wages/salaries of admin. backup staff
- telephones and postages
- office consumables
- systems and procedures (eg post-training questionnaires)
- hire of rooms.

'Materials' costs:
- films and tapes
- distance learning packages
- materials used in practice sessions
- protective clothing
- books and journals.

Large-scale initial costs relating to buildings or major items of training equipment (eg a simulator) will normally be 'capitalised' – that is, they represent a transfer of liquid funds into 'fixed assets', the costs of which are spread over a long term via the annual 'depreciation' item. Additionally, the upkeep of a training centre (ie a purpose-maintained building) will incur all the normal costs usually associated with buildings eg community charge, insurance, cleaning, heating, lighting, decorating and general maintenance. Training and development departments will also usually be required to carry a proportion of the organisation's overheads.

Ideally, the relationship between learning costs and training costs should be such that both are minimised, because any expense is justified only if it reduces the costs of unplanned learning. However, the degree of certainty attached to any estimates will vary, and decisions usually have to be made on incomplete information. This demands that an organisation must set an upper limit in advance, ie a 'budget' on what can be spent in a given period (usually a year).

Training budget

Exactly how the budget is compiled will depend upon the following two key factors:

- the organisational structure, which affects the way in which the training and development department relates to the rest of the organisation. For instance, as in our example on page 181, some departments are designated as *profit centres*, supplying services to line managers on request and charging accordingly, and sometimes contracting their services and resources (premises, equipment) to external clients for a fee. Such departments are expected to pay their way, costing their services and overheads to determine the prices charged and operating a profit and loss account. In other organisations, the training department is regarded as an *overhead*, and allocated a budget.
- the financial systems and controls that operate throughout the organisation. For instance, *zero-based* budgeting assumes starting with a blank sheet and receiving an allocation justified by the estimated cost of carrying out the training plan, and possibly limited to agreed priorities. More usual is the *annual budget allocation*, the content and size of which depends on many factors. Of particular significance are the importance accorded to the training and development function, the level of its activity, and the training and development manager's tenacity and professionalism in 'fighting his or her corner' when the budgets are being finalised! The size of the budget is likely to vary from year to year depending upon the profitability of the company, or in a public sector organisation, upon government policy. This is an added challenge because training or retraining needs can be greatest when financial resources are at a premium. It is always necessary to plan well ahead and to assess the probable future requirements carefully so that whatever finance is available goes to the real, and acceptable, priorities. Regular monitoring of expenditure is essential, so that any discrepancies are noticed at an early stage, and corrective action taken before the situation becomes out of hand.

Whether the budget consists only of amounts earmarked for specific purposes is likely to depend on the organisation's accounting norms: most 'active' training budgets now contain contingency sums which are *not* so earmarked and which can therefore fund unanticipated costs. Where such contingency sums are included there may be a temptation to create or 'find' ways of spending them: unspent budgets may be thought to promote future budget reductions. It is unwise, however, to risk the charge that training money is being spent on interventions that do not show a worthwhile return: like all management decisions, training and development decisions involve the allocation of limited resources to alternative uses, and in the final analysis contingency sums that are wasted are less likely to be renewed than those that are saved.

Although budgets vary from one organisation to another, all need appropriate systems of forecasting the financial resources required and of controlling the money that is allocated. Singer (1977) has specified certain main requirements of a budget and budgetary control in the training function. These are:

- an adequate training and development plan
- the expenses incurred in achieving the training and development plan must have been identified and estimated
- the responsibility for items of expenditure must have been allocated between training specialists and other managers
- account classification must have been made so that expenditure can be allocated to specific cost areas
- cost information must be recorded accurately and a mechanism for feeding back the collated information must be present so that individuals can take corrective action when required.

Cost/benefit analysis

It will be apparent that a proper cost-benefit analysis, whereby *all* the results of the training intervention are systematically quantified and compared with *all* the training costs, is rarely possible or economic. The management of training remains a situation-specific art. This in turn means an *organisation*-specific art: the extent to which costs and benefits are assessed will often be determined by organisational norms. If periodic budgeting operations happen, they may require some sort of cost-benefit support for new items, for items over a certain sum, for capital proposals, for 'earmarked' items – or again budgets may be determined solely on the basis of comparison with past actuals or by allocating a new finite sum to a variety of uses in a prescribed way. New, unbudgeted proposals may similarly require detailed supporting evidence and face-to-face 'selling' – or they may naturally follow from a committee minute. A simple rule might be 'the bigger and more innovative the training proposal, the more a cost-benefit spotlight will be expected and is in fact needed'.

Nevertheless, the growth in importance attaching to training makes it desirable for trainers and their organisations to improve their ability to judge specific proposals in cost-benefit terms. In most organisations with a recognisable training function, however disparate it may be, the days are long gone when approaches to training involve no more than allocating expected costs to a welfare budget, and assuming as an act of faith that hoped-for benefits must follow.

Cost-benefit judgements might be best made in league with accountants: in any organisation, they have 'conventions' and 'norms' that they use in other fields to give money-values to things that are not at first thought convertible into money. They also tend to appreciate readily the consequences of decisions. For example, cutting production times can also cut overtime payments; adding competence can lead to wage claims, resignations and recruitment; and improving the image of staff who have consumer contacts can dramatically improve the frequency of those contacts. But regardless of whether help is available from accountants or others, the cost of training must be compared in some way with what it is expected to achieve. The more explicitly it can be demonstrated and quantified (and, usually, the more sophisticated the accompanying detail – although here it may be necessary to judge the requirements of those whose approval is sought), the easier the task will be of persuading the organisation to 'buy' a proposal, and the more convincing the result.

Comprehensive coverage of cost-benefit analysis in relation to training has been offered by Talbot and Ellis (1969) and by Pepper (1984), but has not figured prominently among the many publications on employee development that have appeared in the last decade – a surprising gap, in view of the ongoing debate on the economic significance of training. However, an American professor (Campbell, 1994 and 1995) has to some extent filled the gap by offering a variety of simple cost-benefit methods. We now describe three of these methods, and then illustrate them with a fictional case-study (although based on a real-life situation) of our own. (Unusually, we have decided to omit here all our relevant money figures from the case, because they may tend to distract from our main purpose, which is to emphasise the ideas and attitudes in a cost-benefit *approach*. The three methods are 'payback', 'cost-benefit ratio' and 'return on investment'.

Cost-benefit method 1: 'payback'

A 'payback' judgement involves asking the question, 'How long will it take for training to pay for itself?' The implication is that from a break-even time that can be calculated, savings and/or new income will be realised. The simple formula to define the 'payback period' is:

$$\frac{\text{Full cost of training}}{\substack{\text{Annual operational savings} \\ \text{and/or new income}}}$$

In Campbell's words, 'payback' offers 'a quick initial look at a potential investment'. The shorter the payback period, the stronger the case for training – provided the annual improvement can be expected to last.

Cost-benefit method 2: the cost-benefit ratio

This method projects the ratio between total training cost and total estimated benefits. It is especially useful where benefits are difficult to quantify, not least because it forces judgements on those benefits and their monetary values. Its formula immediately shows whether expenditure is likely to pay for itself of not. The formula is:

$$\frac{\text{Projected full cost of training}}{\text{Predicted total operational benefits}}$$

If the resulting ratio is less than one (1.0, or 100 per cent), training clearly looks 'profitable' – provided the prediction of operational benefits can be trusted. This latter point is critical, however. To begin with, what is the assumed time frame? Unlike payback, a cost-benefit ratio does not of itself show up how soon results will accrue. Are the benefits expected to appear at the end of weeks, months or a number of years? And will other factors soon intervene to change the details of the operation? Equally significant, all assumptions must be rigorously vetted, and estimates used that are both realistic and prudent. Finally, it must be remembered that costs and benefits tend to be multi-dimensional – that is, a saving in one area may affect another, which itself may involve both costs and savings – and hence an attempt must be made to estimate and include any knock-on effects.

Cost-benefit method 3: return on investment

This is perhaps the most used method within the private sector, where a saving or a surplus is likely to be judged against others in relative rather than absolute terms, and a specific yield is often required to match or better another that uses and 'ties up' the same amount of cash. ROI is usually calculated as a 'per annum' percentage:

$$\frac{\text{Operational savings each year + increases in annual income}}{\text{Total costs}}$$

This is the cost-benefit ration in reverse – or rather, upside-down. Here a *high* resulting percentage ensures further consideration. As such, it still demands great care with its assumptions. If the expected yield is higher than that from using the money in another way, there is a *prima facie* case for transferring the money to this purpose. If not, or if there is no prospect of such a transfer, *but* the yield is still higher than the cost of borrowing, then organising a loan immediately looks a worthwhile option.

> Our case-study involves a Further Education College with a complement of 350 staff and over 5,000 students, whose main 10-storey building is now over 25 years old. The building still uses its original three lifts, which serve all floors. During the last 10 years the cost of keeping these lifts running has itself escalated, involving both consultancy and breakdown maintenance – but they are not yet fully depreciated, and the college governors do not see any possibility of replacing the lifts for at least another decade.
>
> The running of the building, including the lifts, is the responsibility of the estate manager supported by an assistant at manager level; neither has any real knowledge of lifts management. The estates manager is due to retire in some five years' time when, it is hoped, his highly committed and enthusiastic assistant will succeed him. All lifts maintenance is currently handled by an outside firm which operates an annual planned maintenance schedule and is called in whenever a breakdown occurs. The estate manager has several electricians and

mechanical fitters on his team, but they are not multi-skilled and do not work on the lifts.

Jane Simpson is the head of adult training; she has also been made responsible (part-time) for college-wide staff development. She reflects on the lifts problem when she reads annual appraisal reports on the estate manager and his assistant, both of which refer to the issue without allocating criticism to the appraisees. It occurs to Jane that a training intervention might be a cost-effective option. How about upgrading the estate manager's – or his assistant's – technical knowledge of lifts and lifts management?

Jane talks with the lifts manufacturers and learns that they them-selves run an expensive residential course in lifts management, which should go a long way to making anyone who attends something of a consultant. They are also developing their own training operations and plan multi-skilling courses for groups of qualified engineering staff, although again at fairly high cost – but that cost can be almost halved if team training can be mounted on an operator's own premises. Jane's training budget can cover the estate manager or assis-tant attending the residential course, but she has no budget for the engineering staff and multi-skilling; such training would have to be specially funded by moving money from a non-training college use.

Jane and the college accountant look at the options from the points of view of (a) payback (b) cost-benefit ratio (C-B) and (c) return on investment (ROI). The following chart summarises their discussion:

		Payback	*C–B*	*ROI*
1	Estate mgr	Quick – but not lasting	C>B	Minus qty
2	Assistant	Quick and lasting	Some extra costs year one B>C from year two	Minus in year one OK year two Good year three onward
3	Multi-skilling – away from base	Two years minimum – but probably lasting from then onward	Knock-on costs year one and two Probably B>C from year three or four	High once training completed
4	Multi-skilling	Quick and lasting	Few knock-on costs if mounted during college vacation B>C from year two	High once training completed

It is not difficult to establish a preference for *both* items 2 *and* 4. The discussion uncovers a clear link in operational terms between the two training proposals – the value of the manager acquiring lifts management skills is improved by his having a team of trained engi-neers at his disposal, and the team training is more valuable if the team works for and with an informed specialist in lifts management. Jane and the college accountant can easily 'sell' to governors the unbudgeted investment – largely on the ground that the ROI is unusually high and the annual saving can be earmarked for lifts replacement, allowing replacement well before 10 years.

Our brief case-study has ignored reality in some respects: for example, we have assumed constant money values, and in the summary chart we have not offered quantified conclusions where some would have existed. The case remains fictional, although some aspects of it are taken from real life; its key assumptions are, we believe, realistic.

The three cost-benefit methods outlined above are by no means the only ones available, nor do they adequately explain all the issues that might be addressed when judging viability, choosing between alternatives or evaluating past or present norms. Other relevant issues and approaches – some of which involve complex-sounding terms to summarise what are essentially simple concepts – are as follows:

- inevitability: must the training be carried out regardless of cost or benefit? Examples include legal directives, safety imperatives, and – more simply – new equipment or systems that can be used only if new learning takes place.
- 'waiting cost': the estimated cost of waiting (ie *not* training until a specified future date), compared with the cost *and benefits* of moving ahead without delay. This highlights the issue of *timing* (especially if the intervention is not already backed by a budget): *when* is the best time? The calculation may need to include any costs of specially raised finance, but also any expected *operational* benefits from the time the training is completed. An inflation element may properly be applied to either, but not simultaneously to both.
- 'opportunity cost': what is the value of any *alternative activity* that must be given up if the training goes ahead? What alternative activity benefits (eg work output) will be foregone? What alternative activity costs (eg work materials) will be saved – or (eg overtime payments) incurred? Care should be taken to estimate both within the context of the specific training plan: for example, the estimates will differ widely if training is planned to take place during or outside normal working hours.
- 'interference cost': what is the cost of interfering with 'normal' work routines? This cost can be wide-ranging, extending beyond the immediate workplace to sales figures, and/or to other intermediary functions which depend on the ouput for their own work.
- 'establishment cost': what part of the organisation's standard training overheads (eg full-time training staff. training centre running charges) should be included, if any? Will establishment resources actually be involved – as planners, trainers, space providers, etc? (See 'Cost-benefit ratio' below.)
- 'marginal cost': what additional (ie over and above any 'interference cost' and 'establishment cost') money must be spent to carry out the training

activity? This can reflect a long list of items (see pages 192–3), including course fees, travel, accommodation, allowances and backup administration.

- 'work benefits': how are trained employees expected to influence work – in terms of such things as output, worktime per unit produced, utilisation of equipment, efficiencies, tolerances, raw material wastages, 'rejects', system improvements – even morale, absenteeism, accident histories? As with interference cost above, can benefits be expected beyond the immediate workplace? Will trained employees release others for different work? Might any such benefits be offset by any possible adverse effects?
- 'employee benefits': will employees become more skilled, more versatile, more motivated, more knowledgeable of related activities, more committed to a new or revised work system, more contented? Are these benefits likely to be offset by new fears, hopes, ambitions? Might employees be likely to look for new rewards, new equipment, new – maybe external – opportunities? Will they need or want more or different information in the future?

It is worth stressing yet again that many of the elements included within the issues listed above contain *qualitative* elements that cannot easily be transformed into monetary or numerical values readily agreed by everyone. Four related points are worth remembering. First, an overall approach that builds contingency sums into training budgets will make 'unproven' decisions easier to take. Second, the ultimate results of training will be in part a reflection of the degree of commitment behind the decision. Third, if trainees' learning is monitored as training proceeds, the training process can itself be adjusted with greater chance of success. And fourth, trainees themselves might sometimes with advantage be helped, urged or allowed to share the responsibility for both the decision to train and for managing training's 'bottom line' as the training evolves. A decision to move ahead with a training intervention is not an end in itself, but the prelude to activity that must still be managed, and in many cases the person in the best position to justify the training intervention is the one who trains.

CONCLUSION

The content of this chapter can be briefly summarised as follows:

- All managers need to understand mainstream *operational goals and priorities*, and to seek ways whereby training and development can contribute towards them.
- The *training policy* clarifies the purpose of training, defines responsibilities, and provides guidelines for decision making.
- It should be frequently reviewed.
- The *training plan* translates the policy into *training/learning events* to meet specific situations.

- Large organisations with a stable bureaucratic culture and planned training programmes for different categories of staff are more likely to have long-term training plans.
- Rapidly developing organisations have the most difficulty in producing detailed training plans and may be constrained to operate on an *ad hoc* basis. In any organisation, however, written policy statements and plans are extremely useful documents.
- *The training budget* may be drawn up in one of several ways, usually depending upon the financial systems and controls in the rest of the organisation.
- Because the budget is likely to be a fixed amount, it may affect the details of the plan, and the training officer may have to prioritise.
- As training needs unfold progressively, training budgets should be constantly reviewed.
- Training almost always involves both *costs and benefits*, although a clear-cut reliable quantifiable cost/benefit calculation may be impossible, but training specialists should be able to think in cost/benefit terms.
- Trainers can add value to their own roles by discussing needs, options, priorities, methods and follow-up with other operating managers, not least line management and accountants.

As a little revision, think of your own organisation, or one you know well. Has this chapter helped you in recognising how the training and development unit operates? As a profit centre? A cost centre? Does it have a training budget? What system is used? Work out the costs of any one training intervention in this organisation. Try to work out a cost/benefit analysis on any training intervention in which you have been involved, using the most appropriate of the three methods above.

FOR FURTHER REFLECTION AND DISCUSSION

1 **What do you see as the key requirements of a policy that aims to promote 'learning from everyday experience'? Explain the influence of these requirements on the following:**

   - **job descriptions**
   - **job training manuals**
   - **performance appraisal**
   - **departmental meetings.**

2 **What are the main difficulties of translating corporate objectives into human resource objectives and plans, both generally and in any organisation with which you are familiar? How can these difficulties be tackled?**

3 **What in your opinion are the key areas to be addressed in an organisation's corporate learning strategy? What arrangements would you recommend within your organisation to ensure that departmental training plans reflect such a strategy?**

4 What are the main influences on an organisation's policy or policies for employee development? Draft a proposed policy statement, including each of the following issues, for an organisation that does not yet have a written employee development policy:

- identification of training needs
- work experience opportunities for non-employees
- performance appraisal
- paid leave/release for educational purposes
- line management's training role.

5 As part of a zero-based approach to budgeting you will have to review the total training needs of your organisation for the next year. Draft proposals describing how you would do this. Indicate which content areas you would consider high priority. Prepare a briefing note for senior management. (IPD Examination Stage 2, Employee Development, November 1994.)

6 Give examples of the type of data you would need in order to carry out a cost/benefit analysis of a training programme.

SUGGESTED READING

FRIEDMAN B. *and* HATCH J. *et al. Delivering on the Promise: How to attract manage and retain Human Capital.* The Free Press, New York, 1998. A useful practical approach to investing in people as a means of attaining strategic business objectives.

HARRISON R. *Employee Development.* Institute of Personnel and Development, London, 1997.

MOORBY E. *How to Succeed in Employee Development.* McGraw-Hill, London, 1991. (Particularly Chapter 6 and the Appendix to Chapter 6, for an illustrative case of an employee development plan.)

RICHARDS-CARPENTER C. *Relating Manpower to an Organisation's Objectives.* Institute of Manpower Studies, Report No. 56, 1982.

SLOMAN M. 'Coming in from the cold: a new role for trainers', *Personnel Management.* January 1994. pp 24–27.

9 Assessing training needs – the job and the individual

Job training analysis – techniques of analysis – carrying out an individual training needs analysis – assessing the performance of others – self-assessment: creating experiential learning opportunities – the influence and role of the line manager

INTRODUCTION

In Chapter 7 we demonstrated how an assessment of organisational needs can highlight problems revealing a variety of job-specific training needs for groups of people or for individuals. It is these with which we are now concerned. We shall consider three main questions:

- *how to identify the requirements of a particular job or task*
- *how to assess the existing competence and potential of the employee against these requirements.*
- *how individuals can assess themselves and how their managers can assist them to do so.*

Fairbairns (1991) suggests that a fourth question is required, namely:

- *what skills/knowledge/personal attributes are likely to be encouraged, recognised, rewarded by the organisation?*

As you read this chapter you might like to consider the implications of this fourth question and, in particular, to relate it to the title of this book. We shall return to this issue later in the chapter. We shall now approach the first question by considering some of the different ways of analysing jobs for training purposes and some of the techniques that are commonly used, and then proceed to the second question of how an individual's performance may be assessed. However, the situation is not always quite so clear-cut, because changes in organisations, such as the trend towards flatter structures, or matrices of project teams, may mean assessing the capability and potential of the team rather than the individual. In fact, individual needs may vary according to the team mix; of equal importance as technical expertise may be the role each person plays as a team member, and this may have to be assessed during the process of the teamwork itself. In addition, theories of experiential learning tell us that we need to reflect on what has happened and assess our own performance, determine how to improve and what help we need, and that this process is an essential part of the learning itself. In both these instances, the boundaries between our two main questions become less clear, but we will return to a consideration of these issues later in the chapter.

JOB TRAINING ANALYSIS

The use of job analysis is not confined to purposes associated with training and we therefore use the term 'job training analysis' to distinguish it from analyses carried out for recruitment, job evaluation, ergonomic or other reasons. Although the emphasis and the detailed information will vary, there is likely to be some overlap of the results of different types of analysis; for example, it might be found that an analysis for job evaluation purposes provides a useful starting-point, and, conversely, a job training analysis might be an aid in recruitment and selection.

In practice, jobs are varied and have many facets. Some consist of few tasks, others of many, some are relatively static and others subject to frequent changes, some require a high degree of discretion whereas others are mainly prescribed. Additional complications are caused by the range of social and physical environments in which they are carried out.

A wide variety of skills and knowledge may need to be analysed: for example, job skills may be manual, diagnostic, interpersonal or decision-making. The knowledge component may be technical, procedural or concerned with company operations. Moreover, jobs vary widely in the range, variety and degree of skills and knowledge needed to perform them. With many different combinations of these components in jobs, different analytical approaches and techniques are necessary. Until the advent of NVQs, to which we shall return later, it was customary to view a job as having requirements of knowledge and skill (and sometimes attitudes). This provided a framework in which to collect and organise information about a job, as well as a useful foundation from which to derive the appropriate content of a training programme, methods used to impart knowledge being different from those required to develop skills, which require opportunities to practise. From the analysis it is possible to determine 'behavioural objectives' specifying what the successful trainee is to be able to 'do' at the end of the programme, the standards required and the conditions under which the work will be carried out (see pages 234 ff).

The ITBs introduced rigorous job training analyses, which fitted the higher proportion of routine manual jobs which existed at that time, and were also in accord with the philosophy of the day. Although these systems had the drawback of being inward-looking, time-consuming to produce and neglectful of the needs of a team, or of problems of role conflict, they were in many cases a marked improvement on the previous 'common skills' or 'welfare' approach to training. Some of the techniques that evolved continue to be useful because, although automation and new technology has resulted in a trend away from routine manual to more technical jobs, some of the 'old-type' skills are still required today. We therefore consider it relevant to give some examples. Currently we have the rapid development of

NVQs, which employ different terms and methodology. We shall briefly describe both approaches, terming the former 'traditional' job training analysis and the latter 'approaches to competence'.

The process of 'traditional' job training analysis

As Boydell (1977) points out: 'Job analysis is a *process* of examining a job. Thus it is not a particular document, but rather gives rise to certain documents, the product of an analytical examination of the job.' A variety of documents can arise as a result of the analytical techniques. The main ones are as follows:

A job description

'A broad statement of the purpose, scope, responsibilities and tasks which constitute a particular job' (MSC, 1981). It contains the job title, the department in which the job holder works, to whom he is responsible and for whom he has responsibility, the purpose of the job, a list of the major tasks and, if appropriate, a brief description of any resources for which he is accountable. In a large organisation, it may be advisable to add the hours and precise place of work, because it can provide useful information in determining availability and suitable timing for any proposed training programme.

A job specification

'A detailed statement, derived from the job analysis of the knowledge and the physical and mental activities involved in the job, and of the environment within which the job is performed' (MSC, 1981). These activities are normally classified under the two headings of 'knowledge' and 'skill', and sometimes a third heading, 'attitudes', is added. In the case of a secretary's job, two of the tasks in the job description might be typing letters and answering the telephone. Associated physical and mental activities might be the interpersonal skills required in dealing with irate customers on the telephone, or knowledge of organisation style and format of letters.

A training specification

'A detailed statement of what a trainee needs to learn, based on a comparison between the job specification and the individual's present level of competence' (MSC, 1981). Methods of determining the latter may be by comparison with experienced workers' standard in the case of an operator or, in the case of a manager, by staff appraisal.

Task analyses

Give details of each of the tasks of the job, often in the form of Stages and Key Points (see Figure 9.1). In the secretary's job an example might be the stages and important points to remember in using a piece of office equipment, such as a fax machine (see pp 209–11 below).

Faults analyses

Give details of the faults that can occur in specific tasks (see page 212).

Types of analysis

The comprehensive analysis

In this approach, all facets of the job are examined with the aim of producing a detailed record of every task in the job, and the skills, knowledge and attitudes required for each. A less comprehensive and less expensive approach may often be adequate, and the following criteria should be confirmed before a comprehensive analysis is carried out:

- The majority of work tasks that the trainee will have to do are unfamiliar to her, difficult to learn and the cost of error unacceptable.
- Time and other resources are available for a full analysis – the job is likely to remain basically unchanged and the resultant training programme used frequently by a number of trainees.
- The job is closely prescribed and the 'correct' method of doing it must be learned.

A situation in which an exhaustive analysis might be worthwhile could be where new plant is to be installed in a factory, and because totally unfamiliar operating skills are required, the staff concerned need total retraining.

Having decided that a comprehensive analysis is necessary, the first step is to examine the job to gain an overall picture and write a job description. The next step is to examine in depth and produce a job specification. A useful sequence is to identify the main responsibilities of the job holder and record the constituent tasks for each of these, together with the skills and knowledge involved in carrying them out. For example, the responsibilities of a barman will include serving drinks to the customer and accepting payment. Taking the first of these, a number of separate tasks can be identified, such as serving beer and serving wines and spirits. Each task is then analysed to find out what knowledge and skills are necessary. In the case of serving beer, these will include knowledge of the beer on sale, the ability to change a barrel of draught beer, together with knowledge of when it is right to serve to the customer, and so on.

Key task analysis

This is concerned with the identification and detailed investigation of the key or core tasks within the job. As far back as 1970, Wellens pointed out that job analysis as a means of determining training needs is at its most effective at the lower end of the organisation: the discretionary and ever-changing nature of supervisory and managerial jobs means that they cannot be predetermined or prescribed accurately. Indeed, often the most important task facing a manager is to determine what in fact he or she ought to be doing, and this can involve a complicated balance of priorities. Although a breakdown into tasks and their requisite knowledge and skills can be of some use at supervisory and middle management levels, a total analysis would be costly, cumbersome and likely to obscure the critical areas of the job. At management level, therefore, job descriptions and specifications are usually expressed in more general terms, concentrating on objectives, targets and key areas. (However, definitions of responsibilities common to a number of supervisors and managers may be useful as a basis for standard in-house courses.)

Key task analysis is appropriate for any type of task where the following conditions apply:

- the job consists of a large number of different tasks, not all of which are critical for effective performance; it is assumed that the job holder does not normally require training in minor or non-key tasks, and
- the job is changing in emphasis or content, resulting in a continuing need to establish priority tasks, standards of performance and the skills and knowledge required.

Problem-centred analysis

This approach differs from those described previously in that no attempt is made to produce a description or specification of either the whole job or all of its key tasks. Analysis is limited to a difficulty considered to have a training solution, such as the chief chemist asking the training department to organise a report writing course for her technical staff because their reports were unclear and poorly structured. The analysis is concentrated on this particular aspect of the technical staff's work and excludes others unless they are directly relevant to the specific problem. A problem-centred approach is appropriate when:

- the need for training is urgent but resources are not available for a more extensive analysis
- the operational goal is essentially and uniquely linked to the resolution of one or more identified problems
- a fuller analysis is unnecessary, for example, where an employee's work is satisfactory except in a specific area.

Approaches to competence

The concept of 'competence' has evolved over a number of years, originally in relation to management development, and it received a further impetus when researchers were trying to find ways in which young trainees could be provided with learning experiences in one organisation that would stand them in good stead in another. The original solution was to identify a number of 'Occupational Training Families', 'Key Competences' and 'Transfer Learning Objectives' (Hayes *et al*, 1983). Later, the Management Charter Initiative (MCI, see page 321) adopted the competence approach and a national framework of management competences has been devised. Over the course of time, a number of different methodologies have been used to identify desirable competences, two of which are outlined below.

'Input' approaches

During the last 20 years there have been many studies of what it is that effective managers contribute to the job. Mintzberg (1975) identified eight basic groups of management skills, but the most comprehensive study involved 2,000 US managers and was carried out in 1979/80 by the American Management Association and documented by Boyatzis (1982). The researchers were trying to answer the question, 'What are the characteristics that distinguish superior performance by working managers?' They defined competency as 'an underlying characteristic of a manager causally related to superior performance in a management position.' This suggests that it is more than a set of skills; it is a mix of aptitudes, attitudes and personal attributes possessed by effective managers. In a useful discussion of the competency-competence debate, Woodruffe (1992) stresses that a competency is 'a dimension of overt manifest *behaviour* that allows the person to perform competently'. He explains that the reference to behaviour is important to the definition, stressing that a job analysis should isolate the behaviours that distinguish high performance.

The 'outcomes' model (NVQs)

Here we have a different methodology. Whereas 'input' models are concerned with what it is that effective employees bring to the job, 'outcomes' models focus on what high performers *achieve*.

The method of analysis used for NVQs is dominated by two factors. They are *outcome-led*, and are based on *national standards* of competences ideally assessed in the workplace. Competence is defined as 'being able to perform "whole" work roles to the standards expected in employment in real working environments' (NCVQ, March 1991). The implication here is that 'whole work roles' involve more than just specific skills and tasks. As already mentioned in Chapter 2, identifying these competences is the remit of the NTOs, and the technique used is functional analysis (see pages 214 ff). The approach assumes that the competence will be used at the workplace both to define training needs and to assess 'qualified' status, because standards are set in the form of performance criteria.

In this text we have used the term 'competence' in relation to the 'outcomes' approach and the term 'competency' with reference to the 'input' approach.

TECHNIQUES OF ANALYSIS

Many different techniques have been devised to enable the variety of job skills to be analysed and recorded. Among the best known are the following:

stages and key points analysis, manual skills analysis, faults analysis, critical incident analysis, job learning analysis and functional analysis and benchmarking (see page 160).

Stages and key points analysis

Imagine you are Nellie Brown, an assistant supervisor of an office in a branch of an international company. You have a very busy day ahead of you and a pile of queries to sort out. Your manager asks you to look after Mary, a trainee who started yesterday, and show her the work of the office – in particular, how to use the fax machine. There are messages going out all the time, so there is plenty of opportunity; the only problem is that you have very little time this morning. You take her to the machine and let her watch you transmitting several messages. You ask Mary if she has any questions and are assured that she can manage, so you leave the last message for her to send to the United States, and just as she is starting you are called away to the telephone. When you come back you find Mary in tears because, although the letter has gone through the machine, and cost three minutes of telephone time, the concluding report indicates that transmission was not OK. One of the staff sitting nearby tells you that Mary had difficulty in putting the paper in straight at the beginning, causing the alarm bell to ring. Several people had come to help her, and eventually the fax went through. However, because there was now a queue at the machine, she had pulled the paper to hurry it as it came through, thereby interfering with the transmission. There were a number of key points that you should have made plain when you demonstrated to Mary, but because you were busy and your mind was on your own work, they did not come readily to your mind. The result was wasting money in useless telephone time, some disruption to others in the department, as well as the emotional upset to Mary and feelings of inadequacy on your part. When discussing this with friends over lunch, you discover that other departments have previously prepared analysis sheets which state very simply the main stages in routine tasks and the key points associated with them. Anyone demonstrating to new recruits can use these sheets to check that they have not omitted any important part of the instruction.

This technique can be applied to relatively simple tasks which are part of a more difficult job, but it is unsuitable for complex work or tasks that require the frequent use of judgemental skills. A stages and key points analysis is normally undertaken by a trained instructor, supervisor or senior operator.

The analyst watches and questions an operator at work and using a stages and key points breakdown sheet (see Figure 9.1) records in the 'stage' column the different steps in the job. Most semi-skilled jobs are easily broken down into their constituent parts and a brief summary is made of what the operator does in carrying out each part. The analyst then examines the stages separately and for each one describes in the 'instruction' column, against the appropriate stage, how the operator performs each task. The description of the operator's skill and knowledge is expressed in a few words. At the same time, the analyst notes in the 'key points' column of the breakdown sheet any special points such as quality standards or safety requirements, which should be emphasised to a trainee learning the job. A 'stages and keypoints' breakdown sheet serves two purposes: it provides the pro forma which aids the analysis and, when completed, it is used as the instruction schedule. This is an efficient method of analysing relatively simple jobs. It is long established and has been used widely since its introduction from the USA as part of the TWI (Training Within Industry) Job Instruction programme during and after the Second World War.

Figure 9.1 **A 'stages' and 'key points' breakdown sheet**

JOB TITLE: How to make a job breakdown		
Stage (what to do in stages to advance the job)	Instructions (how to perform each stage)	Key points (items to be emphasised)
1 Draw up table	Rule three columns. Allow space for column headings and job title	Use this sheet as example
2 Head the columns	On top line insert the title of job Insert: Column 1 (Stage) Column 2 (Instructions) Column 3 (Key Points)	Headings – summarise what worker needs to know to perform each job Watch for steps which are performed from habit
3 Follow through the job to be analysed	After each step, ask yourself – 'What did I just do?' Note places where the worker could go astray. Note items to be emphasised. Note hazards. Stress safety points	Write notes clearly and concisely Keep stages in order Ensure directions are complete – never assume they are
4 Fill in Columns 1, 2 and 3 as stage 3 above is performed	Make brief and to-the-point notes	Review and emphasise these 'Key Points' decisively
5 Number the stages	Follow the sequence a worker must follow when learning the job	
6 Follow the job through using directions in Columns 1 and 2	Follow the instructions exactly	
7 Check that all 'Key Points' are included	Record in Column 3 all points where the worker may be confused	

(Reproduced with acknowledgement to the former Ceramics, Glass and Mineral Products Industry Training Board.)

Manual skills analysis (MSA)

This is used to isolate the skills and knowledge employed by experienced workers performing tasks requiring a high degree of manual dexterity. It can be used to analyse any task in which precision, manual dexterity, hand-eye co-ordination and perception are important features.

The hand, finger and other body movements of an experienced operative are observed and recorded in great detail as he carries out his work. This is a highly specialised technique and should be used selectively; those parts of the job which are relatively easy to learn are analysed in much less depth (a stages and key points approach may often be adequate) and an MSA is limited to those tasks (or parts of tasks) which involve unusual skills. These are the 'tricky' parts of a job, which, while presenting no difficulty to the experienced operative, have to be analysed in depth before they can be taught to trainees. In Figure 9.2 we give an example of a typical pro forma used in an MSA which illustrates the breakdown of the task of filleting raw fish in a food processing factory. It will be seen from this example that an experienced operative's hand movements are recorded in minute detail, together with the cues (vision and other senses) that the operative uses in performing the task (see Chapter 3). Explanatory comments are added, where necessary, in the 'comments' column. Special training is needed to apply this type and level of analysis and, in particular, to identify the cues on

Figure 9.2 **Manual skills analysis**

DEPARTMENT : Fish–filleting		TASK: Fillet/trim small plaice		DATE:		
Section or Element	Left hand	Right hand	Vision	Other Senses	Comments	
Select fish	Reach to trough– grasp fish with T and 1 2 3 4 around belly, p/u and bring forward to board	P/u knife with T and 1 2 3 4 around handle. With sharp edge of blade to right of filleter	Glance ahead for knife position on board Glance ahead for fish position on trough	Touch LH on fish		
		Knife hold:				
Position fish	Place fish on board so that the dorsal fins fall to the edge of the board and the head lies to the right hand side of the filleter.	Hold knife handle against first and third joints of the fingers. Place upper part of T (1st joint) against lower blunt edge of knife and the lower part of T against upper edge of handle. Do not grasp knife tightly. Do not curl tip of fingers into palm of hand.	Check position of fish	Touch LH on fish	Knife is held in the RH during the complete filleting cycle. If knife is held correctly it should be possible to move the knife to the left and right by 'opening' and 'closing' the knuckles (when T is removed from handle).	

Key. LH = left hand, RH = right hand, p/u = pick up, T = thumb. 1 = first finger,
2 = second finger, 3 = third finger, 4 = fourth finger. Synchronous movements are
recorded on the same line. Successive movements are recorded on succeeding lines.

(Reproduced with acknowledgement to the former Food, Drink and Tobacco Industry Training Board.)

which the operator depends in both normal and abnormal work conditions, and the senses by which he receives them.

Faults analysis

When analysing a job, information is collected about the faults that occur and especially those which are costly: 'the process of analysing the faults occurring in a procedure, product or service, specifying the symptoms, causes and remedies of each . . .' (Manpower Services Commission, 1981) is termed a faults analysis. The result of this analysis – a faults specification – provides a trainee with details of faults which he is likely to come across in his work, how he can recognise them, what causes them, what effects they have, who is responsible for them, what action the trainee should take when a particular fault occurs, and how a fault can be prevented from recurring. A faults specification is usually drawn up either in a tabular or 'logic tree' form and is useful both for instruction purposes and as a memory aid for an employee after completion of training.

Critical incident analysis

One way of defining the areas of a job with which the incumbent is having most problems is by examining incidents which he sees as the most difficult to handle. This information can be obtained by interview, although depending upon the status of the interviewer, employees may be reluctant to reveal their real problems for fear of making themselves appear inefficient. One of the classical criticisms of the critical incident technique is that people tend to select incidents which they think will put them in a good light, and therefore an atmosphere of complete trust and honesty is necessary if this difficulty is to be overcome.

An alternative way of obtaining the information is to ask the incumbent for a short written account at the end of each day of the one incident of the day which has been the most difficult to manage, and to estimate how frequently he has to deal with a similar difficulty. The exercise is repeated for several days, or for several weeks on days chosen at random. The process is simplified if a special form is designed for the purpose. The forms can be returned anonymously and an overall picture can be gained as a basis for general training programmes. The reported incidents can be camouflaged to make useful case-studies. It is, however, very informative if the respondents are willing to identify themselves so that individualised training can be devised and, in addition, particular problems can be localised, perhaps to one department or to newly promoted supervisors. Assistance can then be given exactly where it is required.

As well as pinpointing trouble spots, this technique is useful in involving the employee. In a turbulent environment, change can be so rapid that management may be unaware of the problems and consequent stress which individuals are suffering and a simple technique such as this can often help to alleviate the situation. It is, of course, recognised that not all problems will have a training solution and that some will expose training needs for people other than the incumbent. Before embarking upon this type of exercise, therefore, it is necessary to be assured of management commitment at least to a *consideration* of possible ways of overcoming problems that cannot be solved by training. Having asked for employees' co-operation in writing daily reports, something must be *seen* to happen.

Job learning analysis

The types of analysis we have discussed so far have been concerned with the *content* of jobs and tasks; in contrast, job learning analysis focuses on *processes*, and in particular upon the learning skills that are required. This technique is described in detail by Pearn and Kandola (1993), who give the definition of a learning skill as 'one that is used to increase other skills or knowledge ... The learning skills represent broad categories of behaviour which need to be learnt.' They identify nine learning skills:

- physical skills
- complex procedures which have to be remembered or followed with the aid of written material
- checking/assessing/discriminating
- memorising facts/information
- ordering/prioritising/planning
- looking ahead
- diagnosing/analysing/solving
- interpreting or using written/pictorial/diagrammatic material
- adapting to new ideas/systems.

The analysis is carried out by interviewing the job incumbent, starting with a description of the main aim of the job, followed by the principal activities. Using nine question cards, each relating to a particular area of learning (see Figure 9.3), the interviewer probes each main activity in more depth, and the resulting analysis enables trainers to design learning approaches and appropriate material to the required type of learning. The aim is not only to ensure that the trainee can learn the content of the job but that he has the skills to master work of a similar type. For instance, in a job where considerable memory work is involved, the trainee should learn the items he needs to know, but he should also be aware of ways of assisting the memory, such as visual association, mnemonics, etc. In this way, he or she is learning to learn.

This method can be used in conjunction with other techniques. It is particularly suitable for jobs the content of which cannot be analysed by observation alone, ie those involving planning ahead, diagnosing, analysing, etc. It also has the advantage of making the job holder aware of his own learning processes. It could usefully be employed by a project group, to determine their own training needs, redefining the nine 'learning skills', if necessary, to suit their own purpose. For further information about the method, see Pearn and Kandola (1993).

Figure 9.3 Job learning analysis question cards

CARD 1

Q1   PHYSICAL SKILLS

Are there physical skills involved in this activity which it took you a long time to get right or become proficient in?
What are they?

Probes

How much time did it take before you got it right?
What would the consequences be if you did not perform the physical skills correctly?

CARD 2

Q2   COMPLEX PROCEDURES

In this activity, do you have to carry out a procedure or a complex sequence of activities either (a) relying solely on memory, and/or (b) using written materials, manuals, etc?

Probes

(a) What happens if you forget the sequence or procedure?
     What are the consequences of forgetting the sequence or procedure?
(b) What written materials, manuals, etc do you use?
     How do you use them?
     When do you use them?
     How accessible are they?
     What are the consequences of not following the procedure correctly?

CARD 3

Q3   CHECKING/ASSESSING/DISCRIMINATING

In this activity, do you make adjustments/judgements based on information from your senses (sight, sound, smell, touch, taste)?
Give me some examples.

Probes

What senses, i.e. sight, sound, smell, touch, taste, do you use?
What adjustments/judgements do you make?
How do you make these adjustments/judgements?
What would the consequences be if you did not make the adjustments/judgements correctly?

Source: Pearn M. and Kandola R. *Job Analysis: A practical guide for managers* (2nd edn, IPD, 1993)

Functional analysis

This is the established process to determine the standards aimed at approval for NVQ use. The statements of competence are derived by analysing employment functions; briefly, a statement of the key purpose of the overall area of competence is the first requirement. The next step is to ask the question, 'What needs to happen for this to be achieved?' This results in a breakdown into the primary functions that need to be carried out to fulfil the competence. The question is then repeated, generating a further breakdown of the primary functions into sub-functions, that are then divided further and so on (see Figure 6.9 and pages 106–7).

   In this way the function is broken down into units of competence and their constituent elements, the latter being accompanied by performance criteria. A unit of competence consists of 'a coherent group of elements of competence and associated performance criteria which form a discrete area of activity or sub-area of competence which has meaning and independent value in the area of employment to which the NVQ relates' (NCVQ, 1989). An example of an element of competence can be found in Chapter 6 (Figure 6.11).

The elements and performance criteria should:

- be stated with sufficient precision to allow unambiguous interpretation by different users, eg awarding bodies, assessors, trainers and candidates
- not be so detailed that they relate only to a specific task or job, employer or organisation, location or equipment.

NCVQ (1989) (now subsumed under QCA)

The NVQ statement of competence has a common format which contains:

- NVQ title
- units of competence
- elements of competence with their associated performance criteria.

Elements of competence are structured as below:

ACTIVE VERB	**OBJECT**	**CONDITIONS**
Implement and evaluate	changes to services, products and systems	related to all operations within the manager's line responsibility

Performance criteria should each contain a critical outcome which defines what has to be done for the relevant function to be successfully accomplished (see Appendix Figure 4.1).

It is also customary to add range statements to the elements of competence. These specify the range of contexts, eg customers, products, settings, to which the element is expected to apply. By extending the range, it is possible to broaden the application of the competence to a national standard, rather than to have it apply to only the narrow requirements of one organisation. This, however, relies on the transfer of learning, about which too little is really known.

When job training analysis is used purely for in-company purposes, the task of distinguishing the necessary knowledge and skills is facilitated because the circumstances under which the function is to be performed can usually be defined, and the necessary knowledge can be deduced without great difficulty. Broadening the competence nationally, to embrace any context, is an infinitely greater task. The first stage is to specify the range of application of each element (the range statement), but in one organisation or educational institution it is unlikely to be possible to practise or assess each element in all applications covered by the range statement. The question then arises as to how to facilitate learning which will transfer to these applications and how to test that it does.

Jessup (1991) argues that if the same *procedure* applied in all contexts, then transfer of learning could be assumed and cites the example of learning to drive one model of car, which transfers to other makes. Where this is not likely to be the case, if it were possible to provide experience and assessment in all likely situations, then there would still be no problem. As, however, the range of work contexts throughout the country is vast, this is unlikely to be feasible. Jessup suggests two possibilities: first, to predict the likely main variations and ensure that learners know how to adapt accordingly; and second, to ensure that the learners understand the principles involved, thus enabling them to choose for themselves the correct responses to new situations.

A further difficulty about national standards based on outcomes is that the different contexts in which functions are performed are so varied that in extreme cases it may be beyond the limit of any one person's competence to perform in them all. Imagine a barman in a public house in a run-down inner city area, who is thoroughly competent in that situation, partaking in good-natured daily banter with his customers, and effectively keeping order. If transferred to the bar of a luxury cruise liner he might never be suitable. The very skills that had contributed to his success in the first context might prove a hindrance in the second. The 'input' model of competence is needed here, despite any apparent national qualification.

Despite the critics of NVQs, there is no doubt that the identification of transferable competences could be a great step forward, particularly when in place in a national framework. This would be of use not just to employers but for trainees, who need to learn skills that will stand them in good stead in entirely different types of employment. A national 'scheme' of competences that can be accessed by anyone and provide certification for units that can be accumulated for qualifications is highly desirable. In addition, NVQ specifications are suitable for comparison with European awards and thus assist in mutual recognition of qualifications.

For a deeper discussion of NVQs see Jessup (1991 *op. cit.*), from which many of the ideas of this section have been taken.

CARRYING OUT AN INDIVIDUAL TRAINING NEEDS ANALYSIS

Steps in the analysis

Figure 9.4 shows the main steps in analysing a job for training purposes. The sequence illustrates a comprehensive analysis but the principles involved also apply to other forms of analysis.

Figure 9.4 The main steps in analysing a job for training purposes

---

Step 1
Gain co-operation of all concerned

Step 2
Carry out pre-analysis investigation

Step 3
Decide appropriate analytical approach

Step 4
Analyse the job

Step 5
Write the job description

Step 6
Write the job/training specification

Step 1: Gain the co-operation of all concerned

Before carrying out any of the steps below it is necessary to inform everyone of the purpose and process of the investigation, or suspicions may be aroused when the analyst starts asking questions. Consulting and involving people at the outset also ensures a better chance of obtaining commitment to any training programme which might result, and constitutes the first step in a training intervention.

Step 2: Carry out a pre-analysis investigation

It is first necessary to establish that a training analysis is needed because a problem that may appear to be due to lack of training may have other causes, such as excessive workloads or poor organisation. When it is agreed that the problem is a training one, the next stage is to decide whether an analysis is really required. Questions, such as the following, clarify this point:

- What is the organisation losing in terms of production or services because the employee has not been formally trained?
- Is sufficient information available (eg from suppliers' manuals) to make an analysis unnecessary?
- How long does it take an average employee to learn the job without planned training? If a matter of hours, then analysis may not be necessary.

Having established that an analysis is needed, a check is made to ensure that the job is unlikely to be changed significantly.

Step 3: Decide the appropriate analytical approach

A stages and key points analysis may be appropriate for most of the tasks within a job, but one or two tasks may need a faults analysis or even a manual skills analysis if a great deal of perception or intricate hand and eye movements are involved.

Step 4: Analyse the job

The analyst needs to know the sources of information available, the appropriate methods of collecting it, and the depth of analysis required.

Sources of information include the following:

- the job-holder, who can often provide the bulk of the data required
- the job-holder's superior, who will specify the purpose of the job and the necessary standards of performance; these points may be obvious for work where the content is largely prescribed, as in the case of most semi-skilled jobs, but it is often much less clear in other types of work, notably managerial jobs
- customers or clients; information can be gained from records of customer complaints, or questionnaires, which are frequently issued by organisations, such as hotels or garages, that provide a service
- organisational records such as job descriptions/specifications, organisation charts, policies, plans, procedures, and sales and production records
- suppliers' manuals can be an essential source of information for training purposes, particularly when new equipment is used for the first time.

Methods of analysis

The analyst first identifies the job-holder's responsibilities and tasks, and then finds out, for each task, what is done, why it is done and how it is done. This involves finding out what plans the job-holder follows, what 'cues' he uses in initiating, controlling and completing a task or part of a task, and what skills and knowledge are required to respond effectively to the relevant cues at various stages in each task. The following methods are commonly used:

- *Observation by the analyst*
Very detailed and continuous observation is required when analysing the manual skill required by an operative in complex and short cycle repetitive work (see Chapter 3). Continuous observation is not normally warranted for jobs in which tasks are repeated at regular intervals, because sufficient information can normally be obtained by random sampling. Observation by itself, however, is inadequate: for instance, observing a process operator reading a number of instruments on a control panel is of little help to the analyst.

- *Self-observation*

This can be a useful method of collecting data on the purpose and content of a job but relies entirely on the job-holder's willingness to keep a diary of his activities. The technique is used in the analysis of managerial and other work characterised by a high degree of discretion. Disadvantages are that the observer may be too close to the job to see it objectively and may, for his own purposes, under- or over-emphasise certain aspects at the expense of others. The job-holder may be very busy and at the end of the day his recollections may not be strictly accurate. The required record should be kept as simple as possible so that it can be kept up to date rather than becoming a chore to be completed later. One advantage of diary-keeping is that it obliges the job-holder to consider exactly how he spends his time – a very salutary experience to anyone who has never done so! It may be tempting to overestimate what one can do in a given period, and by drawing attention to this fact keeping a diary may well arouse interest in the management of time. This technique is also usesful as an aid to self-assessment – see below.

- *Questionnaire*

This is a particularly useful technique if a significant number of analyses have to be made and can be used as a preliminary to an interview/discussion. It allows the job-holder to think carefully beforehand and ensure that all relevant detail is included. Questionnaires and check-lists can be designed for any job requiring analysis and can indicate the extent to which different tasks are performed within a job, and their level of difficulty. A further advantage is that they can be subjected to numerical analysis, by computer if necessary.

- *Fact-finding interview*

Discussions with the job-holder and other relevant employees are an essential part of the job analysis. The analyst should be competent in the use of interview techniques, such as the framing of questions and careful listening, to gain the maximum benefits from this method.

- *Do-it-yourself*

One way of learning about a job is to try to do it. By putting himself in the position of a trainee, the analyst experiences at first hand the difficulties involved in learning the job. Although this may be impractical or unnecessary, there are certain situations in which it is a useful method of obtaining information. Tasks that are difficult to describe in words, such as those involving a high degree of manual dexterity, are amenable to this form of analysis.

Step 5: Write the job description

It is possible that this is already in existence, but it is still useful at this point to check its accuracy. It might also contain extra details such as the incumbent's hours of work, and this might be helpful to know when arranging

Figure 9.5 The role set of a production manager

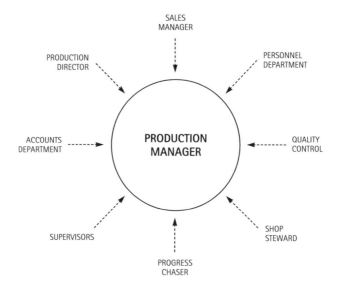

training programmes. It is also sensible to mark the date at the top of all job analysis documents.

Where the job-holder has to liaise with a number of people in the organisation, it can often be illuminating to make an interactive diagram: see Figure 9.5, which depicts a 'role set'. Kahn *et al.* (1964) demonstrated that the conflicting expectations of the same person by various members of staff can be a potent source of stress and difficulty. For instance, a production manager may have to maintain a delicate balance between the requirements of the production director, the sales manager, quality control, the progress chaser, his own subordinates, the shop steward and the production director. Developing strategies to cope with this situation is likely to be a key area of the job, and yet might easily lack emphasis in a traditional job description.

Step 6: Write the training specification

A job specification for training purposes gives much detail of the skills and knowledge (or the competences) required and should reflect the environmental and 'job/role environment skills', as well as the tasks performed. The completed specification provides the yardstick against which a trainee's performance will be measured, and any shortfall identified. It also provides the information necessary to devise an appropriate training programme (see Chapter 10). Before embarking on the training programme, the specification should be verified with appropriate managers and agreement obtained by all parties. It is particularly necessary to check the emphasis given to different items. One of the important benefits of a detailed specification is that it clarifies the job, because the incumbent's conception of his precise duties and responsibilities is frequently different from that of his superior.

ASSESSING THE PERFORMANCE OF OTHERS

Assessing the new employee

A new employee, selected against a personnel specification, may already have, in broad terms, the necessary ability, achievement and experience and may therefore only require limited training. It is, however, advisable to check this, either by discussion with the person concerned, or, if appropriate, by administering a test. The new job may be very familiar in many respects but differ in one or two important aspects in which previous experience can hinder performance. Where safety controls are involved, it is imperative to be aware of the dangers of negative transfer (see Chapter 4). Possibly the only training that might be required would be to discuss the important areas of difference and provide practice in them.

A trainability test is 'a validated test designed to assess whether a job applicant has the potential to reach a satisfactory standard after training'. The applicant is required to perform an appropriate, carefully designed, short task after being given prior instruction . . .' (MSC, 1981). This type of test can be used for a variety of jobs ranging from fork-lift truck driving to bricklaying and bottling, as well as social skills such as interviewing a client for a mortgage with a building society. It is also suitable for all ages of recruit and is regarded as more appropriate for older applicants than traditional selection tests.

Appraisal of existing employees

The two most common methods of assessing the performance of existing staff are performance appraisal and assessment centres. (For comprehensive coverage of a wide variety of assessment methods, including unconventional techniques, see Davey and Harris, 1982.)

Performance appraisal

A small chemical company in the UK received instructions from its parent in the USA to install a performance appraisal scheme as standardised by the parent company. The UK personnel manager protested that it would not suit the UK company, but his objections were overruled and the scheme was set in motion. The managers were called together and given some preliminary training in the operation of the scheme and in appraisal interviewing. Three years later, the scheme was deemed a dismal failure, because managers merely went through the motions of conducting the interviews, many of which took place in the bar of the local public house. The appraisal report forms contained non-committal comments, which were no use for any purpose. The parent company still insisted that there should be an appraisal scheme operating in the UK, but reluctantly agreed that the standard scheme could be altered or modified to suit.

Knowing that introducing a new scheme would now be a tricky operation because of the attitudes that had already been created, the personnel manager enlisted the help of consultants. They set up task groups representing all grades of management, with a brief to discuss the difficulties of appraisal schemes, what the objectives of such a scheme might be, and how they might turn the request from headquarters to their own advantage by identifying the type of scheme that they felt would bring them some benefit. The suggestions from the task groups were modified at a conference where all managers were given the opportunity to voice their opinions. Only when it became apparent that there was general commitment was a new scheme drawn up on the proposed lines; groups of managers came together to clarify how they would operate the new system and, at their own request, to have further practice in conducting the interviews. After a difficult start (because the first task groups still carried over negative views of appraisal from the former scheme) the new system ran smoothly.

Lack of commitment and unclear aims are the main reasons why appraisal schemes fail to realise the hopes of their instigators. It is expedient to use group discussions and participative approaches to draw up the scheme, thus making the design of the system and the assessment criteria the first stage of training. A further cause of failure is lack of ability and confidence to conduct the interview; accepting criticism is painful, particularly if it is given in a tactless manner. Managers are understandably reluctant to create resentment in subordinates with whom they are going to have to continue to work, and are often tempted to 'duck' important issues. Appraisor training, therefore, is an essential part of the process. In fact it is often said that appraisal can indicate more about the appraisor than the appraisee!

Some appraisal schemes emphasise joint assessment, with the final report owned and signed by both parties. In cases of disagreement a two-part report may be submitted, or someone further up the hierarchy may be designated to discuss any points that either party wishes to raise. Performance appraisal needs to be complemented by regular review meetings; it is ineffective to initiate for the first time at an annual appraisal, discussion of an issue that arose several months previously.

Findings from the Price Waterhouse Cranfield Project on trends in Europe indicate that performance appraisal is one of the major tools of management development in the UK as well as in Sweden, Switzerland and Holland, whereas it is less used in France, Spain and Germany, and rarely in Denmark. In all countries, including the UK, figures indicating the incidence of management training in appraisal are considerably lower than those relating to the regular use of the technique (Holden and Livian, 1992) – a disturbing feature in view of the discussion above.

The purpose of appraisal may be to assess and improve current performance usually by defining training needs, or future potential, as well as salary review. It is not normally deemed advisable to attempt all three objectives at one time. Fear of losing monetary reward or promotion may inhibit an open discussion of training and development needs. It is indeed possible that one appraisor may not be appropriate for all three. For example, an immediate superior may be the most suitable person with whom to discuss current performance, but potential and promotion prospects may be the domain of someone further up the hierarchy. Some organisations make a practice of using more than one appraisor. For instance the 'grandfather' or superior's superior may be present at the interview, and we know of one organisation where a colleague of the appraisee is also present.

A relatively new development is that of upward appraisal, whereby subordinates are given a formal role in assessing their superiors. To avoid embarrassment, this normally takes the form of anonymous questionnaires. Sometimes the questionnaires are collected and collated by independent consultants who feed back the results individually and in strict confidence, and where required, give assistance in compiling action plans. It usually complements, rather than replaces, more traditional forms of appraisal. Its supporters claim that it facilitates employee empowerment and makes for a more participative management style. It certainly has the potential to provide a new and useful perspective on training needs, but a number of studies suggest that it can be a highly political process. (See Redman and Mathews, 1995.) Another variation is appraisal by colleagues.

It is normally good practice to give advance notice of the interview and ask the appraisee to write a report on his or her own performance, and use this to start off the discussion. Some of the first appraisal schemes were designed on the basis of personal qualities such as enthusiasm, commitment, loyalty, etc, but current schemes are usually output-based, reviewing performance against targets during the period under review, and formulating new targets for the forthcoming period. The interview should terminate with the identification of developmental steps, action plans and targets, with dates.

Objective-setting and formal appraisal are at the centre of *performance management systems* (PMS), where individual goals and responsibilities are linked to the objectives of the work unit and key corporate objectives as a whole. A survey commissioned by the former Institute of Personnel Management found that organisations that operate PMS normally have a mission statement which is communicated to all employees, and express performance targets in terms of measurable outputs, accountabilities and training or learning targets. They use formal appraisal to communicate performance requirements and produce personal improvement plans, and they also have a tendency to link performance requirements to pay, particularly for senior managers (Bevan and Thompson, 1991). Although the majority of companies in the survey had instigated PMS to improve organisational effectiveness, the researchers found no evidence to indicate that this link existed. Some PMS systems make use of computer programs to subject data to statistical procedures and produce results that are as objective as possible. For a more detailed acount of such a scheme, see Moorby (1991). Despite the survey findings, the incidence of PMS is likely to increase and, as the example in Chapter 7, page 151 demonstrates, it links up very conveniently with NVQ competences.

Assessment/development centres

These have a history based in selection procedures and are still used for this purpose today. Many companies, however, have extended their usage to assessment for promotion and/or development centres to indicate strengths and weaknesses. Dulewicz (1989) claims that assessment centres were designed primarily as a predictor of potential, *not* as a method for appraising current performance, and that their record for doing this is far better than that of any other technique.

The first step in devising an assessment/development centre is to identify what strengths or characteristics are to be tested. As we have seen in considering the competences, two approaches are possible: the input approach, in which case personal attributes such as leadership might be tested, or the outcomes approach, in which discrete units of the job might be given as assessed tasks. In practice, most companies seem to employ input approaches, testing competencies such as basic reasoning, strategic visioning, confidence, control, flexibility, interpersonal skills, etc, although with the advent of NVQs there may be a trend towards testing 'output' defined competences.

There are a number of important questions to ask, namely:

- What are the essential competences/(ies) the organisation/job requires?
- How can we monitor the competences/(ies) required in a changing environment?
- Can we devise tasks that really do assess these competences/(ies)?
- Does performance on the task actually transfer to the working situation?
- How can we evaluate the scheme as a whole?

Ways of arriving at answers to the first of these questions include: the use of the Repertory Grid technique (see Fransella and Bannister, 1977) to generate a list of the critical competences/(ies) exhibited by effective managers; surveys among staff; comparing results with those of similar organisations and interpreting any differences; considering the findings of other researchers; or adapting national standards such as those established within NVQs. Whatever methods are used it is necessary to check that the dimensions being assessed are still relevant to work aims and objectives, otherwise there is a danger that managers and assessors will subconsciously select in their own image and that this process of 'cloning' may hinder organisational development. Some organisations attempt to answer the last three questions by careful performance appraisal of staff who have previously been through the centre, to compare their marks with actual performance. This is, of course, open to the criticism that since being assessed some development should have taken place. A more rigorous approach would be to rate managers in their current jobs, put them through the assessment centre and compare their scores with the ratings. Few organisations do this, because of the inconvenience it would cause. It may be thought ironic that standard selection tests are not marketed unless they have been thoroughly validated, and yet important career decisions may be made in many companies on the strength of procedures that have not been subjected to this rigour.

The training of assessors is obviously a crucial factor. Not only must they be capable of assessing the dimensions in question, but fairness also demands inter-assessor reliability; continuous training and updating is therefore required. Assessors may be senior managers who have themselves been through the centre and possibly assisted in its design. The full support of top management is vital in order to gain the commitment of managers at all levels, as the following quotation from L. Jackson (1989) shows:

> If anything, we underestimated the level of inertia and opposition which faced us . . . It was fortunate we had the full support of the directors . . . it was noticeable that the psychological barriers were more daunting than the administrative and technical ones.

Now imagine that you are Jim Unlucky and have just returned to work on Monday, having spent the end of last week going through your organisation's assessment centre. Attainment of certain standards is a prerequisite for being considered for promotion, and you have just been informed that unfortunately you did not make the grade, although after a suitable period you can apply for reassessment. You have been provided with a profile and asked to produce an action plan, to be discussed with your superior and training officer if required. You feel resentful about the whole business. You did not understand what one of the tests was getting at, and do not agree with the comments on your assessment sheet. You have just been to see your boss, who said he did not understand them either. You wonder whether it is worth trying to make an action plan and apply for reassessment or whether to start looking for other jobs, because you do not seem to be getting very far in this one. You wonder whether your assessment centre scores will feature in an employer's reference.

A number of organisations (see, for example, L. Jackson, 1989), have found that merely feeding back the profile of strengths and weaknesses does not necessarily equip those assessed to take the required action. Short off-the-job follow-up courses may be necessary to give a fuller understanding of the meaning of the profile and to assist the manager to come to terms with it. Such a course is also a convenient occasion for drafting and discussing personal action plans, making learning contracts and enabling managers to begin to take charge of their own learning. This will not necessarily be related to weaknesses because, although 'training needs' are usually associated with limitations, one of the features of an assessment centre is that it also brings out strengths. Perhaps in the past we have dwelt too much on 'training gaps' and paid too little attention to helping people to learn how to build upon their strengths.

Griffiths and Goodge (1994) describe 'third-generation' development centres where participants are actively involved in generating their own assessments.

For further accounts of assessment centres see Cockerill (1989), Dulewicz (1989) and Woodruffe (1990).

SELF-ASSESSMENT – CREATING EXPERIENTIAL LEARNING OPPORTUNITIES

As the rate of change accelerates rapidly, detailed job analyses become quickly outdated, necessitating increasing emphasis on *self*-analysis, *self*-development and situations where employees take charge of their own learning. We are at the turning of the tide, and this trend is likely to continue, so that situations where a training and development professional produces a job analysis and prescribes the necessary training are likely to become confined to lower-level routine jobs. In Chapter 7 we raised the question, 'How can we help people to develop themselves?', and one way in which we can do this is by helping them to learn from experience.

In Chapter 3 we explained the cyclical process of experiential learning (see Figure 3.2), and implicit in the reflection and conceptualisation stages of that cycle is the recognition of one's own shortcomings. Mumford (1989) has pointed out that managers tend to think in terms of managerial activities and problems first, whereas recognition of learning/training needs is a secondary stage in their thought processes. The requirement, therefore, is to accelerate this procedure and 'trigger' an acceptance of these needs and an awareness of remedial opportunities, many of which already exist in the working environment. There are numerous ways of encouraging this recognition; for instance, Mumford suggests a review based on the learning opportunities identified in Figure 3.3, which can encourage managers to realise how they can create learning events for themselves, often without the word 'need' being mentioned at all. (For a comprehensive treatment of this topic see Mumford, 1989, and Honey and Mumford, 1989.)

Action learning 'sets' can provide a similar kind of 'trigger', particularly when the discussion centres around what is needed to overcome a particular problem. Regular entries in a personal logbook help towards the gradual identification of needs and opportunities. This type of activity is at the heart of the process of continuous development and the concept of learning organisations, where *reality* is the vehicle for learning. External help can be obtained through discussion with other people, but the process itself is internal and essentially self-developmental because the assessment is an intrinsic part of the learning. It is a skill, the most vital of the 'competencies' that has to be acquired and gradually cultivated as a prerequisite of 'learning to learn'. A recognition of one's own learning style is a helpful step forward, and the Honey and Mumford Learning Styles Questionnaire (see Chapter 3) is a useful diagnostic instrument. Advice on how to practise and improve styles other than that originally preferred helps the learner to become more versatile in completing all four stages of the experiential learning cycle.

Various kinds of planned interventions can be used as stimulators for experiential learning, such as courses consisting of 'contrived' experiences (eg group task assignments, or in their extreme form, Outdoor Training). The debriefing that follows such activities can afford significant insights into strengths and weaknesses, and into the role each participant has played in the group.

Programmes can also be structured around questionnaires which identify preferred team roles, the two most notable being the Belbin Team Roles (see Woods and Thomas, 1992), and the Margerison McCann Team Roles (see Margerison, 1992). Both of these feed information from a self-perception questionnaire into a computer and produce individual print-outs relating to the way participants see their roles as team members. The new Belbin programme has an added dimension in that it incorporates information provided by colleagues or other course participants, thereby providing a more objective profile. The analysis into identifiable 'roles' assists an individual in making the most of opportunities for practice which arise in the course of his or her work. These programmes and the learning needs they diagnose are particularly important in view of the increasing use of teamwork in organisations. They are also useful tools to help in the diagnosis of *group* training needs.

Other ways of helping people identify their own training needs are individual action plans. Sometimes it is useful to start these with a blank sheet; otherwise a little helpful structure can be provided in the form of such questions as:

- Where am I now?
- Where do I want to be?
- What is stopping me from getting there?
- What do I need to know?
- What do I need to do?
- Where can I get help?
- What targets am I going to achieve by . . . (*dates*)?
- How am I going to monitor and evaluate my performance?

When completing action plans, it is important that the targets are sufficiently specific to be recognised. For instance, to plan to 'delegate more next year' is not a meaningful target, because it can be very loosely interpreted. A more specific target would be 'By 13th March I will have reviewed all my work activities and found a suitable way of delegating 20 per cent of them.'

For further discussion of self and team development and 'reflection in action' see Chapter 12.

The role of the coach in self-assessment

The coach helps the trainee (or sometimes group of trainees) to assess his own performance, realise his own shortcomings and identify his own learning needs, develop and carry out a learning/action plan, reassess his competence and constantly review progress. The essence of coaching is to help the learner recognise and take advantage of the learning opportunities that occur in his working situation.

Fred is an assistant editor in a local newspaper, which is a 'learning organisation'. He is fortunate in that his manager, Tom, realising that developing his staff is an important part of his responsibilities, has himself undertaken an open learning programme on coaching. He helps Fred to assess his strengths and weaknesses and take a critical look at his performance. Together they make an assessment of his training needs and consider the best ways of meeting them. They make a learning/action plan and, wherever possible, they try to identify suitable learning opportunities in the working situation. For instance, Fred is praised for always producing the latest 'hot news' but, on the other hand, is sometimes criticised for holding up all his copy until the very last minute. This has caused great difficulties in the production department and has occasionally cost money in the form of overtime for production staff and loss of sales due to late delivery to retail outlets. Tom suggests that Fred might spend two afternoons in the production department, shadowing the assistant production manager (see page 325) and discussing problems with him. As a result he is to produce a report on better handling of last-minute 'hot items'. (This might also provide a training opportunity for the assistant production manager, as well as for the supervisor who is to deputise for Fred on the two afternoons.) Tom and Fred agree to meet on a regular basis to reassess Fred's skills, and set new targets and action plans. In this way the coaching became a continuous cycle and gradually Tom learns to manage the process for himself.

Companies using functional analysis might be able to find a relevant job analysis, prepared by the appropriate NTO, which could be used to determine the required units of competence. The performance criteria and range statements could then be used as a guide in assisting the learner to assess his performance. The skills of coaching range from those of listening and giving feedback (see page 85), skills of setting up and managing a discussion, interview skills, to knowledge of the learning process. For an example of a framework for training in coaching, see Moorby (1994). Although in certain circumstances a coach and a mentor may be the same person, coaching should not be confused with mentoring, which involves advising, counselling and sometimes acting as a role model. (See page 241.)

THE INFLUENCE AND ROLE OF THE LINE MANAGER – A SUMMARY

The ideal situation is one where people can recognise their own needs, (as the act of recognition is an important part of the learning process), can promote their own learning opportunities, and recognise and take advantage of those that occur naturally during the day's work. The most important person in helping or hindering them to achieve this is usually their own immediate superior. This is true in all sizes of organisation, but in small companies, where there is no training and development specialist, the management contribution is absolutely vital. Although we have mentioned this in many places in this book, and have devoted a section of Chapter 6 to line management's responsibility for training, we feel that it would be helpful here to provide a summary of the practical ways in which managers can help their subordinates.

- Most importantly, managers can act as *role models*. In Chapter 4, we explain how each encounter with a superior involves learning of some kind for the subordinate, and often for the superior too. Managers can themselves profit from experiential learning and, in particular, from using the reflective stages of the Kolb cycle. Managers who commit themselves to continuous development (see Chapter 3), and in so doing are realising their own needs, are likely not only to improve their own performance, but that of their subordinates. In this way, they can help to create a 'learning culture', see Chapter 12.

- Managers can act as *coaches*. (See page 227 and page 85.)

- They can prepare members of staff about to take part in training programmes by discussing the content and demonstrating an interest in the application to the job or department. A debriefing session afterwards can be very important in obtaining value from an external course. (See pages 245, 249 and 271).

- They can also act as *mentors* (see page 241), not necessarily to their own subordinates, but possibly to those of other managers, or to trainees more than one tier below.

- They can help subordinates to realise their own needs by becoming skilled in the processes of staff appraisals, helping to draw up effective action plans (see pages 221, 223, 227), target-setting, or compiling personal development files. (See Chapter 10, page 246.)

- In addition to formal appraisal systems, they can realise the importance of *immediate feedback* or knowledge of results, and have informal discussions such as the second example on page 85, Chapter 4), without waiting months for the formal occasion. By adopting a constructive approach they can help their subordinates to learn from their mistakes and understand *why* they went wrong as well as *what* they did wrong. People do not learn and 'stretch' themselves if they are discouraged from taking any risk. Managers can also recognise that *favourable feedback* is as important as criticism.

- Managers can create *on-the-job learning opportunities* which will widen subordinates' horizons and help them to see the whole picture. (See in particular, Alan Mumford's examples on page 70, Chapter 3)

- They can *delegate* in a helpful and progressive manner, making sure that the subordinate knows exactly what is expected, has been given appropriate guidelines, has a defined action plan and knows that advice and help are readily available if required.

- They can help to remove some of the barriers to learning. See pages 74, 249 and 250.

At the beginning of this chapter, we quoted Fairbairns (1991), in suggesting a third question which might be relevant in determining an individual's training needs:

'What skills/knowledge/personal attributes are likely to be encouraged, recognised or rewarded?'

This question brings us back to the title of this book, which is based on the philosophy that whatever approach is taken to training, or even if no formal training exists, an organisation is a learning environment with its own system of rewards and punishments of varying kinds. If training is required to run directly against the organisational flow, trainers must be prepared to overcome resistance. In assessing needs, therefore, some attention must be paid to the organisational context.

You should now realise that there has been an historical development of methodologies to determine training needs, influenced by the dominant job characteristics at different periods, as well as the philosophies propounded by national institutions such as training boards and the QCA. We are fortunate in having a heritage of approaches and tools from which to choose for specific occasions. It is likely, however, that the real challenge is yet to come; it is that of giving further impetus to the trend of encouraging individuals to assess their own and their team's needs. Start now and look at Mumford's table, Figure 3.3, and identify occasions at work when you could take advantage of opportunities to practise some of the skills in the right-hand column. Which skills do you think it would be most useful for you to develop further, and why?

FOR FURTHER REFLECTION AND DISCUSSION

Consider how you would answer the following questions:

1 **By what means should an organisation determine (a) when operational problems justify formal training solutions, and (b) how to make use of normal work activities as training opportunities?**

2 **What steps would you take in identifying the training needs of a group of college lecturers who have been in their posts for a number of years? What arrangements do you think colleges might make to ensure a regular updating of knowledge and skills?**

3 **How would you establish the training needs of a small group of experienced sales representatives, externally recruited following their being made redundant by a competitor?**

4 **How would you identify and assess the competences required for a job of your choice? Illustrate with detailed performance criteria, range statements and evidence requirements. Can you think of at least two methodologies for doing this?**
(IPD Examination, Stage 2, Employee Development, May 1995)

5 **You are planning to arrange a learning programme for 30 women who will take up their first managerial appointment over the next 6–12 months. They currently undertake a wide range of occupations within your organisation.**

How will you assess their needs? Identify the steps you would take. (Adapted from IPM Examination, Stage 2, Employee Development, May 1992)

SUGGESTED READING

FRANSELLA F. *and* BANNISTER D. *A Manual for Repertory Grid Technique.* Academic Press, London, 1977.

JESSUP G. *Outcomes: NVQs and the emerging model of education and training.* The Falmer Press, London, 1991 (particularly Chapters 5, 18 and 19).

MOORBY E. 'Mentoring and Coaching', in J. Prior (ed.) Handbook of *Training and Management Development.* Gower, London, 1994.

MUMFORD A. *Management Development: Strategies for action.* 2nd edn, Institute of Personnel Management, London, 1993.

PATRICK J. *Training: Research and practice.* Academic Press, London, 1992.

PEARN M. *and* KANDOLA R. *Job Analysis: A practical guide for managers.* 2nd edn, Institute of Personnel and Development, London, 1993.

MEGGINSON D. *and* WHITAKER V. *Cultivating Self-Development.* Institute of Personnel and Development, London, 1996. Gives comprehensive and practical guidance on using a variety of methods to diagnose one's own needs and to formulate a self-development and action plan.

10 Determining and evaluating training interventions

Training interventions – determination of training objectives – determination of the appropriate training strategy – planning and implementation of the training – evaluation of the programme

INTRODUCTION

Imagine you are the training director of XYZ Store, which has a large number of retail outlets situated throughout the UK. You have just attended a board meeting, at which disturbing figures were produced showing that in the past quarter retail shrinkage has increased dramatically. The situation is regarded as very serious and was discussed as a matter of major concern and priority. Some of the comments made by your fellow directors were as follows:

'Our branch managers need training – they don't seem to understand their responsibilities; they need to be made to see that shrinkage in their own branch is their pigeon. We should call them all in for a compulsory conference, and tell them it's not good enough.'

'That would be expensive. After the amount we have lost in shrinkage, we can't afford it. Perhaps the regional managers could hold their own conferences – make them realise their responsibilities as well.'

'I disagree; what we need is not more training, but better security equipment and alarms.'

'I agree. It will cost the earth to run a conference, and anyway it isn't the managers who need training: it's the counter staff who let it all happen, and there is quite a high turnover there. We would be training forevermore.'

It was finally agreed, however, that you should produce a report to be discussed at a special meeting of the board in two weeks' time.

This chapter will help to provide you with some criteria to use in deciding upon your recommendations. You will also see, however, that getting your recommended course of action approved by your colleagues could be a political matter which you will have to take into consideration.

In Chapter 7 (page 158), we gave an example of an incorrectly identified training need, and therefore before attempting to determine any training strategy, it is first prudent to verify that training really can contribute to the situation. Once you have confirmed that this is the case, the main stages in devising a planned training intervention are illustrated in Figure 5.2 and are as follows:

- *identifying the training requirements; what do you want to achieve in terms of outcomes?*
- *setting training/learning objectives*
- *selecting the training strategy*
- *designing and planning the training*
- *implementing the programme*
- *evaluating the training.*

We considered the first of these stages in Chapter 9, with an investigation into methods of determining individual training needs. We now consider the formulation of specific objectives, the choice of strategy, and the planning, implementation and evaluation stages of training.

TRAINING INTERVENTIONS

We use the term 'training intervention' to include any event that is deliberately undertaken to assist learning to take place. It includes a wide range of activities from formal courses to structured work experiences, and we refer to these activities as strategies.

The logical first stage is to determine exactly what it is hoped to achieve by a training intervention, ie formulate the objectives. It is then necessary to decide the best means of achieving these objectives, select a strategy, plan the training accordingly, and implement and evaluate it.

Although it is convenient to consider these stages in logical progression, it should be realised that they are not entirely discrete; for instance, well-defined objectives or competences should provide criteria that can be used as a basis for evaluation. It is sometimes necessary to employ training techniques, such as structured exercises, which will provide feedback of the learning taking place and which will thus form part of the evaluation. The final evaluation serves a number of purposes: it provides the trainer with feedback or knowledge of results, and draws attention to aspects of the objectives that have not yet been achieved. This involves a reconsideration of residual objectives and a return to the beginning of the cycle. Self-evaluation involves consideration of mistakes and errors made, and is a valuable part of the learning process. In the interests of clarity, however, we shall deal with each of these activities in turn.

STAGE 1 – DETERMINATION OF TRAINING OBJECTIVES

A learning objective may be regarded as an intent, expressed in the form of a statement, describing a proposed behaviour change in the learner. The term 'criterion behaviour' is used to define what the learner is expected to do at the end of the training. It specifies the tasks, procedures and techniques that he should be able to carry out, the standards of performance required and the circumstances in which the work will be undertaken (see Mager, 1984). There are, therefore, three stages in compiling a behavioural objective. These are:

- Specify the behaviour the learner is required to demonstrate for the objective to be achieved.
- Determine the important conditions in which the behaviour must be demonstrated: for example, the type or range of equipment to be used or the environmental constraints.
- Determine the standard to which the trainee must perform. This can vary from a precise production specification to criteria such as absence of customer complaints. It is frequently the most difficult aspect to define, but it is usually possible to find a way of describing what would be regarded as acceptable performance, even if in some instances it has to be 'to the satisfaction of the supervisor'.

An example of a behavioural objective is ' On completion of the training, the word processor operator should be capable of typing 'x' words per minute with no errors, using 'y' system, under normal office conditions'.

It is worth noting that some words in the English language, such as 'understand', 'know', 'appreciate', are open to many interpretations. For instance, if a person 'knows' how a refrigerator works, he might be able to design one, to assemble one, to repair one, or merely to describe its operation. Words such as these should not be used in compiling behavioural objectives. Preference should be given to more precise terms such as 'identify', 'differentiate', 'construct' or 'solve', which are more capable of describing specific behaviour.

It should also be noted that there is a difference between 'learner' objectives and 'trainer' objectives. Examples of the latter might be 'to give an appreciation of . . .', 'to provide an adequate foundation for . . .' These do not specify what the trainee is expected to do at the end of the training and should not be listed as behavioural objectives.

It is not always easy to structure an unambiguous behavioural objective in a training context, but the clearer the objective that results, the more likelihood there is of successful training. A trainee cannot be expected to know what he should be learning if the trainer's own objectives are uncertain! In some areas, such as management development, it is much more difficult to describe training objectives in strict behavioural terms, because the specific behaviour required may not be known at the time of training, or the possible behavioural outcomes may be too numerous to list. In such circumstances, one solution proposed by Gronlund (1978), is to state the general objective first, and then clarify it by listing a sample of the specific behaviour which would be acceptable as evidence of the attainment of the objective. For example:

> At the end of the training programme the manager will be able to take greater responsibility for the development of his own staff. Indicative activities will include
>
> - carrying out satisfactory appraisal interviews
> - enabling his subordinates to recognise and accept their own training needs
> - conducting effective coaching and counselling sessions
> - delegating successfully to his subordinates.

Objectives can also be formulated in this way without necessarily predicting the precise outcome. Many learning experiences raise open-ended questions, the answers to which have to be worked out when back on the job. It is unrealistic to set as a behavioural objective for a course on management styles 'participants will change styles immediately on returning to work', but it is possible to determine indicative activities, such as demonstrating an interest in developing new interpersonal skills, or initiating discussion on management styles with colleagues.

Training can often act as a catalyst for change, and it may be useful to make a distinction between training objectives and the ultimate outcome of an intervention. For example, a management conference might be called with the objective of arriving at some common agreement on the solution of a problem. A sub-objective might be that each manager would be able to identify the implications of the problem for his own department, and contribute to the solutions by putting forward practical suggestions. A second sub-objective might be attitudinal in that although possibly not in entire agreement with the ultimate solution, each manager would have recognised the many facets of the problem and display some commitment to the final recommendations. In other words, the learning experience of discussion with colleagues holding varied viewpoints would give each manager a broader perspective and an understanding of the reasons for the decisions, rather than an opinion based on his own narrow experience.

A record of conference proceedings including the contribution of each manager, and a subsequent follow-up of the implementation of the proposals, would be methods of ascertaining the fulfilment of the objectives. What could not be specified beforehand, however, would be the nature of the conclusions reached, ie the ultimate outcome. Top management may well have had some desired solution in mind and the conference may have approved it, but if, in the course of debate, sound reasons emerged for adopting a different approach, top management's credibility would be lost if these findings were to be totally disregarded and the pre-determined solution imposed from above. In these circumstances, such a conference may well have done more harm than good! Similarly, an intervention such as a series of courses using team roles exercises may have as its purpose an examination and evaluation of the work of a team, but the precise outcome of that programme cannot be predicted. As we move further towards self-development and experiential learning for the individual and the group, the outcome may be to trigger change in a variety of ways which could not have been predicted.

It does not necessarily follow that the trainer or coach alone should be formulating the objectives. The concept of continuous development implies that employees should be able to take increasing responsibility for their own learning, and therefore must be capable of drawing up their own objectives, although there may be some conflict between the desired objectives of the employee and those of his or her employer (see page 148). Assisting in the determination of training objectives can be an important motivator, and indeed part of the learning process itself for any trainee but in particular for young people undertaking a general basic training. The same principle applies to students from schools, colleges or universities who are undertaking work experience placements.

Objectives and NVQs

In earlier chapters we described how NVQs are based on the concept of competences, and both the learning required and its assessment are governed by statements of competence. The elements of competence bear some relationship to behavioural objectives in that they are defined by means of an active verb and also include a statement of the conditions. In addition, each element has performance criteria setting out what must be achieved for successful performance. The performance criteria must always contain a critical outcome and an evaluative statement. The critical outcome stipulates what has to be done for the element to be successfully accomplished, and the evaluative statement qualifies it in a quantitative or qualitative way. The performance criteria must relate to outcomes and not processes or procedures. They are concerned with *what* the learner can do rather than *how* he has acquired the competence. Further detail about the required outcome is given in the Range Statement, which indicates the range of applications to which the element applies. The terminology of 'behavioural objectives' is not used, and Jessup (1991) suggests that a major difference between the two methodologies is that in the NVQ approach the statement of outcomes is not limited by considerations of assessment. Some of the earlier attempts at defining behavioural objectives were focused on educational programmes with conventional assessment schemes.

STAGE 2 – DETERMINATION OF THE APPROPRIATE TRAINING STRATEGY

The link between job analysis and behavioural objectives should now have been clarified. At this stage it becomes obvious whether the necessary knowledge and skills, or in the case of NVQs the 'competences' have been investigated and described in sufficient detail. For instance, 'communication skills' is too broad a description to be of much assistance: it could give rise to a wide variety of objectives, for which appropriate training could range from report writing to learning how to chair a meeting. On the other hand, 'ability to give accurate and speedy information about train times to all telephone inquirers' gives a very clear indication of what is needed. Precise details are therefore essential to the design of a programme that requires specified outcomes.

At this point there may be a range of choices, and selection of the most suitable strategy can be critical. We have classified the possibilities under six main headings:

1 training on-the-job
2 planned organisation experience
3 in-house programmes
4 planned experiences outside the organisation
5 external courses
6 self-managed learning.

We shall shortly consider each of these in more detail. The four 'decision criteria' to use in determining the appropriate training strategy are:

• compatibility with objectives
• estimated likelihood of transfer of learning to the work situation
• available resources (including money, time and staff)
• trainee-related factors.

It is not possible to give specific rules which will hold good in every situation, not least because most cases are likely to result in a compromise between what is desirable and what is possible. The decision-making process is likely, therefore, to be one of 'best fit' and is exemplified in the following case:

An HRD manager was requested, as a matter of urgency, to arrange team-building training for a group of managers about to embark on a new project, the success of which depended crucially upon group effort. There was little time to undertake the training. Using the four criteria, the salient factors were:

• the objectives embraced knowledge of skills of group membership (for example of group interaction), as well as of attitude formation
• learning transfer to the work situation was essential; the organisation climate was influenced by a practical 'down to earth' management style, which was likely to be supportive of training based on real, rather than theoretical, issues
• resources were very limited: time was short and there was little money left in the budget
• trainee-related factors; the managers had family commitments and

would not have welcomed being asked to stay away from home, although they might ultimately have been persuaded to do so. They could not be spared from their departments for long periods.

The HRD manager considered the possible strategies. He rejected on-the-job training as being unlikely to achieve the objectives because each manager was isolated in his own department. Planned activity inside the company satisfied the criteria of good learning transfer, acceptability and credibility to the managers concerned. He deliberated how it could be arranged. He then considered external courses and re-read a brochure for an outdoor training course which he had previously thought looked useful. He knew this type of training was often effective in creating a team spirit, and if all the managers were to go together there was a good chance the learning would transfer to the work situation. The timing was suitable, but the course lasted a full week. It would be difficult to arrange for all the managers to be absent from their departments so near the commencement of the project and the cost would use all that was left of the training budget. He recollected that one of the managers had a heart condition, which might cause difficulties. He considered other external courses and rejected them for similar reasons.

He then thought about the possibility of an internal course and decided that, because the objectives included attitudes and skill requirements, a course involving discussion sessions and group activities would be appropriate. There would be a better chance of learning transfer if it were possible to base sessions on real problems the managers would face in carrying out the project. From a resource perspective, the cost would be less than an outside course, and the timing could be arranged to suit the managers' availability. Although evening sessions might be included, they would not have to stay away from home, which would save money; that could not be considered an advantage in achieving the objectives, but the training officer judged that in the circumstances it was the best compromise he could reach. A conference room and syndicate rooms were available.

The main difficulty was that time was short for him to prepare the programmes, but having considered his own commitments and those of his staff, he decided that it would be possible, especially as it might be beneficial to arrange certain problem-discussion sessions after the project had actually started. This would enable the course to be based partly on 'real' material, which would help to ensure learning transfer similar to that provided by on-the-job training. He decided to consult senior management about the possibility of building some of the later sessions into the conduct of the project itself, and also to investigate what assistance he could obtain from his local college. In this way, he would be able to combine two strategies: an in-company course consolidated and made relevant by structured in-house activity. Training would thus be playing a direct and integrated role in implementing organisational plans.

This example is not intended to demonstrate that an in-house course is necessarily superior to outdoor training, which on another occasion might have been more effective; nor does it illustrate that courses are always the answer, but rather that each decision as to the most appropriate training strategy is contingent on the circumstances, and the resultant decision will reflect the 'best fit'.

We now turn to each of the six main forms of training strategies and the four 'decision criteria' in more detail, and give examples of how they relate to each other.

The six main strategies

1 Training on-the-job

A discussion of the merits and demerits of off- and on-the-job training will be found in Chapters 4, 5 and 9. On-the-job training accounts for about half of all training, and a survey carried out for the IPD in 1996 in manufacturing companies indicated that it worked 'tolerably well' particularly for simple tasks, but that improvements could be made. (IPD 1998). Jobs vary from the very simple to the highly complex, and it is therefore difficult to generalise, but knowledge of the learning processes described in Chapters 3 and 4 and the analytical techniques discussed in Chapter 9 are equally appropriate for on-the-job and off-the-job trainers. In general, the success of on-the-job learning depends upon:

- well-trained trainers, who are not only competent at the job, but have skills in coaching and giving feedback, and who are knowledgeable in appropriate learning processes, such as those discussed in Chapters 3 and 4).
- adequate recognition of the on-the-job trainer role. Many on-the-job trainers have other responsibilities and if, for instance, they are supervisors or fellow workers, they may well not regard training as their main concern. They need to be given sufficient time allowance from their other work, kept up to date with new developments and, where possible, should be given regular opportunities to act as trainers.
- adequate preparation. For an operator's task this includes not only the necessary materials, and learning aids but a competent job training analysis (see Chapter 9). For simple tasks, the stages and key points analysis illustrated in Figure 9.1 is extremely useful. See also page 209. For a feedback or coaching session for any type of job (see pages 85 and 227 ff) preparation would include careful study of all relevant details of the learner's progress to date.
- safety considerations (see Chapter 3). These should be paramount, and potential dangers should always be key points on a training analysis.

Training on dangerous equipment should be preceded where possible by experience on a simulator, and should at all times be monitored with extreme care.

• appropriate target setting, performance testing and monitoring procedures to assess progress and provide knowledge of results for trainer and learner.

In the case of management development, on-the-job training may take the form of coaching and advice from immediate superiors or, in some instances, merely seeing the example of a good superior's work practices, and trying to perform according to his standards (ie modelling) may suffice. (See Chapter 9 page 229). The whole process of agreeing key areas and targets, whether as part of a formal performance management scheme or by individual agreement between boss and subordinate, may also be viewed as invaluable on-the-job training in such aspects as time management, work organisation and planning.

On-the-job training is obviously likely to take place in small companies where there is no training specialist, but it can also be an appropriate option for larger organisations, where the specialist's role may be in training the trainers. An important additional advantage of on-the-job training is that can be a useful developmental experience not just for the trainee, but also for the trainer or coach.

Considered against the four 'decision criteria', the advantages of on-the-job training are that it is likely to be high in learning transfer to the specific job and to appear inexpensive in terms of resources (but see examples of learning costs in Chapter 8). The learner may take longer to reach the desired objectives, because the environmental conditions may be unfavourable, but there can be some compensation in the fact that he may well be performing some part of the job during the training period. However, the training may be narrow and job specific, without the necessary underpinning knowledge, and may not transfer to other environments. For many jobs a mixture of on- and off-the job training might well be the best strategy – a view which can be reinforced by the suggestion that those who have just completed off-the-job training cannot usually be considered 'completely trained' until they have had the benefit of consolidating what they have learned by on-the-job experience, and may still require careful monitoring and coaching for some time.

See Cannell (1997) for useful case-studies and tips on on-the-job training. See also IPD *Key Facts On-the-job Training* (1998), for an informative but concise summary, including how to implement an OJT programme, two short case-studies and further reading list.

2 Planned organisation experience

This can be designed within existing organisational processes and wherever possible as an integral part of mainstream developments (see Figure 3.3). It can include planned experience in other departments or within the same department, or the assignment of special responsibilities, problem-solving discussion groups, quality circles, special projects, developing fresh aspects of activity such as a new sales promotion, or a system of records. These are likely to provide positive transfer of learning provided there is organisational support. On the other hand, it is counterproductive to ask someone to undertake projects and special assignments when there is little hope of eventual implementation. Action learning (see pages 108 and 294 ff), involving 'learning by doing', provides a means whereby managers learn on the job as well as acquiring awareness of their own developmental processes.

Opportunities for planned in-house activities are sometimes deliberately created or may be planned to assist day-to-day running of departments. One organisation arranges for its graduate trainees to take over a production section for four weeks while the supervisor is on holiday. The graduate prepares for this by spending some time beforehand in the section, and actually takes over the week before the supervisor departs, continuing for a week after her return. This provides a challenging work experience for the graduate, while allowing the supervisor the privilege of taking her annual leave at a time other than the normal factory holiday.

Another form of training in this category, which is growing in popularity, is the use of coaches and mentors. It is suggested that mentoring originated in the concept of apprenticeship, and a mentor has been described as a 'role model . . . a guide, a tutor, a coach and a confidant' (Clutterbuck, 1991). The mentor is usually eight to 15 years senior to the protégé, and may be the immediate boss, although this is not always satisfactory, because the two roles can conflict. A more common arrangement, therefore, is that the mentor is a more senior individual above, and frequently to the side of, the protégé's own boss. Mentoring has the advantage of inducting newcomers efficiently to the organisation and of assisting them with organisational problems and personal development, thereby increasing motivation and job satisfaction. The mentor can also pass on the organisational 'culture'. A properly organised scheme of mentoring is an inexpensive and efficient method of employee development. (For an example of a framework for a training course on coaching and mentoring see Moorby, 1994.)

3 In-house programmes

Many large organisations have a regular programme of in-house courses for what might be regarded as 'maintenance' training. These can include updating courses in specific topics or they may be general courses, such as those for junior, middle or senior managers, and attendance by those eligible for promotion is a routine practice. Other courses and conferences may be organised for specific needs, such as changes in legislation, company policy or industrial relations practice. Some internal courses may be consultative in nature, for instance conferences to discuss future organisational development, or changes in structure or management style. Some organisations run their own part-time qualification courses, and the NVQ framework, assessed in the workplace and offering certificates for the successful completion of units which can be accumulated to qualify for awards, lends itself admirably to this arrangement. For instance, 'retail skills' apprentices in a well-known supermarket chain undergo in-company programmes for the National Retail Certificates. Because these must be assessed to a national standard, they should be recognised by other employers, and can be used as a basis on which to build during later career development. Staff from local colleges are usually very happy to assist and help to plan in-house courses.

There is likely to be better learning transfer from internal, compared with external, courses, particularly if senior management are involved in some of the sessions. The training can be directed at real organisational problems, which is likely to increase face validity and chances of effectiveness. Courses are useful when many employees require similar training at one time. A variation is open access in-house training. This can include the provision of computer-based training and the use of interactive video. For example a large motor vehicle manufacturer had the problem of training 600 engineers, within a six-week time-span, in a new specification system for vehicle components. With the help of a grant from one of the national schemes, the target was achieved on time by the use of interactive multimedia computer-based methods at half the cost of traditional training. This type of training has a number of advantages in that it can be undertaken very near the trainee's place of work, and progress can be at his own pace and convenience. Training times can be reduced by the use of pre-tests, which enable the trainee to omit any items with which he is already familiar, whereas intermediate and final tests ensure that the material has really been mastered. This type of intensive course is now being used by many other large organisations. For instance, a large building society which was in the process of altering its operational systems was able to train all the staff very effectively by means of computerised packages. Although the initial outlay was considerable, the overall cost per head was much lower than the estimated expenditure on 'traditional' hotel-based courses entailing travelling and residential expenses. Furthermore, the programme is always ready and available to train new members of staff.

A recent survey (Xebec 1998) suggests that more and more in-house training will be delivered over company intranets. The research showed that two-thirds of organisations now have a corporate intranet and 22 per cent already use it to deliver on-line training. At present the majority concentrate on IT/technical skills and corporate issues, but the intranet is also used for training in personal skills (presentation skills, time management and assertiveness) and customer care training (telephone skills, handling complaints). The researchers predict that in the future although IT skills will remain the most frequent type of intranet training, with corporate skills following closely, there will be a considerable increase in the use of this medium for the delivery of personal and management skills, customer care and finance skills.

Once the equipment is installed and used for other purposes as well, this is a convenient and inexpensive medium for training, with the possible added advantage that, where appropriate, it allows 'just-in-time' delivery. It can allow self-paced and flexible learning, can deliver training to many people on different sites, is particularly useful in global organisations and, where appropriate, can offer instant contact with a trainer. A number of imaginative uses have been suggested, such as 'virtual classrooms' where people from geographically spread sites can exchange knowledge, or individual tuition from a 'trainer' who may be located miles away. There may, however, be a number of difficulties to overcome. As with any other form of training, management support is paramount, and pilot studies suggest that a culture change may be required, so that learning and development are valued. For instance, managers need to understand that staff using on-line programmes on a PC are 'working' and arrangements need to be made so that they are not disturbed. Time management is likely to become of increasing importance as staff assess their priorities and possibly struggle with information overload.

Research commissioned by BT (Scope Ketchum 1998) suggests that there is likely to be a time lag as HRD specialists assess the results of pilot studies and 'the next two years will see steep learning curves for those responsible for training, after which time on-line learning will come of age'. Although this method of delivery appears to have great potential, it is worth pointing out that there is often a social aspect to learning, and taking part in 'virtual classrooms' and 'group discussions' over an intranet demands new skills from the participants. For instance, during a 'traditional' discussion, participants interpret each other's 'body language' and voice intonation. They rely not just on *what* is said, it is *how* it is said that conveys the complete meaning. The absence of these additional modes of communication puts a greater emphasis on the exact wording of contributions to avoid misunderstanding. Video clips and video conferencing can help to overcome this difficulty. In addition, consideration has to be given to differences in learning styles, and it is possible that not everyone can happily learn from the type of material that can be presented over an intranet. Furthermore, it is unlikely to be suitable for all types of learning; for instance, social skills require practice and constructive feedback, although as technology develops and interactive programmes become more readily available, this difficulty may in part be overcome. The advent of voice control to eliminate the use of a keyboard would also help to make the process more widely acceptable. It would be fair to say that, at the time of writing, more pilot studies and experimentation are needed. If it becomes widespread, this medium could obviously influence the role and required skills of the HRD specialist, as the accent is likely to be upon *selecting, designing, script writing, and editing* self-learning programmes or materials for virtual classrooms; and providing *support and counselling* rather than upon direct training.

4 Planned experiences outside the organisation

Secondments and visits to suppliers or to the premises of important customers in order to obtain external views of the organisation's products and services can provide valuable insights. Visits are sometimes arranged to competitors or suppliers abroad, although these may be expensive. These experiences can, however, fulfil a number of objectives because, as well as imparting information, they often result in attitudinal change and can be used to provide a tangible reward for a recent job well done.

Although training objectives are derived from organisational needs, there can be circumstances when management is justified in encouraging employees to undertake self-developmental activities to further their own careers, eg when promotion prospects are minimised and when current jobs afford little opportunity for challenge or development. Examples of such developmental activities include undertaking a role within an appropriate professional body (resulting in contact and discussion with colleagues in other organisations), experience in chairing or addressing meetings, or assisting in external projects for the local community or with local educational institutions.

Learning transfer will depend upon the particular experience, but some attitudinal change is likely to result which will enable the incumbent to view her job in a different light. Although there can be dangers in arranging learning activities of this kind, in that employees may gain useful experience which will enable them to move to other organisations, the importance of mental activity and stimulation is a central feature of the process of continuing development. There is therefore a case for making allowance for this factor when setting training objectives. It is necessary to balance the likely costs involved against the possibility of disillusioned employees who, having loyally carried out unchallenging tasks for the organisation over a number of years, discover that they are unable to adjust to change and find it difficult and threatening to learn new techniques and methods.

5 External courses

A plethora of leaflets and brochures advertising external courses is constantly arriving on the desk of every training officer, and to send someone on a course appears an easy, although frequently expensive, option. External courses are broadly of two kinds: the short full-time variety, run by consultants, colleges and universities, and longer (usually part-time) courses often leading to a qualification. Educational institutions are usually very happy to co-operate and organise part-time programmes specially tailored to the needs of individual organisations or, by agreement, of a consortium of organisations. Because there can be dangers in an organisation becoming too inbred it is useful for employees to find out what happens 'outside': discussing the problems of others can often throw new light upon one's own situation. Where only one or two people require specialised knowledge, a course at the Open University or Open College or at one of the many distance learning programmes on offer is likely to be the best alternative.

Learning transfer is not likely to be high unless the organisation climate is supportive and the immediate manager has an important role to play. (See page 245 below.) Furthermore, if external courses are to be effective, they must be chosen with care. Having determined whether it is policy to cater for the particular need by an external course, and whether the trainee would be prepared to attend, the main factors to be considered are the precise objectives:

- What are the course objectives? Do they match the particular training need?
- Do the training methods and length of the course accord with its declared objectives? For instance, if the intention is to improve an employee's communication skills, what aspects of communication are covered, and do they match the employee's requirements? Is there any opportunity for supervised practice and feedback? The acquisition of skill does not come through knowledge alone.
- Is there any indication of the level of the course?
- Who are the organisers?
- What experience have they had in the field?
- Is there any information to indicate their competence?
- What other organisations have supported the course?
- Is it possible to obtain feedback from them?
- Is the cost related to the expected benefits? There is a temptation to judge the merits of a course by its price, but that can be misleading.
- A considerable proportion of the price of a residential course is the cost of the accommodation. Does the venue appear to be suitable? This may seem to be unimportant but if, for instance, a senior manager is asked to attend a course held in surroundings that he considers uncongenial, he may approach the learning material with negative attitudes.

HRD specialists should satisfy themselves on these points before committing their organisations to the expenditure and opportunity cost of sending their staff on external courses.

Briefing and debriefing sessions, preferably by the participant's superior, really are a prerequisite to gaining maximum advantage from an external course. Although they are very obvious and inexpensive steps to take, managers frequently fail in this respect, with the result that the participant may not have a clear idea of the objectives in sending him on the course, and on return may fail to implement any new ideas through lack of opportunity or because he feels that no interest has been taken (see also page 249). To overcome this difficulty, some courses for supervisors and junior managers are preceded by short preliminary courses for participants' superiors.

Part-time courses, particularly those leading to a qualification, constitute a relatively long-term commitment and a considerable amount of personal study time. For instance, an MBA programme is likely to have broadly based objectives, be extremely demanding, and might be difficult to manage at times of work crisis and overload. Requests to attend such courses often come from the employee, and are sometimes negotiated on a joint payment basis. From the company perspective it is very important that such a programme is integrated with the career development programme for the employee, and that at least one person from senior management takes an active interest in progress. Without this type of support it is likely that if, on successful completion of the programme, the employee sees no immediate prospect of promotion or recognition, she will seek better opportunities elsewhere. There are now many types of MBA programmes; some have become specialised for particular categories of participant, such as staff from the Health Service, from engineering or for personnel staff, to mention but a few examples. Some are 'executive programmes' for relatively senior managers who must be sponsored by their organisations. Such programmes will normally have a steering committee composed of representatives of sponsoring organisations as well as staff from the university to advise on the programme and monitor its development. It is useful for the HRD manager from a sponsoring organisation to find out about this committee, because it is a vehicle through which she can exert influence on the conduct of the programme. Some MBAs are designed entirely for one organisation, or for a consortium. These and other part-time courses, such as those leading to professional qualifications, for instance those of the Institute of Personnel and Development, are normally regarded as a stage in career development rather than a remedy for an immediate training need.

6 Self-managed learning

In Chapter 4 we suggested that any organisation is a learning environment, but the efficient self-management of that learning requires particular skills and will only come about in special circumstances. Self-managed learning is therefore not an option that an HRD manager can suddenly decide to implement, but should be regarded as an ultimate aim that may be fulfilled to a greater or lesser extent. People cannot be *ordered* to manage their own learning; for this to be a sustained organisational strategy a number of conditions must be present. Most importantly, learning must be seen to be valued by the organisation; in other words, there must be a learning culture (see Chapters 4 and 12) in which people will be given help to learn both regularly and rigorously from their work. They should be able to identify their own needs, draw up and prioritise a plan of action and evaluate the results. Self-evaluation and the realisation of new ability and competence inspire confidence and act as a spur for further learning (see the continuous development spiral on page 73). Help will come from managers, coaches, mentors and colleagues, reinforced by organisational systems and processes such as regular discussion of needs and individual appraisal, as well as assistance in finding appropriate training and education. Logbooks and records of progress provide a focus, as well as stimulus to further development. Some organisations have instigated voluntary systems of 'personal development files' in which an individual employee agrees with his line manager to create a personal development plan based on a two-way commitment but emphasising personal responsibility. The file is owned by the individual and can hold certificates or portfolio documents belonging to the employee, and for young people it provides a follow up to their Record of Achievement.

Self-managed learning can be experiential through recognising and making full use of learning opportunities at work (see Figure 3.3), but it can also be derived from courses and programmes, possibly using company open learning centres and/or educational schemes. An increasing number of organisations have recognised this and provide open learning facilities, many on site, where employees can book their own access times and embark upon programmes of their choice. There is often no requirement that the programmes they choose are directly related to their current job. However, as we pointed out in Chapter 7 (page 148), the perceived needs of an individual may relate to self-development and may not necessarily coincide with the immediate requirements of the organisation. Open learning centres are very costly; the evaluation of benefit to the organisation can be difficult to calculate and quantify, particularly in the short term, and important debates may take place relating to responsibility for the choice of programme, and who should pay. The culture and ethos of a learning organisation would suggest that *any* learning is beneficial to the development of the whole person, and that the gain would ultimately be fed back to the organisation in the form of increased maturity and learning capacity of its personnel.

Some organisations have gone a stage further and have set up education schemes offering employees a wide choice of programmes for their own development. The well-known Ford Employee Development and Assistance Programme (EDAP) courses started in July 1989 with the stated objectives of offering employees 'a wide range of personal and career development education and training, retraining and development activities and to make available a variety of employee assistance services to encourage a healthier life style'. A national tripartite committee comprising representatives from the staff and hourly unions and Ford management is responsible for establishing and reviewing the programme's goals and objectives and monitoring progress. Budgets, based on numbers of employees on site, are controlled by local tripartite committees at each of the 19 British locations. As well as approving individual applications for assistance, up to a predetermined limit per annum, these committees can also undertake larger projects such as establishing their own training and learning centres in order to cut down costs and make facilities available for shiftworkers.

Courses under EDAP are not job related and take place in employees' own time; 32 per cent of courses are held on site and employees are also allowed to take non-work-related courses at local authority skill centres and evening classes, including NVQs and degree programmes. Traditionally, over 50 per cent of employees have applied for assistance each year and they receive advice on the most suitable courses from local education advisers funded by the programme. Approximately one-third of applications are for educational courses and one-third for new skills courses such as bricklaying, car maintenance and decorating. The remainder are for courses in health, leisure and hobbies. Although the direct benefits of the scheme accrue to the participants, it is felt that the scheme helps in various ways: to break down barriers within the workforce; to provide a foundation for further joint initiatives between unions and managers; and to make for a healthier and more adaptable workforce (Willoughby, 1996). As we noted in Chapter 2, from an employee's standpoint a new perspective may be beginning to emerge. The pace of change and economic circumstances are gradually bringing the realisation that instead of relying totally on an organisation for their career progression, employees need to manage their own learning in order to gain flexibility and their own portfolios of qualifications, experience and marketable skills.

Paradoxically, whereas a learning culture is necessary for self-managed learning to flourish as a recognised organisational strategy, enthusiasm for learning can become infectious and help to bring about that very culture. Enthusiasm may be generated by a number of individuals or stimulated by organisational intervention such as programmes like those described above. In fact, research at the University of Michigan is being undertaken to investigate the 'spill over' into the wider community by identifying and quantifying the intergenerational effects of learning at Ford (Gibbs *et al*, 1995).

An estimate in July 1995 by the Individual Commitment Division of the Department for Education and Employment was that 350 companies were involved in Employee Development Schemes; the indications are that this figure is already likely to have increased, and with the interest shown by the TECs, LECs and NTOs progress in this direction is gaining momentum.

The decision criteria

Objectives

Although we have argued that objectives should be formulated in terms as precise as possible, it does not necessarily follow that each can be fulfilled by matching it exactly with a particular strategy. Indeed, more that one strategy may be necessary to achieve a single objective. For instance, a junior manager may be unskilled in presenting a persuasive case at committee meetings: one way of bridging this 'gap' might be for him to attend an appropriate course which incorporates suitable skills demonstration and practice sessions; another method might be for a more senior member of management to give him appropriate coaching, followed by on-the-job experience including making presentations at specific meetings. In practice, probably a combination of all three would be useful.

Questions such as the following may assist in determining an appropriate strategy:

- Is the strategy consistent with the organisation's training policy and/or culture?
- Is the objective mainly concerned with long-term career development, or a shorter-term need? For instance, seconding a manager to a long-term part-time course is not likely to be suitable for overcoming his immediate problem of time management, and might even exacerbate it!
- Is the main requirement theoretical knowledge, or is the real need that of a thorough understanding of the organisation's policies and procedures? It has not been uncommon for managers to be sent on external courses covering, for example, principles and practices of marketing, when what is really required is a better understanding of company marketing policies, procedures and objectives. It is acknowledged, however, that a familiarity with general principles helps to set company practices in perspective (and

possibly bring about an improvement in them) and that what is often required is a mixture of both theory and company practice.

- Is the main need really knowledge or practical skill? A course on computing that does not give 'hands on' experience may help to change attitudes and arouse interest for further training, but is unlikely to help the participants with operational skills or overcome possible anxieties about interacting with computers.
- Is part of the training requirement a general understanding and discussion of common problems? An important aspect of training can be an awareness of and sensitivity to the total situation, and although this need might be partially met by dissemination of information, it will almost certainly require some kind of relevant experience – either a problem-solving discussion or possibly brief secondments to other departments. Training can sometimes assume the form of consultation: an example might be when a conference is called with a dual purpose of consultation about the introduction of total quality management, and possibly modifying the original plans as a result, as well as defining the knowledge and skill required to take part in the new style of management. It may be necessary to include general and theoretical material, but the organisational objective would not be met by sending staff individually on external courses.
- Does the objective involve introducing fresh ideas and new perspectives? Would it be best served by contact with people from other organisations, either by external course or visits or secondments?
- Is the objective associated with a need for reinforcement, reward or prestige? Managers have sometimes claimed that they have been offered the chance to attend a course as a reward. In the right circumstances this can be a valid training strategy. It is likely that the manager will approach the training with a favourable mental set and, if impressed, she may give more encouragement to her subordinates to attend courses.

Likelihood of learning transfer

In Chapters 3 and 4 we demonstrated that learning is an inevitable feature of organisational life. The provision of planned training is therefore considered as an intervention into an informal, continuous and powerful learning process, which affects the transfer of learning to the workplace in a way which should not be underestimated. It is not uncommon for staff returning from a course to be greeted with 'You've had your holiday, now get on with your work.' A backlog of problems awaits, and often there is not even an inquiry into whether anything useful was learned, let alone a follow-up session about the implementation of new ideas. Sometimes there might be direct opposition.

On page 74 we referred to barriers to training, and it is certainly necessary to be aware of the many forms these barriers can assume, including inertia, autocratic opposition, bureaucratic procedures, work overload, interpersonal relationships, vested interests, fear of change and insecurity. Such barriers must be taken into consideration when devising a training strategy, as must the overall climate, dominant management culture and style, and sophistication and previous training experience of the organisation. For example, where there has been no previous planned training it might be unwise to start with a sophisticated form of interpersonal skills development for middle-aged supervisors who have been employed in the organisation since leaving school. A short, practical course where the job relevance is easy to determine would probably make a better beginning. They might then be encouraged to ask for further provision. In Chapter 3 we suggested that training might be regarded as the process of opening a door: when it is pushed ajar, it opens up vistas of other rooms with more doors. The view often generates a desire to penetrate further, but before this first door was opened, it was not possible to realise that there was anything beyond. A wise HRD manager will help to facilitate this process.

As a general rule, the more the HRD manager can take part herself in the mainstream organisational activity and can involve the sources of power in the actual training, the greater the likelihood of learning transfer. Examples might be:

- organising learning sessions as an integral part of mainstream events (see example on pages 237 ff)
- emphasising the personal responsibility of managers in training their subordinates (see Chapter 6, pages 122 ff and Chapter 9), and assisting them to do this
- assisting managers to coach their subordinates
- ensuring that managers are directly involved in briefing and debriefing sessions for staff undergoing training
- if the occasion is appropriate, arranging for top management to attend a course first
- developing managers and supervisors as trainers in their own departments
- asking senior managers to lecture or lead sessions on in-house courses
- the use of mentors.

Some of these suggestions may involve training for superiors and achieving a particular objective may initially require an indirect approach.

Available resources

These include such items as:

- accommodation for running internal courses, or environmental constraints such as noise and space, for on-the-job training
- equipment, or availability of money to purchase the hardware and software required for the use of new technology; many organisations have a microcomputer on every desk, providing a ready-made facility for the reception of in-house training programmes
- staff expertise in training techniques (eg coaching, writing programmes, delegating, acting as mentor)
- time span: how much time is available, and must the training be completed to particular deadlines?

- finance: is there a training budget? If so, is each item already allowed for at its expected cost? If not, is contingency money included and available? If not, can money be 'moved' from another use? If not, will the proposal have to wait for the next budget? Or can new finance be specially arranged? If yes, will there be an added cost (eg interest)? The existence or otherwise of a training budget is of considerable importance. (See also 'Training Budget' on pages 193 ff, and the section on costs and benefits of training interventions on pages 195 ff).
- available external help: are there good facilities and staff in local colleges? Is suitable help available from other organisations such as suppliers or professional bodies?
- availability of relevant external courses: some expertise is specific to organisations and is therefore unlikely to be found externally
- availability of external funding (eg in the shape of grants from the local TEC or the European Social Fund).

For a further discussion on resources see Chapter 8.

Learner-related factors

These include the following:

- the experience and current expertise of the learner; superfluous training in aspects well known can result in deteriorating performance through annoyance and boredom. Most computer-managed programmes incorporate pre-tests which enable learners to 'skip' aspects with which they are already familiar.
- learning style: the ultimate aim may well be to encourage employees to use a variety of different learning styles, but in the early stages of training, particularly if the content may be difficult for the learner, it is better to use a mode that appears to accord with his preferred or natural learning style. When attempting to convince trainees of the value of using different learning styles, it is advisable to start with content that is likely to be acceptable. For instance, many managers are interested in finding practical solutions to industrial relations problems. If training is required in this field, it might be useful to start with concrete examples and exercises which purport to find solutions, and subsequently progress to conceptual and theoretical aspects of the role of trade unions. On the other hand, a group of graduates with little or no experience of management might well prefer the sequence reversed. It must also be noted that an overall objective should be to improve learning potential; an understanding of learning styles is one way of achieving this.
- age factor (see also pages 88 ff): older people should not be made to feel inadequate in front of younger people, particularly if they are feeling insecure because they are being retrained in entirely new skills. If, for instance, they have a knowledge deficiency in arithmetic, they may find it more acceptable to undertake a computer-assisted programme or a

distance learning course where they can work in private at their own speed and convenience.

- size of group: this has an obvious influence on the technique to be used. It is not practicable to organise a discussion for one person! Closely associated with group size is the availability of trainees because, although the number may be considerable, if they are separated by geographical location, or shiftworking, the effect may be to reduce numbers available at any one time, and computer-assisted learning or distance learning packages may be suitable. These have the additional advantage of standardising instructions throughout a large organisation. For instance, British Airways uses computer-based sales training, which is fully integrated with the training of booking clerks and includes such tasks as reservations, fare quotation and departure control.
- motivation: the likely attitude towards different styles of learning is relevant here, but other practical factors such as the necessity to be away from home on a residential course should be taken into consideration.

STAGE 3 – PLANNING AND IMPLEMENTATION OF THE TRAINING

Where practicable, it is always advantageous to consult those concerned about the design of their programme; in all circumstances, careful briefing of trainees and their superiors is essential if learning is not to be inhibited by conjectures as to why the training is taking place. Exactly what is involved in planning and

Figure 10.1 Stages in the design of a structured training programme

---

Step 1
Review the training objectives

Step 2
Determine appropriate learning activities

Step 3
Assess training times

Step 4
Construct the timetable

Step 5
Brief the trainers

Step 6
Organise the preparation of material and equipment

---

implementing will depend upon the form of training that has been chosen. Because the most comprehensive preparation is likely to be required in planning an in-house course, we have selected this training strategy for fuller discussion. The steps in the design of a structured in-house course are shown in Figure 10.1.

Designing and planning a structured internal training course

Step 1: Review the training objectives

The objectives, and the knowledge, skill and attitudes required to achieve them, might be regarded as constituting the 'syllabus'. It is necessary to determine which objectives are the most important and therefore where the emphasis of the programme should lie, and then to arrange the material into a suitable sequence. This may be determined purely by logic but attempts should be made at the outset to create interest and utilise the participant's natural curiosity (see Chapter 4). It is important to arrange the material in steps of suitable size for the trainee to master and (unless structured discovery learning is intended) to ensure that the programme proceeds methodically from the known to the unknown and that, where appropriate, each session serves as preparation for and introduction to those which follow.

Although Figure 10.1 does not include any reference to monitoring and evaluating, the point must be made that these activities are intrinsically related to the objectives. At the stage of reviewing the objectives, therefore, prudent trainers are already considering how they will monitor and evaluate. The more specific the objectives the easier these tasks will be.

Step 2: Determine appropriate learning activities

Decide what sessions will be necessary and set sub-objectives for each, anticipating how the attainment of each objective might be evaluated. Determine the most appropriate training technique (or method), bearing in mind that a particularly important objective might require several sessions using a variety of training techniques. For example, during a course on organisational change, one of the objectives might be that the participants should be able to identify the barriers to change. This could be introduced by syndicate discussion sessions, where each participant describes some change he has experienced and indicates areas of concern. Syndicates could then discuss the origin and alleviation of those worries and whether they could have been avoided. A case-study might then follow, allowing participants to apply and reinforce some of their findings and, after discussion of the case, the session might conclude with a short summary of the whole topic, accompanied by a 'handout' of the salient points. The trainer would receive some evaluation of the learning which had taken place by listening to the contributions to the case-study, although there are dangers of evaluating group performance. It might also be possible to use a self-administered test before the final summary session.

The criteria for determining the most suitable training technique for each session are similar to the decision criteria for the strategy (see pages 248 ff).

The following example helps to explain the need for care in the structuring of precise behavioural objectives:

> A group of craft trainees had to learn an electrical coding comprising nine colours, and the job required instant association of a number (one to nine) with a particular colour. The objective would not be met if they learned the sequence of colours by rote, because each time they wanted to pair a colour and a number they would have to repeat the sequence, causing delay and allowing the possibility of error, which could have serious effects on safety. The training technique which was devised consisted of a visual presentation of well-known objects associated with each colour, such as one brown penny or five green fingers. The use of vision and the association with previous knowledge quickly enabled the trainees to learn the information in the exact form in which it was required, a green wire immediately bringing to mind the number five.

The age of the trainees can also influence the suitability of a technique. Belbin and Belbin (1972) discovered that certain methods were more effective than others with older trainees. Discovery learning or forms of 'deductive' learning (ie where the requirement is to reason out the answer) show the best results. Techniques that rely upon memory are not likely to be successful. Unlike older people, younger trainees enjoy a competitive approach, such as a quiz, and prefer frequent changes of topic. The former learn more effectively by concentrating on the same subject matter for longer periods; variety can be introduced by changing the training method. (For a more detailed investigation into methods of training older employees, see Plett and Lester, 1991.)

If course participants are at different levels of ability and have differing degrees of practical experience, then flexible methods, such as computer-assisted learning, or sometimes discussion groups and case-studies, can be useful. Those with experience can be encouraged to assist but not dominate.

Step 3: Assess training times

The time available for each session must be determined: participative methods may be the most effective in enabling learning transfer but they can be time-consuming, and it is therefore practical to employ them for the most important aspects of the training. A further consideration is the time of day of each session; for instance, it may be considered wise to arrange a participative session straight after lunch, or after dinner in the evening of a residential course. Estimating the exact time required for each session is to some extent a matter of trial and error, and the requirements for the same programme can vary for different groups. An experienced course organiser can usually gauge the timing reasonably accurately by consulting with those responsible for the various parts of the training, using the duration of similar programmes as a guide and taking into account the age, experience and motivation of those to be trained.

Step 4: Construct the timetable

The course organiser should ensure that the timetable is flexible enough to be modified if required without affecting the whole programme, and determine the trainers for each session.

Step 5: Brief the trainers

This is an important, and frequently neglected, step in the design process, and misunderstandings can easily arise if the objectives for every section of the programme are not fully discussed and understood. The training technique to be used may well be discussed with the trainer but the final choice cannot be left to her entirely because of the need to obtain an overall balance. It is the course organiser who has to take this overall view. Otherwise, to quote the extreme case, it would be possible for each of several trainers to decide to show a film on the same day. Variety has to be planned: it cannot be left to chance. After briefing, the trainers then prepare the detailed material for their sessions. Information about the use of different training techniques will be found in Appendix 5.

Step 6: Organise the preparation of material and equipment

Professionally prepared programmes, course manuals, log books and other references create a favourable impression. Unprepared or inadequate equipment suggests that the training is of secondary importance, and this can quickly affect the attitude of trainees.

STAGE 4 – EVALUATION OF THE PROGRAMME

Although it is generally accepted that there is a strong case for attempting to evaluate training, particularly in view of the very large sums of money spent on it, the attendant problems often appear insuperable. In fact, evaluation is one of the more difficult of the HRD manager's tasks, but it need not be impossible. Although we are considering it last, it must not be considered as a discrete 'add on' activity. As we pointed out at the beginning of this chapter, consideration must be given to evaluation when originally formulating objectives. It is a well-known truism that people who do not know where they are going can never know when they have reached their destination; on the other hand, precise and well-defined objectives are the key indicators in recognising when one has arrived. Evaluation therefore begins at Step 1.

The first difficulty is that it is necessary to know the exact knowledge and skill of each trainee before the start of the training. Without this information it would be impossible to assess what they have learned at the end. This would necessitate a pre-test, which is practicable in programmed or computer-assisted learning. It becomes more difficult when we consider an in-house course for managers. The first objective of every trainer in that situation is to establish rapport with the course members.

Presenting them with a pre-test, especially if they are unlikely to be able to complete it, is hardly in accord with this aim, nor is it likely to inspire them with confidence and a favourable mental set. Even if a pre-test were to be arranged, it could be argued that participants had learned from the pre-test not the training, and it would therefore really be necessary to set up a number of control groups. This is unlikely to be practicable, and therefore the HRD manager will realise from the outset that she can only do the best that circumstances permit.

A second difficulty is that an ongoing review tends to result in changes to the detail of the programme (and even to some of the objectives) before it can be evaluated.

The questions that need to be answered in evaluating a particular training programme are as follows:

1 Why is the evaluation required?
2 Who should do it?
3 What aspects should be evaluated and when should this be done?
4 What kinds of measurement will be used?
5 When will it be done?

1 Why is the evaluation required?

The answer to this question will affect the appropriate response to the other four. Five main reasons can be given:

- The evaluation enables the effectiveness of an investment in training to be appraised in general terms and provides data that can justify expenditure on training. One of the difficulties in obtaining money for a training budget is that the results are often regarded as intangible, and the training as an act of faith.
- It provides feedback to the trainer about her performance and methods, and is therefore a part of her learning experience.
- It enables improvements to be made, either on the next occasion, or if the evaluation is ongoing, as the training proceeds.
- Reviewing and evaluating his achievement to date is an intrinsic part of the learner's progression round the experiential learning cycle, and therefore should be a part of the learning process itself.
- The evaluation indicates to what extent the objectives have been met, and whether any further training needs remain.

2 Who should carry out the evaluation?

This is a most important decision, as any suspicion of bias can invalidate the results, and also because receiving feedback can be a sensitive issue and may therefore need to be handled with extreme care. As, however, the process is itself a learning experience, it is obviously advantageous to involve those who could learn the most from it.

Tracey (1968) makes the point that:

> Evaluation must be co-operative. A one-man evaluation is little better than no evaluation, regardless of who does it, how competently he does the job, or how valid his findings may be. All who are a part of the process of appraisal, or who are affected by it, must participate in the process.

Obviously the HRD manager, relevant line managers and the learners need to co-operate in the process. However, each will bring a different perspective, and it may well be that the overall responsibility is best vested in a neutral party. This may be difficult, because even external consultants can have their own bias. Whoever takes overall responsibility, it is important that they are seen as impartial, having credible expertise and knowledge of the relevant processes, as well as possessing tact to deal with sensitive issues.

3 What aspects of training should be evaluated and when?

A number of different models have been suggested. The structure we describe below is after Whitelaw (1972) and Hamblin (1974), but for alternatives see Warr, Bird and Rackham (1970) or Jones (1970). See also Bramley (1996). Hamblin and Whitelaw suggest that training can usefully be evaluated at different levels, each of which requires different techniques. An example of this type of model is given below.

Level 1: Reactions of trainees to the content and methods of training, to the trainer and to any other factors perceived as relevant. What did the trainee think about the training?

Level 2: Learning attained during the training period. Did the trainees learn what was intended?

Level 3: Job behaviour in the work environment at the end of the training period. Did the learning transfer to the job?

Level 4: Effect on the trainee's department. Has the training helped departmental performance?

Level 5: The ultimate level. Has the training affected the ultimate well-being of the organisation, for example, in terms of profitability or survival?

It will readily be seen that these are sequential stages in the process: if it is found that behaviour on the job has not changed after training, unless evaluation has been carried out at Level 2 it will not be possible to ascertain whether the failure was due to lack of learning transfer or to the fact that the learning never took place at all. If the evaluation is to perform any of the functions we have outlined then this type of detail is essential.

To facilitate evaluation, it is possible to set objectives at each of these levels. For instance, the objectives of a course providing an introduction to the organisation's networked computing facility might be:

- that participants would recommend the course to their friends and wish to attend a further course themselves. This would involve a favourable 'reactions level' evaluation (Level 1).
- that participants should be competent in the use of a variety of software. This would involve objectives at Level 2.
- that participants should request terminals on their desks and suggest how they could be used to make daily work practices more efficient (Level 3).
- that the introduction of desk terminals for the course participants should result in increased output in the department (Level 4).
- that this increased productivity in the department should contribute to the profitability of the organisation (Level 5).

It will be seen that the easiest levels to evaluate are 1 and 2 and that the process becomes increasingly difficult as Level 5 is approached. This is partly because of difficulties of measurement, but also because the problem of establishing cause and effect. Organisational changes are multi-causal: for example, it is usually impossible to determine how much of an increase in profitability is the result of a specific training intervention. There is also likely to be a time lag between the completion of the training and its effect on the organisation, and the relevant learning may have arisen from a later source. It can be said, however, that the more successful the evaluation at the earlier stages, the more likely is the training to affect overall departmental or organisational performance.

4 What kind of measurement will be used?

Different techniques and yardsticks are appropriate for each level of evaluation.

At Level 1, where an attempt is being made to assess the recipients' reactions to their training, techniques such as questionnaires, interviews, group discussion, individual interview or asking trainees to write a report can be employed. Care must be taken with the timing of these methods. For example, if participants have enjoyed a course, they may finish in a mood of euphoria which may not last after they return to work, and therefore a misleading impression might be conveyed if they are asked to complete a questionnaire at the end of the course (see Easterby-Smith and Tanton, 1985).

Similarly, trainees may not be in a position to know immediately whether what they have learned will be useful. It may be necessary to wait some considerable time before being able to obtain informed opinion. Furthermore, although learning should ideally be a helpful experience, it can at times be painful, and trainees may encounter difficulty or criticism and attempt to divert this to the training activities. If such trainees happen to be the most vociferous during an evaluation discussion, the trainer may obtain a completely false impression. Experienced trainers learn to interpret this type of feedback and to use a series of techniques to obtain their information. For instance, they might use a short questionnaire and/or hold a general discussion, or interview the participants separately after an appropriate length of time has elapsed. Another method is to issue a questionnaire, ask the trainees to complete it, hold their own discussion session and present what they consider to be the most salient points to the trainer.

A number of other indicators can also be used to provide evaluation at this level, including requests from participants for further training, their recommendation to others to follow the same programme, or the return of past trainees for further help and advice. No single one of these can be taken out of context, but they can all assist to confirm or contradict an apparent trend.

At Level 2, the following techniques might be used:

Phased tests, as in craft training

These are beneficial in monitoring progress and providing feedback which can be used to modify the training as it proceeds. In addition, they provide intermediate targets and knowledge of results to trainees.

Final test

Workplace-based tests of competence, such as those required for NVQs, are relevant here, and their incidence is likely to increase as more and more organisations become involved in these qualifications. Because jobs and the contexts in which they are performed are very varied, they can take a number of forms, such as the situation described on page 106, where the learner sends a claim form, and his performance is tested by a visiting assessor.

Final examination

This is still the most common type of evaluation in academic, and some professional, circles, although other types of continuous assessment have gradually been introduced. Final examinations have a number of disadvantages in that they are influenced by the trainee's ability to perform on a few chosen days and may therefore be affected by short-term memory, domestic circumstances or health. It is important that they are designed to incorporate a representative sample of the activities to be evaluated.

Projects

As well as being useful learning methods, these can provide valuable feedback on the ability to apply what has been learned to an organisational problem or issue.

Structured exercises and case-studies

Performance on these can give the trainer indications as to how well people are learning. Structured exercises, such as interviews using closed-circuit television, are particularly helpful because it is possible to watch performance improving as the training progresses, and a record remains for comparison. Many of these activities, however, take place in groups, and the trainer must beware of assuming that because a group has performed well, every member of that group has learned what was intended. One or two members can lead or inspire a group to the extent that it is difficult to realise that some people have contributed little.

Participation in discussion during training

This can be another indicator but requires skilled interpretation, because there can be a variety of reasons trainees remain silent. They may feel over-awed by prominent members of the group, or the entire group atmosphere may be alien to them. It is also possible that they have a different preferred learning style. An experienced trainer tries to interpret the meaning of such a situation and manage it.

Level 3 requires assessment of improved performance on the job. This is easiest in the area of operator training, where before-and-after measures can often be made. It becomes more difficult to evaluate performance further up the organisational hierarchy, where jobs are less prescribed and measurement imprecise. There is also likely to be a time-lag between training and the appearance of indicators of performance improvement. For instance, upon returning to work after attending a course on sales techniques, a salesman may immediately practise what he has learned and sow the seeds of extra future orders. These may not materialise for some time, after which other factors in the situation may have changed – there may have been some alterations to the product – and it is difficult, if not impossible, to attribute cause and effect. Attempts have been made to identify any change of behaviour on the job after the completion of training by questioning supervisors and colleagues. These have yielded some positive results, but must always be open to the criticism that if colleagues are asked to look for behavioural change, the implication has been made, and a mental set established, that would allow the perception (or imagined observation) of factors that otherwise might have passed unnoticed.

In general, it might be said that the more care that has been taken in the assessment of needs and the more precise the objective, the greater will be the possibility of effective evaluation. In the case of the salesman above, rather than an overall objective of increasing his sales it might be possible to be more precise by using sub-objectives such as increasing second sales, or reducing customer complaints directed at staff.

Levels 4 and 5 are the most difficult to evaluate for the reasons given, and also because departmental and organisational results depend upon many people, and it is difficult to apportion improvements to the efforts of specific individuals. Evaluation is therefore often related in a more general way to the health of the organisation. Evidence might be found in: overall profitability; lack of customer complaints; a favourable attitude to training; the standing of the HRD manager and the nature of requests made to her (is she, for example, included in discussion of matters that are central to the organisation?); a system of performance appraisal which works; the availability of suitable people to promote from within; and a proactive labour force which will accept change.

The majority of training in the private and public sectors takes place in a busy working environment, and a rigorous scientific approach to evaluation, involving pre- and post-training tests, control and experimental groups etc., although very desirable, is often not practicable. However, if adequate resources are not made available for evaluation purposes, the effectiveness will remain unchecked.

This dilemma can be resolved to some extent by adopting the following pragmatic approach:

- Set clear training objectives, expressed as far as possible in behavioural terms, or in competences, specifying the performance evidence required and the range (see Figure 6.11).
- Include objectives for each level of evaluation.
- Evaluate systematically at as many levels as practicable to obtain the total picture.

Together, these three steps will go a long way towards helping an organisation maximise its benefit from investment in training.

To return to our case-study at the beginning of the chapter: you should now have a good idea of the kind of decisions that would have to be made and of the alternatives available. The training director's report was accepted and the recommendations successfully implemented as follows:

It was realised from the outset that the support of district and regional managers was vital, and a working party of representatives from these groups and from security staff was appointed. A form of 'cascade' training was agreed upon and the store managers therefore had a key role to play. In reality, this was a very large project and it is not possible to give all the details here. In summary, however, it was agreed that the first requirement was to raise managers' awareness of the problem. Secondly, managers needed to define their own key role in decreasing shrinkage, and identify the specific actions and procedures required to bring about an improvement. They then needed to raise awareness in their staff and encourage and give guidance on good practices. As the managers had little experience in training, they also required some assistance in this direction, and it was decided to produce a special training package for them, as well as material that could be used either as a guide for training their staff or as self-instruction material.

The actual package which was produced consisted of: a video giving practical tips and portraying models of appropriate behaviour; posters made from stills of the video, as a constant reinforcement of the message; a booklet to assist managers to identify problems in the store and draw up appropriate preventative procedures; guidance for managers on introducing the staff package to store assistants; and an individual booklet for staff, including a checklist for regular use.

The training programme consisted of four team-briefing sessions in each store. These took place over a four-week period with store and departmental work and discussions during the intervals. The sessions were carried out by training department staff and store managers. The booklets and training materials were made by desktop publishing in-house, and could therefore be updated when required. The investment was therefore not for a 'one-off' training event, but for material that could be used and modified for many years.

In this particular case the evaluation could be carried out on all of the levels above. A questionnaire at the end of the team-briefings gave the reactions of the participants, and a question-and-answer sheet gave an indication of the learning that had taken place. The shrinkage statistics provided evidence for evaluation at departmental and store level, and the overall improvement in shrinkage costs was reflected in company profitability – Level 5.

This case is based upon, although does not exactly replicate, an assignment undertaken and written up in full detail by Bailey (1991).

FOR FURTHER REFLECTION AND DISCUSSION

1 Describe and critically review a course, conference or other learning event that you have attended, either as organiser or participant, during the past year.

2 Your organisation has recently installed intranet equipment. Prepare a report to the directors assessing its potential for the delivery of in-house training and development, and outline the preparatory steps that would be necessary.

3 Choose either
(a) an aspect of managerial behaviour you would like to eradicate, or
(b) an aspect of managerial behaviour you would like to promote,
and draft a suitable training programme to that end – outlining and justifying the learning methods proposed. How would you evaluate the programme?

4 'The trouble with textbooks and journal articles on the subject of "evaluating training" is that they always take a theoretical, scientific and logical approach which ignores mainstream operational aims.' Comment on this statement, and suggest practical evaluation measures within your organisation which can overcome this criticism.

5 **What information would you seek for evaluation purposes from employees in your organisation who attend external courses? Construct an appropriate questionnaire, and explain how you would expect to use the information it provides.**

6 **You have been asked to design a scheme to enable all employees to pursue development activities of their own choice. In a short report to management, specify:**
   (a) **How the scheme would work, with ground rules**
   (b) **who would determine the ground rules to identify what subject matter is eligible**
   (c) **how much each employee would be able to spend**
   (d) **the expected benefits to your organisation**
   (e) **how you would evaluate the scheme.**

Justify your views.

(IPM Examination, Stage 2, Employee Development, May 1993)

SUGGESTED READING

Appendix 7 of this book.

BRAMLEY P. *Evaluating Training*. Institute of Personnel and Development, London, 1996.

EASTERBY-SMITH M. *and* MACKNESS J. 'Completing the cycle of evaluation'. *Personnel Management*, May, 1992.

FOWLER A. 'How to decide on training methods'. *Personnel Management*, 21 December 1995, pp 36–37.

HARDINGHAM A. *Designing Training*. Institute of Personnel and Development, London, 1996.

MEGGINSON D *and* WHITAKER V. *Cultivating Self-Development*. Institute of Personnel and Development, London, 1996.

PLETT P. *and* LESTER B. *Training for Older People*. International Labour Office, Geneva, 1991.

REID M. A. 'Approaches and strategies', in J. Prior (ed.), *Handbook of Training and Development*, Gower, Aldershot, 1994.

11 Preparing tomorrow's workforce

Workforce entrants – making education more vocational – how far should we go in the vocationalisation of education? – employers and educationalists working together – preparing and welcoming the newcomer

INTRODUCTION

The primary purpose of the new national targets for education and training should be **to make Britain more competitive internationally**. *But they will also play a vital role in* **promoting social cohesion** *(*NACETT *Fast Forward for Skills, 1998).*

Imagine you have been asked to give an address, incorporating the above two themes, to a forum of managers and educationalists. Your title is to be 'Education and Training: aims for the new millennium'. What issues would you raise and what do you see as the implications for your audience? Write down your answers, and later compare them with the content of the chapter you are about to read.

    Background information for this chapter will be found in Chapter 2, and we suggest that you refresh your memory by reading it once more. A national system of vocational courses has been introduced with the aim of providing better preparation for work, and employers and educational institutions are liaising in many ways to help to bridge the gap between education and work. Three main themes emerge and are reflected in this chapter. The first relates to the revision and restructuring of educational provision to make it more vocational. However, altering the structure and content of courses cannot alone achieve the desired result; what is needed is increased understanding, leading to a degree of cultural change in educational institutions, and better preparation of newcomers by employing organisations. The second theme therefore relates to collaborative measures between employers and educational institutions, which are resulting not only in providing students with experience of the working environment, but also opportunities at staff level to help to bring the two cultures of education and work closer together. The final theme becomes that of inducting newcomers, including young people starting national traineeships and modern apprenticeships. Induction is necessary not only to help young people in their transition to work, but for all new starters, and possibly for established employees who move to different departments or sites in the course of their career development.

WORKFORCE ENTRANTS

The structure of employment is changing quickly in directions which make increasing demands upon the labour force. Demand for blue-collar, manual jobs is declining, in favour of white-collar non-manual jobs which require high qualifications (see Figure 11.1).

Figure 11.1 **Change in employment[1] by occupation 1996–2006** (United Kingdom)

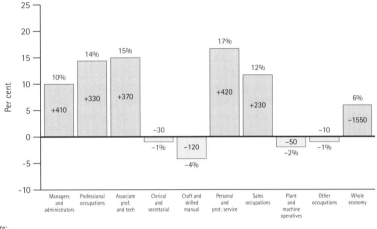

Note:
1 Excludes Armed Forces
2 Figures within bars show absolute change to the nearest 10,000

Source: Business Strategies Ltd, 1996. Reported in the DfEE's *Labour Market and Skill Trends 1997/8.*
© Crown Copyright

There is a decline in production industries, mainly manufacturing, but also agriculture, mining and utilities, (although there is still a need to train some people in these sectors to replace those who leave), and an increase in the service sector. In addition the skill requirement *within* all jobs is rising and there is a move away from manual skills to communication and understanding and monitoring systems. The de-layering which has taken place in many companies, has meant that shopfloor operatives have to show greater initiative and take part in more decisions, and may sometimes have to learn routine engineering or maintenance tasks. There is now a need for flexibility and rapid adaptation to change. The labour force which is required to cope with these developments is changing in structure and has the following characteristics:

- The labour force is growing, but the growth rate is greater for women than for men. Projections vary, but it is generally agreed that during the first decade of the new millennium the number of women in employment is likely to have increased to around 50 per cent of the total.
- Women are much more likely to want part-time work, and the number who have dependent children is increasing.
- The population is ageing. An increasing working population over age 35 is counterbalanced by decreasing numbers in those under that age.

- The numbers of 16-year-olds staying in education continues to increase.
- The share of employees working part time is expected to increase. In 1997, 29 per cent of employees (6.6 million) were part-time, and it is estimated that by 2007 there will be an extra 600,000 part-time workers, about three-quarters of whom will be women. This is part of a wider trend towards progressively greater flexibility of employment through the use of temporary and part-time workers, variation of hours worked, and greater ability to switch staff between different tasks.
- The number of people with no significant skills still gives cause for concern. Research reported in *Skill Needs in Britain 1997*, indicated that over a third of establishments employing people aged 16–19 thought there was a skills gap among this group. The main skills that younger employees appear to lack are general communication skills, practical skills, customer handling skills, and personal skills. (Reported in *Labour Market and Skill Trends 1998/9*, from which much of the information for this whole section is derived.)

Women entrants (and re-entrants) to the employment market

Women are much more likely to want part-time work, and an increasing number have dependent children and some will be lone parents. Women have traditionally been employed in a narrow range of industries, and there is much unrealised potential: they are significantly underrepresented in managerial positions, in many professional occupations and at technician level in a wide range of jobs. It has been suggested that the process of de-layering has resulted in fewer women in management because of a tendency to cut out the middle level.

Many women are returning after a career break to bring up a family. Some may have had little or no working experience and may be apprehensive about entering a totally different environment, and careful induction is needed. Flexible learning provision will increasingly be required so that it can be combined with domestic responsibilities. Courses at the Open University or Open College will be helpful in this respect, as will self-learning materials, technology-assisted learning, distance learning, and open access programmes of all kinds. The free telephone 'Learning Direct', or the 'University for Industry' (see Chapter 1 and Appendix 2) may be very useful in helping women to find flexible learning courses most suited to their needs. If, during their previous education, the new entrants have 'learned to learn' then the task will be much easier. For this and many other reasons a 'learning to learn culture' is rapidly becoming an essential requirement of modern life.

Flexible arrangements will also be required to cope with career breaks. Some organisations already have internal schemes to enable women to return for short periods to update themselves and maintain their skills during a career break. Corresponding educational facilities will be needed, including part-time work experience. Courses that can be undertaken *during* the career break would be welcomed by the women concerned and would assist the quickest possible return to work.

Many women will have received vocational education earlier in their lives and/or will have work experience. Although they may need refresher and updating courses in certain aspects, they will not necessarily require to undertake a whole programme from beginning to end. Courses that have rigid entry requirements, and offer no facility for accrediting previous experience or learning, are likely to be unsuitable, prolonging the necessary education and training time, as well as running great risks of boring the participants. The national framework provided by NVQs (see Chapters 2 and 5 and Appendix 4) together with the flexibility of CATS and APL schemes (see page 272), which afford facilities for the accreditation of appropriate prior learning or prior experience, should go a long way towards helping vocational education meet the needs of these women. Financial assistance in the form of career and development loans, which provide an interest-free 'holiday' are available to encourage people of both sexes to invest in their own training. The government's National Childcare Strategy under which tax credits are available to low-income working families from April 1999, as well as increased provision of childcare places and help with childcare costs, should also be of assistance.

Lone parents

Under the New Deal for Lone Parents on income support a personal adviser contacts all lone parents whose youngest child has reached the second term of full-time education, to assist in job search, and accessing appropriate training.

Disabled people

The main provisions of the Disability Discrimination Act are now in force and should extend the number of disabled people in the labour market. For a brief summary of the employer's legal obligations relating to training, see Chapter 7.

Older workers

By 2002 the percentage of people of working age over 35 is projected to increase by 1.4 million, or over 8 per cent. A significant number of people over 65 remain in the labour force; the figure for 1997 was 408,000 and it is forecast to increase marginally to 410,000 by 2002 (*Labour Market and Skill Trends 1998/99*). Although they are a valuable source of skills and experience, older people tend to be less qualified, their qualifications are often outdated, and overall they receive less training. 'Downsizing' during the 1990s often involved early retirements, resulting in a considerable number of people looking for 'post-first retirement' jobs. There is a need for others to create jobs for these early pensioners, a striking example being a large self-service DIY chain store which opened one branch staffed entirely by people over 50, and has found the experiment extremely successful. The new workers were found to be better at product knowledge and customer care than their younger counterparts in other stores, and there was less incidence of absenteeism and labour turnover (Hogarth and Barth 1991; Worsley, 1996) Some of these 'older returnees' may reappear in the educational system (possibly to take NVQs as an addition to existing qualifications). They are also likely to require flexible programmes, which they can carry out at their own pace, and through which they can be credited for prior experience and knowledge.

A discussion on special methods for training older people will be found in Chapter 4. See also Plett and Lester (1991).

Young people

Young people represent an investment in the future. In these days of rapidly changing technology, they are an important source of new skills and can bring energy and ideas into an organisation and rejuvenate an ageing labour force. They represent an invaluable resource which the nation cannot afford to underutilise, but those with no qualifications are likely to find the job market difficult. Quality education and training for young people has a critical role to play in ensuring that the skills and international competitiveness of our workforce will continue to improve, and the National Learning Targets (see Chapter 2) provide a stimulus to this end. Fortunately, the proportion of young people participating in education beyond the statutory school leaving age has been increasing (see Figure 11.2).

Figure 11.2 Destination of school leavers

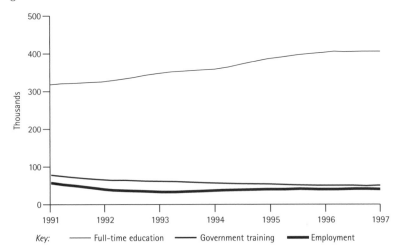

Key: ——— Full-time education ——— Government training ━━━Employment

Note:
During this period, a majority of 16-year-olds from independent schools were not included on careers service records. Other groups which may not be included are those not in school in Year 11, those switching school, and those recently arrived from abroad.

Source: Careers Service. Reported in the DfEE's *Labour Market and Skill Trends 1997/8*.
© Crown Copyright

Those continuing in full-time training are drawn from the entire ability range. The levels of qualification attained by those staying in compulsory education continues to rise, but the fact that two-thirds of 16-year-olds do not achieve a GCSE grade C or above in maths and English (two of the key skills stressed by employers), gives rise to considerable concern, as well as the revelation that one in 12 attains no GCSEs at all. Proposals to overcome these problems include: taking steps to ensure that each pupil acquires the basic skills of numeracy and literacy at an early stage; improving the quality of teaching; involving parents and local communities in education. Some new FE centres are concentrating on new methods, such as group projects and computer-based methods, for underachieving students.

Of all 16–17-year-olds in full-time state education, 57 per cent were in further education in 1997/8 (*Labour Market & Skill Trends 1998/9*). The range of post-16 educational courses is broadening, and much of the growth in full-time education is accounted for by vocational courses. GNVQs are an important factor, and in 1995/96 185,000 students had registered for these courses, the vast majority being 16–19-year-olds. The proportion of young people taking only GCSEs post-16 has fallen rapidly and vocational courses are seen by young people as a more attractive option than GCSE resits (*Labour Market and Skill Trends 1997/8*). A major recommendation of the Dearing Report (1996) was that vocational and academic courses should enjoy equal status, and it is hoped that the national vocational awards will help to bring this about. The majority of schools and colleges can now offer GNVQs (see Chapter 2 and Appendix 4) at Intermediate and Advanced Levels, equivalent to NVQ Levels 1 and 2.

MAKING EDUCATION MORE VOCATIONAL

The field of vocational education and training is vast and rapidly developing, and here we can do no more than outline the main trends and emergent issues. You are recommended to update constantly by means of newspapers and journal reports.

The National Curriculum

Under the Education Reform Act 1988 the National Curriculum for state schools in England and Wales is prescribed by the Secretary of State for Education and Employment, who consults and is advised by the Qualifications and Curriculum Authority. The aim is to give pupils adequate preparation for adult life (including *working* life) by providing a broad and balanced framework of study for all throughout the whole period of compulsory education, and the Curriculum sets out what children should be able to do at each key stage from age 5 to 16. (The system in Scotland is somewhat different and has its own overseeing body.)

In England and Wales, the curriculum is made up of Core Subjects (science, mathematics and English) and Other Foundation subjects (such as design and technology, information and communications technology, a modern foreign language, and physical education). With the addition of religious education and sex education, this work takes about 60 per cent of teaching time, leaving 40 per cent for options. For each subject there are:

- *levels of attainment*, or end of key stage descriptions, which define the knowledge expected of pupils at each level or stage
- *programmes of study*, which detail what pupils should be taught in order to reach the levels
- *statutory assessment at the ages of 7, 11 and 14*, which is based on the levels as they are defined in the National Curriculum. There were originally 10 levels, but the Dearing Reports (1993 and 1994) have resulted in changes in the way that the attainment levels and programmes of study are defined for each subject. As well as evaluating progress, it is intended that the assessments will be diagnostic in that they will pinpoint where pupils need help.

In addition, five focal themes are seen as essential:

1 economic and industrial understanding
2 careers education and guidance (including a period of work experience)
3 health education
4 education for citizenship
5 environmental education.

The National Record of Achievement (NRA)

The NRA was introduced in 1991 with the idea that it should be maintained for every pupil whose property it would be. It contains a record of main assessments and also an account of experience and attainments written by the owner. It is available for inspection by prospective employers and should provide information about attainment and all-round performance, and is intended to be continued into adulthood, thus providing a lifelong record of achievement in education, training and employment. Following the Dearing Report (1996), a comprehensive review of the NRA was undertaken which concluded that the new Record should be simple to keep, and support materials should be provided to help users review and record their personal achievements, set targets, plan, and seek appropriate advice. The resulting new materials, under the name of *Progress File*, give individuals much more responsibility to plan and manage their own lifelong learning. Trials are still taking place, and it is planned to make the materials available to schools in the form of a CD-ROM.

National developments in further and higher education

A few years ago it would have been possible to structure discussion of education under neat headings such as 'Initial Full-Time Education' and 'Further and Higher Education'; the flexibility of today's system no longer makes this possible. For instance, the work of the Qualifications and Curriculum Authority ranges from schools to colleges. General NVQs can be taken in schools or by students in colleges of further education or in adult education institutes; most vocational courses can now be pursued on a part-time basis while working, or by studying full-time. Boundaries are becoming blurred and some of the features of Further and Higher Education that we shall describe below are also applicable to the National Curriculum. The term 'Further and Higher Education' can be used in a general sense to cover all post-school education. Accessibility to learning facilities is an essential ingredient of continuing development and the flexible system (full-time, part-time, distance and self-managed learning) allows people to acquire whatever level of qualifications their abilities, time and motivation permit.

Many students take advantage of part-time or distance learning facilities, which enable them to complement their employment with relevant study. The employer's support is of the utmost importance; this can include the granting of day release and the facilities to undertake a work-based project, but of equal importance (often not realised by employers) is the *interest* shown by management. Imagine undertaking a year's work-related course, either by day release or in your own time in the evenings, and your own manager giving the impression of having no interest! Attempting to integrate learning with the work environment or with general career planning is also critical, and will usually cost very little; it will not only make the educational programme more effective, but will help to retain the employee afterwards. As well as discussing progress with students, employers/managers can contact tutors, or in many cases can attend 'open days' or sponsors' evenings when they can also meet other participants on the programme. They can often offer useful visits of students to their premises to discuss aspects of particular interest.

The range of post-16 educational courses is broadening and much of the growth is accounted for by vocational courses. A number of common themes can be observed, which include:

- the provision of many diverse qualifications within a co-ordinated national framework within defined levels, subject to one Qualification and Curriculum Authority (see Chapter 2)
- the necessity for an education system that imparts the knowledge and skills required for adult life and a competitive workforce
- desire for parity of esteem of academic and vocational qualifications
- transfer of credits from one programme to another (CATS – details given below)
- accreditation of prior learning and experience (APL and APEL details given below)
- assessment based on targets and outcomes
- records of achievement
- work experience for all
- change in orientation from academic to workplace-led programmes and qualifications

- more collaboration between educationalists and employers, and greater opportunity for the latter to influence and become involved in national training and education schemes.

In the following sections we outline ways in which some of the above requirements are being achieved.

Credit Accumulated Transfer Scheme (CATS)

This is a national scheme to ease progression from one programme to another, by which specific courses (ie qualifications or parts of qualifications), may be given a credit rating towards exemption from similar content on other programmes. These credits may be transferable from one institution to another. It is for individual institutions to decide precisely how many credits are given for any specific qualification, but the candidate may be required to 'confirm' the notional points score by undertaking a 'portfolio exercise' as determined by the institution to which application is being made.

Accreditation of Prior Learning (APL)

There is now greater readiness on the part of further and higher educational institutions to take account of prior learning, thus avoiding situations where students are obliged to cover the same ground twice. There are two forms of recognition:

- Accreditation of Prior Learning based on evidence of successful completion of a relevant formal programme (APL)
- Accreditation of Prior Experiential Learning (APEL) based on evidence of learning through work experience. This evidence will normally consist of a portfolio of relevant documents and may also include such written assignments relating to work experience as the educational institutional concerned deems relevant.

Both APL and APEL enable students to gain exempting credits (entry with advanced standing) on many degree courses. Some professional bodies are co-operating to link APEL with second degrees and professional qualifications. Accreditation of prior learning can also apply, where appropriate, to entrants on NVQ programmes. These schemes, as well as the provisions under CATS, are in harmony with the concepts of continuous development and continuing professional development, and make further and higher education more accessible and attractive to adults.

Assessment based on targets and outcomes

The way in which performance on many formal courses is assessed has gradually been changing, so that rather than a pass or fail, or an overall grade, they give more detailed indication of what the student can actually do. Older traditional forms of assessment might be described as 'norm-referencing', because the results would be expected to conform more or less according to a normal curve of distribution (where the majority cluster around the average – small numbers obtaining either very high or very low marks). Although these systems afford the facility of comparing trainees with each other or with a given standard, they provide a general grading rather than a clear picture of where strengths and weaknesses lie. The extreme case might be where one student obtains a first-class honours degree and another student obtains a third-class degree; an employer might judge the first student to be a better resource than the second. It is, however, still not apparent what either student can actually do; the second student might have other attributes, such as self-presentation skills, that might make him a better choice for an appointment in sales management than the student with first-class honours. Leading graduate recruiters have called for the existing system of degree classification to be scrapped and replaced with more detailed grades of skills and achievements, describing the current system of rating the quality of degree as 'outmoded and discredited' and are pressing for ratings that give a clear indication of the standard of academic study, core business skills, the outcome of their work experience and what the degree means (Welch 1997).

In contrast to the traditional method of 'norm-referencing', 'criterion-referenced' assessment gives more detailed information. It involves assessing the performance of trainees, pupils or students on a number of specified dimensions. These may be competencies (such as leadership, tolerance of stress, negotiation) or outcomes (such as ability to use a micrometer or to operate a duplicating machine). The assessment may consist of awarding a grade for each dimension, which can then be recorded on a 'profile'. Ideally, learners should draw up their own profiles, which should be completed with more than one tutor or workplace supervisor in more than one context (eg shopfloor, classroom, lecture room). In this way the 'profile' serves both as a record and a learning tool. The ability to evaluate one's own strengths and weaknesses might be regarded as one of the essentials of self-development. A useful dimension of the assessment profile is 'the ability to learn new competences', which is of interest to any prospective employer.

Criterion-referenced assessment requires explicit trainee/pupil objectives. In the case of the National Curriculum, these are expressed as targets in the form of standard assessment tasks for each level, and assessment takes the form of assigning one of 10 grades. In the NVQ context, what is assessed is stated in terms of competence, performance criteria and range statements, which give details of the conditions under which the competence is to be measured. Those conditions are designed to equate as closely as possible with those of the working environment under which the activity normally takes place. Although this is a laudable concept, its implementation is not without its problems. The implication is that assessment will be delivered locally, but as the context of the working environment can vary greatly from one organisation to another, the achievement of national standards at the workplace might be disputed, and there is no guarantee that all supervisors/managers will be impartial, and external verification is likely to be expensive. Assessment bodies require those who are to undertake the assessment to be properly trained to do so; this can be an expensive undertaking.

Change in orientation from academic to workplace-led programmes and qualifications

One example of a new approach to higher education based on a partnership between education and industry is being piloted in Leeds. Entitled 'Learning Power', it is offered by the Leeds TEC and the two local universities; it is not a taught course, each learner agreeing a flexible programme specially tailored to meet individual needs, and involving a wide variety of learning methods. Credit can be given for previous experience and learning through APL and APEL. The focus is on live work-based projects, supervised by an appropriate university specialist and a workplace mentor, and students are encouraged to make use of 'learning sets'. They must also compile a portfolio of learning. All university facilities are available to them and the programmes can lead to full university awards at all levels from Certificate of HE to Masters Degree. At the present time the scheme is a local pilot, but it is attracting considerable national attention.

HOW FAR SHOULD WE GO IN THE VOCATIONALISATION OF EDUCATION?

There is no doubt that changes were needed within the educational system to prepare young people for work in a modern environment. The quality of life in the UK depends upon competitive firms to provide good jobs for everyone, and a well-trained and efficient labour force, where continuous learning is the norm, is a main ingredient for this success. It is not acceptable to have school leavers who have not acquired basic skills such as numeracy, literacy and information technology, which are necessary to hold their own in modern society. Young untrained people are particularly vulnerable to unemployment; in times of high skills shortages, the country cannot afford to waste this resource, and in times of recession, the social consequences of sizeable numbers of unemployed youngsters cannot be contemplated. No longer are people employed for their muscle power or manual dexterity alone, globalisation, downsizing and technological change have brought about a situation where it is not sufficient to have a well educated élite; *all* young people must have adequate preparation. At the higher educational level, employers have expressed their concerns about the value of degrees and have called for a 'revamp of the system to make common competences a fundamental part of passing the test' (Welch, 1997). A recent survey shows that graduates have high job and career expectations, but employers continue to complain that university leavers have little general business knowledge, and lack communication and IT skills. (Prickett 1998). The Dearing Committee into Higher Education (1997) believed that this issue should be addressed and that the four key skills of communication, numeracy, IT skills and the ability to learn should be integrated long-term to the higher education curriculum. In Chapter 2 we point out the very high percentage of small firms and medium-sized firms, and this is where most employment growth is likely to be. Graduates entering small organisations are likely to be required to make a useful contribution straight away, and key skills are likely to be prerequisites. In addition, higher education needs to stimulate graduates to become entrepreneurs and equip them to start up a business.

There is, however, another side of the coin; the definition of education on page 7 draws attention to the wide function of education, and one can argue that its prime function is to produce good citizens who, as well as being highly employable, can also use their increasing spare time wisely and, if necessary, can stand back and indulge in healthy criticism of organisations and institutions, and can also pose pertinent questions and cope with a changing environment. Reg Revans (1983) argues that in times of change when no one knows what to do, one needs not only what he describes as 'programmed knowledge' (P), but questioning ability (Q) and the skills to explore the possible answers. In our next chapter we develop the theme that employees who concentrate solely on the efficient maintenance of the *status quo* are 'yesterday's men', and we elaborate on the theory of 'reflection in action'. One can ask whether learning to attain NVQ competences derived from functional analysis (basically of the *status quo*), and teaching taking place in schools that are judged and rated publicly on their ability to 'get pupils through' prescribed tests, are actually good preparation for this creativity and initiative. Individuals need to be able to think flexibly and across traditional disciplinary boundaries, which is an argument for a broadly based education and an increase in the range of interdisciplinary studies. This country has always been famous for its inventors and creators and one wonders, for instance, whether NVQs would have helped the young Isaac Newton to question why the apple fell to the ground? In Appendix 4 we outline a number of worrying criticisms of NVQs. Not least of these is that they emphasise the ability to perform a given task at a particular time, and tend to neglect the background knowledge and concepts that might help the learning to transfer to different times and places. This point is perhaps exaggerated in the comment of the owner of a large food store, whose praise of the new NVQ system included the following remark – 'We don't teach people *about* meat any more: we teach them how to use the bacon-slicer!'

Furthermore, we have stressed in many parts of this book that the employee of the twenty-first century will have to have 'learned to learn'. This can be a function not just of *content* of syllabuses, but the *way in which* that content has been learned. The preoccupation with test results and targets does not appear to encourage attention to this fact. The concept of learning organisations has been proffered for some time, but there are still comparatively few real learning organisations to be found. One of the reasons for this is the lack of the necessary skills and methodologies to create such cultures. We give a few suggestions to this end in Chapter 12. Such skills and thought patterns are unlikely to be engendered by narrow vocational education.

Mistakes may have been made in the past, and some spheres of education may have tended to isolate students from the needs of industry, instead of encouraging them to take part in the creation of national wealth (on which, in the last analysis, our educational institutions rely for their own funding). However, an ability to think for themselves, to question, to think laterally and creatively, and to research, are all requisites of tomorrow's workers, and it can be argued that a broader education would provide wider perspectives, enabling employees to look at their jobs from the outside and take a more balanced view. We must not lose sight of the fact that academic education directed at making people *think* is an invaluable asset. In making education more vocational it is important not to throw the baby out with the bathwater, and we must constantly bear in mind that tomorrow's citizens will require more than the sum of a collection of workplace competences.

EMPLOYERS AND EDUCATIONALISTS WORKING TOGETHER

The recent revisions to the structure and content of courses aim to make education a better preparation for working life, but full benefit will not be obtained without a change of ethos. Although it is neither practicable nor desirable for the cultures of education and the working environment to be exactly the same, one way of assisting to bridge the gap between school and work is to bring these cultures closer together. In further and higher education greater collaboration can ensure that course design keeps pace with the changing demands of employment. However, the need is not totally one-sided; a better understanding of the educational system, the teaching/learning methods used and the objectives of tutors is helpful to employers in recruitment policies as well as in formulating realistic expectations of new entrants and providing appropriate initial training and induction programmes. At another level there is potential benefit to both parties from collaborating in research to solve organisational or industry-wide problems, particularly at the 'leading edge'. Universities and colleges can be particularly helpful to small and medium-sized business in terms of advice, research or use of facilities. On a local basis there are numerous examples of partnerships between educational institutions and industrial and commercial organisations, many initiated and sometimes pump-primed by local TECs to meet the specific needs of the locality. Education Business Partnerships (EBPs) have been set up throughout the country to bring education and business closer together in ways that best meet local needs, and in 1995 the National Business Education Partnership Network was established to promote and give greater coherence to the work of the EPBs. We give below a few examples of the ways in which the gaps between educational institutions and employing organisations are being bridged.

Work-related experience

This can take a variety of forms, some examples of which are given below:

- visits to organisations by individuals or groups
- assignments, projects and research
- work shadowing (See Appendix 2)
- compacts (See Appendix 2)
- teaching companies (See Appendix 2)
- sessions in school or college by staff from organisations acting as visiting lecturers.

These activities can be time-consuming and the benefit gained from them is likely to be in proportion to the quality of preparation beforehand by *both* parties. For instance, it is unlikely that a group of schoolchildren who have received no prior briefing will have a profitable experience from a 'standard' organisation visit, where no effort is made to consider their particular needs. How much better it would be to lead up to such a visit by integrating it with other aspects of the curriculum, providing lead-in sessions beforehand, working with the host organisation to define exactly what is required from the visit, and following up with a debriefing session. Similarly, careful discussion is required as to what help or facilities will be provided when a student undertakes a project in a host organisation, and a visiting lecturer needs to be briefed very carefully about what it is hoped to gain from his or her session.

Work experience

Work experience is distinguished from work-related experience in that the student actually carries out the job as closely as possible to the conditions in which an employee would work, although the emphasis is obviously on educational aspects. If carefully planned, supervised and debriefed there is no doubt about its value. Since 1997/98 all pupils in their final compulsory year at school have been entitled to two weeks' work experience (*Labour Market and Skill Trends 1997/8*) and many programmes and sandwich courses require much longer periods. The Dearing Report of the National Committee of Enquiry into Higher Education (July 1997) recommended that the government should work 'with representative employer and professional organisations to encourage employers to offer more work experience opportunities for students'. In 1998 a new National Centre for Work Experience was launched. It is a subsidiary company of the Council for Industry and Higher Education and aims to promote and support work experience for the benefit of students, organisations and the economy. It also hopes to bring about greater recognition in the academic world of various ways in which students can obtain experience of the working world. However, although work experience is a commendable inclusion in the educational curriculum, it is not an easy option. To be successful it demands careful planning, time and resources from the host organisation and the young person's tutor. Timescales for placements, realistic objectives, work programmes, visits by the college tutor during the placement, discussion time with the student and evaluation, all have to be agreed, and some large organisations have found it necessary to appoint a work experience tutor or co-ordinator. The (former) Institute of Personnel Management (since 1994 the IPD) urged its members to manage work experience professionally by taking the following steps:

- finding out about the programme of which the work experience will form a part
- setting learning objectives for work experience in collaboration with the young person's tutor
- bringing young people together for common briefing sessions, eg induction which is essential – particularly the health and safety items. (See Chapter 3)
- reviewing the work experience against the learning objectives at the end of the placement
- producing written material to avoid duplicating instruction
- updating the work programme continuously in the light of experience.

The attitude and commitment of teaching staff is of prime importance, and proper time allowance must be allocated for initial discussions with the student and the host organisation, and for appropriate follow-up. Unless students have a very clear idea of what they are trying to gain, there is a great danger that within the short time available they will obtain a superficial impression or will not take the opportunity seriously. Some programmes require work experience overseas, and with increasing globalisation this requirement may become more commonplace; such placements require even more care in preparation and monitoring. Work experience is increasingly in demand for teachers and tutors, but the timing can cause particular difficulty for employers if there are only certain times of the year, such as school holidays, when they can be spared. There have been a number of imaginative developments, such as offering places on company management development schemes to head teachers, and some Compact schemes (see Appendix 2) include placements for teachers.

PREPARING AND WELCOMING THE NEWCOMER

Careers guidance

Careers Services exist to provide guidance to individuals in matching their ambitions and skills to suitable occupations. The White Paper *Competitiveness: Helping business to win* (HMSO 1994) specifies that young people have an 'entitlement' to careers guidance and that advice should be given at ages 13, 15 and 17 for those still in full-time education. The Green Paper *The Learning Age: A renaissance for a new Britain* (DfEE (6)) stresses the importance of careers advice for lifelong learning, and government programmes have set aside funds to improve this service by increasing the numbers of careers advisers and providing training and updating. Flexible and innovative methods of delivery have also been used, including group discussions for young people, action plans and planned programmes of career education. Careers education takes place in schools and the careers libraries initiative helps schools update their careers information. The 'Progress File' CD-ROM mentioned on page 270, currently being piloted in schools, embraces the much wider area of careers education and guidance and includes material on careers information and effective action planning. In addition, the TECs, with assistance from government, created around 3,000 Training Access Points to provide information on learning opportunities, and the free national telephone helpline 'Learning Direct' (see Appendix 2) is also available. Provision for special groups of people, such as lone parents, or those under the New Deal (details of which are given in Chapter 2), include the service of a personal adviser.

National Traineeships

Following the recommendations of the Dearing (1996) report, National Traineeships have replaced the former Youth Training. These offer work-based training up to NVQ Level 2, normally to people within the 16–18 age range. The National Training Organisations, which have representatives from both large and small organisations, design the structured framework and standards for each industry. National Traineeship frameworks are now available in most of the main industrial and service sectors. Prospective employers work with their local TEC and training providers to determine what form the young person's training will take to meet both the standards and the needs of the business. The local TEC may provide financial support to help pay for the training provided. Where the organisation has a qualified assessor, the assessment can take place in-house, or a number of organisations can pool resources and employ or train their own assessor. Alternatively, the assessment can be made by a local college or training provider. This is a flexible system designed to suit small companies as well as large ones. Trainees under this scheme can also carry on to modern apprenticeships.

Modern apprenticeships

Modern apprenticeships should not be confused with the old-style time-served schemes associated primarily with manufacturing and construction. The old schemes existed for a very limited range of occupations and many were unsatisfactory for a variety of reasons. The result was that overall the UK compared very badly with its competitors in the supply of skills at craft, technician and supervisory level. The advent of new technology brought the need for additional skills, and de-layering in many organisations increased the importance of this intermediate level. The new schemes were introduced nationally in September 1995 as a major initiative to remedy the situation by providing employer-based learning to NVQ level 3 or above for young people. The schemes have been developed by TECs throughout the UK working with NTOs and employers in a wide range of industrial and commercial sectors to develop their respective sector models based on a common framework of core criteria to ensure quality and consistency.

Training – contents and outcomes

Training must lead to an NVQ at Level 3 or above and provide for breadth and flexibility according to sector and employer needs, drawing on units from related GNVQ or NVQs to make a modular structure. Sectors also allowed for multi-skill schemes. The core content emphasises standards of literacy and numeracy as well as job-specific and technical skills and broad occupational knowledge. Problem-solving, the ability to get on with people, assuming responsibility and selling ideas are also prominent. There is no time serving: training outcomes are achieved in the shortest and most realistic timescales and progress is measured by target milestones.

Trainees – rights and expectations

The programme provides equal opportunities for both sexes. The normal age range is 16–24. There must be a written 'pledge' between the employer and the young person underwritten by the appropriate TEC. Apprentices normally have full-employed status, although in a small minority of industries there can be exceptions.

Progress to date

Modern Apprenticeships are currently available in some 80 areas across a wide span of industry and commerce, as the following examples show: marine engineering, craft baking, floristry, horse industry, electricity supply, electronic systems service, banking service, insurance, and museums, gallery and heritage sector. 'Employer Case Studies' [DfEE 1998 (10)] demonstrate the possibility for flexibility and innovation. For instance, the steel industry has devised two types of modern apprenticeship; 'Model A' is job-focused to produce multi-skilled operatives, generally in production, technical, or engineering. 'Model B' covers elements of production, technical, engineering, sales, marketing and administration. At Tinsley Wire, a company which helped to pilot the 'Model B' scheme, it is felt that people who go down this route are more likely to become future team leaders and middle managers. The apprentices start with a 14-week induction course, which includes health and safety procedures, as well as knowledge of all the company's departments. In the next stage they learn to operate machines and to control processes, and spend time in marketing, planning and accounts. They then specialise in production, business administration, sales or technical, and undertake the Steel Industry Operations NVQ Level 3. One of the key partners in the Steel NTO acts as overall manager in its member companies, providing any external training required and assessment for the key skills. An important feature of the programme is that each apprentice has his or her own in-house mentor, (a senior manager).

By way of contrast, the owner of a floristry business consisting of three shops, has four apprentices undertaking a programme including both the retail aspects and floristry. It is estimated that the programme will take a school-leaver three or four years before reaching the level of NVQ 3. A local college provides support in units such as key skills and amenity horticulture, which the staff are unable to teach in-house. Two members of staff are training to become assessors, one in retail and the other in floristry. The local TEC provides some funding, and it is hoped to use this to send the apprentices to flower schools in Holland. They regularly go to Covent Garden Market to help with the buying, and have had the opportunity to help with the Chelsea Flower Show.

There are many more examples from small and large organisations, from the apprentice stonemasons at the works department of a cathedral, to the apprentices at London Broncos Rugby League Football Club, or the business administration apprentices working for a chartered accountant who is prepared to support them beyond NVQ Level 3 to train as accounting technicians. The modern apprenticeship scheme is flexible and can be adapted to suit the needs of small and large organisations, in many types of industries, as well as the specific interests of the trainees.

Induction

Although all the measures we have described help to reduce the gap between education and work, the way in which new entrants are received into an organisation remains a critical factor in forming their attitudes and ensuring that they reach the desired standard of performance as quickly as possible. The process of induction begins with the initial contact between the new employee and the organisation, as this is when first impressions are formed which can be long lasting; induction can thus be considered as including the whole of the recruitment process. This includes recruitment literature, which should be well-produced, attractive, but realistic and truthful, to avoid later disappointment and the creation of negative attitudes, as well as to everything pertaining to the interview process and its ambience. Our main concern here, however, is with welcoming the new employees into the organisation and department, ensuring that they understand core information about the job and its environment, and helping them into their new jobs. Thus it is the one type of training necessary for all types and levels of newcomers, whether young or old, qualified or unqualified, whether they are recruits or have changed their work within the same organisation. Labour turnover is frequently highest among those who have recently joined an organisation and the term 'induction crisis' is used to describe the critical period when new starters are most likely to leave. A well-planned induction programme can help to decrease labour turnover by ensuring that new starters settle quickly in their jobs and reach an efficient standard of performance as soon as possible.

Legislation – for example in the field of health and safety – has caused employers to review the content and effectiveness of their induction arrangements and these reviews have led to two major conclusions. An awareness that the traditional 'standardised' induction course which all employees attend often disregards the particular needs of special groups such as school leavers, national trainees, immigrants, the disabled, adults being trained for new jobs, managers and work-experience students. Although such staff will share some common induction needs, their programmes must also reflect the differences and, as a result, should vary in both content and duration from one category to another.

The wider induction objectives for young people cannot be achieved in an initial short course of training. The following quotation from the MSC (1975) study on the vocational preparation of young people is still highly relevant:

> What is needed . . . is a personnel policy specifically for young entrants which recognises the special problems they face in the transition to the new environment of adult working life, at a time when they are also experiencing the personal problems of growing up. Such a policy would reflect awareness of the teaching methods in use in schools, the common attitudes of young people towards work and the community; their ideals and expectations; the difficulties faced by young people in . . . adapting to working life, in working with older people and in understanding and accepting the discipline of the workplace. Particular attention would be given to trying to see that those close to the entrants, particularly their supervisors and workmates were able to guide them in their development, both as individuals and as capable members of the working community, and that the young people themselves know where they can go to get advice whenever they need it.

From this it follows that induction cannot be fully carried out by the HRD specialist or central HR department alone, but must be an overall managerial responsibility. Many induction needs are concerned with the immediate working environment; a most important part must be played by superiors and those working in the vicinity. For these reasons, induction should be regarded as an integral part of the corporate training plan and its importance should be stressed in the training given to all employees, and especially to managers and supervisors.

The following list indicates the types of material that are likely to be generally relevant to newcomers:

- *conditions of employment:* the contract of employment, payment procedures, holiday arrangements, relevant legislation, absence and sickness procedures, meal and tea breaks, disciplinary procedures. Care should be taken to ensure that new employees really understand these matters, and that they sign a document verifying that they have read any relevant matter. This is important not only for the welfare of the employee, but from an organisational perspective, to avoid misunderstandings which, in extreme cases, could lead to industrial tribunal procedures, when proof that the employee received the necessary information may be required.

- *welfare:* pension and sickness schemes, welfare and social activities, medical services
- *the organisation:* vision and objectives, products, standards, market, future developments
- *introduction to workplace:* meeting the supervisor and fellow employees, geography of department (eg canteen, toilets), the job, who's who, any impending workplace changes
- *safety:* hazard areas, fire alarm procedure, fire points and exits, no-smoking areas, first aid and accident procedures, safety rules (eg safety clothing), security arrangements, safety committees, safety representatives. (Thorough instruction in safety aspects is a legal requirement. New starters, including those on short periods of work experience are particularly at risk – see Chapter 3.)
- *training and education arrangements:* person(s) responsible for training, content of training programmes, further education, including release arrangements and awards made
- *organisation facilities:* clubs, discount schemes
- *pay and rewards system:* how to read a pay slip, performance-related schemes, overtime and incentive payments, share option and pension schemes, overtime and incentive schemes, income tax and other deductions
- *non-financial benefits:* rest rooms, canteens, clothing, products
- *discipline and grievance procedures:* rules and regulations, how to register a grievance
- *trade unions and staff associations:* the role of trade unions, joint consultation.

The content, approach and methods of delivery should be planned around the needs of the learner. In some cases a few hours' induction is adequate but in others it may last for several weeks. Appropriate timing of sessions can be a decisive factor in effectiveness. It is usually preferable to split the content of longer programmes into several sections, sometimes over a number of weeks, providing the learner with the information as he or she needs it. As an extreme instance, school-leavers are unlikely to be interested in the details of the pension scheme the minute they arrive on the premises. Their first concern is likely to be 'Will I be able to do the job, and what will my supervisor and 'mates' at work be like?' On the other hand, in a certain chemical company, safety conditions are so paramount that no new starter (or visitor) is allowed into the production area without satisfactorily completing an interactive computer-based program on the safety requirements and regulations, and signing a statement to verify that they have done so!

Training methods will vary, depending upon the subject matter and the type of trainee. Self-study methods which allow self-pacing and choice of timing, such as computer-based programs, or by means a company intranet, may be useful for giving certain types of information to employees in dispersed locations in this country or overseas, or possibly for employees transferring from one department to another. If the software contains a facility to record who has undertaken the programme and how they scored, this is obviously an advantage. With the aid of computers and word processing systems, some companies with dispersed sites have standardised their induction and early training by producing templates or 'proformas' of induction and training manuals. These contain basic information and training programmes for all employees, but have blank spaces and 'prompt' points for management at different locations to add site-specific information and to adapt the programmes to their own needs. A language translation facility can be included in the software for multi-national organisations.

> The UK company Safeway, which has comprehensive training programmes that cover both 'technical' and 'people' skills, issues each new recruit with a 'Career Passport' in the form of a folder containing information on induction and providing the new recruit with 'Milestone Checklists' that outline the basic skills he or she will learn within the initial phase of the job training. Achievement can then be recorded against these checklists.
>
> The Career Passport gives information on how, after the initial training has been completed, the learner can develop his skills within his current role. Additional sections covering basic skills required for other departments, competency development and management training, and development can be added to guide him as he progresses through the business.
>
> A Coach's Guide gives the line manager or trainer information in three main areas:
>
> 1 hints and tips on how best to cover particular areas and information on what materials are available, such as videos, workbooks or CBT
> 2 validation questions and exercises for each of the milestone checklists
> 3 ideas on how to provide staff with on-going development 'challenges' and reviews to improve individual, team and overall store performance.

Figure 11.3 and 11.4 give an overview of the content and structure of the basic store induction module. It will be seen that the first part of the mornings are spent in welcoming and informative sessions, and the second part in familiarisation with the process area. The methodology is varied with interactive sessions so that participants are not expected to spend too long merely trying to absorb material. An important feature of the programme is a review of corporate goals, which are communicated by means of exercises and discussions to demonstrate in a meaningful way how behaviour in store relates to these goals.

Figure 11.5 gives a checklist to be completed and signed by the new recruit to ensure that all necessary areas have been covered. Two or three weeks after the formal programme, participants return as a group for customer service exercises, consolidation and emphasis of points made during the initial programmes

Management trainees

Management trainees have special requirements, which are likely to fall into four main categories:

Figure 11.3 SAFEWAY – Content and structure of store induction programme: Day 1

Module 1 Introduction	Module 2 The shop floor
Approx. Timing 9.00am–10.30am Day 1 *(90-minute session)*	Approx. Timing 10.30am–12.20pm Day 1 *(105-minute session)*
• Welcome and domestics (5 mins) • Ice-breaker (10 mins) • *Welcome to Safeway* video (15 mins) • What you need to know (5 mins) • Who you need to know (5 mins) • Break (Canteen intro) (15 mins) • Introduction to senior team and talk (15 mins) • Shop steward talk (10 mins) • Retail handbook and principal statement (5 mins) • Staff dress/locker keys (10 mins)	• Store tour (30 mins) • Break (10 mins) • *Health and Safety* video (15 mins) • Safety search (20 mins) • Safety discussion (5 mins) • Lifting (5 mins) • Hygiene and temperature control (10 mins) • Introduction to process areas and 'buddy' (10 mins)
Location = Training room	Location = training room, shop floor and process area

Reproduced by kind permission of Safeway Stores plc

Figure 11.4 SAFEWAY – Content and structure of store induction programme: Day 2

Module 3 Customer service	Module 4 Launch Pad
Approx. timing 9.00am–10.45am Day 2 *(105-minute session)*	Approx. timing 10.45am– 12.15pm Day 2 *(90-minute session)*

• Review of Day 1 (10 mins)
• Safeway goals (5 mins):
  – 1st Safeway goal – customer promise exercise (25 mins)
  – 2nd Safeway goal – current initiatives (10 mins)
  – 3rd Safeway goal – store performance measures (5 mins)
  – Safeway goals summary (5 mins)
• Product location exercise (20 mins)
• Product location summary (10 mins)
• Break (15 mins)
	• Telephone/tannoy (5 mins)
	• Absence reporting (10 mins)
	• Payslips (5 mins)
	• ALS (5 mins)
	• Break (10 mins)
	• Security – trolley exercise (10 mins)
	• Pensions and benefits (10 mins)
	• Retail handbook and launch pad quiz (20 mins)
	• After launch pad (10 mins)
	• Final checklist (5 mins)
	• Finish

Location = Training room and shop floor	Location = Training room and shop floor

Reproduced by kind permission of Safeway Stores plc

Figure 11.5 **SAFEWAY – Store induction programme: employee checklist**

Welcome ☐
Own-brand awareness ☐
Base store details and buddy system ☐
Store structure, process areas, key personnel, senior team ☐
Store tour ☐
Staff dress ☐
Health and safety video ☐
Temperature control ☐
Hygiene ☐
Safe lifting ☐
Safeway goals ☐
   – Customer promise ☐
   – Current initiatives ☐
   – Store performance measures ☐
Product location ☐
Telephone and tannoy system ☐
Absence reporting ☐
Payslips ☐
ALS ☐
Security ☐
Pensions and benefits ☐
Retail handbook and principal statement ☐
Career route ('After Launch Pad') ☐
Process area introduction ☐
Post launch pad questionnaires ☐
Customer service focus ☐
4-week review ☐

I have received training in the above and understand the performance standards required.

Employee ....

Line manager .... Date ....

Reproduced by kind permission of Safeway Stores plc

- organisational knowledge encompassing most of the items mentioned above
- the political system and in particular the types of managerial behaviour that tend to be respected and rewarded; sensitivity to organisational culture
- management skills, such as time management, delegation
- technical and/or professional knowledge and skills. Although they should provide an excellent basis for further learning, even highly specialised degrees are unlikely to encompass the precise needs of an organisation, or be 'at the leading edge' of the company's particular interest.

Care should be taken that such trainees, recruited as top managers for the future, do not receive conflicting messages. If the recruitment brochure has given the impression of immediate responsibility and rapid career progression, it can be demoralising to be given a lengthy (12–18 months') 'Cook's Tour' of the organisation. It is likely that attitudes to the job are developed at an early stage and become internalised, and it can therefore be extremely beneficial to set reasonably demanding projects, which will not only help to solve problems but will require the learner to find out useful information about the company. Technical graduates, whose university course has prepared them for a particular profession, such as engineering, may require considerable information about the organisation's specific technology and particular niche. General Arts graduates will, of course, require much more. One problem is that the student culture is very different from that of a business organisation, and unless they have had a significant amount of work experience, graduates are likely to require assistance in this direction. Senior managers acting as mentors and coaches can be an invaluable resource in helping the development of awareness and sensitivity to organisational culture and practices. They can also play a major role in assisting with career planning, drawing up action plans and identifying 'milestones', which are particularly important when the training is lengthy, so that the trainee can work to objectives and see what progress is being made.

At the beginning of this chapter we asked you to imagine you were to give an address on 'Education and Training: aims for the new millennium'. We hope that by now you have identified more issues than you are going to be able to explore in one hour, and that you appreciate the ambitions and contradictions of the current scene: for example, closely defined competences for NVQs alongside a need for initiative and creativity, the requirement for people with ever deeper technological knowledge and ability who must still have generalist competences and key skills. The challenge is enormous and complex, but we cannot afford to fail. You should now be able to distinguish the main current trends in vocational education and training: if you are not already familiar with the situation, a useful exercise would be to investigate what is happening in your own local schools and colleges and see how many examples you can find of liaison between educational institutions and employers. If you are employed, what does your own company do in this respect, and how effective is it?

FOR FURTHER REFLECTION AND DISCUSSION

1 'The National Record of Achievement' is an attempt by the educational world to provide potential employers with comprehensive information. What other benefits might there be in keeping these records, and how might their use influence initial training/teaching decisions? What would you like to see included in the record, and for what length of time do you think an individual could realistically maintain it?

2 Draft a short report to your top management team, explaining the National Traineeships or Modern Apprenticeships programme, incorporating firm recommendations concerning your organisation's future involvement or otherwise.

3 Draft a letter to the journal *Personnel Management*, in which you offer personal comments on current moves at national level to ensure that vocational qualifications are valued by employers and reflect competence at the workplace.

4 FE college bodies now contain a proportion of 'employment interest' governors. What do you see as the main responsibilities which these governors must carry? What would you look for when identifying suitable people to undertake this role?

5 You have been asked by your organisation to prepare plans for a conference which will bring together a mixed group of internal managers and external teachers, the theme being 'Making Work Experience Work'. Summarise your draft plans and compose a briefing statement which explains the conference aims and method.

6 Describe your organisation's induction training arrangements. How would you set about improving these arrangements?

SUGGESTED READING

Vocational education and training is a rapidly developing and changing field. The best way of keeping up to date is to read the publications of the DfEE and your local TEC. The DfEE Skills and Enterprise Unit, Moorfoot, Sheffield operates a membership scheme which supplies the particularly useful annual publications *Labour Market and Skill Trends* and *Labour Market Quarterly Report*, as well as executive briefing and updating papers. The DfEE journal *Insight* is available from PO Box 5000, Sudbury, Suffolk CO10 6YJ.

The Times Educational Supplement and *Higher Educational Supplement* are useful sources of information.

People Management is also an excellent source of updating material and critical commentary (the latest edition can be read on www.peoplemanagement.co.uk).

BURKE J. *Outcomes, learning and the curriculum*, Taylor and Francis, Basingstoke, 1995.

FOWLER A. *Employee Induction: a good start*. London, Institute of Personnel and Development, 1996.

12 An agenda for the future: learning to learn

New horizons – ideas still awaiting followers – learning to learn.

INTRODUCTION

This is our last full chapter. Although we have throughout Section B regularly reminded you that management remains a situation-specific art, and that there is no 'best approach' to determining training interventions, much of what we have written has been based on what most writers and practitioners have accepted as 'standard practice'. Standard practice has naturally been based on traditional assumptions relating to workplace organisation, the relationship between employees and employment, and management. We now want to explore ideas which, though not new, have to date failed to achieve general currency but should, we believe, significantly influence tomorrow's 'standard practice'; these ideas are (a) socio-technical and contingency theory (b) action learning (c) continuous development (d) learning organisation, and (e) knowledge creation. We end with our list of 'preferred' training interventions for the future – for individual learners, for teams and groups, for middle management, and finally for top management.

NEW HORIZONS

If we compare UK life in 1999 with that in 1900, we have no difficulty in noting widespread and substantial differences affecting how and what we learn. To begin with, there is much more knowledge available: a high proportion of what is now known was not known back in 1900, and by far the greatest part of today's knowledge is accessible to anyone who wants to use it if they have, or can acquire, some basic accessing skills. It can also be reasonably argued that most of this growing mountain of knowledge is needed by a steadily expanding number of potential users, the essential point being that new knowledge has usually emerged in response to a 'practical' purpose. Further, the pace at which it has emerged has escalated, directly mirroring the increasing frequency with which innovations intrude into our lives.

It is now over 40 years since Drucker (1954) predicted a forthcoming 'knowledge society', and nearly 30 since Toffler (1970) alerted us to the notion that any idea in general circulation might already reasonably be considered redundant in terms of its practical value. This notion has changed the way in which some people think of knowledge. Knowledge now no longer consists only of reliable, stable, finite data, but extends to cover opinions, preferences, values, likes, dislikes, and so on – and many more 'knowledge-based intangibles' (Nonaka and Takeuchi, 1995). And even those things that *can* be proven to exist are themselves regularly superseded by inventions designed to serve equal purposes more efficiently.

Drucker and Toffler were two early examples of writers who argue that organisations' health will in future rest upon intellectual assets rather than land or machinery, or even money. The greatest asset, it is suggested, will be the 'knowledge worker', meaning a person who continuously updates his or her knowledge, continuously questions what has traditionally been accepted, continuously redefines old and senses new problems, and continuously searches for new solutions. Competitive advantage will rest with organisations that employ or create and retain such people: the successful organisations will develop new-style 'learning cultures' in which employees are naturally helped to learn on a continuing basis.

Learning cultures will, if and when established, reflect new philosophical assumptions. Figure 12.1 offers a comparison between traditional assumptions, which accepted the possibility of stability and order at the workplace, and assumptions that accept change. During the lifetime of this book, the latter have been increasingly the norm in articles which explore how learning systems and learning cultures are likely to develop.

Figure 12.1 Assumptions underlying learning systems and cultures

Traditional	Future
Stability	Transience
Bureaucracy	Contingency
Homogeneity	Heterogeneity
Dependency	Confidence
Hierarchy	Heterarchy
Division of labour	Teamwork
Quality control	Social accountability
Problems defined academically	Problems defined operationally
'Disciplinary' knowledge	Transdisciplinary knowledge
Teaching	Learning

The assumptions in the right-hand column of Figure 12.1 are not simply the products of fertile imaginations. In general terms, they reflect society's realisation that workplace certainty is a rare phenomenon – a realisation that has sprung from experience. But they also spring from real-life developments, usually technological in nature, that have served society's widespread determination to meet more efficiently its needs for new, superior products and services. These developments – notably developments in information and communications technology – are real, and have bred confidence among commentators and managers alike. Where once the 'modern' approach was to set and manage by objectives, the more confident 'post-modern' view is proactively to create products, methods, and systems – which are themselves capable of further development. Learning systems both exemplify and serve this post-modern ideal.

Computerised processes are already well-established throughout the commercial world, and are involved in most workplace communications. The Internet is available to all, given a computer, a modem and a telephone line. In the UK, virtually everyone can now link directly to servers which transfer knowledge at will throughout the entire world. Already there are examples of large organisations having established internal 'intranets', allowing groups of employees to have access to their own endlessly increasing internal data banks. Soon also we shall have voice-activated computers, reducing the need to sit at a keyboard to communicate. Fast-flowing electronic mail discussions will often replace meetings, and 'attendance' at conferences will be possible without leaving home. 'New' knowledge will be available more quickly at the specific workplace than in purpose-built learning sites.

It is also worth noting that as time moves on, the young people who enter the world of work will be used to new learning norms. Children may before long be given a 'smart card' at birth which will give them access to individual learning guides who, in collaboration with parents, will help them continuously to plan their formal learning paths; formal learning achievements will be centrally logged as they happen, and will not be tied to age. Indeed, while educational qualifications are still likely to be the prime aim of full-time education experience, later learning will be assumed to follow. Schools, colleges and universities as we have known them may no longer be needed: the need for lecturers, for example, seems likely to decline, although such people may well exist in different capacities serving new learning processes which are essentially aimed at facilitating self-development. Future workers may therefore be more likely to practise self-development, more likely to expect managers to have 'facilitator' roles, and more likely to commit themselves to group learning activities.

It is these processes, roles and activities that we aim to explore in this chapter. But first it is worth studying in rather more detail a variety of conceptual approaches to establishing what the processes, roles and activities should be.

You might at this point like to remind yourself of the contents of Chapter 5, which explored learning system dimensions, and defined a number of differing systems. The key dimensions described there were (a) their learning orientation (to the individual or the organisation), and (b) their structure (evolutionary or designed). Now we must think in terms of a further, and somewhat complex, dimension – namely, the extent to which a learning system can develop itself. We are now looking at how organisations as well as individuals can learn – and how both can 'learn to learn'. And how both might endlessly learn to learn into the future. This is the ultimate training intervention: one that ensures that future training interventions happen naturally.

IDEAS STILL AWAITING FOLLOWERS

There have been several relevant approaches during the past 40 years.

1 'Socio-technical' and 'Contingency' theory

The first suggestion that training interventions might recognise stability as unnatural, and might instead aim at creating work units that sought to manage change on a continuing basis, came from the Tavistock Institute's researchers, and their advocacy of socio-technical theory, during the 1960s. These researchers were mainly psychologists and sociologists, who spent much time investigating the relationships between employees and their employing organisations (and indeed between employees and their work) at a time when automated processes were on the increase.

Socio-technical (ST) theory offered a model for flexible organisation and change management. Its basic model charted four key contingent (ie interdependent) organisational elements – 'tasks', 'technology', 'structure', and 'people' – which must be collectively managed in the service of the organisation's goals (see Figure 12.2; a much more sophisticated version, showing 'management' as a fifth and co-ordinating element, is in Morgan (1997), Exhibit 3.3). The key message was that as each of these elements varies through time, the *relationships* between them must be continuously monitored and frequently adjusted to maintain a 'healthy' operation. For example,

Figure 12.2 **The socio-technical system**

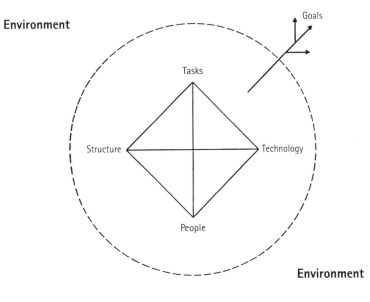

if new technology or bureaucracy subordinates creative workers to routine, low-discretion jobs, an abrasive interaction is likely, calling for conscious changes to either or both; the lack of such changes might lead to absenteeism, job turnover and a variety of behaviours that 'interrupt the main work task'. While this was not an explicit 'learning to learn' message, it did imply that each unique organisation should promote among its management an endless acceptance of change, an endless need to see or feel the need to change, and an endless attempt to create unique situation-specific answers to relationship problems.

There were several other messages. First, adjusting the relationships between any two elements might of course demand the adjustment of either or both. Hence, new technology might demand employee learning, and trained employees might justify changed tasks, and new tasks might lead to new management systems, which might again demand new employee learning. But second, each element's *internal* stability might be expected to fluctuate – a phenomenon that certainly applies to the 'people' element (for example, people do not all learn at the same pace), and justifies time spent away from the mainstream work tasks on 'process review' discussions, which means *unscripted* interpersonal learning activities. Taken together, these messages establish that 'managing the process' is as important as 'managing the task'. Moreover, they lead to a third message: group or team learning must itself be continuously reviewed and influenced 'as it happens'. These three messages were enshrined in the general view that a healthy work team will learn, and must manage its own learning without waiting for an external training imposition.

ST theory influenced a wide body of consultancy-oriented researchers in the field of organisation development (OD), who conducted OD seminars and projects in many of the UK's larger firms during the 1970s. These interventions usually accepted the basic 'contingency' view, and hence adopted the entire organisation as the basic unit to be researched or studied. If the human element was usually studied as part of the organisation's culture, learning methods and processes were often ignored – except perhaps during discussions on specific options for forward cultural change. OD activity did nevertheless involve much open discussion, especially at senior management levels, and undoubtedly improved awareness throughout management that the various socio-technical elements need to be both internally consistent and adapted to outside environmental conditions. This in turn gave rise to much internal talk with T&D/HRD management about training needs and options in organisations where senior management found OD useful; in a few firms, it led to the training of staff specialising in process consultancy. It is unfortunate that so little of contingency theory and process consultancy were retained during the expansion years of the 1980s.

2 'Action learning'

In Chapter 5, we included 'action learning' (AL) as one of our 'broadly defined' learning systems. The philosophy behind AL makes it much more than a set of procedures. AL's creator Reg Revans developed and preached his ideas relating to management learning from as early as 1945, yet they have never been widely understood, despite being wholly relevant to the task of improving performance in a changing environment.

AL starts with the assumption that change means uncertainty. Managing uncertainty demands more than drawing on stored memory: decisions must also be based on ideas about the future and the probability or otherwise of a given decision being adequate. When a problem occurs, it is risky to assume that the way a similar problem was dealt with in the past must also now be the 'best solution'. In such a situation, the manager needs to *update* his or her view of what must be taken into account – aims, constraints, options, and likely outcomes – and then needs to *create* a new view of what should be done. In the process of doing this, the manager may need to do some research – that is, to 'understand' the implications of the problem more deeply by gathering new information. This is what Revans meant by 'action learning': *finding things out* while getting on with the real management task. The process is essentially question-based, ignoring established answers unless or until they satisfy whatever questions are being asked.

Some questions are likely to be useful in all, or at least most, situations. Revans listed a few: for example, 'What am I trying to do?' 'What is stopping me from doing it?' 'Who can contribute to a solution?' But for the most part, real problems demand tailor-made questions which must be specially created – and Revans judged that the most useful questions are often posed by people who are not familiar with the problem. Hence he suggested the best vehicle for AL is a group or 'set' of several members from different backgrounds, disciplines and cultures. A variant is a group of colleagues who are joined by one or more 'outsiders' to work on a given problem. The AL set is typically a group that is meeting for the first time; it is introduced to the problem by the manager who 'owns' the problem (and who remains part of the set); it has the help of a 'co-ordinator', who essentially acts as secretary, arranging meetings, writing up findings, collecting material, and so on.

AL philosophy holds that the best opportunities for management learning lie in everyday management jobs. A few organisations (notably within the large multi-nationals, where trans-national and inter-company sets still appear, and in the health service) continue to support the approach, and at least one university degree course is based upon it; but industry as a whole rarely saw it as a major alternative to sending managers on external courses.

3 The 'continuous development' approach

Continuous development (CD) originated in the late 1970s with a group of training practitioners who formed the then Institute of Personnel and Development's national committee on Training and Development. They had become concerned at the frequency with which reports and papers, often from quasi-governmental sources, were advocating bureaucratic solutions to the nation's overall economic problems. Most of them had acquired an understanding of the main socio-technical principles; and they had also adopted Kolb's experiential learning ideas (see page 67). They had doubts about the 'total organisation' approach of the OD consultants; in their pragmatic view, training specific to any given work unit could dramatically improve both the organisation's and the nation's economic health, and its absence was often the result of the need for it never being appreciated by top management. They believed that the relationships between people and work should be adjusted to allow the people who were closest to the work significantly to influence decisions on their own training, and again to allow time for that training to happen.

CD emerged in the form of a five-year Institute-led 'ABCD' ('A Boost for Continuous Development') campaign. It was preached not as a theory, and not primarily even as a group of work practices, but as an attitude – justifying and explaining the term 'continuous'. Two mainstream ideas were preached as front campaign runners: first, self-development, and second, the integration of learning within work. If managers, and especially personnel and training managers, could adopt the CD attitude, both these ideals could be realised in a myriad of unique, situation-specific ways – national prescription would be redundant – with organisations coming to value, to create where necessary, and to *use enthusiastically* (a) already-known systems for appraisal of weaknesses and identification of training needs in line with forward operational plans, and (b) process review. To stimulate cultural change in this direction, the Institute launched a Code of Practice, which stressed the importance of

- clear organisation-wide *CD policies* (eg corporate commitment to CD, interdependence of technical and social systems, self-development as a responsibility of every employee, all employees to learn as much as possible about learning processes, facilities for learning during work time, etc)
- *CD responsibilities and roles* (eg senior management to promote CD policy, and to demand adherence to the CD concept from management; management to spend a substantial amount of their time on CD activity; PM/HRM professionals to take the lead in arranging discussions wherever they felt learning activity is inadequate to operational results; ALL LEARNERS to clarify their own learning goals with their superiors and colleagues, and without waiting for directives endlessly to propose ways of learning which minimise operational disruption, etc.)
- several CD *practices* (eg learner involvement in appraisal processes; mandatory CD agenda items for standing committee (including board) meetings; explicit reference in contracts for the introduction of new plant or equipment to the early involvement of staff during commissioning processes; regular process review discussions, wherever possible aided by facilitators, for all work teams)
- *CD training* (of managers, and especially training specialists, as facilitators).

The ABCD campaign drew sustained interest from a number of professional bodies, and from the academic world. Along with the later-named IPD, some of the former have since developed 'continuing professional development' systems for their membership, which promote CD's self-development aim. The academic world's interest was also sustained, but (as we shall shortly explain) soon tended to follow more ambitious theories covering the integration of learning with work. Most training specialists and line management viewed the campaign with caution, however, searching for hidden motives that did not exist. Government's training advisers flirted with CD briefly, then quickly abandoned their involvement in the campaign in favour of the employer-led Management Charter Group development (which included the CD ideal in its Charter but did nothing to promote it) and the introduction of the qualifications-based NVQ system (which initially claimed to ensure competence at the workplace, but which explicitly avoided the issue of how to integrate learning and work).

4 The 'learning organisation' approach

The 'learning organisation' (LO) approach came from academic sources at roughly the same time as training practitioners were promoting CD. This school of management thinking moves several theoretical notches further than socio-technical and contingency models. LO theory makes an important distinction between the 'adaptive' organisation (in which change is managed by 'reading' opportunities and constraints, and training plans are created to produce improvement, and a higher level of 'generative' organisation that aspires to take the lead in controlling its environment. LO proponents argue that people's ideas and behaviour do not have to be subordinated to corporate strategy and centrally-defined working procedures; policy, operations, ideas and action are all viewed as being in the ideal evenly balanced and linked (see Figure 12.3).

Figure 12.3 **The learning organisation**

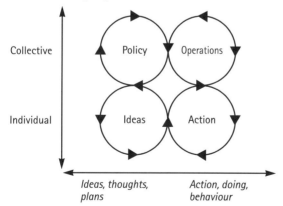

Reproduced with permission from J. Burgoyne's article 'Feeding minds to grow the business' in *People Management*, 21 September 1995.

In this ideal 'learning organisation', learning is seen as the *process* element that links the other four essentials – but the process is *two way*, with people and practices continuously influencing each other, with learning and change management following naturally.

Garratt (1994, 1995) has described the historical flow of management thinking that has led to this conceptual position. He maintains that as early as 1947 a convergence of disciplines (eg psychology, sociology, cybernetics, economics) established basic ideas about:

- the key role of people as the only source of organisational learning
- learning having both an intrinsic (personal development) and extrinsic (organisational asset-creating) value
- the necessity for multiple feedback loops of learning to create continuous organisational learning.

Garratt (1995)

Garratt (1994, 1995) also credits the Tavistock Institute's research on socio-technical systems in the 1950s and 1960s with demonstrating the critical nature of learning processes in healthy work groups; he finds it surprising that these ideas have taken so long to become accepted within the world of work, more especially because a host of management thinkers (Weber, Revans, Lewin, Emery, Argyris, Hodgson, Schumacher, Mintzberg, Handy, Pedler, Burgoyne and, latterly, Senge are among many that are named) have built upon ST ideas.

Senge (1990) calls the learning organisation 'an organisation that is continually expanding its capacity to create its future'. His four basic management disciplines are:

- personal mastery
- mental models
- building shared vision
- team learning.

His *fifth* discipline is systems thinking, which is for him the discipline that integrates the others, the pay-offs of integration being immense – put simply, creating the fused ensemble prevents the individual disciplines from being gimmicks or fads. According to Senge, these five disciplines allow the 'learning organisation' to be built systematically and not just to happen.

Burgoyne (1995) is less ambitious than Senge. He proposes the following practices as necessary to ensure the 'balanced' corporate learning process that is inherent in Figure 12.3 (page 297) (which we have reproduced from his article):

- a learning approach to strategy
- participative policy-making
- 'informating' (internal openness, plus dialogue/communication via IT)
- internal exchange (mutual adaptation between people and work units)

- reward flexibility (reward systems that incentivise learning and openness)
- enabling structures (simple enough to allow learning and accommodate its consequences)
- interorganisation learning (learning with, learning from, benchmarking for development as well as imitation)
- a learning climate (cultural norms that support shared learning from experience)
- processes that support self-development.

All these practices are immensely difficult to prescribe, even within a theoretical ideal. Burgoyne concedes that the learning organisation is 'not a standard formula, or a proven winning formula to be benchmarked and imitated'. He calls it a 'proposal, an invention and a broad concept – the best suggestion about how work and organisations proceed in this period of history'. It remains a powerful set of ideas to challenge and condition the thoughts of anyone whose responsibilities extend to managing the relationship between learner and organisation.

These ideas are not merely an academic brainchild. Carling and Heller (1995), provide forceful practical arguments in favour of learning organisations as a foundation for success. They point out that a learning climate is by no means new in the field of sport: great champions act as both master and pupil, giving lessons to others and learning themselves both from experience and from other coaches. They quote Drucker's maxim that information is replacing physical assets as the backbone of business and add that as information constantly becomes obsolete those who would be winners must update continuously, which involves learning. The adaptive learner and organisation *react* to changing circumstances, but those who devote all their energies to techniques such as 'just in time' and maintaining the lowest rate of defects are 'fighting the last war' and will not win the competitive race. Victory will go to the leaders in creativity. Carling and Heller quote from Alan Kay: 'The best way to predict the future is to invent it.' The learning organisation seeks to *generate* the future it wants, a philosophy in total opposition to worn-out clichés such as 'That's the way we've always done it here.' It is vital to know and to reinforce one's strengths, and recognise and eradicate one's weaknesses; *this involves learning*, and applies to winners who want to stay ahead, just as much as to losers. In the learning organisation everybody learns, which means everyone is taught – an idea with which many senior managers feel uncomfortable.

5 The 'knowledge creation' approach

During the 1980s, at roughly the same time that the LO approach was becoming well known, academic journals in the USA carried a number of articles by one or both of two Japanese business experts, putting forward the elements of a new theory of 'organisational knowledge creation' which they were constructing from research into successful Japanese organisations. The full theory was published in 1995 (see Nonaka and Takeuchi, 1995), and although we offer our summary here, we would recommend that it should be read in the original to ensure understanding of all its complexities.

Briefly, knowledge creation (KC) theory starts by defining knowledge broadly, to include not merely factual information but also attitudes and skills. The simple definition is 'justified belief', which at the level of the individual incorporates virtually every assumption, preference, and even intention. Knowledge is said to be either 'tacit' or 'explicit'. The former is personal and 'context-specific', which means that it has been experientially acquired by the individual, is subjective in nature, and cannot easily be formalised or communicated to others. The latter is objective, 'situation-free', removed from the individual's personal bias, and can be transmitted in formal, generally recognised language. The first need in knowledge creation is to stimulate the conversion of tacit knowledge to explicit knowledge; four modes of knowledge conversion are defined at length, these being sequentially required in a 'learning spiral' that moves knowledge from the individual outwards to an ever-widening group and eventually to an entire organisation. (A key stage in the conversion is 'triggered by dialogue or collective reflection', with discussion making use of metaphors, analogies, concepts, hypotheses and models). The learning spiral is said to function only when several supportive conditions (eg clear strategic intention, relatively unhindered autonomy) exist.

If KC is mainly geared to suggesting operational ways to satisfy these learning spiral conditions, it nevertheless offers significant pointers to what can reasonably be termed possible training interventions, and clearly aims at real integration of learning and work. We shall return to these later, when we look closely at practical training options for the future.

You may recall that in Chapter 5, where we explored organisational learning systems, we included an example of a so-called 'knowledge management' system. 'Knowledge management' (KM) is not, as has often been suggested, a set of concepts that naturally stem from KC, although some observers have described it (wrongly) as part of KC. The recognition and growth of KM has come with the development of information technology, which has dominated technological progress across the entire world since the mid-1980s. The important point to record here is that while KC has a lot to say about learning, and acknowledges that people are the essential agents of learning at all levels, KM says little or nothing about the human dimension; personnel management issues which follow the establishment of new information networks are treated as 'hygiene factors'. Most writers on KM are communications experts or information scientists: their ideas relate essentially to ensuring that information flows widely and smoothly, the assumption being that 'more people with more information means more learning' – a conclusion that is not shared by those influenced by any of the previous approaches.

It remains true that the increased availability of computer-based information, and the increased speed at which it can be accessed, plus the opportunity to establish forum-type electronic discussions on a worldwide basis, offer significant incentives and new levels of motivation for individual learners and organisations alike. Several large UK companies are now committed to extensive KM activity, and they view this as more than mere information processing. It seems that in these companies personnel management are working with IT specialists, and view KM as an in-house resource which will continue to grow in importance alongside further developments in learning. It is for this reason that we included KM in Chapter 5, and again why we feel the progress of KM should not be ignored.

LEARNING TO LEARN

During 1998/9, the Institute of Personnel and Development commissioned research into KM and LO, aiming to determine the importance of each for short-term operational success and long-term organisational renewal, the contribution employees must make to each, and the implications for the PM/HRM function. The first stage, a literature search (see Scarborough, Swan and Preston (1999)), yielded disappointing conclusions. KM and LO were reported as representing 'new approaches to the problems of competitiveness and innovation', but judged as approaches which 'will eventually be blown away'. According to the researchers, the literature confirms 'an alarming gap in the treatment of people management issues' – a remark that perhaps sprang from the fact that in recent years KM articles have ignored KC and severely outnumbered articles on LO. Moreover, academic studies on LO were seen as 'failing to generate useful implications for practitioners'. Knowledge was criticised as an 'over-theorised and under-specified concept that admits of too many interpretations to be useful'.

These judgements appear harsh, to say the least. There is no doubt that LO writers such as Burgoyne, Garratt and Senge have shown as large an interest in people, and again in operational practice, as in systems. Senge *et al.*'s *Fifth Discipline Fieldbook* (1998) is a good example of an attempt to be operationally specific (and one that does not appear in the researchers' reading list). Nonaka and Takeuchi's KC theory is similarly accompanied by a very practice-ordered set of recommendations, albeit recommendations that assume large-scale cultural change. And if articles in *People Management* during 1998 (Mayo 1998, Lank 1998, Young 1998, John 1998) vary in their views on the practical value of KM, all quote actual organisations that are experimenting with the KM concept.

Our own attempts to reflect constructively on all the approaches that we have described in this chapter, within the wider context of attempting to predict the likely future for training and development, lead us to believe that they collectively suggest a number of key messages that will or should influence the future practice of people management, and that they individually highlight important training interventions for the future. First, a few 'general' messages:

- Change will continue to be a, and quite possibly *the*, major influence upon life, and especially life at work.
- The most important requirement for the ongoing management of change is that of 'learning to learn'.

301

- Within the changing environment, competitiveness and efficiency needs will demand that management roles are, where necessary, extended to incorporate the management of learning.
- While information technology will make more information more accessible more quickly, learning will remain essentially a human activity.
- 'Learning to learn' has varied implications for the individual, the manager and the organisation, and involves the development of experiential learning alongside, and not instead of, more formal traditional learning processes.

Now, some messages which are geared more to operational practice, and are inevitably in the form of recommendations:

- Operational management must continue to be based on 'top-down' decision flows.
- Organisational learning requires a 'middle-up-down' flow of new ideas.
- New-style training interventions should address new learning processes and activities alongside their traditional teacher-led predecessors.
- The concept and practice of self-development should be adjusted to become '*assisted* self-development'.
- Team development should incorporate 'team learning' activity.
- New learning processes demand new roles (some old roles should decline) for (a) senior management (b) management generally (c) individual learners, and (d) training specialists.
- Training interventions – which may often ignore the use of the word 'training' – should be managed primarily to serve performance at three levels – those of the individual, the work team, and the organisation.

We now present our own suggestions on how the more important of these developments might be helped to happen.

Individual learners

Changes in society's attitudes toward learning will happen steadily, albeit slowly. These changes will increasingly tend to acknowledge and promote ideas about thought processes involved in learning rather than teaching, facilitating development beyond instruction, and creativity instead of dependence. All levels within the organisation need to appreciate that this cultural change is taking place, and that the term 'individual learners' extends to all levels, *without exception*. The new thought processes are important for both short-term operational performance and for long-term organisation renewal; senior management need to appreciate this and set about devising strategic plans explicitly aimed at stimulating their use.

The new thought processes all centre on 'reflective' behaviour. It has been clear since Kolb's research (see page 67) that experiential learning requires the learner to reflect; Argyris' work pointed to ways whereby reflection can be helped to happen; and LO writers have more recently redefined its nature in detail. Nonaka and Takeuchi quote Schön (1983, p68) as follows:

> When someone reflects in action, he becomes a researcher in the practice context. He is not dependent on the categories of established theory and technique, but constructs a new theory of the new case.

We can do no more here than give a cursory explanation of this concept; personnel and training specialists must themselves read more widely and reflect on it to give the concept personal meaning, and must use traditional methods to *teach* or *sell* their conclusions to management, especially middle managers. Basically, the 'researcher' practises 'double-loop learning' (see page 97), which involves an endless attempt to find a use for new information, an answer to a problem, a modification to an assumption, and so on. The key to this is the introduction of *questions* into the thought process, which in turn helps build new or 'polished' ideas that can be communicated to others. Learners must be helped – again by traditional methods – to develop the habit of using questions, and again to devise or accept questions relevant to their jobs and appropriate to varying situations. Figure 12.4 offers a few generally relevant options for questions.

Figure 12.4 Examples of questions to promote 'Reflection in Action'

'REFLECTION IN ACTION'

Situation	Questions
New experience	Is this likely to happen again? If so, should I behave differently? Do I need to be better informed for a repeat?
New information	Will I need this information in the future? If so, how can I ensure access to it then?
New problem	Has anyone else experienced this? Is this problem analogous to . . . ? How can I share the problem with others?
Clash of opinions	What are the assumptions underlying each? How fundamental is the difference?
Request for advice	Am I the best adviser? How can I advise without creating dependency?
All situations	Do I need to communicate this to others?

While 'generally relevant' questions can be the subject of collective train- ing interventions, each job – and especially each management job – should have its own list of questions that are specifically relevant to its ongoing operational management. A 'prompt list' should ideally be created for each, containing essentially questions which inevitably command 'opinioned' answers, ie answers that the job-holder is expected to own but which are liable to change or are far from finite. [Marketing people are used to this type of question. To manage a brand, one must take decisions about con- sumer needs and preferences, which change through time: hence the exis- tence of continuing market research programmes, which provide regular data on which up-to-date decisions can be taken.] If such questions are for- mally established, and the job-holder is committed to always having the 'best available' answer, a 'research in action' attitude exists, and the attempt to stay abreast of new knowledge is naturally prompted.

Accessing the Internet and/or intranets will probably become a standard method of updating one's knowledge in future, although traditional methods will not be overtaken. Where new knowledge is directly relevant to the learner's prompt list, the general question is 'In what ways will, can or should this new knowledge influence my work in the future?' But where knowledge does not seem to be immediately relevant, there is another, more complex thought process, that ideally will be brought into play – that of looking for parallels between the new knowledge and the prompt list, or searching for 'analogies'. LO writers stress the value of this type of thinking, and claim that it lies at the heart of most creative learning. Learners, and especially manage- ment learners, should be helped to practise it by traditionally-mounted ses- sions on lateral thinking, and practice in brainstorming (synectics sessions, which provide practice in *metaphorical* thinking, are even more useful).

If the job-holder is known to be the custodian of clear, informed, up-to- date views, plus a range of creative suggestions, other job-holders tend to contact that person as an 'authority' when searching for answers to their own related 'prompt list' questions. This is perhaps the main incentive for the job-holder to practise self-development: it generates prestige and builds confidence, providing the overall culture does not give superior recognition to other values.

Teams and groups

As we have just implied, a key reason why the organisation as a whole should promote self-development is the generation of a strong internal source of up-to-date information and opinion held by confident, articulate employees. We also saw that self-development can be 'helped to happen'. The opportu- nity grows with three further key conclusions:

- First, 'reflection in action' is easier and more likely to happen when two or more people work on it together.
- Second, if an 'openness' culture exists, group learning helps individual learning to happen at a faster rate than simple self-development.

- Group learning tends to be more creative than individual learning.

These are not new conclusions. They were in general circulation over 20 years ago among those who led study group activities based on the earlier Tavistock Institute's socio-technical research. The fact that they have not been adopted by industry in general confirms that the culture inside most organisations has favoured defensive routines which have acted as a deterrent to learning about learning, and still makes us report them as suggestions of what should, rather than predictions of what will, happen in the future.

We mentioned the 'prompt list' as an aid to self-development. If the job-holder's 'boss' understands the value of these open-ended questions, he or she can use them as an aid to face-to-face, one-to-one, operational discussions with the job-holder. The job-holder's views are then tested against further operational realities, and against the boss's own problems, and are likely to be stretched. If they remain strong, learning is being reinforced; if they have to give way, new learning is happening. Senge (1990) and others describe this joint activity as 'dialoguing' – having adopted the idea from the work of the quantum theorist, David Bohm. 'Dialoguing' is 'open' discussion in which assumptions are suspended, and the participants regard each other as equals in a process which allows incoherent thinkers to become 'open to the flow of a larger intelligence . . . in dialogue, people become observers of their own thinking'. Nonaka and Takeuchi (1995) use the term 'collective reflection'.

The process becomes even more useful in terms of operational learning if the group is more than a pair – although it simultaneously becomes more difficult to manage, especially if the group is a real-life operational team. As we have said, the necessary stimulus for 'reflection in action' is the introduction of questions, and 'dialoguing' requires a culture of openness. But the operational grouping incorporates differing operational roles, and unless the meeting is explicitly named as a learning session, these roles inevitably intrude on the 'open' dialogue, transforming the process into a traditional operational discussion. Senge maintains that the prime role of the team leader (usually the most senior person present, or the person who has convened the meeting) involves *balancing* the process between learning dialogue and operational discussion: in the former, complex issues are presented as questions, while in the latter, different answers are presented and defended, consensus views emerge, and authoritative judgments are made. What this means is that the team leader must be able to pose the questions, listen to members' contributions, sum up alternative views, judge when to shift the process into operational mode, extract or expose the operational implications, call on those with operational responsibility (including him or herself) to declare their own commitment or otherwise – and then return the meeting to dialogue mode.

You might call this normal chairmanship – but it is a formidable task that only few currently perform with any real confidence, and calls for formal training in what we shall call 'modern' chairmanship. To maximise the learning opportunity, the natural tendency to move forward into operational decision-making must be resisted, more questions being fed into the discussion. Senge quotes Bohm again in insisting that a 'facilitator' is needed alongside the team leader, at least in the early phases of developing a true 'learning team'. Here is a new role for the personnel or training professional – but of course, anyone who values the role and commits time to learning what it involves can perform it. The facilitator is required to 'hold the context' of the dialogue – that is, he or she must monitor the flow of ideas and inject new questions aimed at ensuring that understanding is widespread and contributions are not ignored. The role demands skill – in listening, watching, interpreting, intervening to pose new questions – and judging when to encourage operational discussion, which is effectively returning the reins to the team leader. A strong mutual respect is needed between the team leader and the facilitator, who ideally will meet before the meeting and share views on who the members are, how the dialogue might be helped to happen, and so on. In some circumstances, and especially in the early phase of a team's development, they might agree to split the meeting into two, three or four meetings – covering sequentially team briefing (traditional style, incorporating some explanation of their own roles), the 'learning dialogue', the 'operational discussion', and feedback on the process.

But there is even more on which the team leader and facilitator must cooperate. We cannot here go into a lengthy explanation of how people variously respond to new ideas, or to their own ideas being challenged; suffice it to say that in addition to the learning process, and the operational process, there is also an *interpersonal* process to be continuously monitored, understood, and managed. Individual learning is at its strongest when ideas are being accepted and further developed in a way that confirms the assumptions behind those ideas. In practice, confidence is dissipated if colleagues seem to ignore or reject those assumptions, or prefer alternative ones of their own making. Loss of confidence shows up as silence, or attempts to 'pair' with another member, or aggressiveness – or a host of other behavioural symptoms, the most dangerous of which was described well over 30 years ago by Bion (1961) as 'the basic assumption' – in which the individual behaves 'as if' believing in the majority or strongest view, while showing a lack of commitment to or enthusiasm for it. Such behaviour usually goes unnoticed, and draws no comment, although the person/s concerned is/are actually building defensive behaviour – they are 'learning how to avoid learning'. Such behaviour needs to be recognised and to form the basis for further work – this is how 'learning to learn' acquires a collective meaning. A 'healthy' team will be prepared to suspend its knowledge-creating process and work on any such process issues *if and when the situation is clear to them*, but such clarity does not normally emerge naturally. Here is the justification for formal training in process consultancy (to add to that in modern chairmanship) on the part of team leaders and facilitators alike.

There is much more that could be written about 'reflection in action' and 'learning teams'. (for example, Mayo and Lank (1994) explore the wide variety of possible 'team' groupings that exist). These are the twin bases of the continuously developing learning organisation. Together, they form the means whereby – in Senge's terms – 'personal mastery' can flourish *as a discipline* (ie a series of practices and principles that should be applied and can be taught) and 'team learning' can be forged via a system of situation-specific ground rules that evolve to promote both dialogue and operational decisions. In our opinion, a culture of this type will ideally be developed by any organisation that aims to stand out in its changing environment as flexible, confident, and determined to manage its own future.

Middle management

Middle management are the main generators of knowledge creation and distribution. We have seen how as team leaders they can help team members to extend and articulate what they know about workplace reality, collecting *en route* ideas for future improvement, and judging when and if operational changes should be made within their own areas of responsibility. Organisation-wide learning and development require that the new knowledge should be spread among others, both laterally and vertically; indeed, middle management must carry information and ideas from their own team meetings as contributions for others they attend. Where once they may have created minutes for a named distribution circle, in future they will increasingly place the record on an intranet (voice-operated computing will help enormously with this task) for a wider audience who can access it in their own time. While security matters may dictate some sophistication in the way the material is presented and made available, the main point to remember is that *keeping information to oneself is NOT efficient management within the context of the learning organisation*. Not least among their responsibilities is that of quickly alerting their superiors to matters which have significant strategic or organisational implications.

The overall learning process is modelled in a simple form in Figure 12.5. It shows how important are middle management's roles, and calls into question the current tendency to 're-engineer' in medium-sized organisations by reducing the number of middle management.

Top management

All that we have written about individual and team learning applies at the 'top' of organisations as well as elsewhere. But top management have their own extra responsibilities and roles. Leadership is still needed, albeit in a different form from the past, to install and maintain the learning culture.

Earlier in this book we have stressed the need for learning policy and strategy. UK organisations traditionally manage their operations from the top downwards, and authoritarian top managers have tended either to avoid consulting others or to listen only to their immediate subordinates before taking their decisions. In the ideal learning organisation, a more complex process is needed, with top management spending very much less time in operational management decisions, and more on managing the overall learning/decision-making process – while retaining their traditional roles in

Figure 12.5 **The organisational learning process**

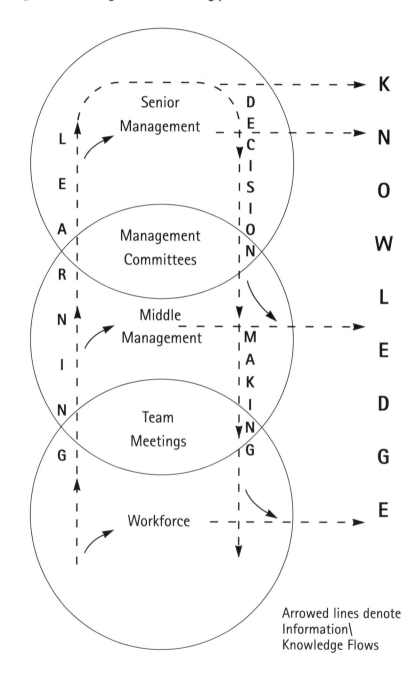

determining and maintaining strategic, political, organisational and resourcing control. Figure 12.6 attempts to chart a continuously developing management system in more complex schematic detail than Figure 12.5, although it remains, of course, no more than a simplistic and contrived attempt to consolidate the ideas we have learned from the many sources quoted.

Several principles must be stressed:

1 Top management does not *'know better' than subordinates about everything,* and must be prepared to collect up-to-date information (including ideas and opinions) before using their decision-making powers. Middle managers will ideally become used to being *asked* for advice or information, with their requests for time (and even new resources) being treated sympathetically. It should nevertheless remain clear that just as middle management are being trusted to know and understand the reality of the workplace and its operating problems, so top management's frame of reference is wider – they must continue to carry the responsibility for boundary management (ie how the organisation should impact on the outside world), strategy (ie the direction in which the organisation must head), policy (the philosophy underlying operations), internal organisation (how people will relate to work), and resources (people, and what they will have to work with, including money and *time*).

2 The first role of senior management is that of questioner. As in the ideal prompt list, the questions will deal with issues that are not clear-cut, and therefore require opinioned answers. As we have just implied, they should carry implications for boundary management, strategy, policy or organisation (the first of these includes anything that involves movement across the boundary – which therefore covers money, products and services).

3 A sequential dialogue/discussion process is even more dramatically relevant at this level than it is within middle management levels. But in pressurised times it may be useful to delegate much of the dialoguing task. One-off research projects, *ad hoc* value analysis groups, special brainstorming sessions, study visits, literature searches – these are merely a few of the many ways (including, of course, agenda items on standing internal committee meetings) which might be made to happen, all offering substantial middle management development opportunities if the work is managed and led internally, and not least if external sources are tapped. In every case, however, the knowledge collection process must include a final stage in which findings are fed back *upward* to those commissioning the work. There is much to be said for overlapping this stage with the discussion stage: separating the two prevents the important see-sawing between dialogue and discussion that makes for decisions that anticipate much of what will follow, and the presence of middle management at top management decision meetings provides a powerful opportunity for developing the former.

Figure 12.6 **The 'continuous development' management system – learning and knowledge integrated with work**

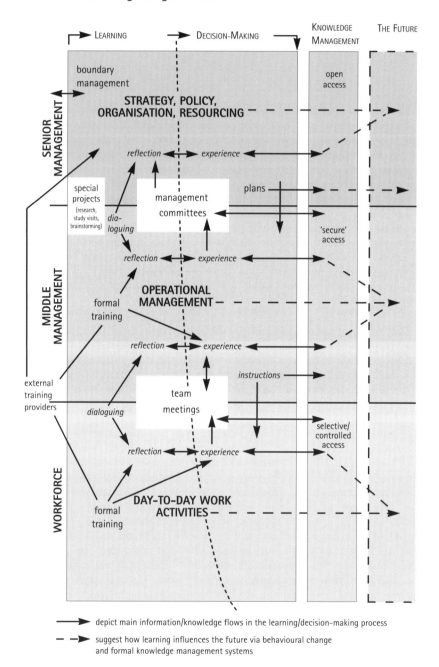

depict main information/knowledge flows in the learning/decision-making process

suggest how learning influences the future via behavioural change and formal knowledge management systems

4 Top management must commit themselves to trusting their subordinates – which means finding and developing people whom they can trust, if the feeling of trust is not already there. This need has considerable implications: for recruitment (top management must be part of the process of recruiting direct into management or management trainee positions), for appointments (top management must identify with each and every management appointment), for appraisal (top management must personally confirm promotability ratings), and even for counselling (top management must learn to understand middle management 'problem behaviour' in much the same way that team leaders manage process review activity).

What these four key points add up to is a system in which top management promote the learning culture while retaining their responsibility for managing the entire organisation. Mayo and Lank (1997) quote Garratt as offering five key conditions that top management 'need to consider' (which we would suggest might read 'must promote'):

- clear formulation of strategy and policy
- taking time and space to think and learn themselves
- demonstrating their own willingness to learn from each other
- delegating problem-solving operational issues to others
- setting a climate that encourages continuous learning.

We should perhaps add one more important condition:

- ensuring that staff in general, and especially middle management, similarly have time and space to think, engage in dialoguing, communicate, develop knowledge management facilities, and make endless training interventions.

This is our last message. It could well have been included in our list of 'principles that must be stressed' above. Time spent on learning must be accepted not as an alternative to work, but *as* work, without question. Training interventions must be based on the firm belief that they are *part of* work, and wherever possible they must be integrated, and not merely dovetailed, with work. Middle management must be assessed on their ability to manage *both* learning and operational decision-making processes concurrently; top management must become used to asking for information and advice from their subordinates before imposing plans. Staffing levels must recognise all this – the very existence of widespread computer terminals and expanding data banks itself demands the rethinking of levels upwards, but the opportunities provided for creative learning disappear if there is not time for additional dialoguing and team learning. Once top management grasp this, they will find that their own lives become more creative, and indeed more interesting as a result.

Whatever the future, learning must surely grow in importance in the eyes of the community. That being so, greater interest in continuous development and learning organisations seems more rather than less likely.

Strategies that seek short-term financial reward by reducing the time and space available for learning work in the opposite direction, and delay, if not prevent, the operational success that can only come from encouraging the training interventions that a changing world requires. If the nation reaches a point where the majority of its workforce believes in continuous development, and a larger majority of its management strives to maintain a learning culture, the ultimate move will have been made, endlessly generating its own infinite number of interventions into the nation's ongoing learning organisation.

FOR FURTHER REFLECTION AND DISCUSSION

1 How do you yourself view the idea of 'lifelong learning'? Do you think of it as geared to formal or informal learning activity, or both? Do you expect it to be reflected in personal educational qualifications? If you were asked to recommend ways to promote it on a national scale, what would you suggest?

2 Try to create a few 'prompt list' questions that you can use to keep your own ideas on something (perhaps something from this chapter, such as 'knowledge management' or 'knowledge creation') up to date. How 'factual' will the answers be at any one time?

3 How do you expect the following to influence your own activities in the future:
   (a) the Internet?
   (b) 'dialoguing'?
   (c) process review discussions?

4 Can you think metaphorically? If you think the answer is 'No', how might you set about developing this skill?

5 Can you think of a metaphor for training interventions?

SUGGESTED READING

Apart from the major titles named in our text (especially those by Garratt, Senge and Nonaka and Takeuchi – see Bibliography) the 1999 IPD-commissioned 'literature search' report by Scarborough, Swan and Preston, provides an in-depth commentary on the key ideas in this chapter.

The four 1998 *People Management* articles noted on page 301 deserve to be read in order to obtain a balanced view of what LO, KC and KM offer.

The only title on CD is the IPD's *Continuous Development: The path to improved performance* (ed. Sue Wood) 1988.

For a more comprehensive overall guide to organisational learning, see Mayo and Lank (1994), who incorporate an appendix entitled 'a complete learning organisation benchmark' – which provides over 20 pages of prompt-list questions aimed at helping the reader to identify which components a given organisation (ie 'yours') might need to establish a continuous learning culture, and how to plan moves towards the new ideal.

Senge deals well with the minutiae of dialoguing and team learning. Schein (1969,1970) is still the best source for facilitator skills and process review. Hardingham (1996) has two chapters on training options to develop process review skills. Barrington (1998) deals with prompt lists and their application.

To review learning organisation within a very much wider conceptual study of organisation into the future, see Gareth Morgan's *Images of Organisation* (1997).

Appendix 1

List of abbreviations

ACAS	Advisory Conciliation and Arbitration Service
ACCAC	Qualifications, Curriculum and Assessment Authority for Wales
AI	Artificial Intelligence
AL	Action Learning
APEL	Accreditation of Prior Experiential Learning
APL	Accreditation of Prior Learning
BIM	British Institute of Management
BTEC	Business and Technology Education Council (formerly Business and Technician Education Council) (now retitled EDEXCEL)
CATS	Credit Accumulation and Transfer Scheme
CBI	Confederation of British Industry
CBT	Computer Based Training
CD	Continuous Development
CG	City and Guilds
CPD	Continuing Professional Development
CRE	Commission for Racial Equality
DE	Department of Employment (since 1995 merged with DfEE – see below)
DfEE	Department for Education and Employment
DVD	Digital Versatile Disc
DV-I	Digital Video-Interactive
EDEXCEL	Current title of the Business and Technology Education Council (abbreviation for 'educational excellence' – used since 1997)
Employment NTO	Employment National Training Organisation
ES	Employment Service (a branch of the DfEE)
EU	European Union (superseded the European Community 1993)
FA	Functional Analysis
FE	Further Education
FEFC	Further Education Funding Council
GCSE	General Certificate of Secondary Education
GNVQ	General National Vocational Qualification
HE	Higher Education
HRM	Human Resource Management
ICT	Information and Communications Technology

IiP	Investors in People
ILB	Industry Lead Body (ILBs are now properly termed NTOs)
IMS	Institute of Manpower Studies
IPD	Institute of Personnel and Development
IPM	Institute of Personnel Management
IT	Information Technology
ITB	Industrial Training Board
ITD	Institute of Training and Development
ITO	Industry Training Organisation (ITOs were renamed NTOs in early 1998)
KC	Knowledge Creation
KM	Knowledge Management
LEC	Local Enterprise Company
LEN	Local Employer Network
LO	Learning Organisation
MA	Modern Apprenticeships
MBA	Master of Business Administration
MCG	Management Charter Group
MCI	Management Charter Initiative
MSA	Manual Skills Analysis
MSC	Manpower Services Commission (no longer in existence)
NACETT	National Advisory Council for Education and Training Targets
NCITO	National Council of Industry Training Organisations (now succeeded by the NTO National Council – NTONC)
NCVQ	National Council for Vocational Qualifications (now replaced by QCA)
NGL	National Grid for Learning
NIACE	National Institute for Adult and Continuing Education
NLP	Neuro-Linguistic Programming
NRA	National Record of Achievement
NROVA	National Record of Vocational Achievement (now replaced by NRA)
NT	National Traineeships
NTA	National Training Awards
NTO	National Training Organisations (created in 1998, incorporating and replacing most ILBs, ITOs and OSCs)
NTONC	National Training Organisations' National Council
NTT	National Training Targets
NVQ	National Vocational Qualification
OC	Open College
OSC	Occupational Standards Councils (replaced in 1998 by NTOs)
OU	Open University
PMS	Performance Management System
PSLB	Personnel Standards Lead Body (now subsumed within Employment NTO)

QCA	Qualifications and Curriculum Authority
ROI	Return on Investment
RSA	Royal Society for the Encouragement of Arts, Manufacturers and Commerce
SCAA	Schools Curriculum and Assessment Authority (now replaced by QCA)
SCOTVEC	Scottish Vocational Education Council (now replaced by SQA)
SQA	Scottish Qualifications Authority
ST	Socio-Technical
SVQ	Scottish Vocational Qualification
TA	Training Agency (no longer in existence)
TDLB	Training and Development Lead Body (now replaced by Employment NTO)
TEC	Training and Enterprise Council
TQM	Total Quality Management
TUC	Trades Union Congress
TWI	Training Within Industry
UfI	University for Industry
VR	Virtual Reality
YC	Youth Credits
YOP	Youth Opportunities Programme (now YT)
YT	Youth Training ('National Traineeships' – NT – replaced YT in 1997)
YTS	Youth Training Scheme (replaced first by YT, and more recently by NT)

Appendix 2

A 'quick guide' to national and European training schemes, institutions, programmes, initiatives

Accreditation of Prior Experiential Learning
A national methodology whereby, in some circumstances, educational institutions may accept evidence of learning through work experience, normally in the form of a portfolio of documents and relevant written assignments, to enable students to claim exemption credits from national and university awards.

Accreditation of Prior Learning (APL)
A national methodology which in some circumstances enables students to claim exemption from examinations or exemption credits from college/university awards on the basis of evidence of successful completion of a different but relevant and similarly rated formal programme. This avoids a situation where students have to cover the same ground twice.

Awarding Bodies
Independent bodies who design course curricula and administer examinations leading to recognised qualifications. Jointly responsible with national training organisations (NTOs q.v.) for the design of national vocational qualifications (NVQs q.v.), and individually for the implementation of specific NVQs. Issue qualification certificates to successful examination candidates.

Business and Technology Education Council (BTEC)
(see EDEXCEL)

CEDEFOP
EU training research agency. Its UK wing is at the IPD in Wimbledon q.v.

City and Guilds (CG)
An independent examining body which for over 100 years has set nationally recognised standards for operatives, craftspersons and technicians through its wide range of certificates. Individual subject exams are usually classified into three performance levels. Many CG awards are now also approved as National Vocational Qualifications (NVQs) q.v.

Compacts
Partnerships between specific employing organisations and specific educational institutions, offering to students training opportunities, to educationists updating in changing techniques and processes, and to employers a flow

of potential recruits. A key service is the provision of Work Experience q.v. for students and staff alike.

Continuing Professional Development (CPD)
An uncoordinated series of initiatives designed to promote the ongoing development of professional people. Most initiatives emphasise formalised learning.

Continuous Development (CD)
An approach to learning, pioneered by the former Institute of Personnel Management (now IPD), which emphasises self-development and the integration of learning with work.

Duke of Edinburgh's Award Scheme
To achieve these awards, young people must successfully participate in some type of service to the community, develop practical and social skills relevant to their own particular interests and participate in some form of organised physical recreational activity.

EDEXCEL
Major UK awarding and examining body, based in London. Formed from the amalgamation of two earlier bodies – the Business and Technology Education Council (BTEC) – a leading provider of vocational qualifications – and London Examinations – one of the main GCSE q.v. and GCE q.v. examining boards. The name 'Edexcel' stands for 'educational excellence'. Closely associated with the University of London. Continues to use the term 'BTEC' for its professional development certificate/diploma, higher national certificate/diploma, national certificate/diploma, first certificate/diploma, and key skills awards; also offers Foundation, Intermediate and Advanced GNVQs q.v., and NVQs q.v. at Levels 1 to 4.

Education and Business Partnerships
EBPs are set up across the UK to co-ordinate education and business links and strengthen liaison between educational institutions and the world of work. They do not conform to one model but have developed their own structures, financial arrangements and specific activities in line with local needs. There is a national EPB with representatives from local Partnerships, which provides support and a national voice for the network.

Employment National Training Organisation (Employment NTO)
Formed from the amalgamation of three previous lead bodies – the Training and Development Lead Body (TDLB), the Personnel Standards Lead Body (PSLB), and the Trades Union Sector Development Body (TUSDB). One of UK's many National Training Organisations (NTOs), q.v. Responsible for setting and maintaining national standards, and for 'prioritising and securing the development of' N/SVQs q.v. in the three areas mentioned.

Further Education Funding Council (FEFC)
Created by the Further and Higher Education Act of 1992, the FEFC must 'ensure that all reasonable needs for further education in England are met' – which means that in addition to administering a funding system, the Council issues strategic plans, manages an inspection service, and exerts a major influence on FE Colleges' activities generally. FEFC circulars, addressing virtually all aspects of College management, are frequently distributed to Colleges.

General Certificate of Secondary Education (GCSE)
UK's single system of examining at 16+, introduced in 1986/8, and designed to cater for all abilities. Emphasis is on using knowledge and skills, not just memory. The exam is taken on a 'subject by subject' basis: grades are awarded against performance in each, grades A to G being considered 'Pass' grades, with work below grade G remaining unclassified.

General National Vocational Qualifications (GNVQs)
Qualifications approved by QCA q.v., available to full-time students in schools and FE colleges. GNVQs are 'broader-based' than NVQs q.v., and are grouped under 14 occupational headings (see also Appendix 4).

Industry Training Organisations (ITOs)
Voluntary (ie non-statutory) bodies representing industries and advising/influencing their respective industries towards 'best training practice'. Most but not all have since 1998 become government-funded *National* Training Organisations, with added responsibility to promote government strategies. NTOs q.v. draft national standards for national vocational qualifications (NVQs q.v.), for modern apprenticeships q.v., and for national traineeships q.v.

Institute of Personnel and Development (IPD)
Formed in 1994 from the merger of the former Institute of Personnel Management (IPM) and the Institute of Training and Development (ITD). Substantial membership (ca 75,000), more than half being trainers. Professional qualification scheme incorporates Certificate in Training Practice plus a variety of stand-alone Employee Development modules.

The Internet and Intranets
The 'Internet' is a worldwide network of sites offering computerised information accessible to computer users who are themselves linked into it telephonically and electronically via computer hardware and an external 'server's' software. Each site has its own Internet address; 'home pages' (each of which may be many pages long, and lead to a vast range of subsidiary sites or pages) ensure that information is automatically available to anyone who makes contact. Messages can be sent to and from sites, thus allowing 'forum dialoguing' as well as simple information retrieval. 'Intranets' are networks which group together a number of Internet sites

usually, but not necessarily, within a given organisation, managing the flow (and availability) of information to the various users.

Investors in People (IiP)

An initiative aimed at increasing employers' commitment to training 'activities and attitudes' throughout the UK. Although managed and promoted by an independent organisation 'Investors in People UK Ltd', Training and Enterprise Councils (TECs) q.v. have been given the role of assessing employing organisations against a 'standard' (see Figure 2.5, pages 42–3, for details).

Lead Bodies

Industry- or occupation-wide bodies set up to identify, define and update employment-based 'standards of competence' in their area of interest. Submit to the Qualifications and Curriculum Authority (QCA, q.v.) proposals for standards which when approved form the basis of national vocational qualification (NVQ q.v.) awards designed by 'awarding bodies', q.v. Since 1998, most Lead Bodies have been reformed as 'National Training Organisations' q.v. and are funded by government, with a wider remit covering a range of education and training strategies.

Learning Direct

Free telephone helpline (managed as part of the UK government's University for Industry (UfI q.v.) arrangements) offering nationwide information and confidential advice to adults and employers on courses and qualifications available.

Leonardo

Major, multi-stranded EU vocational training action programme, offering both a policy framework and operational support, including funds, for projects and exchanges under three headings: Vocational Training Systems (including the development of common training modules, the promotion of continuous learning, trainer training, the networking of guidance centres, and measures to help the unqualified become qualified); Vocational Training Measures; and Language Training, Leonardo subsumes and builds on earlier EU programmes named Petra, Force, Comett, and Eurotecnet, together with part of the Lingua programme and the Iris initiative. These are the types of measures supported:

- pilot projects to design new training approaches, content and materials
- placement and exchange programmes
- analyses and surveys examining training problems
- networks and dissemination projects
- open and distance learning.

A call for proposals is made annually. Funding does not fully match costs; approval demands a trans-national element, which in practice means operational arrangements with one or more organisations in at least one other EU state; research-type activities must also provide for dissemination of results.

Local Enterprise Companies (LECs)
See Training and Enterprise Councils (TECs) below.

Management Charter Group (MCG)
An independent network of UK employers who have put their names to a new charter promoting management education and training, and a linked 'management charter initiative' (MCI q.v.).

Management Charter Initiative (MCI)
A UK initiative in which employers combine to promote higher standards of management practice by sharing resources, exchanging information, devising new management qualifications and observing a Code of Practice. MCI have issued lists of management competences which they recommend as the bases for future management qualifications. MCI-defined competences are accepted by NCVQ q.v.) as meeting their criteria for national standards as defined within NVQs q.v.; several National Training Organisations (NTOs, q.v.) have 'imported' MCI-defined competences into their own standards.

Modern Apprenticeships
Initiative launched 1994 with target of 150,000 'apprenticed' young people following new-style programmes (developed by National Training Organisations (NTOs) q.v.). A key element in each programme is training and education to NVQ/SVQ q.v. Level 3. Training and Enterprise Councils (TECs) q.v. co-ordinate arrangements involving employer commitment to 'start-to-finish' training, and similar pledges from the trainees.

National Council for Vocational Qualifications (NCVQ)
and
Scottish Vocational Education Council (SCOTVEC)
See Qualifications and Curriculum Authority (QCA).

National Curriculum
Prescribed parts of UK's secondary education curriculum – introduced via the 1989 Education Reform Act and implemented via a timetable over the following six years. The prescription comprises 'Core Subjects' – Science, Mathematics and English – and 'Other Foundation Subjects – Design and Technology, Information Technology, a Modern Foreign Language, and Physical Education.

National Grid for Learning
A UK government initiative launched in January 1998 to harness technology to raise educational standards, and to provide up-to-date teaching and

learning materials for teachers of all kinds and at all levels. All schools, FE colleges and libraries should be connected to the Grid by 2002.

National Learning Targets (NLTs)

Targets originally devised and launched in 1990 by the Confederation of British Industry as 'World Class Targets' for the UK; adopted and renamed by government as 'national' targets in 1991. Monitored, reviewed and revised by a National Advisory Council (NACETT). Specific goals relate to NVQ/SVQ attainments by young people and employees generally, and the attainment of 'Investors in People' (IiP) q.v. status by employers. See Figure 2.7 page 50 for details.

National Record of Achievement (NRA)

A sequential portfolio system of collecting and collating qualifications and reports on vocational studies and training.

National Traineeships

Introduced in September 1997, national traineeships are the UK government's attempt to offer 'a job with training' to young people who are not able to match the requirements of Modern Apprenticeships q.v. Replacing earlier youth training programmes, they focus on a combination of workplace skills training and the educational achievement of level 2 NVQs q.v. Structured 'frameworks' and standards have been devised by a large number of national training organisations (NTOs, q.v.); it is usually possible for a successful trainee to proceed to a Modern Apprenticeship. Delivery and funding are arranged by TECs/LECs q.v., involving partnership arrangements between employers, schools, FE Colleges, and careers services.

National Training Awards

A national awards scheme, giving public recognition to organisations and training providers who claim to have demonstrated 'excellence in the training field'. Award-winners are selected from an annual batch of entrants.

National Training Organisations (NTOs)

Network of UK industry-wide or occupation-wide bodies (often technically 'employer-owned', but since 1998 funded from the Treasury) recognised by government as the strategic bodies responsible for defining the needs of their respective industries or groups, and ensuring that these needs are addressed. In particular, the NTOs are approved as the bodies that will set national standards for NVQs q.v., and frameworks for Modern Apprenticeships and National Traineeships q.v. NTOs have their own NTO National Council, which represents and supports the network by (a) influencing government and other key bodies (b) developing and strengthening partnerships at national level, and (c) promoting the benefits and concept of the NTO network. See also Industry Training Organisations q.v.

National Vocational Qualifications (NVQ)
A term used to describe any qualification that has been approved by the National Council for Vocational Qualifications (NCVQ q.v.). Over 600 subject headings exist (end 1998), most fronting qualifications at more than one level, and overall applying to well over 500 occupations. Over 2 million NVQ awards had been made by summer 1998. Qualifications are initially awarded by independent organisations (eg CG, BTEC q.v.), but the 'NVQ' kite-mark appears alongside that of the awarding body. NVQs are arranged in a hierarchy of five levels, from 1 (the most basic) to 5 (management and professional level). 'General' NVQs (GNVQs) are available for those young people still in full-time education. (See also Appendix 4.)

New Deal
UK government initiative aimed at helping young people aged 18 to 24 (who have been unemployed for over six months) to find work and improve their prospects of employment. Consists of (a) 'Gateway' provision (help with job searches, careers advice) and preparation for (b) a range of four education, training, and/or work options (see main text, Figure 2.8 page 53 for details), together with (c) a follow-through strategy. Delivery is an Employment Service (branch of the DfEE, q.v.) responsibility, achieved via local partnerships of TECs/LECS, q.v., employers, local authorities, and voluntary associations.

Open College (OC)
A 'distance learning' organisation, established 1987 on lines similar to those of the Open University (OU) q.v. – but primarily addressing vocational skills training needs.

Open University (OU)
A 'distance learning' organisation, offering degree-level and other courses on a national basis through flexible learning methods. Apart from receiving learning material by mail, students study by watching prepared TV programmes, completing planned assignments and attending residential workshops.

Qualifications and Curriculum Authority (QCA)
Established in 1997, the QCA brings together the work of the earlier National Council for Vocational Qualifications (NCVQ) with that of the Schools Curriculum and Assessment Authority (SCAA). London based. Keeps under permanent review all aspects of the UK's statutory and non-statutory curricula, including the National Curriculum q.v. Accredits proposals for National Vocational Qualifications (NVQs q.v.) developed by national training organisations (NTOs, q.v.) and awarded by awarding bodies q.v. QCA also itself develops and accredits GNVQs q.v.

Records of Achievement (ROAs)
Records issued (from mid-1991) to those leaving full-time secondary

schooling, reporting academic and other successes already achieved. ROAs do not cover the wide range of data that earlier pilot 'Profile' documents covered. See also National Record of Achievement (NRA), which has taken the approach into the post-school education and training field.

Sandwich Training

Arrangements whereby degree and diploma students from UK universities and polytechnics spend periods of time working in industry or commerce (eg in a laboratory or a marketing department) – essentially as part of their course. Sandwich students usually receive special rates of pay and are given 'real' jobs of work.

Scottish Vocational Education Council (SCOTVEC)

See National Council of Vocational Qualifications (NCVQ).
and

Scottish Vocational Qualification (SVQ),

the Scottish equivalent of National Vocational Qualifications (NVQs) q.v.

Skills and Enterprise Network

Free-of-charge service offered by the Department for Education and Employment (DfEE q.v.), providing up-to-date information on skills, the labour market, education and enterprise. Reports research findings, and issues abstracts of all major training reports/publications. Incorporates quarterly labour market and training statistics.

Skills Task Force

Advisory body set up by the UK government to keep under continuing review national skills shortages, skills gaps, and the mismatch between supply and demand. Contains representatives from small- and medium-sized employers, large corporations, further and higher education, trade unions, and local authorities.

Socrates

Major, multi-stranded EU programme for trans-national co-operation in the field of education, covering learners of all ages, types and social groups. Sister programme to Leonardo q.v., with which it shares responsibility for language training. Encourages open and distance learning.

Teaching Companies

An arrangement whereby an employing organisation and a college join together on a project (at the instigation of the former). The college provides a tutor/supervisor and associates to work on the project. The associates may be registered with the college for a research degree, but are paid by the employing organisation.

Training and Enterprise Councils (TECs)
and (Scotland)
Local Enterprise Companies (LECs)
Employer-led bodies, established 1989/90; their main tasks are to manage in the locality national training schemes such as Modern Apprenticeships q.v. and National Traineeships q.v., and to promote skills development in line with predicted local need – for which they dispense government funds. An Investors in People (IiP) q.v. initiative allows them to give public recognition to any employing organisation which meets certain training standards.

University for Industry
A UK government initiative which aims to create a 'national learning network'. Six 'core functions' are stressed: marketing to stimulate mass demand for lifelong learning, in-depth guidance services, brokerage (connecting people with learning programmes), commissioning new materials, 'kitemarking' (to assure users of quality), and market analysis + strategy. This is currently the main national initiative supporting the EU's campaign to promote lifelong learning for all.

Work Experience
Arrangements made between employers and educational institutions whereby students spend periods of time within industry and commerce experiencing the world of work. Schemes vary, sometimes involving projects and group work; some schemes are integral with courses such as TVEI or Business Studies GCSE q.v. Wages are not normally paid.

Work Shadowing
An arrangement whereby a trainee gains an insight into a job by 'shadowing' the incumbment as he goes about his work.

Youth Training (YT)
Government-led programmes for young people – discontinued 1997. Replaced by Modern Apprenticeships q.v. and National Traineeships q.v. together with New Deal q.v. arrangements for 19–24-year-olds.

Appendix 3

The Employment National Training Organisation's National Standards for Training and Development

'Standards' take the form of 'units of competence' (themselves split into 'elements of competence' – not here shown), which describe 'what can be done' by a person who has been assessed as having competence in a given occupational field. These standards were orginally drafted by a 'Training and Development' Lead Body (TDLB) drawn from practising experts and consultants; the TDLB merged with the Personnel Standards Lead Body (PSLB) and the Trade Union Sector Development Body to become the Employment National Training Organisation. NVQ-awarding bodies must use these standards as blueprints for their own study and examination requirements at the prescribed levels. See Chapter 5 pages 106–7 and Appendix 4 for more information on the national vocational qualifications system, and Chapter 6 pages 136–40 for more information on these standards *per se*.

KEY: M = Mandatory (ie 'Core' units of competence)
     O = Optional

Area/Unit Title Basic Requirement	Level 3 T&D All 'M's + 3 'O's	Level 4 T&D (Lng Dev) All 'M's + 5'O's	Level 4 T&D (HRD) All 'M's + 5 'O's	Level 5 T&D (Strategy) All 'M's + 3 'O's
Identify T&D Needs				
Identify individual learning needs	M			
Identify individuals' learning aims/ needs/styles		M		
Identify organisational T&D needs			M	
Specify contribution of T&D to organisational development			O	
Identify organisational HR requirements				M
Ensure strategic position of HRD within an organisation				M
Plan and Design Training				
Design T&D sessions	M			
Design, test + modify T&D sessions		O	O	
Design, test + modify IT-based materials		O	O	
Prepare + develop resources to support learning	M			
Design learning programmes to meet learners requirements		M	O	
Devise a plan for implementing an organisation's T&D objectives			M	
Devise HRD policies + implementation plans				M

Area/Unit Title Basic Requirement	Level 3 T&D All 'M's + 3 'O's	Level 4 T&D (Lng Dev) All 'M's + 5'O's	Level 4 T&D (HRD) All 'M's + 5 'O's	Level 5 T&D (Strategy) All 'M's + 3 'O's
Deliver T&D				
Facilitate learning in groups through presentation and activities	M			
Create climate conducive to learning	M	M	O	
Agree learning programmes with learners	O	M	O	
Facilitate learning through demonstration and instruction	O			
Facilitate individual learning through coaching	O			
Facilitate group learning	O	O		
Support and advise individual learners		O		
Co-ordinate provision of learning opportunities with other contributors to the learning programme		O	M	
Implement HRD plans				M
Review Progress and Achievement				
Monitor + review progress with learners	O	M	O	
Assess individuals for non-competence-based assessment systems	O	O	O	
Assess candidate performance	O	O	O	
Assess candidate using different sources of evidence	O	O	O	
Design assessment methods to collect evidence of competent performance		O	O	
Internally verify assessment procedures		O	O	
Externally verify assessment procedures		O	O	
Advise and support candidates to identify prior achievement	O	O	O	
Constructively Improve T&D Performance				
Evaluate T&D sessions	M			
Evaluate + develop own practice	M	M	M	M
Evaluate T&D programmes		M	M	
Manage relationships with colleagues & customers	O	O	M	
Improve T&D programmes		O	M	
Develop T&D methods		O		
Evaluate contribution and role of HRD				M
Introduce improvements to HRD				M
Develop new approaches to HRD				O

Area/Unit Title / Basic Requirement	Level 3 T&D (All 'M's + 3 'O's)	Level 4 T&D (Lng Dev) (All 'M's + 5'O's)	Level 4 T&D (HRD) (All 'M's + 5 'O's)	Level 5 T&D (Strategy) (All 'M's + 3 'O's)
MCI Units				
Initiate & implement change + improvement in services, products + systems				O
Maintain & improve service + product operations			O	
Monitor, maintain + improve service + products delivery				O
Contribute to planning, monitoring and control of resources	O			
Recommend, monitor, and control use of resources		O	O	
Monitor & control the use of resources				M
Secure effective resource allocation				O
Contribute to provision of personnel	O			
Contribute to recruitment and selection of personnel		O	O	
Recruit & select personnel				O
Exchange information to solve problems and make decisions		O	O	
Other Units				
Establish & improve organisational culture + values				M
Comply with professional & ethical requirements				M
Establish effective computerised personnel information systems to support decision-making				O
Establish performance management processes				O
Negotiate & maintain service agreements				O
Provide support for practitioners in service delivery				O

Appendix 4

**National Vocational Qualifications
and General National Vocational Qualifications**

An Outline and a Commentary

THE NATIONAL VOCATIONAL QUALIFICATIONS FRAMEWORK

Historical background

In 1985 the UK Government established a review group to look at existing vocational education and training arrangements, and to make recommendations for improvements.

Vocational qualifications had for long played an important part in the early training of new entrants into work. Those employers who provided training facilities typically used as the keystone of their training programmes for young entrants attendance at further education classes in preparation for the examinations of a number of institutions which awarded nationally recognised qualifications. The leading awarding institutions were the City and Guilds, the Royal Society of Arts, the Business and Technology Education Council (now renamed Edexcel) and the professional institutions – but there were other bodies, national and provincial in scope, that offered qualifications; indeed any educational organisation could issue its own certificates (Further Education Colleges often did) to anyone passing their own examinations and meeting their own criteria.

There had never been any attempt to rationalise or co-ordinate these qualifications, and it is probably true that employers in general had little understanding of what was available. It was sometimes claimed by personnel specialists that the awarding bodies were themselves more 'educational' than 'work-based', that studies were academic rather than practical, that standards varied across the country, and that recruitment officers could not be expected to judge or even to understand the documents that candidates presented at interview. At a time when pressure was mounting to promote training throughout UK industry, proposals inevitably emerged to rationalise and modernise this haphazard system.

The recommendations of the review group were accepted by the Government and formed the basis of a 1986 White Paper entitled *Working Together – Education and Training*. This charged the existing Manpower Services Commission (succeeded later by the Training Agency) with 'working with industry to facilitate the identification of industry standards' which could be embodied in new National Vocational Qualifications (NVQs) and would be accredited by a new National Council for Vocational Qualifications (NCVQ). (The remit was later extended to cover Scotland and Scottish Vocational Qualifications (SVQs), which were to be accredited by the Scottish Vocational and Education Council (SCOTVEC); throughout this book we have taken the liberty of using the terms NVQ and NCVQ to additionally relate to their Scottish equivalents, and our commentary always covers both.)

NCVQ was established later the same year (1986); by 1999, a framework of over 800 NVQs had been established covering over 500 occupations, many at more than one work level, with over 2 million qualification certificates issued. The NVQ model was further extended in 1991 beyond occupationally specific areas by the introduction of 'General' NVQs (GNVQs), which became available in schools and colleges from 1992; although not tied to defined industry standards, these GNVQs were planned to reflect fundamental skills, knowledge and understanding in occupational areas, facilitating progression to NVQs at higher levels (and aimed essentially at those who remain in full-time education beyond age 16, entering the world of work later). By 1996, GNVQs were in existence, or being piloted, or planned for early piloting, in 14 areas; official 1995 statistics gave the number of GNVQ registrations as 163,000, and rapid growth in numbers was forecast.

Prior to 1995, the responsibility for overseeing all qualifications for those in full-time education below age 16 (ie *schools-based* qualifications) had been entrusted to a School Curriculum and Assessment Authority (SCAA). The emergence of GNVQs, plus moves to 'make education more vocational', led to the merging in 1995 of NCVQ and SCAA in a new 'Qualifications and Curriculum Authority' (QCA). QCA now carries the responsibility for accrediting proposals for national vocational standards and for NVQ awards, along with the quality assurance and audit of the awarding bodies; QCA similarly develops and accredits GNVQs.

The NVQ framework and system

Standards for NVQs (as distinct from GNVQ standards, which we shall discuss later) are created and updated by what used to be known as 'Lead Bodies' but are now termed 'National Training Organisations', or 'NTOs'. There are over 150 NTOs, most devoted to a specific industry (eg agriculture, chemicals) but a few addressing trans-industry occupations (eg clerical and administrative work). NTOs are government funded. Standards are essentially 'employment based' – that is, they reflect actual jobs that exist, and define for each job what is considered to be 'competence' on the part of the job-holder. Management standards – which are added selectively by NTOs to their own 'higher level' products – are created by the independently established Management Charter Group (MCG). The overall NVQ system framework currently shows the following 11 national 'framework areas' (not to be confused with the 'areas of competence' charted in a given NVQ set of standards):

- tending animals, plants and land
- extracting and providing natural resources
- constructing
- engineering
- manufacturing
- transporting
- providing goods and services
- providing health, social and protective services
- providing business services
- communicating
- developing and extending knowledge and skill.

The *process* whereby NVQs are created, developed, delivered, awarded, and preserved involves several *organisations*:

1 Within each of the 11 areas mentioned above, an individual NTO identifies the need for an NVQ, and completes the necessary drafting of 'standards' documents, liaising as necessary with awarding bodies.
2 Awarding bodies design assessment and quality assurance systems and content, which must be endorsed by the NTO before 3.
3 Detailed proposals are jointly submitted by the NTO and one or more awarding bodies to the QCA for accreditation.
4 The QCA ensures that the proposed qualification(s) meet particular criteria, and will be broadly comparable across different sectors (we explain the detailed criteria later at some length).
5 The QCA approves (and monitors) the awarding bodies.
6 Awarding bodies identify and approve institutions to implement and assure the quality of the NVQ, together with assessment centres which meet their criteria for assessing student achievement (training providers may also be assessment centres, and in some instances are empowered to mount their own examinations, but for the most part awarding bodies impose external examinations).
7 Training providers, notably FE colleges, include the NVQ in their own syllabuses, enrol students, and administer study programmes and examination arrangements, liaising as necessary with employers to cover work-based learning or work experience (in some specially negotiated cases, the entire programme may be mounted on the employer's premises; similarly, some training providers have negotiate a 'franchise' to cover the necessary preparation for all learners employed by one employer on a number of geographically dispersed sites).

Levels of NVQ Performance, which do not overlap, are defined by QCA as follows, and condition the positioning of a given NVQ in the overall national qualifications picture:

Level 1 – Competence which involves the application of knowledge and skills in the performance of a range of varied work activities, most of which may be routine and predictable.

Level 2 – Competence which involves the application of knowledge and skills in a significant range of varied work activities, performed in a variety of contexts. Some of the activities are complex or non-routine, and there is some individual responsibility or autonomy. Collaboration with others, perhaps through membership of a work group or team, may often be a requirement.

Level 3 – Competence which involves the application of knowledge and skills in a broad range of varied work activities performed in a wide variety of contexts,
most of which are complex and non-routine. There is considerable responsibility and autonomy, and control or guidance of others is often required.

Level 4 – Competence which involves the application of knowledge and skills in a broad range of complex, technical or professional work activities performed in a wide variety of contexts and with a substantial degree of personal responsibility and autonomy. Responsibility for the work of others and the allocation of resources is often present.

Level 5 – Competence which involves the application of skills and a significant range of fundamental principles across a wide and often unpredictable variety of contexts. Very substantial personal autonomy and often significant responsibility for the work of others and for the allocation of substantial resources feature strongly, as do personal accountabilities for analysis and diagnosis, design, planning, execution and evaluation.

(Reproduced from QCA's *Data News*, May 1999)

It can be seen that these definitions signpost ascending degrees of (a) complexity (b) variety (c) autonomy and (d) responsibility for the work of others. Personal accountability for analysis, diagnosis, creative decisions and such competencies (NB not properly called 'competences' in this context) is specified only at the highest level.

Draft standards must be approved by QCA before they are used as the basis for qualifications which carry the NVQ 'kitemark' at any of the five levels. To be approved, standards must meet certain requirements. They must, for example, be based on *work performance*, not learning performance or personal attributes; they must be written in a way that explains what is expected of people in a job or work role, not as a description of the work itself; and they must define learning *outcomes*, not how the learning should happen. To meet these and similar criteria, standard-setters are expected to engage in 'functional thinking' and indeed 'functional analysis': they must draw functional 'maps' which break down work into areas, sub-areas and *units of competence* – which are deemed to be worthy of separate certification

– and, below that, what are termed *elements of competence*, which constitute the basic outcomes required to justify that certification.

The terms *area* and *sub-area* simply explain the logical positioning of collections of 'units' of competence within an NVQ's framework. A *unit* describes a specific competence via a single short statement. The unit of competence is for educational purposes either 'mandatory' or 'optional' – these units of competence being the building blocks of NVQ qualifications. An *element* is a precise description of what someone should be able to do; it must be accompanied by one or more *performance criteria*, which define a characteristic of competent performance of the element (*all* the performance criteria attaching to an element must be satisfied in order for performance to be considered 'competent'), and by a *range statement*, which defines the breadth or scope of the element by setting out the various circumstances or work settings within which it is to be applied. These three things – the element description, the performance criteria and the range statement – constitute collectively the 'standard' (an example – taken from the Employment National Training Organisation's national standards for trainers – can be seen in Figure 6.11 on page 139).

Figure App. 4.1 reflects the tasks of the standard-setters. NCVQ originally held that knowledge and understanding requirements should not be included within standards, for these assets do no more than *underpin* competence and cannot constitute competence *per se*. A more recent (1995) development amended this view by adding the requirement to produce accompanying (ie attached to, but not part of, the standard) *knowledge specifications* and *evidence requirements*. These were meant (a) to satisfy widespread claims from training providers and personnel managers that knowledge and understanding are indeed an essential part of competence in many jobs, and (b) to help awarding bodies and trainers to interpret standards when creating assessment schedules and learning programmes. Knowledge specifications are now expected to refer to national requirements, not to those within an individual work organisation or at a given workplace; evidence requirements are now expected to state the types and amount of evidence that must exist for a positive assessment of performance competence. We have, of course, seen in the QCA's definitions of levels of competence that 'application of knowledge' is now clearly accepted as a fundamental part of competence.

'*Core skills*' were originally seen by NCVQ as covered within each specific standard. The QCA has, however, developed its own list of 'key skills units', and published national standards for these skills in their own right. They are said to be relevant at all five levels, 'can be used *alongside* NVQs' (and indeed alongside GNVQs and even A Levels – their prime use is probably within schools), and 'are about applying everyday skills in a useful way' (QCA's *Data News*, Summer 1998). These key skills units are:

- information technology
- application of number
- communication

Figure App. 4.1 **Developing an NVQ Standard (an example)**

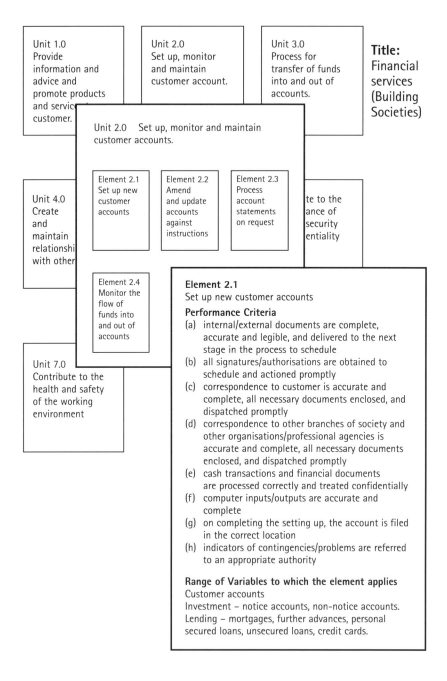

- working with others
- improving own learning and performance
- problem-solving.

Further units are promised.

The reader who wishes to study the NVQ system in greater detail should obtain a copy of the document mentioned in the preceding paragraph: NCVQ's (updated 1995) publication *NVQ Criteria and Guidance*. This is a comprehensive guide to the philosophy underlying NVQs and to all implementation aspects, including assessment, quality assurance and accreditation practices.

Once standards have been approved, awarding bodies can transform them into learning programmes and can establish appropriate assessment processes. Assessment 'should support and draw upon the working and management arrangements of the organisation in which it is used' (*NVQ Criteria and Guidance*, 1995). This requirement has produced many problems, especially in cases where employers' arrangements rely on college staff for assessment, or where workplace supervision is believed to be less than impartial. External assessors and simulation methods are tending to become increasingly accepted where workplace assessment is either not possible or not wanted by employers, and as such methods improve. National standards for assessors are established within the Employment NTO's standards for Training and Development, and NVQ assessors must now be formally certificated in the relevant units of competence.

The QCA must of course approve awarding bodies to award specific NVQs; QCA does not itself make any awards.

The GNVQ framework and system

Despite being linked with areas of work (eg manufacturing, art and design), GNVQs are essentially *non-occupationally specific qualifications*: the underlying philosophy remains the same as that behind NVQs, but GNVQs are aimed essentially at people (mainly young people who are still in full-time education beyond age 16, although some GNVQ studies can start earlier) who are not identified with any given career or industry. The five-level NVQ framework is retained, but because units are largely determined by knowledge requirements, NVQ definitions for each level are irrelevant and ignored. GNVQs are *unit-based*: that is, they comprise combinations of mandatory and optional vocational units, with mandatory core skills interlaced (these core skills are restricted to the prime NVQ fields of communication, application of number and information technology).

Unlike NVQs, all GNVQs at a given level have the same number of units. These units are basically statements of 'attainment', not statements of competence. They are however still described in terms of outcomes (ie what the learner can *do*) and, like NVQs, they contain descriptions of performance criteria, range indicators and evidence indicators. Guidance for teachers is added; colleges and other training providers are expected to design their own courses to meet the requirements of the awarding body with which the student is registered. The three main awarding bodies – EDEXCEL, CG and RSA – have formed a joint council to supervise assessment and accreditation arrangements; as at end 1995, over 70 per cent of all registrations were with EDEXCEL, with CG and RSA accounting for the vast majority of the rest.

The (to date) 14 areas of GNVQ work do not reflect or repeat those used for NVQ purposes. These GNVQ areas are:

- GNVQ Art and Design
- GNVQ Business
- GNVQ Construction and the Built Environment
- GNVQ Engineering
- GNVQ Health and Social Care
- GNVQ Hospitality and Catering
- GNVQ Information Technology
- GNVQ Land and Environment
- GNVQ Leisure and Tourism
- GNVQ Manufacturing
- GNVQ Media: Communication and Production
- GNVQ Performing Arts and Entertainment Industries
- GNVQ Retail and Distributive Services
- GNVQ Science.

Integrating the systems

Much time has gone into debating how to establish progression routes that integrate the NVQ and GNVQ systems (and indeed combine them with the traditional academic route to higher education). The result is a progressive network of all three, as shown in Figure App. 4.2.

Figure App. 4.2 illustrates both the problem and its solution. The collective title, embracing all post-16 qualifications as 'national', and again as 'qualifications for work', recognises the continuing strength of traditional academic qualifications, not least in the eyes of employers. In encouraging movement from *all three* routes into higher education, parity of esteem is established (or at least claimed) for the various choices facing a 16-year-old. And, in giving GNVQ status to vocationally oriented university first degrees and post-graduate work, graduate entry into the world of work and their move on to professional status (at NVQ Levels 4/5) is covered. In allocating the terms 'Foundation', 'Intermediate' and 'Advanced' to GNVQ Levels 1, 2 and 3 respectively, definition problems are swept aside, and the awards become at once more easily related to other forms of college work; moreover, the A level appears to mirror traditional university requirements and can be expected to be more acceptable to higher education in general.

The integrated system is designed to offer:

Figure App. 4.2 **Qualifications for work**

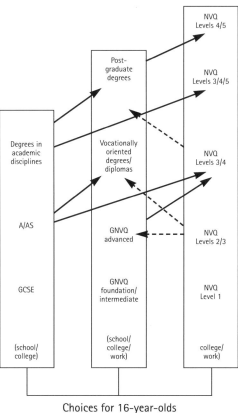

Choices for 16-year-olds

Source: QCA 'Data News', February, 1999

- freedom for the individual to create a personal route of progress in work or education, or in work and education
- choice to stay in education or to move to work, regardless of the age at which the choice is exercised
- the flexibility to transfer skills from one job area to another without starting back at the beginning.

This admirable mixture is achieved partly at the cost of some playing with principles. 'Competence' in its NVQ meaning cannot be developed or claimed within the GNVQ streams, but progression to higher-level NVQs is allowed without its demonstration. The establishment of independent Key Skills Units conflicts with the earlier NCVQ view that 'core' skills should be defined only in their applied form within any given NVQ

337

standard; these units are now defined as standards in their own right and can be accredited alongside both NVQs and GNVQs – suggesting that educational needs have prevailed over workplace logic. Assessment is also a continuing problem: complex demands by the awarding bodies (eg on the collection of evidence) have frequently annoyed teachers who have themselves designed the learning programmes. We shall say more about problems below.

COMMENTARY

During the 10 years since the establishment of NCVQ the voices of many critics and reviewers have been heard. Although the need for a national structure is accepted, and although commitment by the government, lead bodies, colleges, awarding bodies and assessors has resulted in the speedy introduction and establishment of NVQs and GNVQs, concerns have been expressed over matters concerned with the basic philosophy, the assessment methods, and general points relating to the whole administration of the scheme. We shall deal with each of these areas in turn.

Basic philosophy: the competence approach plus functional analysis

It would appear that there are inherent problems in a scheme, national in its coverage, based on competences defined by outcomes and determined by the process of functional analysis. There are two main approaches to defining competences (or competencies): the *input* approach and the *outcomes* model (see page 208). The latter normally involves some type of job analysis and was chosen by the NCVQ, using the technique of functional analysis (see pages 214–16), to determine the desired *outcomes*: in other words, exactly what must be done and to what standard.

As was discovered by trainers in the early days of the training boards, it is not easy to encapsulate a skill using analytical methods, the ensuing description involving an artificial compartmentalisation of knowledge and skill. Wolf (1994) points out that in a regulatory system the more specific one tries to be, the deeper one has to go, and the more cumbersome the result. The NCVQ constantly had to refine its approach – the 'elements of competence' had to be qualified by 'performance criteria', by 'range statements' and finally by 'specifications of underpinning knowledge and understanding'.

The concentration on 'outcomes' led to the neglect of the underlying knowledge and understanding, the pioneers of NCVQ arguing that by defining and testing the outcome they were implicitly including the underlying knowledge. It was recognised later, but only after very considerable criticism, that replication of performance in differing sets of circumstances both current and future requires knowledge and understanding of basic principles, and the specifications of knowledge and understanding were added. These are still held by many critics to be less than satisfactory. For instance, Steedman and Hawkins (1994), to whom we are indebted for a number of ideas and references in this commentary, quote as an example that the advent of NVQs has resulted in the requirement for mathematics for building work being reduced to a level that they claim is substantially below that required in other countries. They argue that the flexibility and adaptability of these trainees will be reduced and suggest that the situation has arisen because NVQs are open not only to young trainees but to experienced workers who, although competent at the work they are currently doing, could not cope with the sophisticated mathematical techniques that might be needed in the future.

Without some mechanism for focusing on 'key areas', minute analysis can lead to attention being devoted to relatively unimportant aspects of the job, to the neglect of those that are critical. Furthermore, Wellens pointed out as far back as 1970 that analysis is at its most effective when applied to routine work and at its least useful in managerial and creative jobs, where it is more difficult, if not impossible, to prescribe the content. An important part of a manager's job may be to determine what in fact he or she ought to be doing and his or her first duties should be to *set* and *reset* standards. The idea of those standards' being defined nationally undermines the very first principles of managerial responsibility. A further difficulty is that analyses require constantly updating; they reflect the position in the 'here and now' and do not necessarily meet the needs of rapidly changing organisations. It is ironic that we have a growing emphasis on learning organisations and continuous development, and a state scheme that relies upon analytical techniques which are at their most effective in a static situation. In Chapter 12 we referred to the suggestion by Carling and Heller (1995) that victory would go to creative organisations that *generated their own future*. One is tempted to ask whether our scheme of national qualifications is devised to maintain the status quo and to encourage companies which, in Carling and Heller's terms, are 'fighting the last war' by devoting all their energies to techniques and practices that have already brought success to our competitors.

In a national scheme, difficulties about the transfer of learning arise in defining outcomes and competences that would apply universally to all types of organisation. This difficulty is compounded where the assessment is carried out at the workplace and certificated as a national (and therefore presumably *transferable*) qualification. Is this possible? For example, can a managerial competence gained and assessed in a large international chemical company be transferred to a small catering company employing 10 people? Have we sufficient research evidence about the transfer of learning to know this? The difficulty is in trying to meet the objective (commendable in itself) of highly job-specific training and assessment leading to a national transferable qualification.

Assessment

Some commentators – for example Marks (1996) – have drawn attention to the huge variation in practice and standards found between centres by the

Government's own researchers. The fact that the system is based on *outcomes* which are assessed *internally, on the job*, or *by project and course work* means that standards must vary and draws the *reliability* of the qualification itself into serious question. Marks compares the NVQs with the vocational qualifications in Germany, where care is taken to ensure reliability and comparability across the country. In contrast to the situation in the UK, there is statutory regulation of all important aspects of course content and structure, as well as external assessment involving written examinations in technical and general subjects and external practical and oral examinations. Prais (1991) maintains that NVQ standards are lower than those in the rest of Europe, and other commentators argue that assessing competence in terms of 'outcomes' results in neglecting the underlying knowledge, theory and understanding acquired by trainees in France, Germany and the Netherlands.

Other assessment issues relate to the objectivity of assessors, who will often be the trainers themselves and will therefore usually know the trainees. Furthermore, Steedman and Hawkins (1994) point out that as Training and Enterprise Councils allocate funding to colleges and other providers based on trainees' success in NVQs, college lecturers and other trainers may well be dependent for their jobs on the success of the very trainees they are assessing. The training of assessors also causes difficulties because of the numbers involved and the cost to the organisation. In short, there are so many variables ranging from type of job, industry, size of company, organisation culture to the number and training of assessors that uniformity of standards must be drawn into serious question. In addition, the concentration on assessment and assessors seems to have diverted attention and interest from developing high-quality workplace trainers.

General points

Shackleton and Walsh (1995) point to the fact that the advent of NVQs has suppressed competitive qualifications. An awarding body seeking recognition must phase out its non-NVQ awards in related fields. Furthermore, Government funding for training schemes and for tax relief to individuals investing in their own training is limited to NVQ awards. They also add that possession of certain NVQs is becoming a statutory requirement for certain job-holders, particularly in relation to health and safety. The competitive market is therefore declining, a situation which they suggest sits rather oddly with recent UK deregulation in other spheres.

Some employers have been put off the scheme because of its cost, bureaucracy and jargon, and in some cases, because they felt that the competences as defined did not meet their needs. Professor Alan Smithers (1993) postulates that rather than being employer-led, the lead bodies are excessively influenced by consultants, who regard them as a business opportunity. Employers consistently ask for literacy and numeracy, and these requests have until recently been disregarded.

Some academics have questioned the adequacy of the NCVQ/QCA definitions of competence, especially in relation to professional and management-level work. Fleming (1991) argues that there are 'higher-order competences' (collectively termed 'meta-competence') which are needed and used in situations that are not predictable, and indeed are central to the management of change. He describes NVQ standards as extending no further than reactive 'contingency management'; proactive change management is described as 'seeing the signs of change in the present' and 'anticipating theoretical and technical advances', then 'imaginatively and constructively' innovating. Fleming is typical of those within UK universities who believe that degree courses, based essentially on the acquisition of knowledge and understanding in an intellectually critical environment, develop this 'meta-competence' which the graduate brings into employment; they claim that graduates typically experience the value of what they have done at the university only later, when meta-competence has had something on which to work. They are also concerned that the current preoccupation with more specific competences may dilute future professional and management studies to the detriment of future innovative work.

Take-up of NVQs

QCA figures show that since 1986 over 2 million certificates have been issued. Shackleton and Walsh (1995) examine the results of the Labour Force Survey 1994 Quarter 1, and conclude that about 5 per cent of the employed population of working age has been or is involved with NVQs/SVQs. However, they draw attention to the fact that this figure does not necessarily indicate a net gain in qualifications, because many NVQs simply replace existing awards. Furthermore, they identify variations in take-up, depending upon:

- *gender*   the take-up figure for women is greater than that for men
- *age*   younger people are more likely to take NVQs than older people, but women in 35–49 age group are more likely to be involved than those of 25–34
- *economic activity*   those on Government schemes are more likely to be involved, whereas self-employed workers are less likely to take part
- *occupation*   workers in clerical/secretarial and personal services are well represented, whereas managers, professionals and plant and machine operatives tend to be underrepresented
- *region*   the Northern, North Western Regions (ie the poorer regions) have higher than average take-up rates, possibly reflecting the influence of government schemes
- *industry*   some industries – agriculture, fishing, forestry, transport and communications – are significantly underrepresented, whereas there is a high take-up of students for awards linked to statutory obligations such as those in energy or water supply.

Figures relating to take-up rates must therefore be interpreted with care. Although overall they may appear encouraging, they are uneven and influenced by a number of factors, not least by government support, and do not necessarily indicate wholehearted and widespread approval.

Monitoring the system

Both the NCVQ and the QCA have been keen to review the progress of their system and products. Many detailed changes have been made – to specific standards, to criteria, and – perhaps most significantly – to the ways in which NVQs, GNVQs and non-vocational qualifications can be understood within an integrated national framework. Problems nevertheless remain. A 1995 evaluation survey, independently overseen by a specially established Evaluation Advisory Group, gathered opinions on the 'Top 100' NVQs and promised a later exercise that would embrace the entire list. The NCVQ press report on this research detailed – after highlighting success stories and judging overall that 'the benefits of NVQs outweigh the costs – the following 'main issues of concern':

- occupational standards do not always reflect the needs of employers
- the language of NVQs . . . makes the standards inaccessible and difficult to understand
- assessment is too burdensome and bureaucratic
- knowledge and understanding specifications are sometimes too vague – some qualifications demand too much and others too little
- external verifiers need a clearer role and better support
- the number of awarding bodies with different systems makes it difficult for employers and individuals.

It is perhaps too early to know if these concerns will lead to major changes; the QCA has been preoccupied during its first two years of existence with establishing its own operations.

There is no doubt that the system has certain attractions that have been appreciated by countries such as Australia, New Zealand, and Ireland, which have introduced schemes along similar lines. It provides 'transparency' of qualifications to enable comparison with European countries – although, as has been pointed out, the knowledge content is currently regarded by some as still not equivalent to that prescribed by our competitors). To an individual, it can provide 'portable' qualifications which can be accessed at times and at levels to suit career progression, and to that extent it supports the concept of continuous development. To an organisation, it offers a consistent methodology, because the defined *standards* can be used for indentification of training needs, coaching, drawing-up training plans and so on, right through to staff appraisal. Some organisations have taken advantage of the system to involve management by adopting a 'cascading' approach, devolving responsibility for defining the standards of their subordinates to line managers. The facility of Accreditation of Prior Experience

(APL) opens the door to experienced workers without the necessity of starting at the beginning to cover competences they already possess. Theoretically, a system of work-based assessment for national certificates should bring training and vocational education closer together. In practice, however, there is a danger that the emphasis on qualifications might turn some employers' attention away from workplace training, under the misguided apprehension that 'the colleges will do it all'. The answer probably is that both training and education are necessary; they should go hand in hand, offering distinctive, but complementary, contributions.

As the system becomes better known, it should eliminate the previous confusion between the awards of many different, but often comparable, qualifications of various awarding bodies, and abolish the situation where trainees possessing one award sometimes had to duplicate studies already undertaken to obtain a higher award from a different body. The NCVQ consistently sought and listened to criticism, and showed itself able to make detailed amendments to the system; the QCA has been equally ready to describe its product as a developing one. The nation's skills are the lifeblood of the economy, and we must therefore hope fervently that our national system of developing people with tomorrow's skills can be made sufficently sound, reliable and robust to maintain our prosperity in the world.

Appendix 5

A 'QUICK GUIDE' TO TRAINING METHODS AND TECHNIQUES

Adapted and expanded from Paper No. 5 of the former Ceramics, Glass and Mineral Products Training Board. Entries have been arranged in an order which moves from traditional and relatively simple methods and techniques, through those which are more complex and require more planning, to those which make use of sophisticated technology.

METHOD: WHAT IT IS	WHAT IT CAN ACHIEVE	POINTS TO WATCH
LECTURE Structured, planned talk. Usually accompanied by visual aids, eg slides, OHP foils, flipchart.	Suitable for large audiences where participation is not wanted. Content and timing can be planned in detail.	Lively style needed. Communication of material may be limited if no provision for feedback to lecturer.
FILMS/VIDEOTAPES 'Visual lectures' – but often presented in dramatised form.	As 'Lectures' – but addition of moving images and drama can significantly aid motivation. Useful as precursor to discussion; can be 'stopped' at key points for discussion.	Tailor-made products are expensive. Care needed to ensure material (not just title) is relevant.
CASE-STUDY Examination of events or situation – often real life – usually aimed at learning by analysing the detailed material or defining, and posing solutions for, problems.	Opportunities exist for both exchange of views on 'what matters' and problem-solving. Especially useful for analysis of financial/statistical data. Can incorporate exercises.	Simple cases may give wrong impression of reality. Difficult to reproduce the 'political climate'.

METHOD: WHAT IT IS	WHAT IT CAN ACHIEVE	POINTS TO WATCH
PROMPT LIST List of 'questions to which a person should have answers'.	Useful basis for self-study or discussion in cases where opinions are important but no clear 'correct' answer exists.	Can highlight inter-personal differences in terms of values – and hence stimulate conflict.
DISCUSSION Free exchange of information, opinions, etc. A 'controlled' discussion may follow a planned path, the leader controlling the agenda; an 'open' discussion may mirror members' priorities.	Especially suitable for development or adjustment of attitudes and opinions. Promotes group cohesion. Also offers feedback to trainer on learning achievement.	May be time-consuming – especially if discussion wanders or 'process problems' emerge. Attitudes may harden rather than adjust. Individual participation may be affected by group composition.
DIALOGUE 'Collective reflection' – two way discussion (or group – often with 'facilitator'). Participants suspend assumptions and work as colleagues.	Shared mental models, and shared understanding of problems/situations; team coherence and discipline.	Facilitator must be skilled; careful line is needed between comment/help and 'expert/intrusion' roles.

METHOD: WHAT IT IS	WHAT IT CAN ACHIEVE	POINTS TO WATCH
INSTRUCTION Formula-based 'teaching' session: 1 Tell – how to do 2 Show – how to do 3 Do (supervised practice) 4 Review process and results.	For introducing skills, usually in line with a planned breakdown of small sequential practice stages. Confidence is built by mastery and link-up of stages. Typically must follow input of knowledge, the skills to be learned being those of application.	Skill may be best addressed as a whole rather than in parts – but lengthy stages 1 and 2 yield memory problems. Design/balance of session important.
LANGUAGE LABORATORY Individual booths equipped with audio programmes and linked to a central tutor.	Allows learner-paced language tuition and practice without 'speaking in public'. Machine management seems to promote motivation.	Good for early stages but cannot replace eventual need to practise in public.
DISCOVERY LEARNING 'Learning without a teacher' – but usually in a controlled (ie pre-designed) set-up, and under supervision.	Offers challenge and builds confidence as learner masters new skills. Best suited to tasks involving dismantling, checking, adjusting, rebuilding. Helps understanding of principles.	Considerable design work needed. Safety paramount – may need special adjustments, and so be unrealistic.

METHOD: WHAT IT IS	WHAT IT CAN ACHIEVE	POINTS TO WATCH
EXERCISE Carrying out a particular task along prescribed lines. Often a test of knowledge communicated earlier.	Highly active form of learning; satisfies need for practice to apply knowledge or develop skill. Often linked with test to judge extent of learning.	Exercise must be realistic, objectives attainable.
PROJECT 'Large-scale exercise', but leaving most of the process within learner discretion. Frequently involves collecting and reporting data, then offering conclusions and recommendations for improvement.	Like exercises, offers practice and simultaneously 'tests'. Stimulates analysis + creativity; also reporting skill.	Like exercises, needs realism and attainability. If 'real life', must have support of those responsible for reality. Ideally will be 'actioned'.
ROLE-PLAY Enactment of role(s) in protected training environment.	Mainly used to practise face-to-face skills (eg selling) combined with review critiques from trainers and/or other learners.	Unless disciplined, can cause embarrassment. Realism of set-up important.
ROLE-REVERSAL Enactment of reversed roles by two or more learners in simulated situation.	Mainly used to help those who operate in face-to-face situations to appreciate their contacts' needs and feelings.	As with role-play, needs discipline and realism.

348

METHOD: WHAT IT IS	WHAT IT CAN ACHIEVE	POINTS TO WATCH
SIMULATIONS/BUSINESS GAMES Dynamic exercises or case-studies – usually involving 'coming to terms with' a situation, then managing it via a set of imposed decisions. Computerised models offer complex data, and often decisions that interact.	Offers practice in management – observation, analysis, judgement, decision-making, etc. Interactive element generates enthusiasm, notably when teams are in simulated competition. Can be linked with team development.	Model can be challenged as unrealistic.
STUDY GROUPS Task-briefed groups which also practise process review, aided by a process consultant, who does *not* operate outside this role.	Offers appreciation of need for both task and process management; also group learning processes.	Some learners dislike lack of structure. May generate stress.
OUTDOOR TRAINING Dynamic open-air exercises, usually carried out in teams.	Offers practice in management, in challenging or problematic circumstances; also leadership and teamwork opportunities, as well as self-analysis.	Physical challenge can be tough. Some learners may not accept relevance of unusual environment.

METHOD: WHAT IT IS	WHAT IT CAN ACHIEVE	POINTS TO WATCH
VIDEO-CONFERENCING AND TELE-CONFERENCING way audio and two-way visual link-up (see Hogan 1993).	Participative training sessions: trainers in different locations. Can interact with each other and with a tutor.	Special training needed for tutor. Careful preplanning Two-essential.
ELECTRONIC BRAINSTORMING Participants sit in a laboratory at individual PCs connected through a local area network. One computer acts as a file server (see El-Sherif and Tang, 1994).	By using special packages eg Meeting Ware, each participant can contribute anonymously by computer to a brainstorming session. The results are analysed by computer.	Careful preparation needed. Experienced team guide required.

350

METHOD: WHAT IT IS	WHAT IT CAN ACHIEVE	POINTS TO WATCH
SELF-MANAGED LEARNING: READING Learner-paced coverage of printed material, with or without basic learning plan	Knowledge retention can be good if learner motivation is high. Learning packages are often augmented by audio- and/or videotapes.	Motivation often declines if reading is difficult/'dull'. Tutorial help can be important.
RADIO + TV BROADCASTS	Large potential audiences permit costly programmes. Often linked with national (eg Open University) courses and qualifications. Satellite TV is likely to offer new and wider subjects. Can be linked with tutorial assistance by phone.	Viewing times often unsocial.

METHOD: WHAT IT IS	WHAT IT CAN ACHIEVE	POINTS TO WATCH
SELF-MANAGED LEARNING: TECHNOLOGY-ASSISTED Learner-managed coverage of programmed material, usually involving keyboard and screen.	Many varied uses. Computer-based training (CBT) can offer workplace simulations and link with videotape to provide still or moving pictures. Compact Disks offer huge information storage, with visual additions. Moves to introduce artificial intelligence (AI) yield prospect of using machine as a tutor and managing one's own learning process.	Hardware may be expensive. Present state of technology makes logic-based programs most reliable.
Computer-based Training (CBT) (Learner uses keyboard in line with screen instructions, calling forth information and responding to questions.)	Screen material can be complex and include animation. Good for presenting statistics. With addition of 'artificial intelligence' (CBT – AI) learner responds to computer question, computer interprets response and adjusts own program.	Compatible hardware and software needed; perhaps also tutorial help.

METHOD: WHAT IT IS	WHAT IT CAN ACHIEVE	POINTS TO WATCH
The Internet, and intranets Worldwide computerised information network, and grouped user sites.	Allows worldwide information gathering, including planned programmes of learning, plus worldwide forums. Useful data source for projects of all kinds. Intranets offer flows of information to specific workplace sites. Some organisations are developing intranet systems in which members continuously input data for central storage which all can access as needed.	Need for discipline in 'surfing' the Net and coping with vast amounts of available material. Security systems may be required to manage 'classified' intranet data.
Compact Disc Training (CDT) and (Video Disc Training (VDT) (Used in conjunction with TV or personal computers)	Compact Disc and Digital Versatile Disc 'Read-Only Memory' (CD-ROM and DVD-ROM) offer high-capacity data-storage facilities. Retrieval can include text, pictures and sound.	Special hardware needed. Limited to retrieval of stored data.
	CD and DVD 'Read-Only Memory – Extended Architecture' (CD-ROM-XA and DVD-ROM-XA) allow learners to 'play with material', practising analysis and synthesis. (DVD allows complex simulations.) Particularly suitable for assembling, dismantling, diagnosis and decision-making.	Learner needs some basic awareness of data in order to manipulate it.

METHOD: WHAT IT IS	WHAT IT CAN ACHIEVE	POINTS TO WATCH
	CD 'Interactive' (CD-I) is similar to CBT-AI (see page 352) in allowing learner much greater control of the learning process, the programme adjusting to learner questions and responses.	May not reproduce realistic workplace language; hence tutor may also be needed.
	'Digital Video' Interactive (DV-I) offers CD-I together with the facility to videotape the learner's own actions, and replay the results. Ideal where the learner must perfect a *physical* movement (eg golf swing, or sign language), and needs to see the result.	Hardware and software are likely to be costly.

NB: VDT are increasingly available as CBT, CDT and 'multi-media programs', which can offer both information and practice in using the information to specific ends eg problem-solving. Program-making equipment, though expensive, can now also be purchased. The DVD's superior data-compression is likely to make it a standard learner-centred aid of the future, employing new style disc-playing equipment linked to the PC.

METHOD: WHAT IT IS	WHAT IT CAN ACHIEVE	POINTS TO WATCH
Virtual Reality (VR) A method of constructing, visualising and interacting with computer-generated three-dimensional worlds. It differs from conventional playback technology, which depends upon previously recorded images. A VR system must rapidly recalculate a fresh image in response to the participant's every move. To appear realistic each new image must be recalculated in under 100 milliseconds.	By using specialist equipment or by viewing the virtual model on the computer screen, users move through the simulated world and interact with it. In use worldwide by Motorola for teaching employees how to run assembly lines. Also in use by British Nuclear Fuels in the design of a control room, the model then to be kept for training purposes.	Currently very expensive to create. Only to be used with large numbers or for reasons of health and safety. A Virtual Reality Simulation Project launched in the UK in 1993 now has 14 members, including British Nuclear Fuels.

Appendix 6

The Institute of Personnel and Development (IPD) is the professional association specialising in the management and development of people for the United Kingdom and the Republic of Ireland.

1 Mission

The mission of the Institute of Personnel and Development is:

1.1 to lead in the development and promotion of good practice in the field of the management and development of people, for application both by professional members and by their organisational colleagues
1.2 to serve the professional interests of members
1.3 to uphold the highest ideals in the management and development of people.

2 Objects

The objects of the Institute are:

2.1 to promote and develop the science and practice of the management and development of people (including the promotion of research and the publication of the useful results of such research) for the public benefit
2.2 to establish, promote and monitor standards of competence, good practice, conduct and ethics for those engaged (or about to engage) in the practice of the management and the development of people, for the public benefit.

3 Purpose of this code

All IPD members of whatever grade of membership should be concerned with the maintenance of good practice within the profession and must commit themselves to this code of professional conduct which sets out the standards of professional conduct to which members must adhere. Attached to this code is a description of the procedure which will be applied to deal with any complaints arising.

4 Standards of professional conduct

IPD members are expected to exercise relevant competence in accordance with the Institute's professional standards and qualifications.

4.1 IPD members provide specialist professional knowledge, advice, support and management competence in the management and development of people. In all circumstances they:

    4.1.1 must endeavour to enhance the standing and good name of the profession; adherence to this code of professional conduct is an essential aspect of this

    4.1.2 must seek continually to improve their performance and update and refresh their skills and knowledge

    4.1.3 must within their own or any client organisation and in whatever capacity they are working, seek to achieve the fullest possible development of people for present and future organisational needs and encourage self-development by individuals

    4.1.4 must within their own or any client organisation and in whatever capacity they are working, seek to adopt in the most appropriate way, the most appropriate people management processes and structures to enable the organisation to best achieve its present and future objectives

    4.1.5 must promote and themselves maintain fair and reasonable standards in the treatment of people who are operating within scope of their influence

    4.1.6 must promote and themselves seek to exercise employment practices that remove unfair discrimination including but not limited to gender, age, race, religion, disability and background

    4.1.7 must respect legitimate needs and requirements for confidentiality

    4.1.8 must use due diligence and exercise high standards of timeliness, appropriateness and accuracy in the information and advice they provide to employers and employees

    4.1.9 must seek to recognise the limitations of their own knowledge and ability and must not undertake activity for which they are not yet appropriately prepared or, where applicable, qualified.

4.2 In the public interest and in the pursuit of its objects, the Institute of Personnel and Development is committed to the highest possible standards of professional conduct and competency. To this end members:

    4.2.1 are required to exercise integrity, honesty, diligence and appropriate behaviour in all their business, professional and related personal activities

    4.2.2 must act within the law and must not encourage, assist or act in collusion with employers, employees or others who may be engaged in unlawful conduct.

5 Complaints

Any person, whether or not a member, may complain to the Institute that a member has been guilty of conduct which is not in accordance with the provisions of this code and/or where that conduct appears likely to bring discredit to the Institute or the profession. Such conduct will be considered under the terms of the Disciplinary Procedure.

Appendix 7

A NOTE ON THE EUROPEAN SCENE

UK national training interventions during the 1980s and 1990s have in part been influenced by the UK government's interest and involvement in the European Union.

The European Union began as the European Economic Community, which was established in 1957 by six European countries (Belgium, France, Italy, Luxembourg, the Netherlands and Western Germany), who that year together signed the Treaty of Rome. Other countries have since joined: the UK became a member in 1973. The Community became the European Union in 1993, when the Maastricht Treaty revised and widened the remit of members, notably on common foreign and security policy, but also on justice and home affairs. The key point is that EU law, which must be based on Articles in the original Treaty, overrides national law, and must be interpreted according to its spirit or purpose.

The original Treaty of Rome included an Article stating that 'The Community shall have as its task . . . to promote a high level of employment and of social protection, the raising of the standard of living and quality of life, and economic and social cohesion and solidarity among Member States'. During the 1980s, European Commission documents underlined the belief that a 'common vocational policy' was being drafted. A 'Social Charter' was adopted in 1989 by all Member States *except the U*K (we shall say more about this later), and details a number of basic human rights, including one related to vocational training ('all workers shall have access to continuous vocational training throughout their working life'), although it stops short of prescribing how this should be ensured.

During the 1980s it seemed possible that any common EU vocational policy might incorporate measures to harmonise vocational qualifications, and that an uncoordinated UK training scene was unlikely to carry much influence – or, put another way, that future EU moves might be expected to draw more from German or French models than from British ones. UK civil servants wasted no time. The result, as we saw in Chapters 1 and 2, was the creation of the UK's national vocational qualifications system, which by the mid-1990s has generally been accepted as worthy of comparison with those of its two main 'competitors', France and Germany.

Competing systems

The *French* system is primarily educational in character and, implemented through a decentralised education network, involves much centralised control, and draws on statutory powers. Clear national aims and objectives exist for all aspects of education and training, including national qualification targets. Government retains control of curricula, examinations and the award of qualifications; teachers are assigned to institutions, not selected by them; regionally appointed subject inspectors assess teacher performance but do not advise institutions. *Lycées* (post-upper secondary schools) are well staffed and well resourced from public funds. Legal obligations rest on employers to contribute to training costs and to release employees to attend courses.

If we ignore the relatively small number of work-based apprenticeships (mainly available within large firms and requiring authorised trainers [*maîtres*]), training takes place almost exclusively in the *lycées*. Pupils study for their *Baccalauréat* qualifications, of which there are three: the 'general' (the Bac. Gen. – not a vocational qualification), the 'technological' (the Bac. Tec. – specialising in medicine or science), and the *professionnel* (the Bac. Pro. – essentially vocational in character). The *Baccalauréat* is the critical focus of the system (indeed, the system has become known colloquially as the 'baccalauréat system'); attaining this qualification is of immense social importance, and to a large extent conditions one's career prospects. Vocational education and development for adults are usually provided by groups of *lycées* administered by local regional bodies and open for six days a week, 11 months a year, which prepare students for further national examinations.

It should perhaps be stressed that French society places a high value on, and is greatly committed to, vocational education, and that France is moving, if slowly, towards a more decentralised system. France now encourages employers to become governors of *lycées* and curricula advisers, and to provide work experience for young people (full-time vocational programmes now contain 16-week work experience programmes). A high priority is given to careers education and guidance, which has ensured high levels of participation in post-compulsory education. However, the French system remains essentially a centralised one, as well as one based on learning away from work.

In contrast, the *German* training system is much more workplace-oriented, emphasising 'learning by doing', with 'apprenticeships' established in all the main areas of work. An apprenticeship combines employer-provided training with part-time vocational education at a vocational school; hence the system is generally described as 'the dual system'. There are no national training targets, but national rules govern learning for each trade: all businesses must register with a local Chamber of Industry and Commerce or a local craft chamber; training contracts (between employer and trainee) are registered with, and supervised by, the chamber (a substantial infrastructure of some 385 authorised chambers regulate the training programmes). No firm is obliged to provide training but virtually all large firms do, and inter-company training centres have been set up by chambers to provide for trainees from small and medium firms (significantly, two-thirds of the companies who train employ fewer than 50 people). On-the-job training is always in the hands of a *Meister* – an accredited 'master craftsman/woman' who is given considerable power over, and responsibility for, the trainee's learning process and progress (Germany boasts 40,000 full-time and 700,000 part-time qualified trainers, accounting for well over a third of all training costs). Off-the-job training usually involves weekly release to attend for 12 hours at *Berufschulen*, vocational extension schools which provide both vocational and general education and which are organised by the states (*Länder*) rather than the national government. The dual system is not merely well established: all political parties and all the social partners involved with the German economy are committed to the system, with its emphasis on the employer as the main training provider.

There is of course no good reason why traditionally rival nations should have similar internal systems. But the French and German training systems could hardly have less in common. The former is easy to describe, the latter complex. The former compels, the latter assumes, and draws on, goodwill from all sides. The French believe in isolating training away from work, the Germans in keeping it close to the workplace. France funds heavily from the centre and levies employers; German decentralises its funding, requiring those employers who train to do so at their own expense. France employs teachers, Germany continuously trains trainers. French qualifications are ends in themselves, influencing social as well as industrial status; German qualifications are routes rather than goals, and no qualification is considered an end in itself. Despite this last point, Germans currently seem less committed or geared to 'lifetime learning', whereas the French have long championed an *éducation permanente* philosophy.

We have seen the main emerging features of the UK training system as:

- centralised government initiatives
- a general lack of compulsory measures (no employer obligations, and no compulsion on learners beyond age 16)
- national training targets, covering organisations as well as individuals, the latter at all ages
- a decentralised system of national vocational qualifications, managed by a network of independent bodies, and committed to accrediting workplace competence
- a network of local Training and Enterprise Councils (TECs)
- emerging support for workplace learning and self-paced learning.

These features are sufficiently unique to suggest that they have not been slavishly copied from either of the UK's main competitors, but they do bear comparison. In promoting a national set of vocational qualifications and aiming at parity of esteem between these and its more traditional academic awards, the UK seems close to France; in insisting that vocational qualifications reflect workplace competence, it equates with Germany. National targets exist, as in France, industry-based standards are closer to the German model. The UK's specially created and geographically based TECs are not, however, to be found in either of the other systems, where influence is exerted through existing institutions (educational in France, local government and commercial in Germany). There is nothing in France or Germany similar to the UK 'Investors in People' campaign, quantified aims for which are established within UK national training targets – and which addresses the key issue of training *organisations*.

Perhaps the most significant differences between all three rest in the way each nation *formally* supports its system: Germany has well-voiced voluntary support, France has statutory requirements, but the UK has little of either, relying (to date) more on targets, dialogue and uncoordinated initiatives from a wide variety of sources, not necessarily government inspired, and not necessarily working towards common ends.

EU aims and actions

As we have noted, the EU's social aims have long assumed the implementation of a charter of human rights (referred to as the 'Social Charter'), including rights to vocational training. Faced with the differences between EU members' training systems, EU initiatives in this context have so far been limited to the following:

- an instrument on *access* to vocational training – for every worker, *throughout* his or her working life
- a stated commitment to the 'rationalisation and co-ordination' of training within 'a common vocational policy'
- comparability of vocational qualifications – including extension of work to cover levels above that of 'skilled worker'
- the promotion of 'lifelong learning' (1996 was designated 'the EU Year of Lifelong Learning').

The UK's Conservative government opposed the Social Charter from its introduction in 1989. The current Labour government has defended and supported it, but without specifically commenting on that part relating to vocational training. It is of interest to note that when in autumn 1997 (during the UK's EU Presidency) the Secretary of State for Education and Employment prepared to introduce a White Paper on lifelong learning, the UK cabinet delayed its appearance by two months and eventually issued the document as a Green (ie consultative) Paper, with many of its proposals rephrased as questions. Senior Cabinet ministers, including the Prime Minister, were said to be concerned that the original document 'lacked rigour' – which suggests that the government wanted more time to explore the implications of some of the EU's more generalised goals and intentions.

The UK is nevertheless signed up to the Social *Chapter*, which is contained within the 1993 Treaty on the European Union (the Maastricht Treaty), and which is effectively the way in which the Social Charter can be transformed into legislation. But the Social Chapter is modified by a 'subsidiarity clause' under which the EU, if it wishes to improve workers' rights by its own directives, must prove that national governments cannot achieve the same ends for themselves. Hence there is room for continued debate.

The scope of the Social Charter is wide: apart from such matters as freedom of movement and the right to receive training throughout one's working life, it covers, for example, rights to information and consultation – including information on planned technological changes and the restructuring of operations. Most importantly, it requires a number of health and safety standards to be met (including arrangements for firefighting, first aid and evacuation, with possible later extensions to include safety induction whenever an employee moves into a new job or area).

There is also the important issue of vocational qualifications and their mutual recognition across member boundaries. Principles for a common vocational training policy were established as long ago as 1963 (at which time such a policy seemed to be limited to establishing common qualifications). At national and transnational levels, the debate on 'integration or diversity' (or a new, acceptable, mix of both) is already being promoted by the European Commission and will continue into the next century. An early 'sectoral' directive required mutual recognition of certain listed professional qualifications (essentially medical practitioners' and other health service qualifications, plus architects'); another, in 1989, extended this to all other 'regulated' professional qualifications (ie qualifications without which a person is not allowed to practise within a member state); and directives in 1992 and 1996 have completed the picture by covering all other regulated vocational qualifications below the professional level. But the problem of detailing precisely what must be mutually recognised has held up, and may even have defeated, *practical* developments; for instance, qualifications might at any given time be in the process of being updated, restructured or at least reviewed, and past awards may not equate with present standards. Perhaps such problems influenced the contents of a 1995 education and training White Paper which heralded two new, parallel goals – an 'accreditation system covering basic, technical and vocational *skills*' plus a 'personal skills card' for individuals to carry. It seems future EU progress in this field may be geared less to establishing common or mutually recognised qualifications than to common skills definition. This in turn means that the UK is unlikely to have to invoke the 'subsidiarity' argument to retain its own qualifications system. The idea of a personal skills card is one that sprang from the UK's presidency period, and is based on the UK's National Record of Achievement (NRA) (see page 270).

Employees' 'rights to training' (as for example in France, where the law requires employers – subject to some defined limits – to grant leave of absence for vocational training) are a more controversial issue. If such rights are confirmed throughout the Single Market, the impact upon UK employers is likely to be considerable. In fact, from 1 September 1999 employees below age 19 in the UK have the right to study-leave. For years an EU directive was expected on 'access to vocational training'; instead, a (less binding) 'recommendation' appeared in 1993. This document states unequivocally that all member states should ensure that *all workers* in the EU have access without discrimination to vocational training throughout their working lives; to that end, it then suggests that each member state should:

- encourage organisations to 'make continual training and development a priority, and establish training plans'
- provide specific incentives (eg financial) to encourage smaller organisations to invest in training
- provide specific retraining incentives for organisations which are 'restructuring'
- develop local and regional networks to 'encourage and assist . . . training which reflects local need'
- ensure that workers know about their organisations' training policies
- promote skills assessment and training needs assessment 'at work or in other countries'
- encourage worker consultation when training plans and programmes are developed
- encourage 'competence-based training which leads to recognised and transferable qualifications'
- promote open and distance learning
- pay particular attention to those who have received little training in the past, are unemployed or disabled, to women – and particularly to women returners.

Despite the inclusion of disabled people in this last prority group, and a succession of EU statements aimed at promoting the social integration of the disabled (more than 10 per cent of the total EU population are said to have disabilities), the EU has not to date drafted instruments relating to their training. The general EU approach has been to urge member states to take action at a national level to enable as many as possible to enter or re-enter the labour market (hence, in the UK, Further Education Colleges can obtain extra funding for 'special needs' students, and the FE Funding Council may pay for them to attend specialist colleges). Member states are also expected to ensure that, to the maximum extent possible, EU 'action programmes' are accessible to the disabled.

The European Commission has already launched and funded a variety of cross-border action programmes aimed at specific goals. In 1995 a major new programme, 'Leonardo', was launched, co-ordinating and expanding these vocational training programmes and offering financial support for trans-national training projects, placement and exchange programmes, surveys into training problems and issues, and open or distance learning developments. The Leonardo programme is currently said to run until the end of 1999, but is likely to be extended in some form. A similar EU programme, code-named 'Socrates', gathers and extends programmes that are essentially based in the education sphere. A long-standing language training programme, 'Lingua', is promoted within both 'Leonardo' and 'Socrates'. 'Leonardo' and 'Socrates' were two of the outcomes of a long-awaited EU White Paper entitled *Growth, Competitiveness, Employment: The challenges and ways forward into the 21st century* issued in 1993. They are 'designed to encourage quality, to stimulate innovation and to implement the concept of lifelong learning' (*Vademecum Socrates* 1995). Lifelong learning is said to be a 'political objective to guide national policies and not just a model for a few one-off experiences' (*Vademecum Leonardo* 1995).

The 1993 White Paper focused on unemployment as the 'main feature of Europe's economic and social crisis' and included among its proposals:

- the promotion of lifelong vocational training
- labour market flexibility through retraining.

These twin goals could be said to represent in a mere dozen words the priorities to which all training interventions at the level of each EU nation might be linked, at least during the next decade.

In 1995, an EU White Paper dedicated to education and training set out a long list of aims and proposals for action at national level. These included:

- exploiting distance learning and IT opportunities
- emphasis on the practical teaching of science and technologies
- 'sound command of the mother tongue' plus knowledge of at least TWO foreign languages
- a focus on the training of those in production
- 'Second Chance' schools (for young people who have left school but lack basic skills), and training of the unemployed to lead to guaranteed jobs
- training for 'new types of engineer and manager', blending technical, commercial and economic disciplines.

The UK's 'University for Industry' and Learning Direct developments clearly serve the first of these (as did a wide variety of UK initiatives during the 1996 'European Year of Lifelong Learning'); the NVQ system serves several; and the 'New Deal' programme/'New Start' projects serve the proposal related to the young unemployed.

During 1997/8, the UK assumed a temporary Presidency of the EU role (the Presidency rotates alphabetically on an annual basis), and marked this with a variety of conferences plus the controversial Green Paper on lifelong learning that we mentioned earlier. The Presidency period also included the launch of the University for Industry and Learning Direct initiatives, and the announcement that 'individual learning accounts' (each opened with a free £150 credit, and allowing credit facilities plus spread payments following course enrolments) are timed for launch in the year 2002.

Bibliography

ADAIR J. *Training for Leadership*. Gower, Farnborough, 1978.

ANNETT J. in *Psychology at Work*. Warr P. (ed.), Penguin Education, Harmondsworth, 1974.

ARGYRIS C. 'Double loop learning in organisations'. *Harvard Business Review*. Sept./Oct. 1977. Pages 115–125.

ARGYRIS C. *Overcoming Organizational Defenses*. Prentice-Hall, New York, 1990.

ARGYRIS C. *Reasoning, Learning and Action: Individual and organisational*. Jossey-Bass, San Francisco, 1982.

ARGYRIS C. *Personality and Organisation*. Harper and Row, New York, 1957.

ARGYRIS C. *and* SCHON D. *Organisational Learning: A theory of action perspective*. Addison Wesley, New York, 1978.

ARGYRIS C. *and* SCHON D. A. *Organisational Learning II: Theory, method and practice*. Addison Wesley, Wokingham, 1996.

ARMSTRONG M. *A Handbook of Human Resource Management*. Kogan Page, London, 1990.

ATKINSON R. L., ATKINSON R. C. *et al. Introduction to Psychology*. (12th edition), Harcourt Brace and Co., Florida, 1996.

BAILEY D. 'Training to reduce retail shrinkage'. *Training and Management Development Methods*, Vol. 5, 1991.

BANDLER R. *and* GRINDER J. *The Structure of Magic: Parts 1 and 2*. Science and Behaviour Books, California, 1976.

BANDLER R., GRINDER J., DILTS R. *and* DELOZIER J. *Neuro-Linguistic Programming*, Vol. 1: *The Study of the Structure of Subject Experience*. Meta Publications, California, 1980.

BARNETT S. *and* RICHERT A. 'Trustworthy'. *People Management*, 28 May 1998. Pages 46–57.

BARON B. in *Managing Human Resources*. Cowling A. G. and Mailer C. J. B. (eds) Edward Arnold, London, 1981.

BARRINGTON H. *Learning about Management*. McGraw-Hill, London, 1984.

BARRINGTON H. 'The prompt list'. *Training and Management Development Methods*, Vol. 12, 1998.

BASS B. M. *and* VAUGHAN J. A. *Training in Industry – The management of learning*. Tavistock Publications, London, 1966.

BELBIN E. *and* BELBIN R. M. *Problems in Adult Retraining*. Heinemann, London, 1972.

BELBIN R. M. *Employment of Older Workers. No. 2, Training Methods*. OECD, Paris, 1969.

BENNISON M. *and* CARSON J. *The Manpower Planning Handbook*. McGraw-Hill, Maidenhead, 1984.

BEVAN S. *and* THOMPSON M. 'Performance management at the crossroads'. *Personnel Management*, Nov. 1991.

BION W.R. *Experiences in Groups*. Tavistock, London, 1961.

BOHM D. *Unfolding Meaning*. Foundation House, Loveland, California, 1985.

BOYATZIS R. *The Competent Manager*. John Wiley, Chichester, 1982.

BOYDELL T. H. *A Guide to Job Analysis*. British Association for Commercial and Industrial Education, London, 1977.

BOYDELL T. H. *and* LEARY M. *Identifying Training Needs*. IPD, London, 1996.

BOYDELL T. H. *and* PEDLER M. (eds) *Management Self Development*. Gower, Aldershot, 1981.

BRAMHAM J. *Practical Manpower Planning*. IPM, London, 1988.

BRAMLEY P. *Evaluating Training*. IPD, London, 1996.

BROMLEY D. B. *The Psychology of Human Ageing*. Pelican, Harmondsworth, 1975.

BROMLEY D. B. *Behavioural Gerontology: Central issues in the psychology of ageing.* Wiley, Chichester, 1990.

BROOKES J. *Training and Development Competence: A practical guide.* Kogan Page, London, 1995.

BURGOYNE J. 'Feeding minds to grow the business', *People Management.* 21 September 1995.

BURGOYNE J., PEDLER M. *and* BOYDELL T. *The Learning Company – A strategy for sustainable development.* McGraw-Hill, Maidenhead, 1991.

BURKE J. *Outcomes, Learning and the Curriculum.* Taylor and Francis, Rankine Road, Basingstoke RG24 8PR, 1995.

BURNS T. *and* STALKER G. M. *The Management of Innovation.* Tavistock, London, 1961.

BUS AND COACH TRAINING LIMITED. *Vehicle Engineering Competence Assessment Scheme.* Bus & Coach Training Ltd, Rickmansworth, 1990.

CABLE & WIRELESS. *Annual Review.* 1998.

CAMPBELL C. P. 'A primer on determining the cost effectiveness of training Part 1'. *Industrial and Commercial Training.* Vol. 26, No. 11, 1994. Pages 32–8.

CAMPBELL C. P. 'A primer on determining the cost effectiveness of training Part 2', *Industrial and Commercial Training.* Vol. 27, No. 1, 1995. Pages 17–25.

CANNELL M. 'Practice makes perfect'. *People Management*, Vol. 3, No. 5, March 1997. Pages 26–30, 33.

CARLING W. *and* HELLER R. *The Way to Win: Strategies for success in business and sport.* Little, Brown and Co., London, 1995.

CASSELLS J. 'Education and training must be geared to match the demand for more skills in British industry today'. *The Times*, 18 June, 1985.

CHAPPLE F. 'A report on the Electrical, Electronic, Telecommunication and Plumbing Union's retraining programme'. *The Times*, 13 March, 1984.

CHILD J. *Organisation: A guide to problems and practice.* Harper and Row, London, 1982.

CLUTTERBUCK D. *Everyone Needs a Mentor*. IPM, London, 1991.

COCKERILL T. 'The kind of competence for rapid change'. *Personnel Management*, Sept. 1989.

COLLARD R. *Total Quality: Success through people*. IPM, London, 1989.

CONFEDERATION OF BRITISH INDUSTRY. *World Class Targets*. CBI, London, 1991.

COULSON-THOMAS C. *and* COE T. *The Flat Organization*. BIM Foundation, Management House, Cottingham Road, Corby, Northants NN17 1TT, 1991. Also cited in *Skills and Enterprise Briefing*. Issue 3/ 92 Feb. 1992, Skills and Enterprise Network, PO Box 12, West PDO, Leen Gate, Lenton, Nottingham NG7 2GB.

CROSS M. *Towards the Flexible Craftsman*. The Technical Change Centre, London, 1985.

CUMING M. *A Manager's Guide to Quantitative Methods*. Elm Publications, Kings Repton, Cambridge, 1984.

DAVEY D. MACKENZIE *and* HARRIS R. *Judging People: A guide to orthodox and unorthodox methods of assessment*. McGraw-Hill, Maidenhead, 1982.

DEARING Sir R. 'Committee of enquiry'. *Higher Education in the Learning Society*, July 1997.

DEARING Sir R. *The National Curriculum and its Assessment*. School Curriculum and Assessment Authority Publications, Dec. 1993. Ref. D/F.

DEARING Sir R. *Review of National Curriculum: Report on the 1994 consultation*. School Curriculum and Assessment Authority Publications, 1994. Ref. COM/94/118.

DEARING Sir R. *Review of Qualifications for 16- to 19-year-olds*. School Curriculum and Assessment Authority Publications, PO Box 235, Hayes, Middlesex UB3 1HF, 1996.

DEPARTMENT FOR EDUCATION AND EMPLOYMENT (1). *Labour Market and Skill Trends 1997/8*. DfEE, Sheffield (Crown Copyright) 1997.

DEPARTMENT FOR EDUCATION AND EMPLOYMENT (2). *Labour Market and Skill Trends 1998/9*. DfEE, Sheffield (Crown Copyright) 1998.

DEPARTMENT FOR EDUCATION AND EMPLOYMENT (3). *Investment in Training and the Growth and Survival of Small Firms: An empir-*

ical analysis for the UK 1987-95. (Report by the Centre for Business Research, Cambridge) DfEE, Sudbury, Suffolk, 1998.

DEPARTMENT FOR EDUCATION AND EMPLOYMENT (4). *Towards a National Skills Agenda. (4)* (First Report of the National Skills Task Force) DfEE, Sudbury (Crown Copyright) 1998.

DEPARTMENT FOR EDUCATION AND EMPLOYMENT (5). *National Learning Targets for England for 2002.* DfEE, Sheffield (Crown Copyright) 1998.

DEPARTMENT FOR EDUCATION AND EMPLOYMENT(6). *The Learning Age: A renaissance for a new Britain. (Green Paper).* Stationery Office, Cmnd. 3790, London (Crown Copyright), 25 February 1998.

DEPARTMENT FOR EDUCATION AND EMPLOYMENT (7). *Design of the New Deal for 18–24 Year-Olds.* DfEE, Sheffield (Crown Copyright) 1998.

DEPARTMENT FOR EDUCATION AND EMPLOYMENT (8). *University for Industry: Engaging people in learning for life.* (Pathfinder Prospectus). DfEE, Sudbury (Crown Copyright) 1998.

DEPARTMENT FOR EDUCATION AND EMPLOYMENT (9). *New Start, Issue 4.* DfEE, Sudbury (Crown Copyright) 1998.

DEPARTMENT FOR EDUCATION AND EMPLOYMENT (10). *Modern Apprenticeships. Employer Case Studies.* Vol. 3, 1998.

DILTS R. B., EPSTEIN T. *and* DILTS R. W. *Tools for Dreamers.* Meta Publications, California, 1991.

DOBSON C. B., HARDY M. *et al. Understanding Psychology.* Weidenfeld and Nicolson, London, 1990.

DONNELLY E. L. 'The need to market training', in *Gower Handbook of Training and Development.* Prior J. (ed.). Gower, Aldershot, 1991.

DONNELLY E. L. *Training as a Specialist Function – An historical perspective.* Working Paper No. 9, Faculty of Business Studies & Management, Middlesex Polytechnic. Middlesex Polytechnic, London, 1984.

DORE R. P. *and* SAKO M. *How the Japanese Learn to Work.* (Nissan Institute/Routledge Japanese Studies Series.) Routledge, London, 1989.

DOWNS S. 'Designing training for competence'. *Competence and Assessment.* Issue 31, February 1996.

DOWNS S. *Learning at Work: Effective strategies for making things happen.* Kogan Page, London, 1995.

DRUCKER P. F. *Managing for Results.* Heinemann, London, 1964.

DRUCKER P. F. *The Practice of Management.* Harper and Row, New York, 1954.

DULEWICZ V. 'Assessment Centres as the route to competence'. *Personnel Management*, Nov. 1989.

DUNCAN K. D. *and* KELLY C. J. *Task Analysis, Learning and the Nature of Transfer.* Manpower Services Commission, Sheffield, 1983.

EASTERBY-SMITH M. *and* MACKNESS J. 'Completing the cycle of evaluation'. *Personnel Management*, May 1992.

EASTERBY-SMITH M. *and* TANTON M. 'Turning course evaluation from an end to a means'. *Personnel Management*, April 1985.

EL-SHERIF H. H. *and* TANG V. 'Team focus electronic brain storming'. *Training and Management Development Methods*, Vol. 8, 1994.

ELMS A. 'Investors in People accreditation: one large organisation's journey to IiP status'. *Training and Management Development Methods*, Vol. 12, 1998. Pages 2.15–2.24.

EMERY F. E. (ed.) *Systems Thinking.* Penguin, London, 1981.

EMI Group. *Annual Report.* 1998.

EMPLOYMENT OCCUPATIONAL STANDARDS COUNCIL. *Training and Development Standards.* EOSC, London, 1995.

EMPLOYMENT SERVICE. *Annual Report & Accounts.* 1997–1998.

ESTES W. K. *Learning Theory and Mental Development.* Academic Press, New York, 1970.

ETZIONI A. *A Comparative Analysis of Complex Organisations.* Free Press, Glencoe, Illinois, 1961.

EUROPEAN COMMISSION. *Leonardo Da Vinci Programme: Vademecum.* EC, Directorate General XXII – Education, Training and Youth, Brussels, 1995.

EUROPEAN COMMISSION. *Socrates: Vademecum.* EC, Directorate General XXII – Education, Training and Youth, Brussels, 1995.

EUROPEAN COMMISSION. *White Paper: Education and Training.* European Commission, Brussels, 1995.

EUROPEAN COMMISSION. *White Paper: Growth, Competitiveness, Employment: The challenges and ways forward into the 21st century.* European Commission, Brussels, 1993.

EUROPEAN UNION, *see* EUROPEAN COMMISSION.

FAIRBAIRNS J. 'Plugging the gap in training needs analysis'. *Personnel Management*, Feb. 1991.

FARNHAM D. 'Corporate policy and personnel management', in *Personnel Management Handbook.* Harper S. (ed.). Gower, Aldershot, 1987.

FAYOL H. *General and Industrial Administration.* Durod, Paris, 1915.

FEFC *see* Further Education Funding Council.

FESTINGER L. *A Theory of Cognitive Dissonance.* Row Peterson, Evanston, Illinois, 1957.

FLEISHMAN E. A. *and* HEMPEL W. E. 'The relationship between abilities and improvement with practice in a visual discrimination task'. *Journal of Experimental Psychology*, 49, 1955.

FLEMING D. 'The concept of meta-competence'. *Competence and Assessment.* Issue 16. Employment Department Group, Sheffield, 1991.

FOWLER A. 'Benchmarking'. *People Management*, 12 June 1997.

FOWLER A. *Employee Induction: a good start.* IPD, London, 1996.

FOWLER A. 'How to decide on training methods'. *People Management*, 21st Dec. 1995. Pages 36–37.

FRANSELLA F. and BANNISTER D. *A Manual for Repertory Grid Technique.* Academic Press, London, 1977.

FRIEDMAN B., HATCH J. *et al. Delivering on the Promise: How to attract, manage and retain Human Capital.* The Free Press, New York, 1998.

FURTHER EDUCATION FUNDING COUNCIL. *General National Vocational Qualifications in the Further Education Sector in England.* FEFC, London, 1995.

FURTHER EDUCATION FUNDING COUNCIL. *Post-16 Vocational Education and Training in France*. FEFC, Coventry, 1995.

FURTHER EDUCATION FUNDING COUNCIL. *Post-16 Vocational Education and Training in Germany*. FEFC, Coventry, 1995.

FURTHER EDUCATION FUNDING COUNCIL. *Inclusive Learning*. (The Tomlinson Report) FEFC, Coventry, 1996.

FURTHER EDUCATION FUNDING COUNCIL. *Learning Works: Widening Participation in Further Education*. (The Kennedy Report) FEFC, Coventry, 1997.

FURTHER EDUCATION FUNDING COUNCIL. *Quality and Standards in Further Education, 1996–7*. FEFC, Coventry, 1997.

FURTHER EDUCATION STAFF COLLEGE. *A Guide to Work-based Learning Terms*. Training Agency. HMSO, London, 1989.

FURTHER EDUCATION UNIT. *How Do I Learn?* 1981.

GARBUTT D. *Training Costs with Reference to the Industrial Training Act*. Gee and Company Limited, 1969.

GARDNER H. 'The theory of multiple intelligences'. *Annals of Dyslexia*, Vol. 37, 1987. Pages 19–35.

GARRAT B. 'An old idea that has come of age'. *People Management*, 21 September 1995.

GARRATT B. *Creating a Learning Organisation*. Director Books, Cambridge, 1990.

GARRATT B. *Learning to Lead*. HarperCollins, London, 1991.

GARRATT B. *The Learning Organisation*. Fontana, London, 1994.

GARRATT B. *The Learning Organisation and the Need for Directors Who Think*. Gower, Aldershot, 1987.

GIBBS R., GLENDENNING R. *and* McCARTHY J. 'Learning in the workplace through employee development: three perspectives'. *Training and Management Development Methods*. Vol. 9. 1995. Pages 1.11–1.25.

GLASER R. *Training Research and Education*. Wiley and Sons, New York, 1965.

GOLDSTEIN I. L. 'Training in work organisations', in *Annual Review of Psychology* 31, 229–72, 1980.

GREGORY R. L. (ed.). *The Oxford Companion to the Mind*. Oxford University Press, Oxford, 1987. Pages 740–47.

GRIFFITHS P. *and* GOODGE P. 'Development centres: the third generation'. *Personnel Management*, June 1994. Pages 40–43.

GRONLUND N. E. *Stating Behavioural Objectives for Classroom Instruction*. Macmillan, London, 1978.

HAMBLIN A. C. *Evaluation and Control of Training*. McGraw-Hill, Maidenhead, 1974.

HANDY C. *The Age of Unreason*. Hutchinson, London, 1989.

HANDY C. *The Making of Managers*. National Economic Development Office, London, 1987.

HANDY C. *Understanding Organisations*. Penguin, London, 1985.

HARDINGHAM A. *Designing Training*. IPD, London, 1996.

HARRISON R. *Training and Development*. IPM, London, 1997.

HAYES C., FONDA N., POPE N., STUART R. *and* TOWNSEND K. *Training for Skill Ownership*. Institute of Manpower Studies, Brighton, 1983.

HAYES C. *et al*. 'International competition and the role of competence'. *Personnel Management*, September 1984.

HAYES R. H., WHEELWRIGHT S. C. *and* CLARK K. B. *Dynamic Manufacturing: Creating the learning organisation*. The Free Press, New York, 1988.

HERZBERG F. *et al*. *The Motivation to Work*. John Wiley, New York, 1959.

HEWSTONE *et al*. (eds). *Introduction to Social Psychology*. Blackwell, Oxford, 1990.

HIRSH W. *and* REILLY P. 'Cycling proficiency'. *People Management*, 9 July 1998. Pages 36–41.

HMSO. *Industrial Training Act, 1964*. HMSO, London, 1964.

HMSO. *White Paper: Competitiveness: Forging ahead.* HMSO (Cm 2867). May 1995.

HMSO. *White Paper: Training for jobs.* HMSO (Cm 9135), London, 1984.

HMSO. *White Paper: Working Together: Education and training.* HMSO (Cm 9832), London, 1986.

HMSO. *White Paper: Employment for the 1990s.* HMSO, London, 1988.

HMSO. *White Paper: Education and training for the 21st century.* HMSO (Cm 1536), London, 1991.

HMSO. *White Paper: Competitiveness: Helping business to win.* HMSO (Cm 2563), London, May 1994.

HOGAN C. 'How to get more out of videoconference meetings: a socio-technical approach: experience of CURTIN University of Technology'. *Training and Management Development Methods*, Vol. 7. Pages 5.01–5.32, 1993.

HOGAN C. 'Water buffaloes get bewitched: observations of a participatory rural appraisal training workshop'. *Training and Management Development Methods*, Vol. 10. In publication.

HOGARTH G. *and* BARTH M. *Why Employing the Over-50s Makes Good Business Sense.* Publications Department, Institute of Employment Research, University of Warwick, 1991.

HOLDEN L. *and* LIVIAN Y. 'Does strategic training policy exist? Some evidence from ten European countries'. *Personnel Review.* Vol. 21, Issue 1, 1992. Pages 12–23.

HONEY P. *and* MUMFORD A. *Using your Learning Styles.* (2nd edition), Peter Honey, Ardingly House, 10 Linden Avenue, Maidenhead, 1986.

HONEY P. *and* MUMFORD A. *The Manual of Learning Opportunities.* Peter Honey, Ardingly House, 10 Linden Avenue, Maidenhead, 1989.

HONEY P. *and* MUMFORD A. *Manual of Learning Styles.* (3rd edition), Honey, Maidenhead, 1992.

HONEY P., BURGOYNE J., CUNNINGHAM I. *et al.* 'The debate starts here'. *People Management,* 1 October 1998.

HUMBLE J. *Management by Objectives.* Industrial Educational and Research Foundation, London, 1967.

INCOMES DATA SERVICES. *European Management Guide: Training and development*. IPM, London, 1992.

INSTITUTE OF PERSONNEL AND DEVELOPMENT. *Continuing Professional Development* (Policy Document and User Guide). IPD, London, 1995.

INSTITUTE OF PERSONNEL AND DEVELOPMENT. *Key Facts: On-the-job-training*. 1998. Website: www.ipd.co.uk

INSTITUTE OF PERSONNEL AND DEVELOPMENT. *IPD Professional Standards*. IPD, London, 1997.

INSTITUTE OF PERSONNEL AND DEVELOPMENT. *Professional Education Scheme*. IPD, London, 1996.

INSTITUTE OF PERSONNEL AND DEVELOPMENT. *Qualification Routes*. IPD, London, 1996.

INSTITUTE OF PERSONNEL AND DEVELOPMENT. *The IPD Code of Professional Conduct and Disciplinary Procedures*. IPD, London, September 1997.

INSTITUTE OF PERSONNEL MANAGEMENT. *The IPM Code: Continuous Development: People and work*. IPM, London, 1984 and 1986.

INSTITUTE OF PERSONNEL MANAGEMENT. *Towards a National Training and Development Strategy* and *An Action Plan for the UK*. IPM, London, 1992.

INSTITUTE OF PERSONNEL MANAGEMENT. *TVEI Recommendations on improved School/Work Liaison*. IPM, London, 1984.

INVESTORS IN PEOPLE UK. *Investors in People: How to get started*. Investors in People UK, London, 1997.

INVESTORS IN PEOPLE UK. *Investors in People: The benefits of being an Investor in People*. IiP, London, 1995.

JACKSON L. 'Turning airport managers into high fliers'. *Personnel Management*, October 1989.

JENNINGS S. *and* UNDY R. 'Auditing managers' IR training needs'. *Personnel Management*, February 1984.

JENSEN E. *Brain-Based Learning and Teaching*. Turning Point Publishing, Del Mar, CA., NY., 1995.

JESSUP G. *Outcomes: NVQs and the emerging model of education and training.* Falmer Press, 1991.

JOHN G. 'Share Strength' (Knowledge Management). *People Management*, 13 August 1998.

JOHNSON P. R. *and* INDVIK J. 'Using brain hemisphericity to enhance career management'. *The International Journal of Career Management*, Vol. 3, No. 3, 1991. Pages 3–10.

JOHNSON R. 'Neuro-linguistic programming', in *Handbook of Training and Development.* Prior J.(ed.) Gower, Aldershot, 1991.

JONES A. M. and HENDRY C. *The Learning Organisation: A review of literature and practice.* The HRD Partnership, London, 1992.

JONES J. A. G. *The Evaluation and Cost Effectiveness of Training.* Industrial Training Service, London, 1970.

KAHN R. L., WOLFE D. M. *et al. Organizational Stress Studies in Role Conflict and Ambiguity.* Wiley, London, 1964.

KAMP D. 'Neuro-linguistic programming'. *Training and Development*, Oct. 1991. Pages 36 and 38.

KAY. H. 'Accidents: some facts and theories', in *Psychology at Work.* Warr P. (ed.). Penguin Education, Harmondsworth, Middx, 1983.

KENNEY J. P. J., DONNELLY E. L. *and* REID M. A. *Manpower Training and Development.* Institute of Personnel Management, London, 1979.

KENNEY J. P. J. *and* REID M. A. *Training Interventions.* (2nd edition, revised), Institute of Personnel Management, London, 1989.

KOHLER W. *The Mentality of Apes.* International Library of Psychology, Routledge, 1973.

KOLB D. *Experiential Learning: Experience as the source of learning and development.* Prentice Hall, Englewood Cliffs, New Jersey, 1984.

KOLB D. A., RUBIN I. N. *and* McINTYRE J. M. *Organizational Psychology; A book of readings.* Prentice Hall, Englewood Cliffs, NJ, 1974.

LABOUR MARKET AND SKILL TRENDS see DEPARTMENT FOR EDUCATION AND EMPLOYMENT.

LABOUR MARKET QUARTERLY REPORT. (Quarterly report issued up to mid-1995 by the Employment Department/Employment Department Group, and thereafter by the Department for Education and Employment, as 'Skills and Enterprise Network Publications'.) Nottingham, 1994 on.

LANK E. 'ICL's information supercafé'. *People Management*, 19 February 1998.

LAWRENCE P. R. *and* LORSCH J. W. *Organisation and Environment*. Harvard Graduate School of Business Administration, Cambridge, MA, 1967.

McGREGOR D. *The Human Side of Enterprise*. McGraw-Hill, Maidenhead, 1960.

MAGER R. F. *Preparing Instructional Objectives*. Fearon, California, 1984.

MANAGEMENT CHARTER GROUP. *The Management Charter Initiative*. MCI, London, 1987.

MANCHESTER UNIVERSITY. *All Our Futures*. Centre for Education and Employment Research, University of Manchester, Manchester, 1993.

MANPOWER SERVICES COMMISSION. *Vocational Preparation for Young People*. MSC, Sheffield, 1975.

MANPOWER SERVICES COMMISSION. *Training of Trainers*. Two reports from the Training of Trainers Committee. HMSO, London, 1978 and 1980.

MANPOWER SERVICES COMMISSION. *Glossary of Training Terms*. MSC. HMSO, London, 1981.

MARCHINGTON M. *and* WILKINSON A. *Core Personnel and Development*. IPD, London, 1996.

MARGERISON C. 'Margerison and McCann discuss the Team Management Wheel'. *Industrial and Commercial Training*, Vol. 24, No. 1, 1992.

MARKS J. 'Britain out of training for world success'. *The Sunday Times*, 2nd Jan. 1996.

MASLOW A. H. 'A theory of human motivation'. *Psychological Review*. 50, 1943.

MAYO A. 'Memory bankers' (re Knowledge Management). *People Management*, 22 January 1998.

MAYO A. *and* LANK E. *The Power of Learning*. IPD, London, 1994.

378

MAYO E. *Human Problems of an Industrial Civilisation*. Macmillan, New York, 1933.

MEGGINSON D. *and* WHITAKER V. *Cultivating Self-Development*. IPD, London, 1996.

MERRICK N. 'The leisure principle'. *People Management*, 11 June 1998.

MINTZBERG H. 'The manager's job: folklore and fact'. *Harvard Business Review*, July 1975.

MOORBY E. *How to Succeed in Employee Development*. McGraw-Hill, Maidenhead, 1991.

MOORBY E. 'Mentoring and coaching', in *Gower Handbook of Training and Management Development*. Prior J. (ed.). (2nd edition), Gower, Aldershot, 1994.

MORGAN G. *Images of Organisation*. Sage Publications, London, 1997.

MUMFORD A. *Making Experience Pay*. McGraw-Hill, Maidenhead, 1980.

MUMFORD A. *Management Development*. IPM, London, 1989.

MUMFORD A. *Management Development: Strategies for action*. 2nd edn. Institute of Personnel Management, London, 1993.

NATIONAL ADVISORY COUNCIL FOR EDUCATION & TRAINING TARGETS. *Fast Forward for Skills: A summary of NACETT's report on future National Targets for Education and Training*. Oct. 1998.

NATIONAL ADVISORY COUNCIL FOR EDUCATION AND TRAINING TARGETS. *First Annual Report (1993)* and *Reports on Progress (1994 and 1995)*. NACETT, London.

NATIONAL COUNCIL FOR VOCATIONAL QUALIFICATIONS. *NVQ Criteria and Guidance*. NCVQ, London, January 1995.

NATIONAL COUNCIL FOR VOCATIONAL QUALIFICATIONS. *National Vocational Qualifications: Criteria and procedures*. NCVQ, London, 1989.

NATIONAL COUNCIL FOR VOCATIONAL QUALIFICATIONS. *General National Vocational Qualifications*. NCVQ, London, 1991.

NATIONAL COUNCIL FOR VOCATIONAL QUALIFICATIONS. *Your Introduction to NVQs and GNVQs*. NCVQ, London, 1995.

NATIONAL ECONOMIC DEVELOPMENT OFFICE. *Young People and the Labour Market: A challenge for the 1990s.* NEDO, London, 1988.

NATIONAL INSTITUTE FOR ADULT AND CONTINUING EDU- CATION *The Learning Divide – A study of participation in adult learning in the United Kingdom.* NIACE, Leicester, 1998.

NATIONAL INSTITUTE FOR CAREERS EDUCATION AND COUN- SELLING. *Helping People to Succeed: The future of the National Record of Achievement.* NICEC. Sheraton House, Castle Park, Cambridge, CB3 0AX, 1995.

NEALE F. *The Handbook of Performance Management.* IPM, London, 1991.

NIACE *see* National Institute for Adult and Continuing Education.

NONAKA I. *and* TAKEUCHI H. *The Knowledge-Creating Company.* Oxford University Press, New York, 1995.

NORD W. R. 'Beyond the teaching machine: the neglected area of oper- ant conditioning in the theory and practice of management'. *Organizational Behaviour and Human Performance*, Vol. 4, 1969.

OTTO C. P. *and* GLASER R. O. *The Management of Training.* Addison Wesley, London, 1970.

PATRICK J. *Training: Research and practice.* Academic Press, New York, 1992.

PEARN M. *and* KANDOLA R. *Job Analysis: A practical guide for managers.* IPD, London, 1993.

PEDLER M. *and* ASPINWALL K. *Learning in Company.* McGraw-Hill, UK, 1995.

PEDLER M., BURGOYNE J. *and* BOYDELL T. *A Manager's Guide to Self Development.* McGraw-Hill, Maidenhead, 1978.

PEDLER M., BURGOYNE J. *and* BOYDELL T. *The Learning Company Project.* Training Agency, Sheffield, 1988.

PEDLER M., BURGOYNE J. *and* BOYDELL T. *The Learning Organisation.* McGraw-Hill, Maidenhead, 1992.

PEDLER M., BURGOYNE J., BOYDELL T. *and* WELSHMAN A. (eds). *Self-development in Organisations.* McGraw-Hill, Maidenhead, 1990.

PEPPER A. D. *Managing the Training and Development Function.* Gower, Aldershot, 1984.

PETERS, T. *Liberation Management*. Pan Books, London, 1993.

PETTIGREW A. M., JONES G. R. *and* REASON P. W. *Organisational and Behavioural Aspects of the Role of the Training Officer in the UK Chemical Industry*. Chemical & Allied Products Industry Training Board, Staines, 1981.

PETTIGREW A. M., SPARROW P. *and* HENDRY C. 'The forces that trigger training'. *Personnel Management*, December 1988.

PICKARD J. 'A yearning for learning'. *People Management*, 6 March, 1997.

PLETT P. *and* LESTER B.T. *Training for Older People*. ILO, Vincent House, Vincent Square, London SW1P 2NB, 1991.

PRAIS S. J. 'How Europe would see the new British initiative for standardising vocational qualifications'. *National Institute for Economic Review*, May 1991. Pages 52–4.

PRASHAR U. 'Evening up the odds for black workers'. *Personnel Management*, June 1983.

PRICKETT R. 'Employers unimpressed by graduates' lofty ambitions'. *People Management*, 3 September 1998. Page 19.

QUALIFICATIONS AND CURRICULUM AUTHORITY. *Data News Issues 9, 10 and 11*. QCA, London, 1998–9.

REDMAN T. *and* MATHEWS B. P. 'Do corporate turkeys vote for Christmas? Managers' attitudes towards upward appraisal'. *Personnel Review*, Vol. 24, No. 7, 1995.

REID M. A. 'Approaches and strategies', in *Gower Handbook of Training and Development*. Prior J. (ed.). (2nd edition), Gower, Aldershot, 1994.

REVANS R. *Action Learning*. Blond & Briggs, London, 1980.

REVANS R. *The ABC of Action Learning*. Chartwell-Bratt, London, 1983.

RICHARDS-CARPENTER C. *Relating Manpower to an Organization's Objectives*. Institute of Manpower Studies, Report No. 56, 1982.

RICHARDSON J. *and* BENNETT B. 'Applying learning techniques to on-the-job development: Part 2'. *Journal of European Industrial Training*, Vol. 8, No. 3, 1984.

RODGER A., MORGAN T. *and* GUEST D. *A Study of the Work of Industrial Training Officers*. Air Transport and Travel Industry Training Board, Staines, 1971.

ROLLINSON D. *et al. Organisational Behaviour and Analysis.* Addison-Wesley, Harlow, 1998.

ROSE C. *Accelerated Learning.* Accelerated Learning Systems Ltd, 50 Aylesbury Road, Aston Clinton, Aylesbury, 1991.

ROUTLEDGE, C. 'Brains, learners and trainers – a three-part series'. *Training and Management Development Methods,* Vol. 13, Section 7.

ROUTLEDGE C. 'Strategies of effective learners on interpersonal skills courses'. *Training and Management Development Methods.* Vol. 9, 1995. Pages 4.07–4.18.

SCARBOROUGH H., SWAN J. *and* PRESTON J. *Knowledge Management and the Learning Organisation.* IPD, London, 1999.

SCHEIN E. H. *Organisational Psychology.* Prentice Hall, New Jersey, 1970.

SCHEIN E. H. *Process Consultation.* Addison-Wesley, Reading, MA., 1969.

SCHON D. A. *The Reflective Practitioner.* Basic Books, New York, 1983.

SCOPE KETCHUM. *Q115 – On-line Distance Learning Research.* July 1998.

SELIGMAN M. E. P. *Helplessness.* Freeman, San Francisco, 1975.

SENGE P. M. *The Fifth Discipline: The art and practice of the learning organisation.* Century Business, London, 1990.

SENGE P. M., KLEINER A., ROBERTS C., ROSS R. B. *and* SMITH B. J. *The Fifth Discipline Fieldbook.* Nicholas Brealey, London, 1998.

SEYMOUR W. D. *Industrial Training for Manual Operatives.* Pitman, London, 1954.

SHACKLETON J. R. *and* WALSH S. 'The UK's National Vocational Qualifications: the story so far'. *Journal of European Industrial Training,* Vol. 19, No. 11, 1995. Pages 14–27.

SHRIVASTAVA P. 'A typology of organisational learning systems'. *Journal of Management Studies.* Vol. 20, No. 1, 7–28, Basil Blackwell, Oxford, Jan. 1983.

SINGER E. *Training in Industry and Commerce.* IPM, London, 1977.

SINGER E. *Effective Management Coaching.* IPM, London, 1979.

SKILLS AND ENTERPRISE NETWORK, see *LABOUR MARKET AND SKILL TRENDS* and *LABOUR MARKET QUARTERLY REPORT*.

SKINNER B. F. *Science and Human Behaviour*. Free Press U S, New York, 1965.

SKINNER B. F. *Walden Two*. Collier Macmillan, London, 1976.

SLOMAN M. 'Coming in from the cold: a new role for trainers'. *Personnel Management*, Jan. 1994. Pages 24–27.

STAMMERS R. and PATRICK J. *Psychology of Training*. Methuen, London, 1975.

STEEDMAN H. *and* HAWKINS J. 'Shifting foundations: the impact of NVQs on youth training for the building trades'. *National Institute Economic Review*, Aug. 1994. Pages 93–102.

TALBOT J. P. and ELLIS C. D. *Analysis and Costing of Company Training*. Gower, Aldershot, 1969.

TANNEHILL R. E. *Motivation and Management Development*. Butterworths, London, 1970.

TAVERNIER G. *Industrial Training Systems and Records*. Gower, Aldershot, 1971.

TAYLOR B. and LIPPITT G. (eds). *Management Development and Training Handbook* .(2nd Edition), McGraw-Hill, Maidenhead, 1983.

TAYLOR M. *Coverdale on Management*. Heinemann, London, 1979.

THATCHER M. 'Campus fugit' (BAe's Virtual University – British Aerospace Case Study). *People Management*, 3 September 1998.

TOFFLER A. *Future Shock*. Bantam, New York, 1970.

TRACEY W. R. *Evaluating Training and Development Systems*. American Management Association, 1968.

TRIST E. *The Evolution of Socio-Technical Systems*. Ontario Ministry of Labour/Ontario Quality of Working Life Centre, Ontario, 1981.

TRIST E. *et al. Organisational Choice*. Tavistock, London, 1963.

UNIVERSITY OF WEST OF ENGLAND. *An enquiry into the training and continuous professional development of members of the Police Federation of England and Wales*, 1997.

VERNON P. E. *Intelligence and Attainment Tests*. London University Press, London, 1960.

VOGT O. 'Study of the ageing of nerve cells'. *Journal of Gerontology*. No. 6, 1951.

WALKLIN L. *Training and Development NVQs* (A Handbook for FAETC candidates and NVQ trainers) Stanley Thornes, Cheltenham, 1996.

WALSH J. 'No stamp for passport to EU training'. *People Management*, June 1998. Page 15.

WARR P. B., BIRD M. *and* RACKHAM N. *Evaluation of Management Training*. Gower Press, Aldershot, 1970.

WARWICK UNIVERSITY, Centre for Corporate Strategy and Change. *Study for Department of Employment*, 1991. Reported in *Skills and Enterprise Briefing*, February 1992, Employment Department, Moorfoot, Sheffield.

WEBER M. *The Theory of Social and Economic Organisation*. Oxford University Press, Oxford, 1947.

WELCH J. '"Discredited" degree grades under attack'. *People Management*, 24 July, 1997.

WELCH J. 'Police admit that £100m of training is misdirected'. *People Management*, 3 September 1998. Page 9.

WELCH J. 'HR blamed for employers' single-currency ignorance'. *People Management*, 30 April 1998. Page 10.

WELCH J. 'Stress ruling ups the stakes for employers'. *People Management*. 16 May 1996. Pages 13–14.

WELFORD A. T. 'On changes in performance with age'. *Lancet*. Part 1, 1962.

WELLENS J. *The Exploitation of Human Resources*. In *The Times*, 16 August 1968.

WELLENS J. 'An approach to management training'. *Industrial and Commercial Training*. Vol. 8, No. 7, July 1970.

WHITELAW M. *The Evaluation of Management Training – A review*. IPM, London, 1972.

WHITTAKER J. 'Three Challenges for IPD Standards'. *People Management*, 16 November, 1995.

WILLOUGBY B., SPENCE C. *and* GORMAN D. Conference paper presented at 'Geared Up for Learning', organised by the International Consortium for Employee Development, University of Salford, January 1996.

WOLF A. 'Measuring competence: the experience of the United Kingdom'. *European Vocational Training*, Vol. 1, 1994.

WOOD S. (ed.) *Continuous Development: The path to improved performance.* IPM, London, 1988.

WOODRUFFE C. *Assessment Centres: Identifying and developing competence.* IPM, London, 1990.

WOODRUFFE C. 'What is meant by a competency?' in *Designing and Achieving Competency*. Sparrow P. and Boam R. (eds). McGraw-Hill, Maidenhead, 1992.

WOODS M. *and* THOMAS E. 'The Belbin Interface 111 – an expert system to assist personnel and trainers in personal and team development'. *Training and Management Development Methods*. Vol. 6, Section 2.01, 1992.

WOODWARD J. *Industrial Organisation, Theory and Practice.* Oxford University Press, Oxford, 1965.

WORSLEY R. 'Only prejudices are old and tired'. *People Management*, 11 January 1996, Pages 18–23.

XEBEC *Intranet Technology and Training: Is the marketplace ready for training on demand?* A Joint Survey between *IT Training* (Journal) and Xebec McGraw-Hill, June 1998.

YOUNG R. 'The wide-awake Club' (re virtual teams). *People Management*, 5 February 1998.

Index